MICHAEL COLLINS'S INTELLIGENCE WAR

THE STRUGGLE BETWEEN THE BRITISH AND THE IRA, 1919–1921

MICHAEL T. FOY

SUTTON PUBLISHING

First published in the United Kingdom in 2006 by
Sutton Publishing Limited · Phoenix Mill
Thrupp · Stroud · Gloucestershire · GL5 2BU

British Library Cataloguing in Publication Data
A catalogue record for this book is available from the British Library.

ISBN 0-7509-4267-3

Typeset in 10.5/15pt Photina MT.
Typesetting and origination by
Sutton Publishing Limited.
Printed and bound in England by
J.H. Haynes & Co. Ltd, Sparkford.

CONTENTS

Map   iv

Acknowledgements   vi

Prologue   1

1. The Road to Conflict: Michael Collins and the Onset of the
   Anglo-Irish War, 1916–1919   5

2. Director of Irish Intelligence: The Organisation Takes Shape, 1919   35

3. Stumbling into the Haze: The British Response, January–July 1920   64

4. Duel: The Struggle between the British and IRA Intelligence,
   July–November 1920   97

5. Seeking a Knockout Blow: Collins and Bloody Sunday,
   21 November 1920   141

6. Slugging it out: Bloody Sunday to March 1921   178

7. Looking for a Way out: The Quest for a Truce, May–July 1921   219

Conclusions   239

Notes   246

Bibliography   272

Index   277

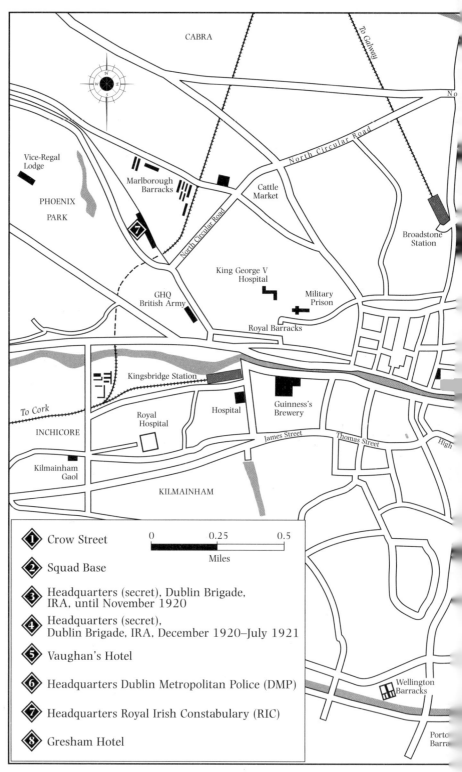

Map 1. Dublin, 1918–1921

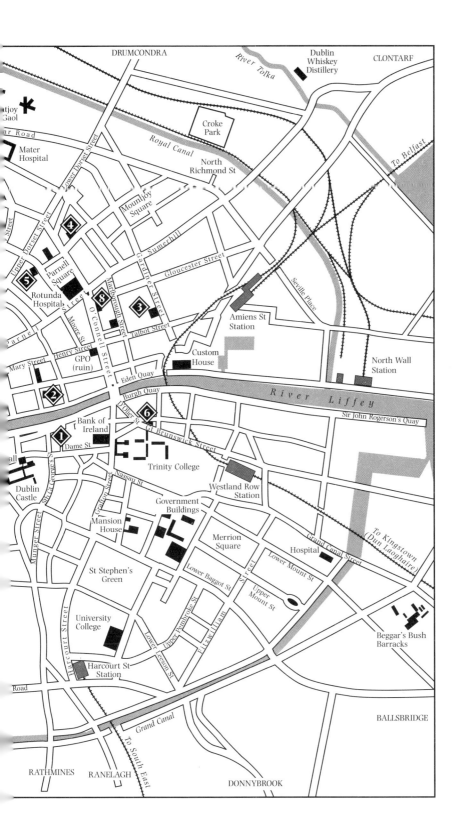

DRUMCONDRA

River Tolka

Dublin
Whiskey
Distillery

CLONTARF

Croke
Park

Mountjoy
Gaol

ar Road

Mater
Hospital

Royal Canal

North
Richmond St

To Belfast

Mountjoy
Square

Lower Dorset Street

Upper Dorset Street

Summerhill

Gloucester Street

Gardiner Street

4

5

Parnell
Square

8

3

Rotunda
Hospital

Parnell

Moore St

Marlborough Street

Talbot Street

O'Connell Street

Amiens St
Station

Seville Place

North Wall
Station

Mary Street

Henry Street

GPO
(ruin)

Custom
House

River Liffey

Eden Quay

Sir John Rogerson's Quay

2

Burgh Quay

6

D'Olier St

Bank of
Ireland

Gt Brunswick Street

1

Dame St

all

Sth George's S

Nassau St

Trinity College

Westland Row
Station

Dublin
Castle

Munger Street

Grafton Street

Mansion
House

Government
Buildings

Merrion
Square

To Kingstown
(Dun Laoghaire)

St Stephen's
Green

Lower Baggot St

Hospital

Lower Mount St

Grand Canal Street

Beggar's Bush
Barracks

Harcourt Street

University
College

Lower Leeson St

Lower Pembroke St

Upper Pembroke St

Fitzwilliam

Upper
Mount St

Harcourt St
Station

Road

Grand Canal

To South East

BALLSBRIDGE

RATHMINES

RANELAGH

DONNYBROOK

ACKNOWLEDGEMENTS

My greatest debt is to Walter Grey, friend and former colleague, who was involved in the project from the start. The book is in large part the product of our continuous dialogue over three years, during which time I relied heavily on his encyclopaedic knowledge of Dublin and Dubliners, his meticulous vetting of many different drafts and the ideas generated in the course of numerous stimulating discussions. Walter also designed the maps. I would also like to thank Dr Timothy Bowman, Michelle Brown and Stewart Roulston, who read and made detailed comments on the text. I am also indebted to Dr Brian Barton, Commandant Pat Brennan, Brother Thomas Connolly, Andrew Cook, Shay Courtney, Jason Foy, Jim Herlihy, Dr Michael Hopkinson, Ivan Johnston, Grainne Killeen, Colin Kirkpatrick, Commandant Victor Lang, Susan Louden, Sergeant Patrick McGee, Peggy Mack (who provided the only existing photograph of her father, Jack Byrnes), Dan Moore, Julian Putkowski, Harry Ramsay, Denis Rice and Alasdair Verschoyle. Finally, I want to thank Christopher Feeney of Sutton Publishing, who commissioned the book, and his colleagues Jane Entrican, Hilary Walford and Yvette Cowles, Allison McKechnie, who edited the manuscript, Jonathon Price, who read the proofs, and Helen Litton, who compiled the index.

Michael T. Foy

PROLOGUE

As the Easter Rising against British rule in Ireland collapsed on Friday 28 April 1916, the rebel Provisional Government evacuated its headquarters in Dublin's General Post Office. Next day it surrendered unconditionally, and two of the leaders, Patrick Pearse and James Connolly, were taken into British custody. Another three, Tom Clarke, Sean MacDermott and Joseph Plunkett, stayed with rank-and-file Volunteers, whom the enemy lined up that evening outside the Gresham Hotel in O'Connell Street.

British officers at the scene regarded the prisoners as pro-German traitors, a defeated rabble that was expected to submit meekly. But instead they remained insouciantly defiant, smashing weapons at their captors' feet and even lighting up cigarettes and cigars. One Volunteer recalled their response when 'orders were shouted by the military to "Stop smoking!" They were an incorrigible bunch – most of them continued smoking. Then came an order in an unmistakable Etonian accent, "Stop that smoking." Some wag repeated the order – and accent – with perfect cadence and this was followed by a peal of laughter from the other side of the street.'[1] The prisoners were then marched a short distance to a grassy space at the front of the Rotunda Hospital, where they were surrounded by armed soldiers and ordered to lie down. Machine guns on the roofs of the Rotunda and nearby buildings covered the area while angry guards using rifle butts threatened anyone who even dared to stretch their legs on the surrounding pathway.

The senior British officer present was Captain Lea Wilson, a 31-year-old Englishman. Sporting a tasselled smoking cap, he circulated with junior officers, asking them repeatedly: 'Whom do you consider worse, the Boches or the Sinn Feiners?' As if on cue, they chorused that the rebels were indeed the foulest.[2] Eventually the G-men, Dublin's political detectives, arrived. After they had identified Tom Clarke as a dangerous subversive, Wilson smacked his face, shouting, 'This old bastard has been at it before.

He has a shop across the street there. He's an old Fenian.'[3] He then frog-marched Clarke to the Rotunda steps and searched him thoroughly; many Volunteers believed, probably incorrectly, that Wilson also stripped him naked. When a British officer disdainfully told Sean MacDermott that 'You have cripples in your army', the limping polio victim retorted: 'You have your place sir, and I have mine, and you had better mind your place, sir.'[4] Another officer confiscated MacDermott's walking stick. Both Clarke and MacDermott were iconic republican figures, and their treatment seemed to smack of deliberate British humiliation. While hardly a sadistic monster, Wilson embodied that injustice, and his face became imprinted on every prisoner's memory.

Saturday night was long and bitterly cold. There was little food or water available, and with no sanitation many Volunteers relieved themselves on the grass. The ground was hard and damp, and an area suitable for about 150 men was eventually crammed with over 400 prisoners as captives arrived steadily from surrendering outposts. Anyone snatching some sleep was liable to be awakened by others trying to work themselves into a more comfortable position or by the torch beam of a British officer searching for rebel leaders. One person who suffered agonising cramps was 21-year-old Liam Tobin. Having barely slept for a week, he was slipping into a dreamlike state, though he remembered Wilson turning down a comrade's request to allow Tobin to rise. 'I know that when he refused to allow me to stand up I looked at him and I registered a vow to myself that I would deal with him at some time in the future.'[5] Nearby, another young man was watching Wilson's behaviour intently. Twenty-five-year-old Michael Collins was already exercising command over others, and he passed along an order to 'get that fellow's name'.[6]

Prisoners debated long over their likely fate, which some envisaged as a specially raised punishment battalion on the Western Front or trans-portation to a Devil's Island on the far side of the world. But Clarke, MacDermott and Plunkett knew that theirs would be a one-way journey terminating in front of a firing squad. In the morning, after twelve seemingly endless hours, they were finally allowed to get up, and nurses crowded at the hospital windows could see a cloud of steaming urine rising from the ground. As it was Sunday many Volunteers knelt and prayed. They were now very hungry and thirsty, having gone without food and water for over twenty-four hours. Finally, at about 9 a.m. they were marched off to Richmond Barracks. MacDermott hobbled far behind under armed escort and arrived three-quarters of an hour late, completely exhausted. Plunkett, who was seriously ill with tuberculosis, had already fainted at the gates and had to be carried inside by British soldiers.

ɪ ɪ ɪ

Four years later in 1920 the political situation in Ireland was utterly transformed. Although Clarke, MacDermott and other leaders had been executed, their revolutionary heirs were now triumphant after Sinn Fein's overwhelming election victory in December 1918, the establishment of an as yet unrecognised independent Irish parliament and the reaffirmation of an Irish Republic. Some Rotunda prisoners had become republican leaders, including Collins, who, besides being an Irish government minister, was the Irish Volunteers' Director of Intelligence and chief organiser of an escalating guerrilla campaign. Liam Tobin was Collins's Deputy Director and manager of a secret intelligence department whose orders were executed by a hand-picked assassination unit known as the Squad. In a remarkable reversal of fortune, Collins and Tobin, once defeated captives, now possessed literally the power of life and death, and their hatred of Lea Wilson was undiminished. In the summer of 1920 they decided to finally settle accounts with him. Collins, as a friend wrote, 'always finished a job'.[7]

Having left the British Army, Lea Wilson had returned to the RIC as District Inspector of Gorey in north Wexford, forty-five miles south of Dublin. Despite its revolutionary tradition, Wexford was relatively peaceful, partly because of a substantial but well-behaved British army and police presence, mountains and rivers that isolated the county geographically and an open terrain unsuitable for guerrilla warfare. A tranquil town of about 3,000 inhabitants, Gorey was an easy posting for a policeman, and Wilson and his wife lived undisturbed a quarter of a mile away. To kill Wilson, Collins had to dispatch his Squad to Gorey. Early on 15 June the District Inspector, unarmed and in civilian clothes, strolled to the police station, cleared up some routine business, bought a newspaper at the railway station and headed home at about 9.30 a.m. Reading as he walked, Wilson probably didn't see a car that was parked a couple of hundred yards ahead with four men gathered round its raised bonnet, apparently examining the engine. As soon as he passed the vehicle, Wilson was shot, staggered fifteen yards and was then hit again. When he collapsed, the Squad finished him off on the ground with bullets to the thigh, chest, shoulder, jaw and skull before climbing back inside the car, which revved up instantly, turned around and headed out of Gorey.[8]

That afternoon Joe Sweeney, a 1916 Volunteer, was standing at the bar of Dublin's Wicklow Hotel when 'Mick Collins in his usual way stomped in and said to me, "We got the bugger, Joe." I said, "What are you talking about?" He said, "Do you remember that first night outside the Rotunda? Lee [sic] Wilson?" "I do remember," I said, "I'll never forget it." "Well, we got him today in Gorey."'[9]

Chapter 1

THE ROAD TO CONFLICT

MICHAEL COLLINS AND THE ONSET OF THE ANGLO-IRISH WAR, 1916–1919

Michael Collins was born on 16 October 1890 at the hamlet of Sam's Cross in west Cork, the eighth and last child of a 75-year-old tenant farmer and his 30-year-old wife.[1] Collins's personality was decisively shaped by his birthplace, family environment and education, all of which permanently instilled distinctive attitudes, values and modes of behaviour and speech. While Collins left west Cork relatively early, in a sense it never left him. Before dying in 1897, Michael senior had taught his son respect for learning, and he read voraciously about politics, war, history, poetry and English literature. Steeped in west Cork's revolutionary past, Collins learned about Irish republican heroes such as Tone and Emmet. He was especially influenced by Denis Lyons, who taught a militantly nationalist interpretation of Irish history at the first of Collins's two local national schools (Lisavaird and Clonakilty), where he also excelled in mathematics, French, Greek and Latin.

Choosing among one of rural Ireland's traditional escape routes for ambitious achievers – the priesthood, emigration or the British civil service – Collins passed the latter's entrance examination in 1906 and became a junior clerk at the West Kensington post office savings bank in London. He resigned after two frustrating years in a dead-end job, but neither a stockbroker's office nor a trust company proved any more satisfying. By his late teens Collins was still a shy and rather socially inept young man, channelling his restless energies into Irish culture, politics and sports. Although friendly with English colleagues, he never assimilated there, staying firmly within the expatriate Irish community, living with his sister Hannie, socialising in Irish clubs and pubs, learning Gaelic and joining the Irish Republican Brotherhood (IRB). Rising political tensions at home during the third Home Rule crisis made Collins even more of a republican revolutionary, and by 1914 he was prominent in the London IRB, honing his conspiratorial ability and talent spotting for new recruits at Gaelic games throughout Britain.

In January 1916 Collins moved to Dublin, partly to evade conscription (which had not been extended to Ireland) but primarily to participate in the coming rebellion. As adjutant to Joseph Plunkett, a member of the Military Council planning the rebellion, he was able to observe the inner circle's expertise in plotting, duplicity and ruthlessness – an invaluable crash course in revolutionary politics. During Easter week Collins performed competently if unspectacularly in the GPO. Subsequently he was interned at Frongoch camp in North Wales, where, according to a fellow prisoner, he 'got his taste of [*sic*] scheming and trickery . . . as well as making friends and contacts with people who were deeply involved with the IRB organisation'.[2] Collins's circle included Joe O'Reilly, who later became his personal assistant, and Mick McDonnell, the first leader of the Squad. In December 1916, when Lloyd George became British prime minister, he released Frongoch's prisoners as a gesture of reconciliation to Ireland. They received a rapturous Christmas reception in Dublin, now literally Ireland's central political battleground and Collins's home for the rest of his life.

Although he returned unemployed and virtually penniless, Collins's head start over more senior republicans who were still incarcerated at Lewes Gaol in England got him the post of secretary to the Irish National Aid and Volunteers' Dependants Fund. Tom Clarke's widow Kathleen had established it, ostensibly as a charity for the relatives of executed and dead Volunteers and former internees, but really to help resuscitate the republican movement. She sensed Collins had the ability to use the Fund as a cover for legally resurrecting political resistance and particularly liked his insistence that 'the fight for freedom must be continued, the Rising to count as the first blow. With his forceful personality, his wonderful magnetism and his organising ability, he had little trouble in becoming a leader.'[3] A Fund employee remembered Collins as

exacting, businesslike and orderly. Sometimes he growled at being asked to do things, but he always got them done. On one occasion early in 1917 I heard him say to a helper, my fiancée, that the office was closed, that he was going out, and that he could not wait, but he did take down the name of a man whom she wanted helped, closed the notebook, put it in his pocket and walked away without a word. He cycled out that same evening to Rathfarnham, saw the man and solved his problem.[4]

While travelling freely throughout Ireland meeting widows and orphans, Collins simultaneously reorganised the IRB, on whose reconstituted Supreme Council he now sat. Already secrecy and power were investing his persona with an aura of command, enhanced by Collins's formidable manipulative skills and an expanding network of republican activists whose names Mrs Clarke had given him.

In the spring of 1917 Collins entered national politics when republicans were challenging a Home Rule party weakened by widespread disillusion at its failure to deliver Home Rule and its apparent subservience to the British war effort. Furthermore, the post-Rising executions had generated enormous popular sympathy for the rebel leaders. The most credible political alternative was Sinn Fein, especially as the British had mistakenly blamed it for the Rising. And, despite republican scepticism about party leader Arthur Griffith's moderate separatism and his espousal of a dual monarchy with Great Britain, Sinn Fein struck lucky in May 1917 when a by-election occurred in South Longford. The contest made opposition unity essential if a traditionally impregnable Home Rule majority in the constituency was to be overcome, and Collins supported a Sinn Fein candidate. But, though he argued for a strong local man, Joe McGuinness, a Volunteer prisoner in Lewes, the doctrinaire McGuinness opposed standing for the British parliament and was backed by the gaol's republican leadership. Collins refused to accept defeat and cunningly circumvented this opposition by appealing to Thomas Ashe, the only prisoner capable of overriding the rejectionists. Head of the IRB and a Volunteer hero after his victory at the battle of Ashbourne in 1916, Ashe agreed that winning South Longford would allow republicans radically to reshape Sinn Fein policy, and he authorised Collins to push ahead with McGuinness's candidacy. As campaign manager Collins marshalled Volunteers as election workers and used the emotive slogan 'Put him in to get him out' to secure a narrow but mould-breaking Sinn Fein victory.

The party quickly followed up by winning East Clare in July and Kilkenny in August – a decisive breakthrough for a resurgent republican movement. South Longford was a nerve-racking experience for Collins but ultimately a triumphant vindication. Having successfully taken a calculated gamble, he had proved his mettle. For the first time Collins had also demonstrated his pragmatism by outflanking revolutionary purists whose dogmatism risked losing everything. The realist who would sign the Anglo-Irish Treaty in 1921 was already in place.

Collins's use of Irish Volunteers as political shock troops was visible proof of that organisation's revival, which had started the previous winter when Cathal Brugha, a hero of the Rising, established a temporary Volunteer Executive. It accelerated after December 1916, as Frongoch's returning internees restored leadership to their local units. When the Lewes prisoners returned in June 1917, Collins worked closely with Ashe, whom he accompanied to public meetings, Volunteer gatherings and IRB conclaves. But in mid-August 1919, after being arrested and charged with inciting disaffection, Ashe began a hunger strike for political status in Mountjoy Prison. He died on 25 September while being force-fed, and his funeral five days later became 'the most formidable act of defiance to British authority since the Rising'.[5] Mourners poured in from all over Ireland, bringing Dublin to a standstill, and sealed off the Castle in a symbolic rejection of British rule. The procession included 200 priests and representatives from every public organisation; 9,000 Volunteers also turned out, most in uniform and some carrying arms. Richard Mulcahy, commandant of Dublin's 2nd Battalion who had been Ashe's second-in-command at the battle of Ashbourne, organised Volunteers to escort the coffin from its lying-in-state at the City Hall and marshal vast crowds lining the route to Glasnevin Cemetery. Chosen by an IRB-dominated funeral committee because of his closeness to Ashe, Collins was to deliver the graveside oration. Despite never having made a major public speech in his life, he was ready for the occasion. Like other prisoners at Frongoch's 'university of revolution',[6] Collins had practised oratory in preparation for future leadership, and his moral and physical courage were not in doubt.

The proceedings at Glasnevin were modelled on those at the same cemetery two years earlier for a venerable republican, O'Donovan Rossa, when Volunteers had fired shots after Patrick Pearse's graveside declaration that 'Ireland unfree shall never be at peace'. Collins's tribute to Ashe consisted of only a few words in Irish and a simple proclamation that 'Nothing additional remains to be said. That volley which we have just heard is the only speech which it is proper to make above the grave of a dead Fenian.' But Collins spoke with great intensity, and his speech, accompanied by a volley of rifle fire, linked Ashe with an undying tradition of national resistance to foreign domination.

The funeral not only transformed Collins into a major republican figure but also established him as a politician in his own right by setting him free of Ashe's dominance. Ashe's pre-eminence had been largely fortuitous, as he had taken the credit for an Ashbourne victory that had really been engineered by his second-in-command, Mulcahy. Subsequently he had displayed insufficient modesty about his very modest abilities, and his continued leadership of the republican movement would have stifled the far more talented Collins. Although Ashe's demise clearly saddened Collins, it also freed him to be his own man. The funeral also fused Dublin's four uncoordinated Volunteer battalions into a new city Brigade whose first O/C was Mulcahy, while his closest associate, Dick McKee, succeeded him as 2nd Battalion commandant.[7]

At a vastly expanded Sinn Fein convention in Dublin on 25 and 26 October 1917, continuing republican reservations about Griffith's moderation forced him to stand aside as leader in favour of de Valera. Collins endorsed de Valera and was himself elected last to the party executive – confirmation that his influence was still largely confined to an inner circle. An Irish Volunteer Convention on 27 October then created a new Resident Executive to equip and train an estimated 60,000 men. Cathal Brugha became chairman, Richard Mulcahy Director of Training, and Collins was appointed Director of Organisation. Mulcahy liked Collins's 'smiling buoyancy, his capacity for bearding tension, clearness of mind, perfectly controlled calm and a devil-may-cariness completely concealed. His clarity of mind, his whole manner and demeanour, together with his power of concentration on the immediate matter in hand, gave him a very great power over men.'[8] Clearly, Collins was a born leader: charismatic, forceful and ambitious, whose all-consuming passion for politics amply compensated for his lack of wealth, a university education and influential connections. A powerful, soaring imagination, a vision of the future and an unbreakable will to realise it accorded with Lawrence of Arabia's dictum that 'All men dream, but not equally. Those who dream by night in the dusty recesses of the mind, wake in the day to find it was vanity. But the dreamers of the day are dangerous men for they may act their dreams with open eyes to make it possible.'[9] Lawrence – a man who shook an empire – was, of course, really describing himself; but Collins likewise dreamed and sometimes achieved the seemingly impossible. In time he too would shake an empire.

In March 1917 Collins's growing prominence prompted G Division to enter him on its suspects register. This was being constantly updated by a 30-year-old clerical officer, Eamon Broy, an unusual political detective who secretly nursed a fanatical hatred of British rule. His farming family lived in a remote area of County Kildare, whose history of rack-renting landlords, agrarian violence and revolution ensured that 'we of the rising generation hated the very name of England'.[10] Broy had only joined the Dublin Metropolitan Police in 1911 because of its excellent sporting facilities, a liberal reputation and an apparently imminent transfer to a Home Rule government. Shifting from the uniformed branch to G Division just before the Rising, he rose swiftly, as many detectives were retired, promoted or transferred in a mistaken belief that the revolutionary threat had evaporated. Increasingly disaffected with British policy, Broy passed many days alone in his office digesting rebellion documents and pondering ways of helping republicans.

> I spent my time thinking what the Sinn Feiners could do to win and whether, in fact, they had the slightest chance of winning. I was well aware of all the dangers that the national movement would have to encounter, some of which were: – traitors in the movement, spies from outside, drinking and boasting by members of the organisation; loose talking, the respectable, safe type of person who wanted to be arrested and be a hero: leakages of information from the USA; accident, papers discovered, on arrest or otherwise, coincidence, chance, unauthorised shooting. Notwithstanding all these dangers, I made up my mind that I would go all-out to help them, regardless of the consequences. The question then was how I could help.[11]

Fascinated by men wrestling with conflicting loyalties or leading lives as double agents inside an enemy system, which they ostensibly served, Broy was a textbook study in duplicity. From espionage literature he knew about Russian Nihilists infiltrating the Czarist secret police. Broy was also intrigued by Lady Gregory's play *The Rising of the Moon* and its depiction of an Irish policeman being torn between duty and fidelity to his own community, foreseeing 'the possibility of acting, as it were, in a highly modernised version of the RIC Sergeant in that play'.[12]

In Broy's version of the play, though, the characters would be flesh and blood and their deaths all too real. Broy relished the prospect of secretly shaping the lives of others and exercising a dramatist's power of life and death by killing off those cast members he most disliked. Clearly he immensely enjoyed outwitting his supposedly more intelligent superiors, settling old scores and watching panic and confusion become etched in colleagues' faces. In March 1917 Broy finally decided to cross over and work for the other – or, as he saw it, his own – side. Calculating that only an extreme republican would risk responding to a G-man's approaches, he tried Harry O'Hanrahan, whose brother Michael had been executed after the Rising. Initially Broy established his credentials by warning about the imminent arrest of two middle-ranking republicans. Then he began passing on every confidential document and police code that came his way, ranging from slips of paper to substantial files, including the Volunteers' own plans for resisting conscription, which an internal spy had leaked to the British. For some time Broy knew nothing about his information's final destination. O'Hanrahan was one of Collins's IRB couriers.

In early March 1918 a great German spring offensive on the Western Front compelled the British Government to mobilise new troops and the possibility that it might extend conscription to Ireland prompted the Volunteer Executive to create a General Headquarters Staff to lead resistance. Although Collins was a leading candidate for the post of Chief of Staff, it went to the better known Mulcahy, who was strongly supported by Dick McKee, the 2nd Battalion commandant who succeeded him as Dublin Brigadier. Mulcahy later recalled McKee's relief at the outcome, 'because there was a certain feeling that Collins was an impetuous fellow; they didn't know very much about him in any case and Dick was quite satisfied that Collins was not the Chief of Staff'.[13] Collins settled for the posts of Director of Organisation and Adjutant-General and shrewdly exhibited no bitterness towards Mulcahy and McKee. He needed them more than they needed him. Only by winning both men over could Collins play a major role in the capital's Volunteer movement. Fortunately for him, Mulcahy had discerned Collins's potential in Frongoch and now began discreetly nurturing it: 'One of my achievements in the work of the Volunteers was that I created a kind of shelter for Collins to get known and to get appreciated.'[14] Collins also worked assiduously to change McKee's lukewarm opinion of him, and the future of the Irish Volunteers – and much else besides – was largely determined by this burgeoning triangular relationship.

* * *

By early 1918 Collins was deeply immersed in the intelligence world through the IRB and Broy's confidential information, an involvement that distinguished him from other Volunteer leaders who had not grasped the importance of intelligence gathering. Although the new GHQ had finally established an Intelligence Department in March 1918, its first Director, Eamon Duggan, was a rather dull solicitor who lacked political drive, conspiratorial ability, personal contacts and mercilessness. He operated out of his legal offices in Dame Street with a single assistant and, like a glorified filing clerk, collated mainly publicly available information. In truth, nothing more seems to have been expected of him. Collins was meanwhile establishing a nucleus of agents in G Division, where two of Broy's colleagues had already defected. Joe Kavanagh, a short dapper 60-year-old clerk with a waxed moustache, spied for Collins from early 1917 until his sudden death from a blood clot in September 1920. At the Castle, James McNamara served as confidential clerk to the DMP's Assistant Commissioner. Both men communicated with Collins through a courier network that included Harry O'Hanrahan, Greg Murphy, Michael Foley and Tommy Gay, a librarian in Capel Street Municipal Library. Broy remembered Gay as 'a tiny Dublin man who suffered from chronic bronchial trouble which made his life a burden. Like nearly all the *dramatis personae* of the revolution, he led a double life; a bookworm openly and also, secretly, a confidential courier for Collins. He was so unobtrusive that neither the library nor his home ever came under suspicion.'[15] The library's reading room, inhabited mainly by down-and-outs, provided ideal cover, though Collins also met Gay at his quiet suburban house in Clontarf.

During April 1918 the German army's seemingly relentless advance forced the British Government's hand over conscription, and, despite Chief Secretary Henry Duke's warning that he might as well conscript Germans as Irishmen, Lloyd George introduced a Military Conscription Bill on 9 April. Although he delayed its application to Ireland, Irish Nationalist MPs immediately withdrew from Parliament and joined Sinn Fein in a national resistance campaign that was endorsed by the Catholic Church. Three days later police arrested Joe Dowling, a member of Casement's Irish Brigade whom a German submarine had landed on the north Clare coast. His orders were to inveigle Sinn Fein leaders – who knew nothing about his mission – into another Rising on the promise of a German expeditionary force. While British Intelligence investigated this so-called German Plot, the Irish situation deteriorated rapidly. Membership of Sinn Fein and the Volunteers soared, armed attacks were made on police barracks in Cork and Kerry, hundreds of thousands pledged to 'resist conscription by the most effective means at our disposal' and a one-day general strike took place on 23 April 1918. On 2 May an exhausted Duke resigned, along with Viceroy Wimborne, and for the next two years Irish policy was shaped by the 64-year-old Colonial Secretary Walter Long.

This former Conservative Chief Secretary, Dublin MP and Irish Unionist leader blamed past British Governments for not arresting republican leaders planning rebellion. Invested by Lloyd George with special authority for Ireland, Long determined never to allow another Rising on his watch. He would help a new Viceroy and Chief Secretary administer the smack of firm government and guide them through the snake pit of Irish politics.

The new Viceroy was Long's old friend Lord French, a 65-year-old former Chief of the Imperial General Staff who had been forced to resign in 1915 after two difficult years commanding the British Expeditionary Force in France. Now languishing as Commander-in-Chief of Home Forces, he welcomed the opportunity to redeem his battered reputation, particularly as he regarded himself as well versed in Irish affairs.[16] Although born in Kent, French always thought of himself as Irish because of his family's origins as Norman settlers in Wexford, and before the war he had served in Ireland, where he subsequently bought a country home in Roscommon. Having strongly endorsed the execution of the rebel leaders in 1916, French became Viceroy as the acknowledged head of a quasi-military Irish administration. Originally he even intended ruling as a military governor and decided only at the last moment to make his old chief of staff, Sir Frederick Shaw, Commander-in-Chief. French's Chief Secretary, Edward Shortt, was a compliant Liberal MP without any previous ministerial experience. He accepted the Viceroy's political seniority and was expected faithfully to implement Long's and French's policy of pacifying Ireland and resisting Irish nationalism.

At a flurry of meetings in London between 6 and 10 May 1918, Long and French formulated a hardline Irish policy in conjunction with Basil Thomson, head of Special Branch and widely regarded as an Irish expert. Although Long expected French to act 'with an unsparing hand',[17] the Viceroy struck Thomson as 'rather old and decrepit'[18] – though he was impressed when French dismissed assassination attempts 'with the greatest composure as a chance you had to take'.[19]

Long regarded Ireland as strategically vital to the Allied war effort, because another rebellion while British and French armies were retreating all along the Western Front might mean the difference between victory and defeat. He demanded that 'the most drastic steps should be taken to stamp out pro-German intrigues'.[20] On 8 May Thomson found Long agitated by Sir Edward Carson's claim in *The Times* that the government had incontrovertible evidence of a Sinn Fein–German alliance. He, in turn, astonished Long by claiming already to have shown proof to Duke and Wimborne, only for them to block the internment of Sinn Fein leaders.[21] This finally confirmed Long's perception of Dublin Castle as an Augean stables needing to be utterly cleansed of such arch appeasers, and he told Thomson that any government that ignored such information deserved impeachment.

Long also instructed Thomson to compile a list of republican ringleaders immediately, and by the time French departed for Ireland three days later, plans for a crackdown were well under way. On Monday 13 May he informed Thomson that large-scale arrests were timed for Friday night and confidently predicted a smooth operation. Reminiscing about his time as Chief Secretary, Long recalled his then chief of police describing an Irish peasant superstition that the deaths of assassins from accidents or disease was 'a judgement, and when the next generation (the present one) grew up they would be too well educated to murder. This is also the view of the Irish police.'[22]

As G Division finalised its arrest list, Broy was leaking the contents to O'Hanrahan, whom he warned on Friday morning, 17 May, that raids would take place that night. After advising that targets avoid their usual haunts, Broy was stunned when over eighty prominent republicans were rounded up. Only later did he learn that, while Collins had tipped off Sinn Fein leaders at a meeting in Harcourt Street, most – including de Valera, Griffith and Countess Markievicz – preferred mass arrest in order to portray British policy as the crude repression of Irish nationalism. Whatever Duggan's formal role, it was on 17 May 1918 that Collins emerged as the Irish Volunteer GHQ's de facto Director of Intelligence. By displaying his access to the enemy's most confidential information and acting as protector of the republican leadership, Collins had transformed his power and standing in his colleagues' eyes.

Having failed to anticipate the Easter Rising, the British authorities were elated at scooping up most of the republican leaders so easily, satisfied, according to Broy, 'that they could lay their hands on anybody they wanted at any time'.[23] Long was pleased that 'the coup seems to have been a complete success',[24] while Thomson crowed that 'de Valera, who had always said he would not be taken alive, went like a sheep'.[25] But any idea that normal service had been resumed was an illusion. Broy noted 'a certain eerie feeling'[26] among fellow detectives when they arrested suspects with their belongings already packed, as if anticipating a journey. But their unease did not percolate to the upper echelons, where Broy saw that, even after Sinn

Fein had filled its organisational gaps with surprising ease, 'there was no suspicion however awakened in the Castle'.[27]

Some republican leaders went on the run. From the end of April to October 1918 Cathal Brugha was in London preparing but eventually abandoning plans to assassinate the entire British Cabinet if it imposed conscription on Ireland. Collins spent the next ten months underground in Dublin, surfacing only briefly at a Sinn Fein Executive meeting to pack the candidate list for December's general election with militants.[28] Mulcahy also remained in the capital, hoping that a republican election victory would lead to the creation of an independent Irish Parliament and government, which in turn would confer legitimacy on the Volunteers as the army of a new Irish state. Until then, he believed Volunteers had to exercise maximum restraint in order to deprive the British of any excuse for cancelling elections and suppressing the republican movement. Mulcahy also worried about an enormous disparity between the British army and the comparatively tiny, untrained and virtually weaponless Volunteers. Since this would have made any premature clashes suicidal, he urged 'prudence, patience and discipline in avoiding situations leading to conflict and exposing the Volunteers and the people to the losses and the danger of disclosing to the aggressors our intrinsic weakness'.[29] But his delicate balancing act was made even more difficult by police raids, arrests and heavy surveillance of Sinn Fein meetings, which Mulcahy feared might provoke local Volunteer units into literally jumping the gun. 'In many areas, where the pressures of aggression were very great and the support of opposition strong, violent reaction by the people created different problems of control for the general headquarters.'[30]

On the British side, Long's grand project stalled quite rapidly after May's apparently successful crackdown, as French discovered that making progress in Ireland was even more frustrating than advancing through the mud of Flanders. Expected to restore order with a government machine that was extraordinarily resistant to change, the Viceroy especially bemoaned the inefficiency of five rival intelligence services, one of which, Thomson's Special Branch, told the military authorities in Dublin hardly anything. He recommended overhauling the intelligence system and increasing its budget in order to locate Irish Volunteer weapons. 'I think all sides feel that the present system should be altered and that it should be replaced by a thoroughly coordinated effort. All the different branches of intelligence appear to be jealous of each other, which is not a good start.'[31]

Later on in early April 1919 French complained to War Secretary Churchill about the crippling lack of a proper Criminal Investigation Department in Ireland and unsuccessfully requested the loan of the head of MI5, Captain Vernon Kell.[32]

Once again, Long blamed the Irish administration and especially Shortt, whom a coterie of Dublin Castle conservatives told him had gone native, by espousing Home Rule to curry favour with nationalists and the Roman Catholic hierarchy. By late August 1918 Long had had enough, and the Chief Secretary became the first – but not the last – Irish official to whom he dealt the black spot. Increasingly isolated, Shortt survived only until December, when he could be quietly jettisoned after the general election. Meanwhile another whispering campaign gathered momentum against the Catholic Under-Secretary, James MacMahon, supposedly in Cardinal Logue's pocket, and his co-religionist Sir Joseph Byrne, the RIC Inspector-General who allegedly lacked zeal in combating republican militancy.

As Mulcahy had hoped, Volunteer restraint held sufficiently for Sinn Fein to win a landslide general election victory in which Collins was returned unopposed for South Cork. Although many Sinn Fein MPs were imprisoned or in hiding, an inaugural meeting of the Dail convened on 21 January 1919 in the Round Room of Dublin's Mansion House. When this direct challenge to British authority fuelled rumours of troop movements and a pre-emptive strike, McKee filled the hall with armed Volunteers disguised as plain-clothes stewards as well as posting scouts outside to warn about any attempt to storm the building. Inside, 3,000 spectators, foreign reporters and honoured guests watched deputies quickly endow Ireland with 'the trappings of an independent state'[33] by reaffirming the Republic of Easter Week, issuing a declaration of independence and electing a cabinet in which Brugha was temporary president (because de Valera was still in jail). Collins became Minister of Home Affairs.

Mulcahy wanted the Dail to meet peacefully, allowing a smooth transition in which new national institutions could be established and new political leaders installed. But he was nagged by the fear of a violent incident in some volatile county like Cork, Tipperary or Limerick. So he was not entirely surprised on the afternoon of 21 January when news filtered through of a Volunteer ambush at a quarry in Soloheadbeg, just outside Tipperary town, in which two policemen escorting a civilian dynamite wagon had been shot dead. As rumours of imminent martial law swept Dublin, McKee assembled armed Volunteers at houses throughout the capital and only stood them down in the early hours after the immediate danger had passed.[34] The Soloheadbeg killers were a local unit commanded by Dan Breen and Sean Treacy, both of whom were imbued with a militaristic contempt for Sinn Fein's timidity. Breen's sole regret was that 'the police escort had consisted of only two peelers instead of six. If there had to be dead peelers at all, six would have created a better impression than a mere two.'[35] His remarks have usually been dismissed as bravado, and many nationalists regarded the killings as a tragic accident, but significantly the gelignite, ostensibly the intended target, lay unused for nearly a year. Undoubtedly, a minority of Volunteers regarded Soloheadbeg as an action waiting to happen.

But, although historians almost universally regard Soloheadbeg as the start of an Anglo-Irish War, the ambush contravened Volunteer GHQ's official policy, and Mulcahy privately denounced it as an irresponsible attempt by extremists to bounce the army leadership into open war. He loathed the Tipperary leaders,[36] and summoned Treacy and his commanding officer, Seamus Robinson, to Dublin, intending, in effect, to deport them. Mulcahy refused even to have them in his office and arranged a street-corner meeting between them and Collins, who as Adjutant-General was responsible for Volunteer discipline. Mulcahy had ordered Collins to have them 'escape' to America, but Robinson was having none of it:

'We don't want to go to the States or anywhere else.' 'Well,' said Mick, 'that is what many people seem to think is the only thing to do.' I began to think that GHQ had begun to give way to Sinn Fein pacifism and with a little acerbity I said 'Look here, to kill a couple of policemen for the country's sake and leave it at that by running away would be so wanton as to approximate too closely to murder.'
   'Then what do you propose to do?'
   'Fight it out of course.'
   Mick Collins, without having shown the slightest emotion during the short interview, now suddenly closed his notebook with a snap, saying as he started off with the faintest of faint smiles on his lips but with a big laugh in his eyes, 'That's all right with me.'[37]

Far from sharing Mulcahy's revulsion, Collins was keen to discover whether Robinson and Treacy were simply undisciplined hotheads or serious revolutionaries. Once they realised that he too believed war was inevitable, and the sooner the better, an unofficial alliance was forged between national and local radicals. In a pub that evening, Dublin Volunteer officer Joe Lawless saw both Tipperary men's contentment and 'from their joking references, I gathered that they had received a formal reprimand with one hand and a pat on the back with the other'.[38] After returning home Robinson and Treacy continued chipping away at what they and Collins regarded as simply an armed truce, doomed to collapse when the British were ready to crush the republican movement.

Convinced that war was unavoidable, Collins was concerned only with ensuring that it began in the most favourable circumstances for the Irish. However, in early 1919 this belief was confined to a small minority, because most republicans, let alone the population as a whole, neither desired nor expected a conflict. But manipulating a reluctant nation into war without a democratic mandate hardly troubled Collins, who only three years before had observed a revolutionary junta, 'a minority within a minority within a minority',[39] brush aside the Volunteers' President, the IRB's Supreme Council and even the secret organisation's own constitution in its unstoppable march towards rebellion. Collins had learned well from masters like Clarke and MacDermott, who had virtually written the manual on duplicity. Unlike the Military Council's seven members, Collins began his road to war in a minority of one, though he was sustained by the same messianic determination and daring imagination. His strategy in 1919 was to first create a radical coalition – a war party – by winning over Volunteer GHQ and the Dublin Brigade, then create a war atmosphere by exploiting British Government mistakes and increasing popular frustration at political stagnation before bringing the crisis to a head through calculated acts of provocation.

Although in the first half of 1919 Collins was not yet strong enough to bring about open war, he strained to get at the police, the British Government's first line of defence. Broy saw his impatience when they finally met a few days before Soloheadbeg, an encounter to which he arrived

very deeply intrigued to know who or what this man Collins was like. The moment I saw Michael at the door before he had time to walk across and shake hands, I knew he was the man. He was dressed in black leggings, green breeches and a trench coat with all the usual buttons, belts and rings. He was very handsome, obviously full of energy and with a mind quick as lightning.[40]

Their four-hour discussion left Broy elated at Collins's scorn for compromise and his belief that the British were only stringing the Irish along in order to split Sinn Fein while preparing an all-out offensive. Broy thought 'there was not a chance of getting anything from the British Parliament by constitutional means' and 'agreed entirely with Michael Collins that force was the only chance, however difficult and dangerous'.[41] After describing a demoralised and ageing police force that was 2,000 men under strength, Broy recommended that Collins begin by driving the RIC from its smaller barracks and weakening its physical and psychological grip on the population. The uniformed DMP should be left alone because it was less politicised, and many nationalist officers with Volunteer relatives would remain passive as long as they were not attacked. Even most G-men were not on full-time political duty and could be persuaded to back off, while a 'ruthless war was to be made on the hard core that remained'.[42]

But, in the shocked aftermath of Soloheadbeg, Collins could not risk assaulting G Division, and instead an uneasy coexistence between British and Irish authority limped along. This stand-off suited Lloyd George, who was immersed in domestic, international and imperial problems and confidently expected Sinn Fein to moderate its republican rhetoric eventually and adjust pragmatically to Britain's overwhelming power. Until then he wanted Ireland kept quiet by French and the new Chief Secretary, Ian Macpherson, a Scottish Conservative who had arrived in January 1919. Sinn Fein, for its part, hoped that American pressure and the Paris Peace Conference would bring about international recognition of Irish independence. But once again provincial bit players refused to stick to the agreed script, and on 23 February Robinson's turbulent 3rd Brigade ordered all British military and police forces out of South Tipperary. Seething at another flouting of his authority, Mulcahy 'refused to sanction this proclamation, but the Brigade authorities went ahead, notwithstanding, and made it public. It was not the first time differences of opinion had arisen between GHQ and the South Tipperary Brigade, nor would it be the last.'[43]

By April 1919 events were moving in Collins's favour. He had forged a new relationship with Dick McKee, an IRB member and revolutionary extremist whose reservations about Collins had been personal, not ideological. As GHQ Director of Training, McKee met Collins regularly, and their burgeoning political alliance was sealed when Collins invited him to supervise an important training camp for Cork Volunteer officers.[44]

Mulcahy regarded theirs as 'one of the great companionships of our period. Linking as it did in the heart of Dublin the striking force of the Dublin Brigade and the information and striking force associated directly with Collins, the Collins–McKee companionship was the core of that aggressive defence which saved our political leadership, Dail and Government from complete destruction.'[45]

McKee's role was pivotal because he made the Dublin Brigade's resources available to Collins, who began attending Brigade Council meetings in February 1919. In addition, through McKee's friendship with Mulcahy, Collins was able to cultivate a relationship with the Chief of Staff. A 26-year-old bachelor, McKee was already an iconic figure to the Dublin Volunteers: a tall, imposing natural leader whose languid exterior and soft beguiling drawl concealed a driven and ruthless personality. At Brigade headquarters McKee had assembled a like-minded inner circle typified by Mick McDonnell, the quartermaster of 2nd Battalion, a firebrand who was constantly baying for action. Early on he had 'advocated the execution of those who were responsible for the identifying of the men executed in 1916 and who were at the same time watching us. This was at first turned down by Dick McKee, who felt that the people would not stand for this action at the time.'[46] But McKee's closest confidant was his future vice-brigadier, Peadar Clancy, who ran an outfitter's shop in Talbot Street that doubled as a revolutionary drop-in centre. These inseparable friends had grown up, conspired, fought and been imprisoned together. Ultimately and violently, they would die together.

Like Collins, McKee thought war inevitable, an idea to which his rhetoric in *An t-Oglach* (the journal that he produced virtually single-handed) subtly conditioned ordinary Volunteers. Frank Henderson, McKee's 2nd Battalion commandant, recalled that 'Nobody exactly spoke as a rule of the coming fight but it was accepted that we were preparing for something which could hardly be anything else than an armed struggle.'[47] McKee prepared by re-equipping his virtually weaponless Brigade with grenades bought or stolen from British soldiers or manufactured at an underground munitions factory in Parnell Street. A large raid at a British military aerodrome in March 1919 had also netted 75 rifles and 6,000 rounds of ammunition. McKee also made Dublin a sanctuary for displaced provincial revolutionaries like Breen and Treacy after they were hounded out of Tipperary in the autumn. He shielded them from Mulcahy in the capital, particularly as he knew Collins was planning to use these enthusiastic gunmen.

By April 1919 Collins still only imperfectly understood G Division's structure and operating methods, and, when Broy offered him a surreptitious guided tour of its Brunswick Street headquarters, he could not resist. Broy was often on night duty, and shortly after midnight on 7 April he admitted Collins and Sean Nunan and escorted them upstairs to the political office. Built into a wall was a small, permanently darkened room containing all G Division's records. It was an archive of failed Irish revolutions brimming with documents and photographs – a rogue's gallery of spies, traitors, *agents provocateurs* and informers. Carrying candles and matches, Collins and Nunan approached like archaeologists entering a long-forbidden secret chamber and, no doubt, with the same hushed expectancy. After five hours reading and note taking, Collins emerged into the morning light a changed man whose questions had been answered, whose ideas had crystallised and who now knew what G-men knew – and did not know – about the republican movement. Having entered and toured his enemy's mind, Collins was now in a position to create 'his own G Division'[48] – one that would emulate and finally outclass the original model.

In February 1919 Collins engineered de Valera's escape from Lincoln Gaol and smuggled him back to Ireland, where he hid for a month until the British Government freed the remaining 'German Plot' detainees. At the same time Collins and others on the run resurfaced. Around April 1919, and probably to his own immense relief, Duggan was shunted aside as intelligence chief. When the Dail cabinet was reconstructed on 2 April, de Valera became President, Brugha switched to the Ministry of Defence and Collins became Minister of Finance. Mulcahy records him then also as definitely being GHQ Director of Intelligence, an apparently routine reshuffle that Brugha must have rubber-stamped without realising that he was vastly expanding Collins's power and authority. Mulcahy claims Brugha 'took no part in the discussion of any matters that could be regarded as purely staff or military matters. And that would almost refer even to the development of policy.'[49] Instead Brugha continued working as a director of a firm of candle-makers and functioning as a part-time Minister of Defence.

Creating a proper Volunteer Intelligence Department would have daunted anyone less confident and resilient than Collins. He started with only a nucleus of police moles and IRB helpers and weighed down by a conviction that time was rapidly running out, that, once G Division had completed gathering intelligence on republicans, the British would destroy Dail Eireann, Sinn Fein and the Irish Volunteers. Collins believed the Irish nation faced a stark choice between the obliteration of its legitimately elected government and an Anglo-Irish War in which victory would be attainable through an effective Volunteer intelligence system. But building such an organisation would take months, whereas Collins's immediate priority was destroying G Division. Just two days after secretly visiting Brunswick Street he began peeling off the division's soft outer layer. Collins had McKee distribute detective lists to his Brigade Council, after which, according to Frank Henderson,

> in all the Battalion areas these junior detectives were rounded up on the same night close to their homes or lodgings as they were returning from duty, taken down quiet laneways and beaten until they solemnly promised to take no further part in such treacherous work against their country's efforts to regain freedom. They were told that if they did not keep their promise they would be shot but that they would not be prevented from doing detective work against criminals. This action had the desired result and drove in the outer ring of police spies.[50]

Broy saw one detective, Denis O'Brien, angrily remonstrating with Superintendent Purcell, who had accused him of not standing his ground. 'He said: "I would like to know what anyone else would do in the same circumstances." He said to some of us afterwards "They were damned decent men not to shoot me, and I am not doing any more against them".'[51] But some senior G-men were beyond intimidation. They included Detective Sergeant Hally, who fired shots at Volunteers raiding his Norfolk Road home on 9 April, and Detective Sergeants Daniel Hoey, John Barton and Patrick Smyth. Broy considered Smyth, an aggressive 48-year-old police veteran, 'most dangerous and insidious when he laughed, and he laughed often'.[52] Hoey retaliated on 9 May with a full-scale police and army raid of a civic reception at the Mansion House, from which Collins only narrowly escaped by slipping out through the back door and climbing a high wall.

* * *

By May 1919 Viceroy French was complaining angrily that 'every day brings fresh proof of the underground actions of these Irish Volunteers which are nothing more or less than a regular constituted and organised Sinn Fein army'.[53] But radical action needed the backing of Deputy Prime Minister Bonar Law, who was in charge during Lloyd George's prolonged absence at the Paris Peace Conference. Law was the Conservative Party leader and a Canadian of Ulster extraction who had unswervingly supported Carson's pre-war campaign against Home Rule. But when Chief Secretary Macpherson met him on 15 May and recommended suppressing Sinn Fein and the Volunteers, Law accepted instead Carson's advice that this would kill off political life in Southern Ireland.[54] He urged Dublin Castle to consider the idea of proclaiming Dail Eireann, and the Chief Secretary, a political cushion wearing the impress of whichever political superior had last sat upon him, returned to break the news to a disappointed French.[55] But Law sensed that 'a big decision'[56] about Ireland was inevitable in the near future.

Soon afterwards French and Macpherson met Long, who was on a fact-finding mission to Ireland. He had found the population sullen, Sinn Fein well organised, and 'more deliberate, cold-blooded crime, than in any previous period'.[57] The Viceroy claimed certain Dublin streets were mined to assassinate him, while Long himself needed the protection of five detectives and armed soldiers. As usual, Long blamed Dublin Castle, which, unless urgently reformed, would make any attempt to suppress Sinn Fein 'suicidal'. 'The moment Government attempted to give effect to the proclamation, the weapon would break in their hands and they would suffer – not the rebels.'[58] Long believed the RIC's Inspector-General, Sir Joseph Byrne, had lost his nerve and that some of his senior police officers were 'either utterly incompetent or hopelessly worn out'.[59] He recommended a complete overhaul, starting with Byrne's replacement by a capable county inspector such as the Belfast Commissioner T.J. Smith. But, as this would take about three to four months, he persuaded French and Macpherson to wait until August or September before renewing their demands for radical political action. Once a reliable police system was in place, he maintained, 'there will be very little difficulty in dealing with these troubles'.[60]

* * *

Collins's decision to eliminate G Division's hard core was endorsed by Chief of Staff Richard Mulcahy. This cautious bureaucrat had finally given up on a peaceful settlement after the Paris Peace Conference had rejected Irish independence and detectives had exerted pressure on republicans by raiding the homes of Volunteer and Sinn Fein activists. Mulcahy regarded this as deliberate British provocation, and was more concerned now with persuading the Irish people that they were being forced into fighting a justified defensive war against foreign aggression. By the middle of 1919 Mulcahy agreed with Collins that British preparations for a pre-emptive strike made decisive action by Volunteer GHQ imperative:

> The authorities were apparently biding their time to have certain preparations made before the Dail was suppressed. The work of men like Smyth, Hoey and Barton and the G Division generally was being effectively snowballed to increase the information regarding the persons who were particularly active and important both on the political and the volunteer side. To have allowed it to develop any way effectively would have been disastrous. The initiative against the detectives was only begun just in time.[61]

Mulcahy's crucial shift to the war party was accelerated by his increasing regard for Collins. The 33-year-old Chief of Staff was originally a post office engineer who had joined the IRB and the Irish Volunteers in Dublin before the war and whose coolness and tactics as Thomas Ashe's second-in-command had really won the Battle of Ashbourne in 1916. Superficially the reserved, bookish Mulcahy had little in common with Collins, but both were products of the British civil service who brimmed with organising ability, and they complemented each other perfectly. Mulcahy was clearly enthralled by the slightly younger man and revelled in their almost symbiotic relationship of 'the completest understanding and effective cooperation . . . I don't think that I ever had occasion to discuss a problem with Collins for more than five minutes or to argue with Collins on any particular kind of line of thought.'[62]

Always happiest behind the scenes, Mulcahy became mentor, friend and an indulgent protector of Collins's somewhat wayward genius, and by skilfully cultivating Mulcahy and McKee, Collins emerged as de facto Volunteer leader. By July 1919 this revolutionary troika – an unofficial Military Council – was ready to attack G Division. Collins's strategy was a masterly combination of defence and aggression. On the one hand, by assassinating G-men he protected the Volunteers from enemy pressure and infiltration; on the other, he goaded the British authorities and police into retaliation and overreaction, encouraging nationalist Ireland to unite behind Sinn Fein. As the outbreak of the First World War in 1914 had demonstrated, national unity in every country depended on the conviction that it had been attacked and left with no choice but to defend itself.

Still, Collins's decapitation of G Division was an extraordinarily daring policy, unauthorised by the Dail government and far ahead of mainstream republican thinking. It was something he had to conceal from almost all his colleagues and superiors. He was helped in this by Brugha's distancing of himself from Volunteer GHQ, and de Valera's departure from Ireland on an extended American tour on 1 June 1919. Just as in 1916, but in a different way, having an absentee Volunteer President enabled revolutionaries to bend the organisation to their will. Collins also shrouded his preparations in secrecy and distanced himself from any disastrous mistake by subcontracting the killings to McKee and Mick McDonnell. In mid-July 1919 they assembled a group of hand-picked Volunteers, but were surprised when a majority of the potential assassins blanched at their job description. Most who signed on, like Paddy Daly, Joe Leonard, Tom Keogh and Jim Slattery, were from McKee's old and super-militant 2nd Battalion. Collins was taking a gamble in sending this embryonic squad into action only six months after Soloheadbeg, especially as this time deliberately killing a policeman could not be passed off as a tragic accident. As the first attack drew near, Broy saw Collins becoming 'extremely anxious as to what effect the shooting of detectives would have on the Volunteers themselves and on the Sinn Fein movement generally, and how it would be taken by the public'.[63]

The Squad's first target was G-man Patrick Smyth. McDonnell ordered Jim Slattery, Tom Keogh, Tom Ennis and Mick Kennedy to shoot him as he passed over Drumcondra Bridge on his way home. But after a fortnight surveying the route and familiarising themselves with Smyth's appearance, it needed a tongue-lashing by McDonnell to spur them into action on the evening of 30 July. However, these novices only wounded the detective, who staggered to his front door and plunged inside. Joe Lawless, who lived nearby, watched as

a few inquisitive people began to drift towards the scene of the shooting and about twenty minutes later the Dublin Fire Brigade ambulance went clattering over the bridge. I walked down myself then, as quite a crowd had collected there and was just in time to see Sergeant Smyth being carried from his house to the ambulance. Joe Connolly, the ambulance driver whom I knew as a Volunteer, remarked to me, rather disappointedly, I thought, 'I don't think he is dead yet', and the crowd silently melted away as the ambulance left with the wounded detective for the Mater Hospital. Smyth died from his wounds a week or two later.[64]

Collins did not authorise another killing for some weeks while he gauged public reaction, which, significantly, was muted compared to that after Soloheadbeg. This was partly because of 'Dog' Smyth's almost universal unpopularity, but also reflected frustration over the continuing political stagnation and mounting cynicism about British Government policy. In early September 1919 an emboldened Collins went after his *bête noir*, Detective Daniel Hoey, whose activities he regarded as especially irksome. Hoey was G Division's rising star: young, intelligent, handsome, energetic and popular with his colleagues. Dublin Castle frequently allocated him important responsibilities such as guarding successive Chief Secretaries. Vinnie Byrne says that Collins 'sent for Daly and told him that he had to get this man once and for all'.[65] But Paddy Daly's team was new to the game, and weeks passed during which Joe Lawless observed an

> increased activity of the protagonist forces and a mounting tension of the public mind which betokened a gathering storm. Towards the end of that summer an indication of the British reaction to the situation was to be seen in a considerable reinforcement of troops and war equipment landed in Dublin from England. Field gun batteries, tanks and armoured cars were to be seen every now and then passing up the quays to the various Dublin barracks, being driven through the city as a demonstration of military power with, I suppose, the idea of overawing the natives.[66]

* * *

By September 1919 Dublin Castle was seriously alarmed by the deteriorating Irish situation. Sinn Fein initiated a nationwide boycott of the RIC in April, and soon afterwards three policemen were shot dead in Tipperary. No arrests were made for the murders, which led to Sinn Fein's proscription in the county in July. Then on 7 September a plain-clothes Volunteer unit ambushed a small detachment of the King's Shropshire Light Infantry on its way to church in Fermoy, County Cork, killing a soldier – the first since the Rising. Their patience exhausted, French and Macpherson appealed once again to Bonar Law. The Chief Secretary argued that, while it had been tactically wise to let the Dail assemble in January, it had now 'sat together and conspired by executive act, which could be clearly proved, to overthrow the duly constituted authorities'.[67] French believed that there was still time to break the enemy's grip on a terrorised population, particularly as he argued Sinn Fein was on the wane: 'These outrages are simply the acts of the few extremists who have got completely out of the hands of their leaders. Every report shows that they are cavilling and quarrelling amongst themselves more and more as time goes on.'[68] The Viceroy predicted that Sinn Fein would soon fragment, with moderates adopting passive resistance and extremists uniting with the Irish Volunteers and Labour's Bolshevik wing.

Basil Thomson's intelligence reports also charted Sinn Fein's supposed decline. They claimed that its campaign for a labourer's minimum wage had alienated farmers and small shopkeepers and that 'when the Peace Terms are published and there is no mention of Ireland, there will be a recrudescence of outrages all over the country but no attempt at open rebellion. The real danger of the future lies not so much in the Sinn Feiners as in the Transport Workers.'[69] In June 1919 Thomson confidently predicted that an adequate military garrison could easily contain any trouble, even though rumours of another rebellion and violent Sinn Fein rhetoric were misleading: 'De Valera and others of the more moderate views are acting as a brake. The outrages are apparently not carried out under the orders from the Central Office, but are local enterprises.'[70]

In July Thomson reported that Sinn Fein was still losing ground. The party's finances were running low because of an apathetic public response to its fundraising appeals, and even Sinn Fein's ban in Tipperary had been quietly accepted. By September it was reported that Sinn Fein 'still seems to be losing its hold on the popular imagination and in the continued absence of de Valera the leaders are facing difficulty in keeping the extremists in hand. It is said that some of the more responsible leaders have sent a message to de Valera threatening their resignation.'[71]

Thomson's optimism probably encouraged Law to respond more favourably this time to French and Macpherson. But the balance was finally tipped on 11 September by an outraged letter from George V protesting at the Fermoy ambush and demanding 'to know what the government was going to do to protect the lives of suffering people in Ireland and what measures were to be brought into parliament for the government of the country'.[72] Within hours of this royal intervention Lloyd George and Bonar Law decided to suppress Dail

Eireann. The announcement was made in a viceregal proclamation the following morning. French knew that the government was crossing the Rubicon ('we are really at war'[73]) but confidently expected victory. So did Macpherson, who, after months of 'incessant anxiety',[74] was sufficiently relaxed to leave Dublin immediately on doctor's orders and recuperate in a Berwick hotel.

Just as the Chief Secretary departed, Detective-Sergeant Hoey was raiding Sinn Fein headquarters in Harcourt Street. Collins only just escaped and went on the run for a second and final time, living underground until the Truce of July 1921. He regarded the British actions as a declaration of war and so did Mulcahy, who argued that 'what turned passive resistance and defensive tactics into an offensive war was the suppression of the Dail'.[75] Although Dublin Castle did not ban Sinn Fein and the Irish Volunteers for another fortnight, Collins retaliated instantly by nominating Hoey as, in effect, the first official British fatality. In the early evening of 12 September, Mick McDonnell reappeared at Jim Slattery's front door with another invitation to a killing, hinting at the identity of the person masterminding their deadly activities. 'He asked me would I mind going on a job. I told him I would not mind, and he said, "They very nearly got him today." – he was referring to Mick Collins. That was the first time I got an inkling that Collins was the heart of things.'[76] Within a couple of hours they located the 32-year-old Hoey. At the end of an eventful day he was on his way back to his living quarters in Great Brunswick Street. As always, he drank a glass of milk in a dairy, an unbreakable routine that enabled McDonnell and Slattery to shadow him down an ill-lit Townsend Street, where they shot him dead in a doorway. By eliminating Hoey, Collins made it impossible for the British Government to retreat without destroying G Division's morale, and indeed that of the entire Irish administration, while simultaneously implanting in Irish consciousness a connection between supposed British aggression and legitimate retribution.

According to Mulcahy, 'as a result of the suppression of the Dail a formal decision was taken to let the Volunteers take an offensive initiative against the administration of that time'.[77] In mid-November the Cork Volunteer leaders Thomas MacCurtain and Terence MacSwiney visited Cullenswood House, Mulcahy's suburban home in Oakley Road, Ranelagh, where Collins also maintained an upstairs office. Reiterating Cork's determination not to repeat its failure to fight in 1916, the fire-breathing MacSwiney wanted to order immediate attacks on a dozen police stations in the county whatever the cost. But Mulcahy told him that 'there was no use having a travelling rising like that but that now that the Dail had been suppressed we had decided that we would have to take the initiative in driving the police in a bit'.[78] Instead, the Chief of Staff authorised attacks on three police barracks in the Cork Brigade area on a single night, provided precautions were taken against loss of life and every man 'involved would be at his work the next day as if no dog had barked in the place'.[79] The successful attack on Carrigtwohill police barracks on 2 January 1920 was effectively the first official Volunteer attack of the Anglo-Irish War.

A week after the Dail's suppression Collins and Mulcahy openly accompanied McKee and McDonnell to another meeting with their gunmen. Collins's performance was mesmerising – part staff college lecture, part history lesson and part indoctrination session. He analysed the British espionage system's destruction of previous Irish rebel movements and revealed his intention of annihilating it through a secret Squad of executioners acting with the Dail government's approval. Paddy Daly claimed that Collins initially appointed four full-time Squad members – Daly himself as leader, Joe Leonard, Ben Barrett and Sean Doyle – while another four Volunteers were soon to be allocated important responsibilities. A longstanding member of both the Volunteers and the IRB, Daly had a reputation for thoroughness, ingenuity and organising ability.

The Squad's first operation after 19 September 1919 revealed how limited Collins's intelligence resources still were and how far the Squad was from becoming the infallible killing machine of legend. Daly received his orders directly from Collins and then had to locate the target (Detective Thomas Wharton) by himself. Collins had warned that Wharton would be accompanied by a double agent who would go through the charade of vainly returning fire but was not to be harmed. However, almost everything went wrong. On 10 November 1919 Daly and Leonard arrived in Harcourt Street and spent two frustrating hours before Wharton suddenly and unexpectedly appeared with three colleagues. After his first shot Daly's gun jammed, and he and Leonard fled, shielded by the police mole, who, apparently inadvertently, stepped into the other two detectives' line of fire. Next day Daly and Leonard were mortified to discover that not only had Wharton survived (though crippled for life) but a bullet had gone through his lungs and wounded a little girl standing nearby. Topping it all, a newsboy selling republican papers was arrested for complicity and later sentenced to fifteen years' imprisonment![80] But, while hardly a model of meticulous planning and execution, the attack had introduced Daly and Leonard to the realities of urban guerrilla warfare in which advanced, foolproof preparation was often impossible, innocent bystanders got hurt and gunmen had to seize sudden opportunities. Even then their weapons sometimes let them down.

* * *

On 25 September Basil Thomson declared that 'the suppression of the Irish republican Parliament had occasioned very little excitement, a fact which points to the small hold the Dail Eireann has on Irish psychology.'[81] But on the very same day a subdued memorandum by French and Macpherson described Sinn Fein membership increasing steadily, along with its grip on the Southern Irish population. They recommended confronting this 'formidable conspiracy' by strengthening the Secret Service's size and budget, especially that of G Division, expanding prison accommodation in Britain, increasing police powers of arrest and giving them a free hand and unqualified support. If these measures failed, there was no alternative to martial law.[82] Within a month French concluded that martial law was indeed necessary but could succeed only with a re-energised and completely trustworthy Irish administration. Feeling increasingly under siege, he complained about 'the terrible state of things existing now at the Castle. The place seems to be honeycombed with spies and informers and men who cannot be trusted.'[83] The Viceroy was particularly concerned about Inspector-General Byrne, who opposed martial law, advocated a settlement with Sinn Fein, got on badly with Commander-in-Chief Shaw and to French represented everything that was detestable about what he regarded as the old regime of appeasers. French's private five-page charge sheet against Byrne accused him of inertia, a lack of imagination and opposition to every effort to restore law and order in Ireland.[84] Byrne had refused for eighteen months to get rid of useless County and District Inspectors, and he had also resisted moves to increase the force's size, recruit in Great Britain, and virtually anything else that was against what he called 'the clear will of the people'. Within a few months of arriving in Ireland French had told the Cabinet that Byrne should go, but he had difficulty finding an adequate replacement.

Several times Macpherson had vainly urged Inspector-General Byrne to act more vigorously, and French believed his failure to do so had encouraged the enemy's assassination campaign in the summer and autumn of 1919. By then, the Viceroy claimed, he had been forced to bring in Belfast

Commissioner Smith as Byrne's deputy. When the Inspector-General continued to resist police reform, he was sent on a month's leave on 10 December 1919 – officially for the good of his health. But French told Macpherson that this bogus excuse was the best he could think of and that Byrne had gone for good. Smith was made acting Inspector-General. Somewhat tactlessly French also informed the Chief Secretary, who was about to take another lengthy recuperative absence in the South of France, that 'I feel sure it will be necessary to increase considerably the numbers of people to be sent away for the benefit of their health'.[85] French had become worried about Macpherson, whose 'health is not good and the continual strain is, I fear, telling badly on him'.[86] The Irish situation had become more or less a military one and only someone accustomed to the sudden alarms of war – like French himself – could handle the pressure.

The Viceroy's difficulties were compounded by Under-Secretary MacMahon, a Shortt appointee who was 'now quite estranged from all of us owing to his violently Catholic leanings'.[87] On 11 December 1919 French denied MacMahon access to all important papers and documents and any contact with his Assistant Secretary, Sir John Taylor. But, despite such humiliating treatment, MacMahon remained on the books, a spineless, time-serving mediocrity who periodically visited Dublin Castle to draw his salary.

It was not a happy New Year in Dublin Castle, where the Viceroy was 'quite sure that the extremists are getting stronger and more arrogant in every direction'.[88] On 3 January 1920 he wrote despairingly that 'Our Secret Service is simply non-existent. What masquerades for such is nothing but a delusion and a snare. The DMP are simply demoralized and the RIC will be in the same case very soon if we do not act quickly to set our house in order.'[89]

* * *

Although the Squad was still finding its feet, Collins wanted to strike a spectacular blow like that of Indian revolutionaries who had bombed and wounded the Viceroy Lord Hardinge in 1912 as he ceremonially entered New Delhi on an elephant. Among the plans Collins considered was assassinating French on the review stand at College Green during an Armistice Day march-past on 11 November 1919. The day before, McKee told Mick McDonnell that the gunman, firing from an office opposite the Bank of Ireland, would not escape alive. He then asked McDonnell to do the shooting! After a minute's hesitation McDonnell agreed, but he did not sleep that night. Next morning he was both surprised and relieved when McKee said Cathal Brugha had vetoed the operation because it endangered civilian bystanders.[90] Then, according to Vinnie Byrne, he, Jim Slattery and Tom Keogh

> were asked to assess the possibility of killing French at the Vice-regal Lodge where he was believed to take a daily stroll around the grounds. It was suggested to us that, if we got over the railings on the RIC Depot side and hid in the bushes, we could let him have it, in the event of his coming along. The three of us went out to the Park and scouted round the whole area to see if there was a chance of carrying out the job. We were unarmed. When we had finished our scouting, Tom Keogh said: 'Well lads, what do you think of it?' I replied: 'I am no Robert Emmet!' So we all agreed none of us were Robert Emmets. Looking back on it now, I realise that, if we had attempted to carry out the operation, it would have been madness.[91]

There was, however, an attempted ambush during a visit by French to Trinity College. A large party of gunmen, including Dail deputies, virtually surrounded the university, only for the Viceroy to slip out by a side gate.[92]

Finally on the morning of 19 December 1919, after a tip-off from Broy that French's train would return just after midday from his Roscommon estate, fourteen men armed with revolvers and grenades cycled out to Ashtown railway station close to Phoenix Park.[93] The Squad party included McDonnell, Daly, Leonard, Keogh, Vinnie Byrne, Slattery and the Tipperary quartet of Breen, Treacy, Robinson and Sean Hogan, whom Collins had attached to the Squad. Leonard had also invited Martin Savage, assistant quartermaster of 2nd Battalion. On arrival they slipped unobtrusively into a nearby pub for mineral water until McDonnell ordered Vinnie Byrne outside to observe an approaching train for any military and police activity. Byrne had gone only a few hundred yards towards the station when a convoy of motor cars passed on its way to collect French. The sound of an incoming train then prompted Daly's group to rush out of the back of the pub and position themselves behind a hedge on the expected route. McDonnell's men rushed into the yard and seized a farm cart to block the way, but it stuck in a dip at the side of the road. Just then a policeman took up traffic duty to allow French's party of three cars and a military lorry to pass unimpeded. On hearing approaching cars, McDonnell's group only just managed to get behind a hedge. Daly saw the flash of uniforms in the first car as it passed, and I threw a bomb through the glass of the second car and I heard a loud crash. The military lorry was advancing and I stooped down to pull out my revolver, but just as I did so I heard Hogan shout 'Look out.' When I glanced down I saw that Hogan had dropped a bomb right between us and that the pin was out of it. I said, 'Dive flat' and did the same myself. The bomb went off. It did not give either of us a scratch but covered the pair of us with clay, which we were able to brush off. The military lorry had passed by this time. Probably the bomb incident had saved our lives, because we would have been very much exposed to the military lorry.[94]

Further on, McDonnell and the others opened fire. Byrne's grenade hit the back of one car and exploded, causing it to crash and blowing the traffic policeman across the road. In another car driven by a soldier, a sergeant lying across the back seat kept shooting until the vehicle disappeared around a wide bend leading to Phoenix Park. Just then Savage shouted that he was hit and collapsed, dead, with a bullet in the jaw. Byrne looked at the crashed vehicle and

saw a hand waving a handkerchief. Someone shouted to him to come out with his hands up, which the soldier did. He was the driver of the car. Mick McDonnell, I think, asked him where was French and the soldier replied: 'Blown to bits in the car.' No one took it upon himself to see whether he was telling the truth or not. As he was standing in front of us, someone suggested that he should be plugged. Someone else replied: 'Oh, it's not him we wanted.' So he was let go in safety.[95]

Because Savage's body could not be carried back into the city on a bicycle, the attackers tried leaving it with the publican, but he had locked the premises. So the corpse was left at the roadside, where the police found it later and brought it to the Viceregal Lodge for identification. The Squad headed back into the city, elated by a belief that French was dead. To avoid being intercepted by troops from Marlborough Barracks, they rode in pairs strung out along the road, and all arrived back without incident. Only later in the day did they learn that French's car had made it through. Although he blamed McDonnell for not blocking the convoy's route with a cart, Daly was sanguine about the affair. He thought that in a pitched battle French's party would have overwhelmed the Squad through its superior numbers and firepower.[96]

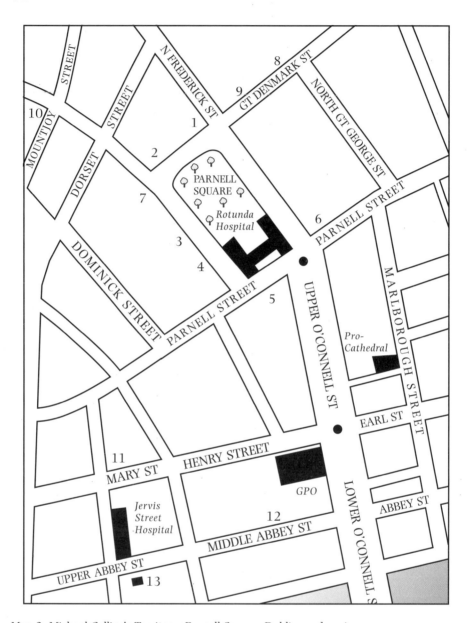

Map 2. Michael Collins's Territory: Parnell Square, Dublin, and environs

1 Banba Hall
2 Gaelic League Headquarters
3 Irish National Foresters Headquarters
4 Keating Branch, Gaelic League
5 Devlin's public house
6 Kirwan's public house
7 Vaughan's Hotel
8 Barry's Hotel
9 Fleming's Hotel
10 Miss McCarthy's boarding house
11 Finance office
12 Collins's office
13 Squad Base

Chapter 2

DIRECTOR OF IRISH INTELLIGENCE

THE ORGANISATION TAKES SHAPE, 1919

When Collins went on the run again in September 1919 after the Dail's suppression, he had plenty of company, because every Irish cabinet minister, government department and Volunteer GHQ was forced underground as well. The survival of this parallel government depended on its relocation to secret offices throughout Dublin, an operation that Collins organised though his trusted fixer, Michael Noyk. As a Jewish solicitor and Trinity graduate, Noyk made an impeccable front man, though politically this long-term republican had (in his clients' vernacular) form as long as his arm. By paying over the odds, he acquired properties that he registered under eminently respectable and frequently fictitious double-barrelled names, making certain that the new tenants followed routines identical to those of their neighbours.[1] This was especially true of 3 Crow Street, a narrow thoroughfare off Dame Street in the city's main banking and business district and, piquantly, only about 200 yards from Dublin Castle. There, in a second-floor office, Volunteer GHQ's Intelligence Department functioned as the 'Irish Products Company', its 'employees' wearing business suits and coming and going at regular hours.[2] Only a small inner circle knew the secret of Crow Street, and even fewer went there.

Collins's personality shaped Volunteer GHQ's intelligence system, validating one historian's assertion that

an espionage service will be largely a reflection of the man who controls it. The success of his agents will depend as much on the inspiration they receive from the top as on their own spying ability and skill. The active work in the field will be determined as much by the organization and administration of the service as by the policy handed down by the government, for unless the agent in the field is backed by the resources of an efficient service, no personal skill can achieve the fullest degree of success, which is the aim of all espionage activity.[3]

The great intelligence director must be an outstanding individual, because, like a commander-in-chief, he wields immense authority as well as carrying always a crushing burden – the power of life and death over others.[4] His persona and the way he exercises immense responsibility must also inspire subordinates, and certainly between 1919 and 1921 Collins proved himself a born leader. In building up and running his intelligence system he consistently demonstrated acumen, flair, inventiveness, efficiency and imagination. The 'Big Fellow' also looked a leader, with a commanding physique and a consummate actor's dignified bearing that accentuated his dominance in any gathering, while he radiated calmness, reassurance and clarity of purpose.

Collins staffed his organisation with competent, strong-willed team players, courageous risk-takers whom he liked testing to the limit. Mulcahy admitted how

reckless Mick was in his daring and in his intensity. When he got men's wills around him moving in a particular way, he was prepared to test them to the full. When Mick got an idea into his head that he wanted to give people an example as to how they ought to step to unexpected situations, he didn't reckon his own value to the organisation or to the danger – he simply plunged into a situation in a daring and reckless and to some extent irresponsible way.[5]

Although Collins planned his major operations meticulously, he knew that perfection was unattainable in the intelligence world. Excessive caution corroded morale as much as foolhardiness and the only mistake greater than underestimating an enemy's strength was to overestimate it. Collins inspired and reciprocated loyalty, evoking in life and death the unwavering devotion of his men. One recalled his 'curious and unusual facility for getting work done by other people. They were all kinds, intellectuals, craftsmen, seamen, hotelkeepers, quay workers and pacifists. He trusted other people and inspired devotion in others.'[6]

Collins also proved himself a superb man manager who, while hardened to espionage's duplicity and cruelty and unburdened by conscience or regret, still retained that core of humanity indispensable in someone to whom men entrusted their lives. An excellent listener, he exuded charm, good humour, patience and interest in other people's lives. Supremely self-confident, Collins never shrank from accepting responsibility, tried to blame others for setbacks or get others to do his dirty work for him because, as Mulcahy insisted, he 'was always prepared to do the things that he would have other people do'.[7] Undoubtedly Collins drove subordinates very hard. One remembered that he was 'full of enthusiasm and energy and could laugh well but he had other very strong moods. He could not stand stupidity and he didn't stand fools gladly. It seems to me that you were afraid of nothing in the world except having to go back to Collins and say that you hadn't done the job.'[8]

Collins's indomitable will reminded Noyk of 'the words of the Spartan mother who said to her son: "Come back with your shield or on it." The word "cannot" did not figure in his vocabulary.'[9] Moreover, his energy and craving for action were those of a young man in a tremendous hurry with a great deal to accomplish in a short time. To many, Collins seemed a driven man, a restless force of nature, unceasingly accumulating information from books, newspapers, written reports, meetings, discussions and casual conversations and absorbing it rapidly through his excellent memory. He conversed with Broy about Russian secret societies and recommended a book on guerrilla warfare in south-west Africa to a professional soldier. And always Collins expanded his boundaries, as Mulcahy discovered once when

> looking in Collins's bag for something and what had he in it only what used to be called one of the little grey books. Not only was his intelligence and will all that it might be, but he was using the little grey books of Pelmanism to work himself up a little bit more to be able to remember telephone numbers etc. That was part of his work and part of his approach to things.[10]

But Collins's tremendous self-assurance, his belief that he could do almost anything – certainly better than anyone else – combined with a compulsive need for absolute control, created the danger of a one-man band. Hoarding intelligence obsessively and doling it out meagrely even to his closest associates, Collins was truly worthy of the spymaster's ultimate accolade: the man who kept the secrets. He also loved accumulating offices and responsibility, occupying four important government and army posts simultaneously for most of 1919. True, as a bachelor Collins travelled light and had a strong constitution, his fitness honed by sport and a generally abstemious lifestyle, but he lived at a headlong pace, constantly overstretching his physical and emotional resources and cramming a dozen lifetimes into one relatively brief career. Eventually even Collins found his workload unsustainable and by the end of 1919 he had reluctantly resigned as GHQ Director of Organisation and Adjutant-General.[11]

Temperamentally restless and burdened by numerous responsibilities, Collins had no intention of being Crow Street's departmental desk manager. Instead he moved unceasingly around an intelligence empire that was concentrated in a relatively small area of central Dublin at the northern end of O'Connell Street. In hotels, public houses, clubrooms and halls clustered around Parnell Square, Collins would meet important contacts, receive messages and documents, issue instructions and convene conferences, usually walking or cycling between his favourite haunts. Although on the run, he never wore a disguise, carried a personal weapon or surrounded himself with an armed bodyguard. Yet Collins's personal security remained intact, something that is explicable only in the light of the British intelligence system's virtually complete breakdown. Until mid-1920 his network's focal point was Vaughan's Hotel in Parnell Square, which Mulcahy regarded as 'a magic mixer', 'a great clearing centre for all who wanted to make contact with him. They could very easily be directed from Vaughan's to whatever "joint" he was occupying at the time.'[12] Within a short radius Collins also transacted business, socialised and sheltered for the night at Barry's and Fleming's hotels on the northern side of Parnell Square and Devlin's and Kirwan's public houses in Parnell Street to the south. After arriving from Scotland in early 1920, Liam Devlin made his more select and discreet establishment freely available to Collins, and it soon displaced Vaughan's as his unofficial headquarters. Collins usually left Devlin's just before curfew, along with Liam Tobin, Frank Thornton and Tom Cullen of GHQ Intelligence Department. But often they stayed overnight because of enemy activity in the area or an early morning intelligence operation. Collins convened more formal meetings at the Gaelic League's headquarters or its nearby Keating Branch, the Grocers and Vintners Association's offices in Banba Hall and the Irish National Foresters' headquarters – all situated in Parnell Square. For a time he also frequented Miss McCarthy's boarding house in nearby Mountjoy Street.

Mulcahy regarded Parnell Square as 'the seat in which Collins generated and used his power and that reputation for leadership',[13] which led many Volunteers to regard Collins as their commander-in-chief. His regular contacts included senior Crow Street intelligence officers, the IRB's Supreme Council, GHQ colleagues like Mulcahy, Dick McKee and fellow bachelors like Piaras Beaslai and Adjutant-General Gearoid O'Sullivan. Among his retreats outside the heartland was the Dublin Whiskey Distillery, situated beside the river Tolka. There Collins relaxed, exercised and meditated in spacious and secure grounds made freely available to him by Denis Lynch, the resident distiller. Directly across the river Collins also used Walter House, the home of McKee's Vice-Brigadier, Michael Lynch. Until January 1920 he expedited GHQ business at Cullenswood House in the southern suburb of Ranelagh – where Mulcahy and his wife also had an upstairs flat – but they all fled these premises after British troops narrowly failed to capture the Chief of Staff. For a time Collins's Department of Finance office was in Mespil Road beside the Grand Canal, but he never felt secure in this residential area and in June 1920 he transferred to Mary Street, a busy thoroughfare not far from Parnell Square. Collins also used a private room at the back of the Collevin Dairies, a shop in Amiens Street used also by railway workers carrying IRA dispatches and sailors smuggling in weapons.[14]

Because Volunteer GHQ Intelligence was Collins's personal fiefdom, its structure was shaped by his inexperience, a need to have it functioning quickly and the fact that Collins's mind was powerful but not genuinely original. For these reasons he settled for creating a mirror image of British intelligence. Crow Street paralleled G Division's Brunswick Street headquarters, Deputy Director Liam Tobin shadowed G Division's superintendent and IRA intelligence officers would first emulate and then eliminate their G-men counterparts. But IRA victory in the intelligence war depended on superseding the original, successful British model – and in this Collins's dynamic leadership proved indispensable. In war and politics his guiding principle was always to seize and retain the initiative, in effect by getting his retaliation in first. He believed that armies and political parties were at their best while advancing, and his assault on G Division was the precursor to other onslaughts.

Operating like a commanding officer, Collins appointed the staff of Volunteer GHQ's Intelligence Department, devised its most ambitious operations, made all key decisions and authorised every Squad execution. This concentration of power and policy-making in his own hands ensured – as he intended – that only Collins ever had the complete intelligence picture, just as in 1916 the Military Council had hermetically sealed information about the Rising. But then, at least, seven men had shared secrets with each other while ultimately Collins trusted only himself. One of his favourite maxims was 'never let one side of your mind know what the other is doing'.[15] Frank Thornton admitted that

> nobody on his intimate staff, from Tobin down, knew more at any time than Collins wanted him to know or more than was essential for his particular work. Each of his agents was kept in a watertight compartment and was frequently reminded by him of the necessity for secrecy. His closest associates on GHQ staff knew the identity of no more than a small fraction of his agents and practically nothing of the service which each was providing. He never mentioned the name of his informant when passing on a fresh piece of intelligence – he was merely 'one of my sources of information'.[16]

Furthermore, Collins rarely committed information – or himself – to paper, routinely memorising and then burning messages. While his hands were on everything, Collins left his fingerprints on nothing. His insistence on absolute control and a dual power base as Minister of Finance and Director of Intelligence also enabled him to coordinate the political and military campaigns for maximum propaganda effect by, for instance, arranging a Squad assassination to occur during a political crisis or at a time of heightened popular emotion.

Collins's monopoly of information, his insistence that all lines of communication ultimately ran through him, could be justified on security grounds. It diminished the risks of leaks to British Intelligence and limited the scale of any leaks that occurred. But clearly it also satisfied some deep need in Collins – a craving even – for absolute control. Collins hoarded information like a miser guarding his pot of gold, a control freak whose operational methods indicated a deeply ingrained dictatorial trait. While many accepted this style as necessary in wartime, whether that would have continued to be the case in future decades of peace is another matter entirely. Even in war it could backfire, especially when he left agents unaware that close colleagues were also working for the IRA. Broy, for instance, was friendly but guarded with fellow G-man Joe Kavanagh, until he risked telling him about his clandestine activities. But Broy was in for a surprise of his own:

> One evening we were walking in St Stephen's Green, and we both made the discovery that we were in contact with Michael Collins. I told him about

Mick's visit to no.1 Great Brunswick Street. He nearly fell, laughing, knowing the mentality in the G Division office and knowing Mick. He got me to tell it to him a second time, and he laughed so much that people looked at him as if he were drunk or mad. Shortly afterwards, when I met Mick, he apologised for not having told me about Kavanagh. I told him that that was what I had been preaching to him since I met him, not to tell anything, that the Irish people had paid too big a price for carelessness like that, in the past. Michael similarly apologised to Joe the next time he met him, but Michael was glad the two of us knew and understood each other.[17]

On this occasion Broy suffered only embarrassment, but a day after he had strolled through the city centre with another police mole, Collins

put his hand over his mouth and, in his usual bantering way, said: 'By the way, did you fellows know you were being followed last night?' I said: 'No, but we took it for granted, in view of what you told us, that British agents might follow us.' 'Because', he said 'Tobin and Cullen followed the two of you last night and lost you.' They crossed O'Connell Bridge as far as Hopkins and Hopkins, and then Cullen said: 'We don't know where the two so and so's disappeared to.' Mick Collins chaffed Cullen then and referred to him as an 'alleged sprinter who couldn't catch these heavy police'. 'Anyhow,' he said, 'I will have to introduce you to the two of them now, because this is too dangerous.' So we were all introduced.[18]

Collins liked organisational flexibility and luckily for him his intelligence machine was created from virtually nothing, staffed by men lacking professional experience and free of rigid bureaucratic attitudes, concern for hierarchy or boundaries of responsibility. Crow Street's agents learnt on the job, and the organisation's relatively small size meant that they frequently performed tasks outside their designated area. At different times even Deputy Director Liam Tobin functioned as office manager, field agent and triggerman.

Because of security considerations, his many responsibilities and a hectic lifestyle, Collins controlled Volunteer GHQ Intelligence from a distance through his devoted assistant, Joe O'Reilly. He called at Crow Street twice a day to collect reports and correspondence and deliver Collins's replies and instructions. A scribbled 'oggs him'[19] on the margins of a document was his written authorisation for an execution. Collins delegated routine administration to

Tobin, the self-contained 24-year-old Deputy Director. His inscrutable exterior masked the intense, somewhat brittle personality of a person whom one acquaintance remembered as 'tall, gaunt, cynical, with tragic eyes . . . like a man who had seen the inside of hell. He walked without moving his arms and seemed emptied of energy. Yet this man was, after Collins, the Castle's most dangerous enemy.'[20] An exceptionally efficient conduit for Collins's orders, Tobin was a laconic keeper of many secrets. Despite their common Cork background, he and Collins were not close, never having met before Tobin's family moved to Dublin before the war. In the capital Tobin had worked in a hardware firm, joined the Volunteers and during the Rising fought in the Four Courts. Afterwards in prison he had become friendly with Dick McKee, who later made him the Dublin Brigade's first Intelligence Officer. As GHQ Director of Training, McKee also dispatched Tobin on provincial assignments, and it was his organising ability and intelligence background, together with McKee's support, and not Collins's friendship, which led to his appointment as Deputy Director.[21]

Collins would meet Tobin almost every evening at Vaughan's or another Parnell Square haunt, and he in turn relied heavily on Assistant Director Tom Cullen and Deputy Assistant Director Frank Thornton. Cullen was originally a Wicklow shop assistant and former GHQ Assistant Quartermaster-General whose loyalty, discretion and bluff common sense Collins valued highly.

The 28-year-old Thornton was from a fiercely republican Drogheda family. In 1912 he moved to Liverpool, worked as a shipyard painter, joined the Irish Volunteers and met Collins, who initiated him into the IRB. An excellent organiser and conspirator, Thornton smuggled weapons to Ireland before returning to Ireland in 1916, when he commanded the Imperial Hotel garrison in O'Connell Street during the Rising. Subsequently in prison he met Tobin, with whom he established the New Ireland Assurance Society in order to challenge foreign domination of the Irish insurance industry. When Collins sent him to Longford in late 1919 to resuscitate the county's Volunteer organisation, Thornton used the Society as a front for his clandestine activities:

As insurance officials both Tobin and I had an excellent cover for our activities in the various areas over which we were operating. In addition, every man appointed to any position of trust in the new insurance company was a Volunteer and, in this way, we paved the way to setting up a very important intelligence organisation and provided a very good cover for all our activities wherever we went.[22]

After his Longford assignment Thornton was back in Dublin on 19 December 1919, only hours after the Squad tried to assassinate Lord French at Ashtown. Next day Collins transferred him to GHQ Intelligence, which Tobin and he managed with an insurance agent's attention to detail and expertise at risk assessment. Indeed metaphorically they still issued life policies, only now with the manner, time and place of a customer's demise predetermined and the company never liable for a single payout. Along with Tom Cullen, they also shielded Collins from his enemies and sometimes himself. The Director could be surprisingly naive when dealing with British agents posing as friends. As Collins's trouble-shooters, they investigated sensitive intelligence-related incidents involving Volunteers. In March 1920 Thornton conducted an inquiry into the killing by one Limerick city battalion of an alleged spy from another battalion.[23] Harmonious personal relations enhanced this senior management team's effectiveness: Thornton, Tobin and Cullen shared a bachelor flat in Rathmines.[24]

Collins was indifferent to intellectual theories about intelligence or its ability to divine the enemy's long-term strategic intentions. He regarded its *raison d'être* as facilitating political and military action and was concerned only with intelligence's immediate and practical application to the Irish conflict. After studying G Division, Collins knew that the four key elements of intelligence were acquisition, analysis, counter-intelligence and implementation, the first three of which he allocated to the Intelligence Department and the last to the Squad. At Crow Street Tobin, Cullen and Thornton functioned as line managers, training and supervising a corps of paid, full-time intelligence officers, whose activities they coordinated with the Squad. Most intelligence officers were IRB members whom McKee had recruited for Collins, and all were Dublin Volunteers. McKee's Brigade was notoriously hostile to using 'outsiders' for operations in the capital, a sensitivity that forced Breen and Treacy to stand down from the Squad after the Ashtown ambush, despite having the backing of Collins and McKee.[25] Initially there were only three intelligence officers: Joe Dolan, Joe Guilfoyle and Paddy Caldwell, whom Tobin, Thornton and Cullen assisted for some months. But, as the war intensified, others joined in July and August 1920. The new recruits included Charlie Dalton, Frank Saurin, Charlie Byrne, Peter McGee, Dan McDonnell, Ned Kelleher, James Hughes, Con O'Neill,

Bob O'Neill, Jack Walsh and Paddy Kennedy.[26] By the end of 1920 Crow Street's expanding personnel and workload necessitated a departmental sub-office, which Thornton ran from rooms situated above a Great Brunswick Street cinema.[27]

Tobin, Cullen and Thornton trained their officers in intelligence acquisition. Charlie Dalton said this 'consisted of tracing the activities of enemy agents and spies, keeping records of enemy personnel, contact with friendly associates in government and Crown service, organising and developing intelligence in the Dublin Brigade as an adjunct to headquarters Information Service'.[28] Dalton himself spent much of his time at headquarters collating information about suspected enemy agents that had been gathered from intercepted mail, tapped telephones and the reports of provincial intelligence officers. Since the IRA knew the RIC's key code word, he deciphered copies of police telegrams which were smuggled out of the Central Telegraph Office in Dublin. These frequently contained details of forthcoming arrests and raids, allowing Crow Street time to warn Volunteers in advance. The Intelligence Department's files also recorded information on IRA agents and sympathisers in the police, army, civil service, prison service, railways, trams, boats, postal service, pubs, restaurants, hotels and newspapers.[29]

Dalton was surprised at the amount of publicly available information in Irish, British and foreign newspapers. He would cut out

> any paragraphs referring to the personnel of the Royal Irish Constabulary, or military, such as transfers, their movements socially, attendance at wedding receptions, garden parties, etc. These I pasted on a card which was sent to the Director of Intelligence for his perusal and instructions. Photographs and other data which were or might be of interest were cut out and put away. We often gathered useful information of the movements of important enemy personages in this manner, whom we traced also by a study of *Who's Who*, from which we learned the names of their connections and clubs. By intercepting their correspondence we were able to get a clue to their movements outside their strongholds.[30]

Volunteer GHQ always feared this intelligence treasure trove might fall into enemy hands and it finally instructed Tobin to burn everything in the event of a British raid. Soon afterwards, Thornton believed that years of effort were about literally to go up in smoke when a large convoy of Auxiliaries (ex-British Army officers serving as policemen) pulled up outside in Crow Street:

> The occupants had all got out of the lorries and were standing in groups on the footpath. We immediately prepared to set fire to everything in the office and sent Dolan, Charlie Byrne and Guilfoyle down to the first landing with grenades; Charlie Dalton was posted at the upper window ready to drop grenades on the Auxiliaries if they attempted to come in. However, the order to set fire was not given until some move was made by the enemy – a sort of armed truce appeared to exist for about half an hour – then to our amazement the Auxiliaries all got back into the lorries again and drove away. We were completely at a loss to understand what all this meant and proceeded to investigate the situation, when to our amazement we discovered that the only reason the Auxiliaries came down Crow Street on that particular day was so that one of their Majors could secure a watch which had been left at a jewellery repair shop two doors away.[31]

Volunteer GHQ Intelligence officers also ferreted out the living quarters and workplaces of enemy personnel, their social haunts, modes of transport and telephone, telegraph and postal communications. The best sources of information were people in regular contact with the targets such as fellow policemen, clerks, typists, waiters, hotel porters, bar staff, dockers, railway officials and journalists. They also conducted covert surveillance of suspected enemy agents, though the risk of being spotted themselves meant that they lived precariously. One recalled that 'during all this time we did not know whether we would be alive in twenty-four hours or not'.[32] The constant danger of capture, torture and execution – official or unofficial – forced them to operate on a need-to-know basis that limited the damage they could inflict on IRA Intelligence if British interrogators made them talk. Tobin ordered them to feign innocence if they were arrested, and to cooperate with the prison authorities to secure their release – even if that meant signing a promise of good behaviour. 'On no account were we to attempt any violent tactics of the IRA such as hunger strikes, etc. Every means would be used through our contacts within to get us out. We were a specially trained body, difficult to replace and had to be got out at all costs.'[33]

While the IRA persuaded or coerced some sources, many volunteered from an uncomplicated patriotism of the 'My Country Right or Wrong' variety.

Whatever reservations many people felt about specific IRA actions, there existed a widespread and instinctive loyalty to popular Irish nationalism and the concept of Irish freedom. The British stoked this emotion by suppressing Dail Eireann, Sinn Fein and the Volunteers – actions reminiscent of continental autocracy, a system utterly discredited in an age of national rights and liberal democracy. Even many policemen and civil servants, on whose continued allegiance its survival depended, had grown to detest British rule. One of Broy's colleagues could see that he 'had only one hate, the British Empire'.[34] For years James McNamara had reported, on behalf of G Division, the inflammatory public speeches of radical nationalists, until eventually he found their arguments unanswerable. Ironically G Division had helped sponsor its own destruction.

Thornton claimed the Intelligence Department wanted to get at least one agent in every Irish government department. It struck lucky when an employee in records supplied the photographs, names, addresses and personal history of practically every typist and clerical worker. GHQ intelligence officers quickly ascertained their political sympathies and recruited many as agents.[35] Pressure from relatives and friends encouraged some people to work for the IRA, but others wanted to avenge some grievance, slight or act of discrimination – real or imagined. Many Catholic policemen knew that a disproportionately high number of senior RIC officers were Protestants, and their sense of injustice was often compounded – and made physically real – by working under mediocre, unpopular superiors. Superintendent Brien aroused physical revulsion in one G Division mole, who remembered him as

> about five feet high and perhaps three in girth. He had a round closed pussy-cat's face and little piggy eyes. Weighing about fourteen stone he had suave oily manners. Like a stage Chinaman, he was forever 'washing' his pudgy little hands, while those little eyes surveyed your face. His only relaxation was to attend the Royal music hall, which he did every night, sitting in the front row admiring the chorus girls' legs.[36]

Others brooded over some incident such as a police or army raid, a checkpoint encounter, a random arrest or a disagreeable interrogation. One man became an IRA agent after Auxiliaries stopped his late-night tram and intimidated its passengers. His brother said he returned home 'furious with indignation about the way that he and the other passengers, particularly the

women, had been treated and the first thing he said to me when he came in
was that, if I got him a gun, he would shoot some of the Auxiliaries'.[37]

Occasionally cash greased the wheels. Even some Auxiliaries became paid
IRA double agents, though Crow Street never fully trusted men whom it
assumed would happily sell it out to a higher bidder. Thornton says they took
the precaution of securing

> two such people in the particular unit or office that they were operating in,
> and the first job that each of these agents would get was to submit a
> complete report on the other. In that way whilst working for us for pay we
> had them continually watching each other, although they were unaware of
> the fact that they were doing so. As a matter of fact in any such case one
> agent did not know of the existence of the other.[38]

Other IRA agents were motivated by a craving for excitement or the
satisfaction of acting out – and getting away with – the double life of a Scarlet
Pimpernel. Broy clearly wanted to ensure his place in Irish history as well as
holding a somewhat patronising vision of himself mentoring an inexperienced
Collins. Disappointingly, although Dublin supposedly had the largest red-light
district in Europe, sex did not feature prominently in the city's intelligence war.
No honey-traps set by seductive colleens compromised gullible British politicians
and army officers, especially as the puritanical republican movement regarded
itself as morally superior to decadent Anglo-Saxons. Robert Brennan of the Dail's
Foreign Affairs Department recalled someone suggesting to Collins that the
Viceroy could be ensnared through his reputed fondness for the ladies:

> The plan was to let one of our girls, whose brother was in prison, go to
> French and appeal to him to have her brother released. She would lead him
> to ask for an assignation and lure him to an available house in Waterloo
> Road, where our fellows would be waiting for him. Mick grinned. 'It might
> be worth trying,' he said, 'keep it under your hat.' The plan was never
> tried. I was pretty sure that some of our people at headquarters would have
> scruples about adopting it.[39]

However, the proprietor of at least one brothel in North Dublin, an English
madam called Betty, would surreptitiously pass on information about her
clients to a British intelligence officer under the cover of an army raid.[40]

Every GHQ intelligence officer had a particular area of responsibility. Frank Saurin, for instance, concentrated on the favourite haunts of British secret service agents and Auxiliaries such as Fuller's restaurant, Kidd's Buffet and the Wicklow, Moira and Central hotels – all in the Grafton Street area.[41] He also controlled the Shelbourne's female telephonist, who monitored every call going through the hotel switchboard. When she reported conversations between an RIC officer and a female British agent enquiring about rewards for captured republicans, Saurin, in a macabre twist, visited the woman's home posing as a life-insurance agent. He intended lining her up for possible execution, but Collins vetoed this because of the adverse publicity it would have aroused. One of Saurin's agents, Lily Mernin, was a Castle typist working for Major Stratford Burton, the British Army's Dublin Garrison Adjutant.[42] She and Saurin would circulate casually around the city's hotel lounges, restaurants and cafés while she discreetly pointed out British officers and intelligence agents. In addition, Mernin provided copies of confidential reports on the Volunteers, British military strength, troop movements and names and addresses of undercover British agents and office gossip. A colleague, Miss Dunne, chatted regularly about two British secret service agents who lived in her block of flats and were friends of her brother. Mernin recalled:

> Suspicion was thrown in my direction one morning when Miss Dunne entered the office and excitedly said that her brother had been missing and that she thought somebody in the office had given information to the IRA concerning the conversation we had in the office about MacMahon and Peel. I found myself in a predicament but I remained cool and calm and bluffed my way out of it and said: 'Who could be a spy?' and put the blame on her brother for talking so much. Some time later the position was eased when Miss Dunne took ill and never again returned to Dublin Castle.[43]

Mernin was never caught.

Sometimes GHQ Intelligence deliberately planted a mole inside the British administration. Bernard Golden, a Dublin Volunteer, joined the British Army's Education Corps as a schoolmaster and reported on troop movements in Ulster. Although he became unemployed in 1920 when his unit was transferred to Dublin, Golden was soon rehired as a clerk in Dublin Castle. He smuggled out a confidential historical record of the Easter Rising and a Crimes Index of raids by soldiers, police, Black and Tans (British recruits to the RIC) and Auxiliaries. Golden also reported a conversation between senior military officers who agreed that any compromise peace would have to include Britain's retention of four Gibraltar-type enclaves in Ireland. This anticipated the naval base provisions of the Anglo-Irish Treaty of December 1921.[44]

Some of Collins's most important agents were policemen. He ran four G Division moles simultaneously – Broy, Kavanagh, McNamara and David Neligan – while Constable Patrick Mannix recruited a dozen uniformed DMP colleagues to leak documents, provide tip-offs about imminent British raids, divert suspicion away from IRA suspects and supply the names and addresses of any British secret servicemen they encountered after curfew.[45] Collins's most important RIC spy in Dublin was Head Constable Peter Forlan, who worked in Dublin Castle and the Phoenix Park Depot.[46] Collins protected him with a safe-conduct pass allowing unimpeded travel day and night. Forlan declined an official police motor car because cycling to and from work enabled him to pass messages to his IRA controller. He leaked confidential documents, including an extensive list of Volunteers who were due to be arrested after midnight. At short notice Forlan smuggled it to a room in Aughrim Street, where female typists copied the names so that couriers could alert the wanted men. Forlan recalled:

The next morning I left the file back in its place. There was hell to pay in the Castle. The military had gone out in their lorries; they visited the nests but the birds had flown. Of course General Tudor and the higher officers could not understand how it had happened that they found no one and they concluded that there must be a leakage. I was never suspected. I was very cautious and knew how far I could go.[47]

Forlan's closest call came after the IRA asked him to retrieve five captured automatic revolvers from a Castle storeroom. After shifting the weapons to another room first thing in the morning, Forlan stuffed them under a trench coat at the end of the day and walked his bicycle, unchallenged, past a sentry:

As I came to the corner of Parliament Street to my great surprise there was a line of soldiers stretched across the street with bayonets fixed walking towards me. I stood near the kerbstone. As the soldiers were within a few yards of me I put up my hands like everybody else. They were searching all comers. I said to the soldier facing me, 'You'll get my pass in this pocket', pointing to the breast pocket of my jacket – my trench coat was hanging loose. The words were scarcely out of my mouth when the officer in charge, who was on the footpath at my right-hand side, said to the soldier, 'Stop that, stop that. You should know Mr Forlan, he is one of our men in the Castle.' I said, 'Thank you, Sir', and if ever these words were true they were true on this occasion. I passed on, trembling all over, knowing how near I had been to my doom.[48]

Although some Irish soldiers assisted a prison break-out, the British army proved less fertile ground for IRA Intelligence, and Major S.S. Hill Dillon's Military Intelligence Service at British GHQ proved impervious to penetration. Thornton admitted that 'contact was never established with this body'.[49]

Although the IRA relied heavily on human intelligence, it also exploited the Post Office's monopoly of written, telephonic and telegraphic communications. According to Dan McDonnell:

we got in every morning a complete pile of letters from all over the country, from England, from everywhere, whether to the Castle Authorities, to GHQ or the RIC Depot. All these letters varied and we got quite an amount of information from them, especially from people anxious to give Crown Forces information. Inter-department, official and unofficial, also came through our hands. Then I discovered we had a complete organisation within the Post Office itself.[50]

Collins had begun organising the postal section in 1918 under Paddy Moynihan, Diarmuid O'Sullivan and Martin Ryan. Initially his spies resisted working under Moynihan, who was under official suspicion for republican opinions, which had led to his transfer from Cork to Dublin. The dissidents persuaded O'Sullivan to face Collins at Devlin's public house, as O'Sullivan reports:

Michael – 'You say they won't work with Paddy Moynihan?' 'Yes', I said, 'that's why I am here seeing you.' Michael: 'Well, now go back and tell these men that I am arranging all this business and that I want them to take their instructions from both Paddy Moynihan and yourself.' But before he said this he asked me very bluntly and lowered his head into my face, 'Will you work with him?' Needless to say I had taken note of the fact that Michael was very determined and immediately answered in the affirmative.[51]

After a major IRA raid on the Central Sorting Office at the Rotunda Rink in the summer of 1919, uniformed police and detectives began accompanying the mail and ensuring that it landed on the table on which all state correspondence was deposited. But Moynihan, O'Sullivan and Ryan ensured that the postman in the State Section surreptitiously extracted those letters Volunteer GHQ Intelligence wanted.[52]

Another useful Post Office agent was Charles McQuaile, a civilian clerk at the Rotunda Rink with access to military correspondence. McQuaile noted:

Letters received into the Post Office did not indicate the location of the officer or soldier; they simply gave the number, rank and name of the individual and serving somewhere in Ireland. It was my job to endorse the address of the unit to which the officer or soldier belonged. In that way I was in possession of a complete list of all the military units and their locations throughout the country. This information I passed on.[53]

McQuaile also intercepted letters to British officers, and supplied a sketch of various GPO branches and the times when military parties collected army mail. When the British intercepted letters to IRA suspects, McQuaile conveyed them to Dublin Castle and the Military Censor at British GHQ – after passing the names to IRA Intelligence. Over time McQuaile became a regular visitor to the Castle and British Army GHQ, where he examined unattended confidential files. One contained details of payments to a couple of civilian agents whom the IRA later shot dead.

Liam Archer, who organised the telegraphist section, recruited a dozen colleagues as IRA agents. He also stuffed into his socks copies of RIC ciphers, which he delivered to Collins's various unofficial post offices in the city centre. Archer also had a lineman trace Dublin's underground telephone cable network and make diagrams of every main Irish telegraph and telephone route. But repeated use of a crude telephone-tapping apparatus failed to crack the British Army connection between Dublin HQ and Cork. Archer provided a detailed plan of the Rotunda Rink building (in which the GPO was temporarily situated) and information about the British intercepting all mail connected with the Dail Bonds:

Our own staff (Intelligence) went straight and got precise details as to where this whole bag of mail was. It was in a cage in the Rotunda at the bottom of a chute. Our contact with the Post Office switched off any means of communication and we got the bag of mail and put it on an ass and cart. We were walking out quite silently when along came the British forces to collect the bag and passed us unwittingly.[54]

Collins also hoped to learn about Lord French's movements from a Viceregal Lodge telephone operator, but she never made good on her promised help.[55]

Saurin claims that much intelligence work was abortive, either through luck, unforeseen circumstances or incomplete information.[56] Sometimes it was dangerously unproductive. After learning that the daughter of Thomas O'Shaughnessy, Master of the High Court, was marrying a British major in the Castle's Chapel Royal, David Neligan secretly obtained the guest list. It contained a cross section of Dublin high society, including the Chief Secretary himself, and Neligan 'gave the list to Collins, who glanced at it and said to me: "We'll plug the bloody lot of them!" I said it was a fine idea.'[57] Tobin arranged an ambush of army officers on their way to the ceremony, and on the day Saurin positioned himself outside a shop in Suffolk Street, along which guests' vehicles were expected to travel. He had licence plate numbers to scrutinise, but 'the only car that came through Suffolk Street was a brown-painted open Humber. It was being driven by a clergyman, and there were three ladies in wedding apparel sitting in it. I had spent the best part of the day standing around with a .45 Colt automatic in my pocket, with the chance of being picked up by some of the enemy, and all for nothing.'[58]

Tobin, Cullen and Thornton analysed intelligence officers' reports, evaluating their reliability, completeness and significance. Dalton claimed that only a small proportion of potential sources were used:

Offers of assistance were many, but the integrity and resourcefulness of the would-be informants in many cases did not qualify them for inclusion in our network of helpers. If, as a result of information supplied by a hotel aide, shooting occurred, this individual, as well as other members of the hotel staff, was subjected to a 'grilling' by the Crown forces. Anyone known to have sympathies with Sinn Fein would receive special attention by the Authorities. Such an examination could possibly result in the informant double-crossing us, with unhappy results. When we got offers of assistance we first had to make up our minds whether we could trust them or not, and then we could only tell them very little. There was the danger that, in their enthusiasm to give information, they could go and ask other people for information without exercising proper caution.[59]

Tobin and his two assistants also recommended the elimination of alleged enemy agents to Collins, but he alone authorised assassinations; they had no independent authority in such matters. The trio also cooordinated counter-intelligence operations against British agents attempting to infiltrate the IRA by posing as friends and unmasked Volunteers whom British Intelligence had turned.

While the Intelligence Department focused primarily on Dublin, it also stood at the apex of a national IRA intelligence system. At the start of the war there were no IRA personnel trained in or detailed for intelligence work outside the capital. There was no organised national system for collecting information, and only a dim appreciation of the practical value of one. But, once the war of ambushes had commenced at the start of 1920, the IRA had to develop a practical intelligence system, especially if it wanted to empty the countryside of RIC barracks. Attacking these installations required systematic surveillance of enemy personnel, armaments, communications and supplies as well as evaluation of the information collected. This meant that every unit had to detail men to organise records, receive reports and check information. This was primarily the responsibility of provincial brigade leaders, but Collins exerted continual pressure through directives and, where necessary, admonition.

Covert action, the Squad's responsibility, involved killing policemen, soldiers, British intelligence agents, Auxiliaries, civil servants and civilians threatening Sinn Fein and the Volunteers. As its target list lengthened during 1920, the Squad expanded and began to work full-time. This change was motivated in part by resentment within the Dublin Brigade at Squad part-timers who were frequently absenting themselves from evening battalion meetings to participate in Squad operations. Initially most Squad assassinations took place in the evening, because Collins believed daylight operations endangered civilians, but when the British reduced the police presence on the streets after dark he abandoned his self-denying ordinance. However, daylight attacks often forced the Squad to leave their workplaces at short notice, and employers and fellow employees soon became suspicious.

When Vinnie Byrne clocked in late after the Ashtown attack, his boss cheerfully derided his excuse about an upset stomach:

'Begorra, Vincent, you have a damn bad shot.' I asked him what did he mean, and he just laughed at me. Everything went well until Saturday morning, when I was called into the office to be paid. Mr and Mrs Mackey were there. The boss said to me: 'Do you know, Vincent, if I thought you were out at Ashtown, I would gladly pay you for your half day.' I did not say anything. Then he said to me: 'I will give you the benefit of the doubt, and have a better shot the next time.' I was paid my day's wages. I might mention here that both Mr and Mrs Mackey were great nationalists.[60]

When the Squad started operating full-time, its members had to be permanently available. Crow Street ordered them to leave home and live in groups at safe houses, subsisting on an allowance of £4 10s a week – a tradesman's average wage.

By early 1920 the Squad's *modus operandi* involved open-air killings in broad daylight carried out by two gunmen, in case one shooter missed or his weapon jammed. After a waiting intelligence officer had indicated the target to them by a prearranged signal like a waved handkerchief or raised hat, the first killer would down the victim while the second finished him off with shots to the head. A three-man covering party was never more than 50 yards away to prevent soldiers, policemen or civilians intervening – though, in fact, this almost never occurred. Most of Dublin's uniformed policemen quietly sympathised with the Volunteers, remained ostentatiously neutral or had been cowed into submission. Occasionally one intervened but got little assistance from bystanders. Vinnie Byrne remembered that once, after he shot a detective in May 1920,

the peeler who was on point duty at Phibsboro' started to run up the Phibsboro' Road to where the shooting took place, and kept on running with a revolver in his hand – an old Bulldog type. He had not a hope in hell of catching them. However, the story is told that he followed them as far as the bridge, where the flour mill is situated. There was a crowd of men standing outside the mill, who were employed there. The peeler said to them: 'Why didn't you stop them?' One of them replied: 'Not likely! Do you want us to get the same as the fellow down there?'[61]

The Squad usually walked but sometimes made a quick getaway by car. Although they were never involved in an actual killing, Ben Byrne remembered that he

> always felt somewhat sorry for the drivers of these vehicles because while we had the active interest to keep us from worrying unduly as to the consequences or results of our activities, the unfortunate driver in each case was perforce left to his own devices, and waiting in suspense for fifteen or thirty minutes under the circumstances was not an enviable position. Actually, as far as I can recollect, three drivers became nerve cases as a result of their work.[62]

Half a dozen Squad members were permanently available at short notice in their headquarters, originally a private house in Seville Place off Amiens Street. Here they passed the time reading, playing cards, chatting and mulling over assassination techniques. But in February 1921, after a botched Brigade ambush nearby, the Squad shifted to Upper Abbey Street, six or seven minutes away from Crow Street via the Liffey footbridge.

The new premises masqueraded as Geo. Moreland, cabinet-makers, upholsterers and builders, fitting well into a district of small shops specialising in timber, plumbing and house repairs.[63] Moreland's was camouflaged by double gates, two high walls, sheds, buckets, fresh shavings, pieces of furniture and tools. Inside, the Squad posed as carpenters, though always carrying concealed weapons under their white aprons. At the front of house a doleful Vinnie Byrne put off prospective customers by explaining apologetically that pressure of work precluded new business for the foreseeable future. Strangely, in the small world of central Dublin, nobody queried a firm that never seemed to carry out any work: perhaps people simply assumed that Moreland's was no worse than any other builders. In case the British raided the premises, there was a quick escape route through an upstairs store with a glass roof and skylight. Plans were in place, but never implemented, to mine the passageways. The Squad secreted its weapons in a mailbag that was lowered by rope into a bricked-up ground-floor lavatory as well as in Mick McDonnell's lock-up garage nearby, a Parnell Street bakery and, across the Liffey, in a yard at Denzille Lane on the north side of Merrion Square. The Squad also had mines and grenades, though these were unsuited to Dublin's confined and crowded streets and unpopular with members, who once drew lots to select the carrier. There were a couple of machine guns, one of which was demonstrated at the Casino, a stone-built summerhouse on the Malahide Road. There, Collins and Mulcahy watched a sharpshooter lift a tin can with his first shot and hit it repeatedly in mid-air. According to Paddy Daly, 'The Casino was a walled-up building which was fairly isolated at the time, and we were confident that if we fired a few rounds we could do so in safety. We were very surprised when one of the Brothers out of the O'Brien Institute came out and told us that we could be heard all over the place.'[64]

McKee recruited the Squad for Collins from the Dublin Brigade, favouring IRB members of his old 2nd Battalion. They were a diverse bunch of individuals. Mick McDonnell, for instance, was an uncompromising, unsophisticated man of action, highly strung with a shrill, high-pitched feminine voice. Charlie Dalton remembered him as a stickler for detail who 'took his duties with intense seriousness, and this, with his irascible temper, made it a bad business to vex him'.[65] By contrast, Paddy Daly was dour, reticent and colourless, while his best friend Joe Leonard was bitter and unforgiving, jeering at victims with puerile puns like a high-ranking policeman Redmond having died outside the Standard Hotel because he simply wasn't up to standard. But Dalton also recalled Vinnie Byrne as invariably 'pleased with all the world and everybody in it. On his round and slightly sleepy face was an expression of incurable good nature.'[66]

Regardless of personality differences Squad members needed to possess certain physical, psychological and emotional qualities in order to function effectively. Above all they were expected not just to kill but to be ready to die – either in action or at the end of a rope. Florence O'Donoghue, a Cork intelligence officer, gave an insightful description of this singular attitude to life and death:

War can be sheer brutality. It can also be a sublime spiritual experience. Living close to sudden and violent death for a long unbroken period is an experience that does not stale, even after years. To give the best of mind and brain to the daily task one must have arrived at an unquestioning acceptance of death, and always be prepared for it. Only in that way is any peace with oneself possible.[67]

And the Squad's resolution was constantly tested as the British garrison expanded and Dublin increasingly assumed the appearance and atmosphere of a city at war. From the middle of 1920 paramilitary Auxiliaries and newly arrived British secret service agents exerted further pressure on the IRA in the capital.

The Squad's work best suited strong and fit young men and most were bachelors in their late teens or twenties. Paddy Daly, a widower in his early thirties, was an exception, while the balding 40-year-old Mick McDonnell was positively ancient. They needed agility for rapid attacks and retreats, which sometimes involved clambering over a wall or dodging a hail of bullets. Joe Dolan of GHQ Intelligence recalled: 'We knew that death would be swift if we were caught. The result was that when we had a job to do we worked fast and got away faster.'[68] Proficiency with handguns, a marksman's keen eyesight, steady hands and natural shooting ability were essential, especially as they got few opportunities for live firing practice apart from occasional sessions in a remote part of Co. Dublin. At headquarters they imitated western gunslingers by drawing, cocking and levelling their weapons. Physical courage was vital, but so too were personal stability and sound judgement: emotionally brittle, volatile and erratic individuals threatened the Squad's cohesion and even survival. Ironically, only Mick McDonnell cracked under the weight of a broken marriage and a nervous breakdown precipitated by his close friend Martin Savage's death at Ashtown in December 1919. After returning to duty, McDonnell was an increasing liability, especially when he became infatuated with a policeman's daughter in the summer of 1920.[69] This entanglement endangered the entire Squad, which now faced the possibility of having to eliminate someone they all revered. Slattery and Vinnie Byrne persuaded Tom Cullen to intercede with Collins, who manufactured a cover story about an imminent British swoop necessitating McDonnell's immediate flight to America. McDonnell's supposedly temporary disappearance extended into a lifelong stay in California. After his departure, Tom Keogh, McDonnell's distraught stepbrother, raged at the Jezebel who had brought him low, vowing to Vinnie Byrne that he

> was going to plug the . . . woman. Keogh said to me one evening 'Are you doing anything, Byrne?' 'No,' I said, 'I'm not.' 'Will you come for a drive?' 'Right,' I said. So he loaded the gun and put it in his pocket and we drove up to the pond in the park. I think he had had an idea that —— was out there with a fellow. He told me to stop there and he went through all the bushes looking for her. I'm sure he would have killed her.[70]

The Squad also sifted out anyone physically and morally squeamish about the blood, screams and final convulsions of a close-order killing. Even a Crow Street intelligence officer like Charlie Dalton 'couldn't sleep that night of Bloody Sunday. He thought he could hear the gurgling of the officer's blood and he kept awake in fright until we told him a tap was running somewhere.'[71] Recruits were usually placed on work experience with an assassination unit, allowing them to gauge for themselves whether they were suitable for such work. Vinnie Byrne, however, was in action within twenty-four hours of meeting Mick McDonnell in November 1919. Sponsored by his long-term friends Slattery and Keogh, Byrne was grilled by McDonnell.

'Would you shoot a man, Byrne?' I replied: 'It's all according to who he was.' He said: 'What about Johnnie Barton?' 'Oh', I said: 'I wouldn't mind' – as he had raided my house. So Mick said: 'That settles it. You may have a chance.' He told me to come along the following evening to College Green at about 5.30 or 6 o'clock. Jimmy Slattery and myself worked together at the cabinet making in Anthony Mackay's, The Irish Woodworkers. Jimmy said to me: 'You had better bring in your gun after dinner,' which I did. [72]

Byrne was told only in general terms what an assassination involved, but, despite never having fired a shot in anger, he wanted to prove himself a soldier. Still, actually killing someone was a personal Rubicon and only by crossing over – or turning back – could a Volunteer discover the kind of man he really was. Byrne was relieved to find after his first operation that he could cope, and was never frightened again.

Members of the Squad, almost all of whom were tradesmen and labourers, were seldom tormented by an intellectual's moral doubts, and their many sleepless nights were caused mostly by British army lorries and raiding parties. Only rarely did anyone express reservations about an operation. But Mulcahy did know about one new recruit who flummoxed his unit leader as they set out on a killing.

He said: 'I'm going to be married in a fortnight's time and I am wondering if we shoot this man, could it bring any affliction on the children of this marriage.' Naturally, this was a surprise and a challenge to the officer, who, however, just said to him 'But you are a soldier and you are acting under orders and you should not let your conscience worry you in that way.' He, however, immediately took the opportunity of meeting the third man on the work and suggested to him 'I think we ought to go home to our tea.' They did so and the immediate problem and difficulty was resolved by going home and giving everybody a chance of thinking over the matter.[73]

Vinnie Byrne even found his priest very understanding at confession:

'I shot a man, Father.'
'What did you do that for?'
'In the fight for freedom, Father.'
'Do you believe in your heart that what you are doing is right?'
'No doubt about that, Father.'
'Then God bless you.'[74]

Since there was no Squad training school, its members learnt on the job or from more experienced comrades. On his unit's first outing, Jim Slattery was surprised when their under-powered weapons almost allowed the target to escape. 'We never used .38 guns again, we used .45 guns after that.'[75] The Squad also refined its assassination locations in the light of such factors as housing and population density and the proximity of police stations and army barracks. After one killing in the quiet Simmonscourt Road area the shooters had to run a considerable distance before melting into the crowds. Slattery recalled: 'scarcely anybody on the road that morning, and if enemy forces had come along we would have had no chance of escaping. That was a lesson that we took deeply to heart and remembered for future occasions.'[76]

In a theatre of war the Squad also discovered that acting ability was a potentially life-saving asset. The guises that its members adopted included corporation employees, priests and even enemy officers. Sean Doyle donned his actor's mask when British soldiers unwittingly stumbled on the weapons dump in Denzille Lane. The Squad had camouflaged it as a builder's yard, though by chance Doyle was the only 'employee' present. He barely had time to secrete his gun in a bucket of putty and slip into a pair of dungarees, but as troops roamed the premises he remained composed, nonchalantly holding a brush, exchanging light-hearted banter and sharing cigarettes with his guard until the search party moved on.[77] Bill Stapleton's ability to mimic a British squaddie's accent saved him when he drove a captured army van towards a planned ambush in Grafton Street. At the time British street patrols were cordoning off the Liffey bridges and grilling pedestrians and car drivers, so Stapleton was taking a considerable risk by crossing over one.

On arriving about the centre of the bridge there was a blast of a whistle and out from among the pedestrians on each footpath a cordon of soldiers rushed across and closed the bridge in front of me. I slowed up and continued moving forward, my intention being to accelerate rapidly. There was some hesitation on the part of the soldiers and I was suddenly prompted to stick my head and arm out of the side window and shout something like, 'Gor blimey, haow are yaow' in an English accent. Fortunately the soldiers concluded, due to the colour of the car and my accent, that we were members of the British forces and passed us through. We continued and reached our point of contact in Dawson Street.[78]

After an assassination they also had to feign normality at headquarters when, as Stapleton recalled, the Squad always reverted immediately to their cover as simple Dublin tradesmen by handling 'pieces of timber as though we had never left the place. This presence of mind was something we all seemed to be able to produce at the right moment.'[79]

Skilled conspirators had a considerable advantage in the intelligence war and almost the entire Squad were IRB members who blended unobtrusively into the general population. Without disguises they posed as ordinary working men, their covers authenticated by proper trade-union cards and an ability to talk credibly about their supposed occupation. Bill Stapleton, whose father was a building contractor, pretended to be a house painter, while Vinnie Byrne, who always carried a ruler, passed himself off as a harmless cabinet-maker.[80] They had to display initiative and quick reactions in unexpected situations but also patience and endurance during futile daily trawls for targets who frequently changed their routines, addresses and places of employment or left the city altogether. Their tours of duty also required a thorough knowledge of the capital's geography, and the Squad consisted entirely of native or long-domiciled Dubliners. Squad life was almost entirely devoid of glamour, and the most common enemies turned out to be tedium and frustration.

* * *

By the winter of 1919 Dublin Castle was alarmed by G Division's embattled situation. Detective Sergeant John Barton's death on 19 November was its third fatality, a quarter of the strength, and represented an unsustainable rate of attrition. Many uniformed officers now avoided confronting the Volunteers, from either political sympathy or an instinct for self-preservation. A British Government report on the DMP in early December 1919 condemned the force as demoralised and inefficient, though, ludicrously, one of the signatories was its own Commissioner, Edgeworth-Johnstone.[81] It recommended that, since 'Dublin City is the storm centre', the Irish administration should concentrate its resources there, especially as further killings were anticipated in the coming months. With the usual sources of information cut off and people afraid to be seen talking with a policeman, the committee urged that an American associated with the republican movement in his own country be imported to ingratiate himself with the IRA and discover its plans. Undercover agents with a skilled trade should be brought into Dublin to work alongside artisans and pick up intelligence. A dozen RIC men, 'young active men of courage and determination, good shots and preferably accustomed to city life', should be lodged anonymously in pairs throughout the city. Licensed to kill, they would shadow G-men on the street and shoot on sight anyone about to attack them. The report suggested: 'The shooting of a few would-be assassins would have an excellent effect. Up to the present they have escaped with impunity.'

Although French regarded him as 'horribly weak' and the DMP as 'simply hopeless',[82] Edgeworth-Johnstone had a dazzling talent for bureaucratic infighting and – unlike many of his officers – dodging the bullets. Instead of getting rid of him, the committee recommended creating a new Assistant Commissioner who would devote himself full-time to revitalising G Division. French speedily appointed District Inspector William Redmond, a pugnacious outsider from Belfast with a reputation as a superb detective. The Viceroy's near miss at Ashtown – an ambush of which G Division had no prior knowledge – had shocked the Irish administration, and Redmond seemed just the man to reinvigorate the detective branch.

Redmond was committed to strangling a Dublin insurgency that increasingly wore Collins's face. When he addressed assembled G-men, David Neligan saw 'a neatly built man of about forty, nattily dressed and wearing a bowler. He looked more like a stockbroker than a policeman. He gave us a pep talk. It was extraordinary, he said, that we, who knew Dublin well, could not catch Michael Collins.'[83] Redmond's appointment had an immediate effect in revitalising G Division, and Collins was alarmed by the possibility that the Assistant Commissioner might sideline or unmask his double agents. So, even before Redmond had taken up his post officially on 1 January 1920, Collins began arranging his demise. He dispatched Thornton to Belfast, where an IRA mole, Sergeant McCarthy, helped him steal Redmond's photograph from the county inspector's office.[84] Redmond then placed himself in mortal danger by appointing Detective McNamara as his principal aide detective. McNamara immediately informed Collins that his new boss was living temporarily at the Standard Hotel in Harcourt Street while his Dublin Castle quarters were made ready. Collins then sent Cullen undercover to the Standard as a hotel guest in order to watch Redmond's evening activities.[85] Redmond had also taken to strolling unescorted to and from his offices every day, an extraordinary security lapse that must have stemmed from either an overconfidence verging on the delusional or a newcomer's failure to grasp Dublin's deteriorating security situation. During a recent visit Walter Long had been

> prepared to find things in Dublin in an unsatisfactory condition [compared to Belfast], but they were considerably worse than I anticipated. Everybody seems to suspect his neighbour; people are afraid to venture out after dark; robberies, burglaries, assaults and raids for arms take place every day. The majority of these cases are not reported in the Press because people are afraid to give evidence to the police, fearing that if they do so worse will befall them.[86]

Since Collins was still vetoing daylight operations that endangered civilians, he planned to assassinate Redmond in the evening on his way back to the Standard. Four hit teams would line the route – at the Castle gate, both ends of Grafton Street and near the Standard itself, a concentration of firepower literally constituting overkill because Collins knew he would get only one opportunity. At 6 p.m. on 21 January, only three weeks after arriving, Redmond left the Castle for the last time. He almost reached the Standard, because winter darkness and dim street lighting obscured this tall military-looking gentleman in a dark grey coat and bowler hat. Paddy Daly was standing close to the hotel entrance when he was startled by the sight of Keogh approaching rapidly just as Redmond crossed the street about six yards away. Although Keogh drew his revolver and began running, it was Daly who fired the fatal shot at Redmond's head; he already knew about the policeman's bullet-proof vest. Redmond fell. Passers-by carried him, bleeding heavily, into a chemist's shop, but he died within a few minutes, still clasping a loaded revolver.[87]

Redmond was the highest-ranking casualty in the DMP's history, and for the Squad his assassination was satisfying compensation for having missed French at Ashtown. His death also helped create the Squad's aura of invincibility, a public belief that it could strike when and where it desired. Furthermore, Neligan recalled it as a grim warning to any like-minded successor: 'Redmond's vacancy was advertised throughout the RIC. An inspector took the job, but did not go looking for trouble and was not interfered with.'[88] After this the Squad never looked back, becoming the 'Twelve Apostles' in September 1920 when Bill Stapleton, Jimmy Conroy, Ben Byrne and Paddy Griffin joined, and expanding to twenty-one during the first half of 1921.[89]

Chapter 3

STUMBLING INTO THE HAZE

THE BRITISH RESPONSE, JANUARY–JULY 1920

From the 1840s Britain's first line of defence against revolutionary Irish nationalism had been detectives of the Dublin Metropolitan Police's G Division, the legendary G-men. Although the DMP's new headquarters in Great Brunswick Street (now Pearse Street) had been built as recently as 1912, G Division's base in it was surprisingly small and antiquated. Modern office equipment was installed only after the Rising, and in 1919 just a third of its fifty-eight detectives were engaged in political surveillance.[1] Ultimately, G Division's effectiveness depended not on its limited resources but on an aura of omniscience that psychologically paralysed many revolutionaries. Even a Collins mole inside G Division was convinced that 'the British had perfected their espionage system at home and abroad. It was the most efficient in the world.'[2]

According to Eamon Broy, G Division's intelligence network of agents and informers included publicans, pawnbrokers, shopkeepers and criminals. Detectives also maintained 'careful and methodical observation of the actions and movements of all persons suspected of being disloyal to the British connection',[3] concentrated especially on railway stations, shadowing suspects to their residences, entering their names into the central register at headquarters and constantly watching their movements and associations. G Division's Superintendent Owen Brien submitted regular situation reports to the DMP's Commissioner, the RIC's Inspector-General, the Director of Military Intelligence and the Chief Secretary for Ireland.

While G-men shadowed suspects, they themselves were hardly shadowy figures, and a republican poem of 1916 even listed the names of ten detectives. Their identities became even better known after the Rising, when they routinely accompanied military raiding parties and by 1919 Volunteers knew more about the G-men than their supposed hunters did about them. G Division had also suffered financial cutbacks, a series of compulsory retirements, transfers and promotions implemented by the Irish administration in a mistaken belief that the revolutionary threat had evaporated. When Collins unleashed the Squad against G Division in July 1919, Dublin Castle went into reverse gear and began appealing for recruits from the DMP's uniformed branch. But the response was very poor. Even 20-year-old Constable David Neligan was snapped up, despite the fact that he had volunteered only to escape beat duty. He knew that his being accepted by the force was

> due to no merit on my part as the shootings had made this service unpopular with the general run of the force. In peace times it was difficult to get in but now the opposite was the case. The Castle was faced with a tough situation. Never before had such a determined and lethal attack been made on the British intelligence forces nor one directed with such ruthless efficiency.[4]

Neligan was originally from Limerick, where his parents had tried to dissuade him from a police career. He was serving at Dublin's College Street station when he joined the detective branch in July 1918. Although initially a loyal if unenthusiastic G-man, Neligan became increasingly disillusioned and resigned in May 1920. After returning home and offering his services to Sinn Fein, he was sent to Collins, who insisted he rejoin G Division. He was accepted back after pretending that a campaign of threatening letters had driven him out of Limerick. Neligan became Collins's fourth mole inside G Division, though at the beginning he knew nothing about Broy, Kavanagh and McNamara working for the IRA.

During the rest of 1920 Neligan witnessed G Division's destruction, as its decades of seemingly unassailable authority collapsed within a few months. The killing of John Barton in November 1919 was particularly damaging, because he was regarded as the finest detective in Ireland.

Although Superintendent Brien was an excellent administrator, he lacked leadership qualities and was unable to come up with new ideas. Brien left after a devastating government inquiry revealed that, in the second half of 1919, three of the nineteen detectives designated as 'political experts' had been assassinated, one had been permanently incapacitated, four had retired, two had transferred to ordinary crime and another three had returned to the uniformed branch. The 'series of murders coming one after another had a paralysing effect upon the Division generally'.[5] Half-a-dozen survivors – including Collins's mole, McNamara – retreated into the Castle, where 'for their own protection they were obliged to be sent out in parties of no less than three or four men which in itself would decrease their value as detectives'.[6]

The Irish administration's attempted rejuvenation of G Division petered out after Assistant Commissioner Redmond's assassination in January 1920. A British intelligence report noted that Redmond had been

> most anxious to assist in working out the military side of Sinn Fein and to collaborate with military intelligence. He very soon became aware that there was a serious leakage of information and at once took steps to ascertain the men in the DMP who were giving information to Sinn Fein. This probably was the cause of his murder early in January, 1920, for there is good reason to suppose that Sinn Fein were informed of his movements by his own men . . . After the death of Mr Redmond the work of G Division ceased to affect the situation, and the force did little more than point duty during the years 1920–21.[7]

Outside Dublin the RIC's Crimes Branch Special, based in Dublin Castle, collated monthly reports from every county headquarters in Ireland as well as Glasgow, Liverpool and Holyhead. Special sergeants forwarded information on extremist organisations based on their own observations and those of rank-and-file policemen, paid informers and loyal civilians such as civil servants, magistrates, shopkeepers and employers. Some sources were coerced – for example, publicans who were threatened with losing their licences – while civilian employees at RIC barracks, street children and people at social gatherings were often recruited after apparently casual encounters. According to Broy,

> when it was thought that members of a family had information which the RIC needed, a constable would be sent on a bicycle to their house. When nearing the house he would deliberately puncture one of his tyres with a pin. Then he would call at the house for a basin of water to locate the puncture and, whilst carrying out the repairs, would enter into conversation with members of the family and gradually lead up to the subject in which he was interested. Members of the family would thus, quite innocently, supply the constable with all the local gossip, and when the 'repairs' were finished the constable would have the information he needed in order to supply the police with clues as to where to institute further inquiries.[8]

Broy even claimed that long-term police 'sleepers' were planted undercover amongst the civilian population. 'Some members of the RIC never served in uniform but spent their whole service period as journeymen, blacksmiths, carpenters or other skilled tradesmen.'[9]

Crimes Branch Special officers throughout Ireland also transmitted confidential reports and cipher telegrams to G Division in Dublin. Broy said that

> when a prominent Volunteer officer from Dublin came to the area, although previously unknown to the police in Dublin he was soon noted by the RIC as a stranger. His movements were noticed and noted, and even if his name was not ascertained, his being in the company of local Sinn Feiners was a clue to his business in the area. All travelling at that time was by rail, and when the Volunteers left by train the RIC ascertained as to where he had a ticket, as, for example, to Dublin. Then either his name, if known, or his description without name if unknown, was sent immediately by cipher wire to G Division. This fact of the menace of the small station in an isolated countryside was the main reason for the ruthless war subsequently made on small RIC stations by the IRA.[10]

The RIC had always been a bulwark against rebellion and rural disorder, but even before the Rising its effectiveness was being diminished by government stinginess about introducing technical innovation and allocating more clerical assistance. After 1916 Crimes Branch Special reports were still written out laboriously in longhand, with copies rarely kept. When the Castle withdrew their special allowances, intelligence officers relied increasingly on memory rather than written records, so that, as the IRA's assassination campaign gathered pace, many took their information with them – literally to the grave. A British intelligence report declared:

> Sinn Fein was not long in recognising that these men and the best and most energetic of the RIC who had accurate local knowledge were the most dangerous of their opponents. From 1919 onwards they carried out a systematic murder campaign, with the result that many of the best of the RIC were killed, many more were transferred to other parts of the country, where for a time at least they would not be recognised, and some resigned. Consequently the police source of information, at that time the only one on which the authorities could rely, was dried up and the intelligence services

paralysed. This was exactly what Sinn Fein desired and intended and was their first distinct success.[11]

In 1914 the British Army in Ireland had delegated intelligence gathering to Ivon Price, an RIC officer who had neither military training nor professional clout. His failure to train intelligence officers, instead preferring to concentrate on catching German spies, actually left the army more dependent than ever on the police for information. After the Rising, Price weakened military intelligence still further by claiming the Volunteers were finished.[12] Yet by May 1918 General Loch was complaining that 'while the Sinn Fein intelligence seems to have improved ours has almost ceased to exist'[13] – a reversal of fortunes which he blamed on a secretive republican leadership, and the rank and file's new sobriety brought on by a wartime scarcity of whiskey.

After Price had returned to RIC duty in January 1919, his successor Major Hill Dillon, a GHQ staff officer, realised that the Volunteers' resurgence made it essential to improve British military intelligence. Yet he had only a few officers at GHQ and the District Headquarters in Dublin, Cork and Belfast. Burdened with non-intelligence responsibilities, most culled their information from police contacts and local newspapers, making no attempt to identify the IRA's order of battle, its key leaders, resources and future intentions. Furthermore, Hill Dillon's organisation was constantly disrupted by transfers of military intelligence officers before they could familiarise themselves properly with their districts.

After Hill Dillon had classified the Volunteers as a hostile revolutionary organisation in May 1919, he sent intelligence officers on courses in England, but any 'who showed an aptitude for this work were sent abroad, and never returned . . . except for the purpose of collecting their baggage'.[14] Yet army high command remained strangely reluctant to break with the increasingly ineffective police intelligence system, even though it knew many RIC officers were

comparatively old men, anxious to keep their areas as peaceful as possible, until such time as they would be entitled to retire on full pension, and therefore they would not cause raids or searches to be carried out unless the information available was very definite. Others were opposed to raids, because, even if arms, etc. were found, and a man arrested and sentenced to imprisonment, the chances were that he would be released within a few weeks, only to murder one or more of those responsible for his arrest.[15]

In May 1919 Hill Dillon took on a group of army officers who had become exasperated by the police, with whom they refused to work. At the end of the year, the British Army was reorganised into divisions and brigades, each of which got its own intelligence officer.[16] The necessity for a professional, independent military intelligence system became urgent as IRA attacks on army units increased and the collapse of RIC intelligence could no longer be denied. In January 1920, when British GHQ decided to deport hundreds of republican activists, it was shocked by the inadequate and out-of-date police files, many of which contained little more than bald assertions about a suspect's unsavoury character. It was army intelligence officers who supplied the IRA status of sixty men who were eventually rounded up – most from Munster and only eight from Dublin. As a result of this fiasco, battalion intelligence officers were appointed, though initially their status was low and they received no extra pay.[17]

At the end of 1919 G Division's decimation and the IRA's neutralisation of Crimes Special Branch forced Dublin Castle to turn the secret service over to Basil Thomson's Special Branch in London. Thomson was the son of an Archbishop of York and had been educated at Eton and Oxford, though subsequently this cynical, adventurous maverick farmed the Canadian prairies, served as prime minister of Tonga in his late twenties and tutored the King of Siam's son.[18] After returning to England as a tough prison governor, he became Assistant Commissioner of the Metropolitan Police in June 1913, with responsibility for Scotland Yard's Special Branch. It was part of Britain's small domestic intelligence system alongside the Secret Service's Home Department, MI5, a military organisation commanded by Captain Vernon Kell. Kell's dozen army officers monitored Germany's spy network in the United Kingdom on an annual budget of £7,000, using Special Branch to arrest and interrogate any civilian suspects. 'The Branch'[19] had been established in the 1880s during a Fenian bombing campaign in England, but it gradually became responsible for combating threats to public order, royalty, politicians and government buildings such as major strikes, anarchist outrages and militant suffragettes. Officers in London and the provinces also investigated aliens and refugees, monitored public protest meetings and protected important public figures. Yet in 1914 Special Branch's considerable workload was carried by only 114 employees on an annual budget of £19,000.[20]

The First World War was a turning point for Thomson and Kell, because home-front stability required the constant vigilance of a fully fledged state intelligence apparatus. The British Government poured resources into both men's organisations, and by the end of the war the combined annual budget for MI5's 844 staff and Special Branch's 700 officers had soared to over £200,000. They intruded into almost every aspect of public life, breaking up Germany's spy network, interning or repatriating over 50,000 enemy aliens, routinely censoring letters and telegrams and compiling dossiers on 100,000 foreign residents. They also maintained surveillance on anti-war and pacifist movements, socialist societies and militant trade unions, raiding their offices and the homes of leading activists. Thomson personally interrogated suspected enemy agents like Sir Roger Casement, and his interest in the Irish situation rose further after the Rising, when he compiled a report on the British intelligence system's catastrophic failure in Ireland.

After 1916 a power struggle developed between Kell, who wanted MI5 to concentrate on political policing, and Thomson, who envisaged an independent Special Branch controlling all civil intelligence. In December 1916 Thomson hived off CID's non-political responsibilities and assumed personal command of Special Branch. Soon afterwards it became responsible for intelligence at Ministry of Munitions factories throughout the United Kingdom, with Thomson reporting directly to the Home Secretary and the War Cabinet on labour unrest and pacifist propaganda. After the Bolshevik Revolution in 1917, the British Government feared a similar internal collapse in Britain, and by the end of the war Special Branch and MI5 were devoting more time and resources on surveillance of left-wing movements than on counter-espionage and enemy aliens. Both organisations had moved far beyond simply preventing and investigating specific criminal acts to become protectors of the state's political system, 'monitors of political opposition in the United Kingdom, whether or not that opposition was controlled from abroad or was breaking the law'.[21] Their intelligence officers, informers and even *agents provocateurs* routinely posed as members in order to infiltrate allegedly subversive groups.

During 1918 Thomson's power base increased steadily because of his close relationship with Walter Long and Viceroy French, for whom he provided a bodyguard in Ireland. From the autumn Thomson also began submitting fortnightly reports to the Cabinet on radical and revolutionary organisations in the United Kingdom.

In early 1919, when Long was drawing up proposals for a new, post-war domestic intelligence system, Thomson suggested placing every agency under an intelligence overlord, a post for which he modestly volunteered himself.[22]

Thomson did not get control over all agencies, but with his greater political influence was able to relegate MI5 to counter-espionage and became the most powerful figure in British Intelligence. His enlarged Special Branch became an independent civil service department, the Directorate of Intelligence, which on 1 May 1919 moved into new headquarters at Scotland House directly opposite Scotland Yard in London. Physically distanced from Metropolitan Police headquarters, Thomson had moved far beyond mundane policing and assumed literally universal responsibilities, monitoring public unrest and domestic subversion, countering foreign threats to the British Empire and acting as Security Officer to the British delegation at the Paris Peace Conference. At the end of 1919 Dublin Castle persuaded him to run the Irish secret service from London.[23]

Thomson had come a long way from the governor's office at Wormwood Scrubs, and from his Scotland House watchtower he surveyed a troubled world that he believed was threatened by a more deadly enemy than Imperial Germany had ever been. Thomson had identified a guiding hand behind British industrial disputes, South American coups, turmoil in central and eastern Europe and revolutionary movements in Egypt and Persia: a vast communist conspiracy striving for world domination by destroying capitalism, democracy and Christianity. And this alien ideology was spreading 'like a cancer, eating away the tissue of society until the whole mass disintegrates and falls into corruption'.[24] Thomson saw 'Moscow Gold' subsidising communist agents, trade-union saboteurs and left-wing agitators in Britain, and fomenting political disorder in Ireland, where sporadic labour unrest and land grabbing was reminiscent of Czarism's final days. Certain that Sinn Fein was a Comintern agent, Thomson hardly skipped a beat as he transformed the party from a pawn of German autocracy into a carrier of the communist virus. As chief sentinel on the watchtower, he was determined to destroy this menace before it spread to the British mainland. But, despite his wartime involvement in Irish affairs, his reputation as an Irish expert and a number of visits during 1920 to Ireland, Thomson never really understood the country or its people. He was handicapped by his quintessentially establishment social background and class attitudes as well as his multifarious intelligence responsibilities. With the entire globe jostling for his attention, Thomson skimmed reports on the Irish situation. By making him its intelligence overlord, Dublin Castle had compounded, not solved, its problems. As an intelligence chief Thomson was, in more senses than one, all over the place.

Thomson's first priority in Ireland was infiltrating the IRA at the highest level and gathering intelligence on those Volunteer leaders annihilating G Division. For this mission he chose an agent who used the pseudonym 'John Jameson'. In republican folklore 'Jameson' has assumed an almost mythical status, supposedly the finest British spy of his generation, a top gun sent to Ireland to eliminate Michael Collins only to be outwitted and destroyed by an Irish master. Tim Pat Coogan describes 'Jameson' with almost complete inaccuracy, as 'plump, sharp-featured, middle-aged, of average height . . . born Burns, the son of a police officer from Limerick. He had been in intelligence work in India before the First World War and during it somehow managed to elude detection in Germany.'[25] In fact, Jack Byrnes was a 35-year-old Londoner of medium build whose only Irish connection was his late grandfather from Wexford.[26] After he had served in Greece as a sergeant major with the Royal Field Artillery, his army career was ended prematurely in June 1918 by a medical discharge for heart trouble. Byrnes returned to the family home in Romford, and his involvement with London's ex-servicemen's organisations and Labour politics attracted the interest of Special Branch, which recruited him during the winter of 1918, almost certainly through his wife Daisy's connections with her former Admiralty employers. Byrnes's motivation for entering the intelligence world was less ideological conviction than a partially disabled ex-serviceman's need for a regular wage to support his family. And he came in at the lower level, because Thomson's best agents were already serving in central and eastern Europe on the front line with communism.

Thomson soon farmed Byrnes out to the army's own domestic intelligence organisation, A2 Branch GHQ GB, which the high command had established in the spring of 1919 to ensure the loyalty of soldiers and ex-servicemen during a difficult post-war transition. With rising unemployment, major strikes and rampant trade-union militancy, Britain hardly felt like a victorious country. The government feared, and a plethora of socialist and radical organisations dreamt, that London might go the way of Moscow. Left-wing rhetoric about overthrowing capitalism by infiltrating the armed forces and police and turning them against the state hardly seemed outlandish when soldiers were mutinying over the slow pace of demobilisation, two strikes had briefly disabled the Metropolitan Police and tanks had been sent in after the Red Flag had been hoisted over Glasgow Town Hall. A former serviceman who founded a Sailors', Soldiers' and Airmen's Union claimed that 'civilian men and women of extreme Bolshevik principles'[27] were manipulating it for revolutionary purposes.

Under Lieutenant-Colonel Ralph Isham, A2's seven staff scrutinised radical newspapers, analysed other intelligence agencies' reports and indoctrinated army officers in anti-communism. As A2's field agent, Byrnes posed as a militant demobilised soldier to infiltrate London's left-wing organisations. According to Julian Putkowski, 'there is no indication that Jack Byrnes was specially trained as a spy',[28] but clearly he was considered a competent middle-ranking agent with a feel for the extremist politics of his home city. A skilled committeeman with apparently limitless free time, Byrnes soon became secretary of the Sailors', Soldiers' and Airmen's Union and a member of the London Workers Committee, a steering group that coordinated the capital's socialist societies and trade unions. He was ideally placed to sabotage both organisations from within by instigating internal wrangling and smearing other leaders as government spies – dirty tricks that worked well in a political environment teeming with ideological nitpickers, cranks, sectarian fanatics, paranoiacs and the clinically deranged. While socialists were nominally fighting capitalism, they mostly enjoyed attacking the real enemy – their left-wing rivals. Byrnes also claimed influence with discontented soldiers and ready access to their weapons and ammunition, a front that impressed many British, Irish and European revolutionary socialists thronging London after the war. They included Sidney Arnold, a Comintern agent, Rose McKenna, a fiery militant nicknamed 'Libertia' who clearly fancied herself as an Irish Rosa Luxemburg, and Art O'Brien, Collins's London representative, who asked Byrnes to supply guns and rifles to the Irish Volunteers.

In late 1919, nervous that its unconstitutional political espionage might be publicly exposed, the British Army high command disbanded A2. Byrnes returned to the Directorate of Intelligence along with the rest of Isham's staff, whom Thomson immediately redeployed to the Irish situation. Thomson intended Byrnes to infiltrate Dublin's republican leadership in the same way that he had penetrated London socialism, and, after telling Art O'Brien that he could smuggle weapons to Ireland, Byrnes was invited to visit Dublin. He arrived in the capital on 6 December posing as 'John Jameson' of Keith Prowse, the theatrical ticket agency.[29] Since the IRA already knew his real name, Byrnes's cover was to maintain the pretence that he was a dangerous radical being sought by British Intelligence. His supposed job facilitated entry to army barracks, where he claimed he could subvert the troops. Byrnes's eight-day visit was not intended to destroy Collins, the mastermind behind the IRA campaign, because at this stage of the conflict British Intelligence did not know that Collins exercised this power within the Irish Volunteers. Rather, Byrnes's mission was to establish useful contacts by winning the confidence of republican leaders as well as assessing the general political situation. He reported British troops as universally 'anxious to give the Sinn Feiners a damn good hiding and settle the matter',[30] and noted that Sinn Fein was mainly confined to the middle classes and workers gravitating towards republican socialism. Dangerously for Byrnes, he might have been lulled into believing that Dublin was a home from home after encountering Sidney Arnold. Arnold was caring for Rose McKenna, who had returned for an operation, and during her convalescence the pair were running a clothing shop in South Frederick Street. Byrnes suspected it was a front for their revolutionary activities and, intriguingly, discovered that Captain Reddy of British Army GHQ's intelligence staff – the husband of a cousin of McKenna – was working occasionally as their shop assistant. Byrnes's association with Arnold and McKenna bolstered his credentials in Dublin's revolutionary circles.

The highlight of Byrnes's visit was meeting Collins, who was obviously curious about someone promising enough weapons to equip the entire Squad and the Dublin Brigade. On 8 December 1919 a runner – possibly Joe O'Reilly – collected Byrnes at his hotel and escorted him just south of the Liffey. He was blindfolded for the last 500 yards, and, when the bandage was removed, Byrnes found himself in a sparsely furnished room containing Collins and three other men, one of which called himself McCabe (which Byrnes assumed was an alias). In fact the trio were Mulcahy, Tobin and Rory O'Connor, Volunteer GHQ Director of Engineering.[31] Byrnes and Collins did not discuss arms smuggling. Their main aim at this stage was to break the ice, assess each other and discuss the general political and military situation. Collins described British military pressure on the IRA and expressed his interest in Byrnes's idea of winning soldiers over by fraternising with them at dances and other social functions. He also handed over a detailed list of British troop strength in Ireland, which identified those units most antagonistic to the Volunteers. He asked Byrnes to find out how well equipped British forces were and by which routes and methods reinforcements would be sent to Ireland.[32]

Byrnes was extremely impressed by Collins's authority, the quality of his information and his power of independent decision-making. Their encounter was British Intelligence's great breakthrough, because Collins had now been identified as standing at the very pinnacle of the republican movement. When Byrnes returned to London, he stressed to Thomson and Isham that 'this man COLLINS is the Chief Director of all active movement among the Sinn Feiners and that he has now taken the place of De Valera owing to the long absence of the latter. Although Collins does not take any active part in the shooting affairs there seems no doubt that he is the organiser.'[33]

Thomson must have been delighted at Byrnes's rapid progress, which allowed him to inform Dublin Castle so quickly of 'definite and trustworthy information that Michael Collins is directing the murders of Policemen; that he has attained such a position that his friends say the Police dare not touch him, and that if any attempt was made to arrest him it would precipitate a Rising in Ireland'.[34]

Byrnes's mission was clearly part of a wider and longer strategy of preparing an intelligence offensive in Ireland. Isham continued laying the groundwork by reconnoitring the battleground when he saw in the New Year at Dublin's Shelbourne Hotel. Isham then ordered Byrnes to resume contact with Collins.[35] Byrnes was back in Dublin between 23 and 29 January 1920, but he could not arrange another meeting with Collins, who was supposedly unavailable. In reality, IRA Intelligence had become very suspicious of Byrnes. Thornton recalled that Tom Cullen 'had forcibly expressed his dislike of the man from the beginning, and possibly this had reactions on myself. In any case there were none of us impressed.'[36] Coogan has argued, unconvincingly, that an IRA super-mole 'close to Basil Thompson [sic] himself'[37] had already betrayed Byrnes. Putkowski speculates that a Collins mole – possibly Lily Mernin – blew Byrnes's cover, but Mernin's written statement does not even mention Byrnes/Jameson. In fact, Thornton says the IRA never did establish beyond doubt that Byrnes was a British spy, and that he trapped himself by failing a series of loyalty tests set by Crow Street. One involved Byrnes handing over a case of weapons in a Bachelor's Walk office. After Thornton pretended to secrete it in the basement, Tobin took Byrnes away, and Thornton immediately transferred the consignment to a nearby location. Later that day one of Collins's police agents told Thornton that the Bachelor's Walk office would soon be raided, and, from the other side of the river, Thornton and Tobin watched as a large force of military and police surrounded the building. 'However, the raid was abortive and they went away, but at about 1 o'clock the following morning they arrived back again and they smashed in the door, and, with picks and shovels, proceeded to dig up the basement looking for secret passages.'[38] In another charade Thornton, Tobin and Cullen staged an argument in front of Byrnes about a supposed evening conference of republican leaders in north Dublin. Byrnes immediately excused himself. When the supposed meeting place was raided that night, Tobin had had enough. But Crow Street could not find Byrnes, who had returned to England in the absence of further instructions from Thomson and Isham.[39]

Believing his cover was still intact, Byrnes arrived back in Dublin on Saturday 28 February. Once again he asked to meet Collins, who instead immediately authorised his execution. Joe Dolan recalled that

> in the last days of February Liam Tobin told me that he would be in D'Olier Street talking to a man. 'Take a good, hard look at him and make sure that you would recognise him again,' he said. At the time arranged I went along. Tobin was on the other side of the road talking to a man about 5ft 8 in. tall, wearing a dark coat with a fur collar. I studied his face – a furtive one. Two days later Tobin said, 'The man I was talking to is Jameson. We know that he is an enemy agent. He must be got rid of.' On March 1, 1920 Paddy Daly and I went out to Ballymun to pick a suitable place for the shooting. We did – a place called Lovers' Lane.[40]

Next day Byrnes was lured in by the promise of meeting Collins again, another trap into which he fell unerringly. It was sprung at a draper's shop in O'Connell Street, where his supposed escorts, Paddy Daly and Joe Leonard, intended for him only a one-way journey to the city's northern outskirts. As the trio boarded a tram, others watched from a distance to ensure that Byrnes had come alone. Joe Dolan and the Squad's Ben Barrett and Tom Kilcoyne had already cycled out to Ballymun. After alighting, Daly brushed aside Byrnes's suggestion of a drink in a pub and instead they strolled on to journey's end in the grotesquely inappropriate Lovers' Lane, where Dolan's party was waiting. With all pretence and hope finally abandoned, Byrnes displayed remarkable courage and dignity in his utterly bleak final moments. Daly 'told him that we were satisfied he was a spy, that he was going to die, and that if he wanted to say any prayers he should do so. The spy jumped to attention immediately and said, "You are right. God bless the King. I would love to die for him." He saluted and there was not a quiver on him.'[41]

Perhaps at the end Byrnes reflected on the unlikely sequence of events that had led him from a Romford semi to these lonely fields. Like Redmond, he had not lasted long in Dublin, although, unlike the Assistant Commissioner, Byrnes had at least gazed upon the face of his executioner, Michael Collins. Soon afterwards a farm worker discovered the body, which was taken to the Mater Hospital and later claimed by his wife, Daisy – a traumatic experience that left her permanently deaf. After a family funeral, she finally laid her husband to rest in a Romford cemetery.[42]

A few months later Walter Long told the Cabinet that Byrnes was 'the best secret service man we had'.[43] But, as Putkowski argues persuasively, his tribute had less to do with the dead agent's ability than with Long's desire to emphasise the seriousness of the situation in Ireland. Although undeniably brave and patriotic, Byrnes had performed like an inexperienced, foolhardy novice completely out of his depth in a country about which he knew little. Perhaps he had been seduced by ineffectual left-wing windbags in a London milieu where exposure as a government spy resulted only in public denunciation and expulsion. Too late, he realised that these new Irish revolutionaries were deadly serious and quite prepared to turn against him the very weapons he had gifted them.

Although Byrnes had pointed the British in Collins's direction, confirmation of his crucial importance to the IRA's campaign came almost simultaneously from another spy who died in virtually identical circumstances. Around 9 p.m. on 18 February 1920 a railway worker on the southern outskirts of Cork heard revolver shots, and at dawn a well-dressed, bullet-riddled body was discovered in a nearby field. The man was dark, fresh complexioned, clean-shaven, thin-featured and of medium height; nearby lay a cap and rosary beads. He had been shot at close range with most of the nine bullets shattering his head and leaving the brains protruding, although one had gone straight through the heart.[44] The absence of any sign of a struggle indicated that the dead man had accepted his hopeless situation. Only a small amount of money was found on him, and his identity remained a mystery for another four days, until Tom Cullen tipped off a friendly journalist that the IRA had eliminated the first spy in its ranks, 23-year-old Henry Quinlisk from Wexford.[45]

Quinlisk was a former soldier in the Royal Irish Regiment who had served on the Western Front until captured by the Germans, whereupon he switched his allegiance to Sir Roger Casement's Irish Brigade. Casement had recruited this misbegotten band of losers from Irish POWs, supposedly to liberate Ireland, though most of the fifty-two members were primarily concerned about their next square meal. Although still a teenager, Quinlisk was well educated and charismatic, and Casement soon promoted him to second in command. He spoke French, German and Gaelic and earned his nickname of Casanova by fraternising compulsively with the local female population. A cocky rogue, Quinlisk was sublimely confident that he could talk himself into and out of any situation.

Unsurprisingly, the Irish Brigade never saw action and after the war became such pestilential nuisances in Berlin that the German authorities issued them with false passports and one-way tickets to Ireland. Quinlisk returned a penniless, unemployed fugitive with few prospects in a country that had changed utterly during his four years away. Adrift in Dublin, he and other Brigade members eventually washed up at Miss McCarthy's Mountjoy Street boarding house, which soon resembled Rick's Café in *Casablanca*, a watering hole for riff-raff and the human debris of war. Collins also used McCarthy's, and doled out funds to help its residents muddle through. Quinlisk also kept afloat by ingratiating himself with republican leaders like Robert Brennan of the Dail's Foreign Affairs Department, who knew his family from Wexford.[46] He introduced Quinlisk to Sean Ó Muirthuile, Collins's colleague on the IRB's Supreme Council, who was initially captivated by the young man.

Thereafter he was constantly to be seen with Sean and his companions. One of them told me they were a bit uneasy about him, not because they distrusted him but because he took no precautions whatever. He had a way with the girls. A few of the lads would go off to Bray or Dun Laoghaire on a Sunday afternoon and before they were half an hour on the Esplanade, Quin [sic] had got off with the best-looking girl in the neighbourhood. A fellow like that might inadvertently give something away. I saw Quin from time to time. He was always immaculately dressed and one would have said that with his good looks, his self-assurance and general bonhomie he would have got anywhere. He liked to give the impression that he was in on all of Mick Collins's secrets.[47]

But Quinlisk's brash, indiscreet behaviour disqualified him from Collins's inner circle, and by November 1919, still unemployed and living hand to mouth, his life was in freefall. Even Collins's financial assistance had dried up, fuelling Quinlisk's anger at the Director of Intelligence. With his feather-light principles and loyalties and a proven track record of betrayal, Quinlisk effortlessly executed another somersault. On 11 November 1919 he wrote to the Castle, claiming that 'since coming home I have been connected with Sinn Fein. I have decided to tell all I know of that organisation and my information would be of use to the authorities. The scoundrel Michael Collins has treated me scurvily and I now am going to wash my hands of the whole business.'[48]

To Quinlisk, working as a paid British agent must have seemed the ideal solution to all his problems. At one stroke he could wipe the slate clean on the Irish Brigade, eliminate his financial difficulties and wreak vengeance on Collins by revealing him as the mastermind behind the IRA campaign. Quinlisk was sufficiently cunning to anticipate Collins learning about his contact with the police, but explained it away as a hamfisted British attempt to recruit him when he enquired about a passport. But it was a dangerous bluff. Collins was on his guard now and ignored Quinlisk's increasingly frantic efforts to re-establish contact. Brennan recalled how

Quin [sic] came in after several weeks absence, and asked me where he could find Mick. I said I didn't know but that Ó Muirthuile should be able to tell him. 'That's the trouble,' he said. 'I can't find any of them. Do you know if there is anything up?' 'I don't,' I said, 'I expect they are lying low for some reason or other.' Which, of course, I did not believe. I reported this to Mick in the afternoon and asked him what was wrong with Quin. He looked up from the desk and said simply: 'Go easy with him.' A few days later Griffith came up and told me that Quin had stopped him in Stephen's Green and asked him where he could find Mick. AG was plainly worried and went off to see Mick about the matter.[49]

Just as it had with Byrnes, GHQ Intelligence tested Quinlisk's loyalties, and, like Byrnes, he fell into the trap. Through an intermediary, Collins told Quinlisk that he was going to Cork, where he would be staying at Wren's Hotel. Soon afterwards, Liam Archer deciphered an RIC telegram to Cork's county inspector warning that Collins, armed and dangerous, would be at Wren's the following night and was to be captured dead or alive. When Archer showed the message to Collins later that evening, his reaction was venomous: 'That . . . has signed his death warrant.'[50] Although Collins accepted that many people were after his scalp, he distinguished between

English spies like Byrnes doing their patriotic duty and someone like Quinlisk, whom he regarded as a traitor who had betrayed his trust and generosity. Using the alias 'Sullivan', Quinlisk travelled to Cork and offered to supply weapons and ammunition to the local IRA leadership, which, surprisingly, had not been told about Collins's ruse. While it stalled Quinlisk and made further enquiries, the Brigade Intelligence Officer decoded a police cipher from Dublin Castle about the imminent arrival of 'Sullivan's' letter. Next morning the Cork IRA robbed two policemen collecting correspondence from the city's GPO, and one letter proved definitively that 'Sullivan' was an enemy spy. When Dublin's permission was sought to shoot 'Sullivan',[51] Collins realised it was the pseudonym of Quinlisk. The failed spy was captured before the police could warn him, and under interrogation he admitted his true identity.

Launched by financial hardship and a bruised ego, Quinlisk's espionage career had lasted only a couple of months. Having changed allegiance once, he found it easier the second time round, and spying probably offered him some welcome excitement and a renewed sense of purpose. Mundane reality had rarely featured in Quinlisk's short life, and after he had experienced war, captivity and treason, it had no appeal anyway. But his time away from Ireland had only encouraged delusions of grandeur, and his failure to appreciate IRA ruthlessness was folly. Over the years Quinlisk had got tremendous mileage from a winning smile and lashings of Irish blarney, but by February 1920 he had run clean out of road. The charm that had seduced so many German hausfraus and Irish colleens had no effect whatsoever on these serious, disbelieving revolutionaries. While deception was an integral part of espionage, self-deception was a dangerous character flaw. Quinlisk's belief that he could run rings around Collins proved eventually to be a serious, fatal mistake.

But British Intelligence had not given up trying to infiltrate an agent into Collins's inner circle. Just over a month after Quinlisk's death Frank Saurin and Vinnie Byrne met Bryan Mulloy, a British Army Pay Corps Sergeant, for tea at the Café Cairo in Grafton Street. Like Byrnes, Mulloy posed as a republican sympathiser anxious to assist the Irish Volunteers and keen to meet Liam Tobin. Crow Street had already concluded that Mulloy was working for Hill Dillon and British Army GHQ Intelligence, and Vinnie Byrne's job was to string him along with the promise of meeting Tobin. He arranged to meet Mulloy the following evening at the corner of Grafton Street. At the appointed time Byrne arrived with the Squad and watched

Mulloy for three-quarters of an hour before he gave up and started walking down Grafton Street. Byrne recalled:

> We made several attempts to get him, but owing to the large number of people in the street, it was very difficult. He turned into Wicklow St. and proceeded as far as the corner of South William St. Here we opened fire and he fell dead. At that time, the Central Hotel in Exchequer St was occupied by British military, so that we could not have let him go any farther, knowing that he could identify at least one Squad man and an Intelligence officer.[52]

During the spring of 1920 Basil Thomson tried another way of crippling the republican war effort through Alan Bell, a former magistrate with a police rank equivalent to Chief Commissioner. Bell carried out sensitive security-related investigations such as the official inquiry into the Squad's ambush of Lord French at Ashtown, and now he was ordered to 'follow the money'.[53] British Intelligence knew that, as Minister of Finance, Collins had salted away Dail Bond funds in the bank accounts of eminently respectable front men. Although hardly any bank manager actually worked for Collins, most knew what was happening, and they felt the heat when Bell, in his capacity as President of the Irish Banks Court, instituted hearings into IRA money laundering. It was a form of inquisition by a financial Torquemada whose relentless probing left successive witnesses squirming. The transcripts of these sessions make for fascinating reading. They were also very funny, as they record how the memories of these meticulous officials short-circuited and collective amnesia descended upon the proceedings. But Collins did not get the joke. Bell was dangerous; Bell had to go. A friendly journalist supplied Bell's photograph, which made it possible to track him to anonymous lodgings on the outskirts of Kingstown (Dun Laoghaire).[54] Mick McDonnell and Vinnie Byrne tried to blow up Bell's car with a large grenade on its way into the Four Courts, but the vehicle simply continued driving along the quayside.[55] A few days later the Squad drove out to Kingstown to kill Bell but found G-men guarding his accommodation. They also met him every morning when his tram arrived in Grafton Street and escorted him to his office in Dublin Castle. Bell was vulnerable only during the journey into town.[56]

On 26 March 1920 Paddy Daly and Tom Keogh sat on their bicycles, watching discreetly from a distance as Bell boarded the 9.30 a.m. tram for the city centre. When it set off, they followed. Daly remembered that 'the tram was going very fast and we found it hard to keep up with it. We saw our group of men at the corner of Anglesea Road and signalled to them that Bell was on the tram. We saw them signal the tram to stop and the whole group got into the tram. The next thing we saw the tram being stopped and Alan Bell being marched out by the group.'[57] The IRA unit included Liam Tobin, Mick McDonnell, Vinnie Byrne, Jim Slattery and Joe Dolan, who recalled that

Bell was sitting on the lower deck near the door. Vinnie Byrne went on the upper deck to give overhead cover. The rest of us stayed on the lower deck. Bell was grey-haired, in his sixties. He looked quite relaxed and happy. I have often wondered since if he had any suspicions when he saw a group of men board the tram. He probably thought we were young men on our way to work. After a few moments Mick McDonnell leaned over towards the victim and asked in a very courteous way: 'Are you Mr Bell?' 'I am,' he said. 'But . . .'. He did not get time to say any more before McDonnell and Tobin grabbed him. People turned round startled as the scuffle started. Just at the corner of Simmonscourt Road we stopped the tram. 'Your time has come,' said Mick McDonnell, as they hustled Bell off the tram. There was a frightened look on his now pale face. I pulled my gun and told the tram passengers, 'Sit there quietly and everything will be all right.' I jumped off and watched in case anyone should interfere. Bell was hustled to the footpath. He was released for a moment, the last of his life. Tobin's gun blazed. So did McDonnell's. And Bell crashed down onto the roadway, shot in the head and heart.[58]

When Bell slumped to the ground, Daly and Keogh cycled away. Shortly afterwards a policeman waved them down and pointed at people fleeing in all directions. But they had nothing to worry about. The constable said he was not going anywhere near a shooting.[59]

Bell's assassination was part of an escalating IRA campaign that made 1920 the bloodiest year in Ireland since the 1798 Rebellion. Although French had not exactly promised six months earlier that troops would be home before the leaves fell from the trees, the situation, far from improving, was getting worse. Now there was just a rapidly receding light at the end of a tunnel, visible to the Viceroy only through his field-marshal's binoculars. On Easter Saturday 4 April 1920 the IRA raided the homes and offices of Dublin's income-tax collectors, destroying records and seriously disrupting the British administrative system.

With Dublin Castle paralysed by internal tensions, Lloyd George reshuffled the Irish Executive in late March 1920. He shifted Macpherson to the Ministry of Pensions, transferred Commander-in-Chief Shaw and offered the combined post of army and police supremo to 58-year-old General Nevil Macready, the Commissioner of the Metropolitan Police.[60] As a former Adjutant General, an admirer of the prime minister and a highly political soldier, it was hoped that Macready would faithfully implement government policy while at the same time Irish nationalists might respond favourably to someone who had alienated Ulster Unionists before the war when military commander in the province. But the vinegary Macready hated Ireland and every Irish faction, and he agreed to take the post only after an appeal from French, his old boss. Having read a damning report on the DMP by one of his own Scotland Yard detectives, he also stipulated that someone else should command the police, whose reform would require one person's undivided attention.

Macready spent three weeks familiarising himself with the Irish situation, reading about the country's history and listening to every shade of opinion to an extent 'that has nearly worn out the drum of my ear'.[61] Meanwhile, Macpherson's successor, Sir Hamar Greenwood, a Canadian Liberal MP, had to win a by-election before assuming his new post.[62] When Macready landed in Dublin during the early hours of 14 April, he discovered French grappling with a major political crisis, started nine days earlier when Peadar Clancy and 100 IRA prisoners in Mountjoy Gaol launched a mass hunger strike for prisoner-of-war status. By now Clancy was Dick McKee's Vice-Brigadier and well known to British Intelligence through his Talbot Street shop, the Republican Outfitters. This was a favourite haunt of Dublin Volunteers, and, short of hanging an IRA sign outside, Clancy could hardly have done more to attract enemy attention. But such brazenness and defiance were typical of someone who intended exploiting the emotive power of a hunger strike to the full. Soon there were vigils outside the jail, the Catholic hierarchy denounced British Government obduracy, clerics flocked to comfort prisoners and newspapers predicted imminent deaths from starvation. Matters came to a head on 13 April, when the Squad assassinated Detective Henry Kells for conducting identity parades at Mountjoy[63] and Clancy warned that men were about to die – a deception that electrified Dublin's rumour mill.

French was determined to hold the line in a battle of wills, which he insisted the British Government could not afford to lose. Four months earlier he had urged it to announce publicly that hunger strikers would be provided with food and left to live or die. In the afternoon of 13 April he telegrammed Bonar Law urging rejection of Clancy's non-negotiable demand for prisoner-of-war status[64] and was heartened a few hours later when the deputy prime minister assured the House of Commons that the Cabinet would never yield to hunger strikers. By now French really should have known better. In the evening a telegram from Law warned of the government's concern 'that if these men die one by one, there will be an outcry in this country which will become exceedingly dangerous and if we were then forced to make any change the effect on the Government both in Ireland and here would be much worse than if a change were made now'.[65] Prisoner-of-war status was conceded, but then Clancy raised the stakes by demanding the immediate release of every hunger striker. Realising that the Cabinet, desperate to avoid more republican martyrs, would ultimately capitulate anyway, French and Macready agreed to release on parole anyone not yet charged with an offence. Nevertheless, despite carefully drafted terms, the prison authorities freed every striker, even serving prisoners, ninety in all. Clancy walked out of Mountjoy a republican legend but a marked man to soldiers and policemen, who regarded him as the architect of their humiliation.

After two hard years staggering from one station of his Irish cross to another, French probably yearned for his old field-marshal's chateau and the simplicities of warfare on the Western Front. There at least lines had been held whatever the cost, retreats forbidden, orders obeyed and deserters executed. Betrayed by the Cabinet, stripped of both his friend Shaw and a compliant – if mediocre – Chief Secretary, the Viceroy believed 'beyond doubt that the Irish Government does not govern Ireland. I have often thought that there is an extraordinary parallel between the situation in Ireland as it exists today and the state of affairs six months before the Boer War. It is the same alternating policy which obliged us to take up arms in 1899.'[66] Even his old mentor Long had abandoned him, complaining that French had recklessly ignored his advice to avoid a confrontation until the government machine was on a proper 'war footing'. Instead, to Long it was 'perfectly clear that there was utter confusion in the Castle and something worse – grave mal-administration'.[67]

Since Dublin Castle could not even manage a prisoner release scheme successfully, let alone defeat the IRA, French was determined to clear out the dead wood once and for all, ensuring that the next, inevitable crisis would end very differently. On 16 April 1920 he asked the Cabinet for an expert investigation into the Irish administration and when Greenwood finally arrived on 6 May he brought with him Sir Warren Fisher, the Treasury's permanent secretary and head of the British civil service.[68] Fisher was a 49-year-old Londoner, a public schoolboy who had graduated from Oxford with a first-class degree and passed at the top – though not the very top – of the civil service entrance examinations. Hard work, determination and luck lay behind a meteoric rise that by 1919 had him at the pinnacle of the civil service.

Behind Fisher's elegant, diffident, unsentimental and even rather effeminate exterior lay a highly strung, emotionally scarred individual, raised by a cold, abusive father and trapped in an increasingly unhappy marriage. But his difficult upbringing had forged an unconventional, fiercely independent, courageous personality, imbued, as Fisher's biographer has perceptively remarked, with an absolute fearlessness in accepting responsibility. He had requested the Irish assignment and would not play safe to protect his career by producing an anodyne report. Furthermore, the politically liberal Fisher had developed a soft spot for Ireland, which he had visited in his youth and whose people he regarded as a 'most attractive race'.[69] If French believed he had found a soft touch who would facilitate coercion, he had utterly misjudged Fisher. After slipping unobtrusively into Dublin, Fisher would light the slow burning fuse of a political bomb that would ultimately blow away both the Viceroy and his Irish policy.

Like a mild-mannered accountant auditing the books, performance and future prospects of a once great but now ailing company, Fisher interviewed senior civil servants, policemen and soldiers. His devastating 'company report' then indicted a 'board of directors' hopelessly detached from reality and trying to sell to an increasingly shrinking market a product that had gone right out of fashion. Now they presided over an institution that was virtually bankrupt, locked into irreversible decline and for which the kindest solution was voluntary liquidation.[70] Fisher's investigation had uncovered a political elite and administrative system metaphorically and literally under siege in a Dublin that had become once again an embattled Pale and whose Castle, for centuries the symbol of Britain's power in Ireland, was now a microcosm of strategic retreat: a Pale within a Pale. Huddled inside it, the Chief Secretary, Under-Secretary, administrative assistants, clerical staff, police chiefs, domestic staff and even a permanent military garrison worked and lived in an atmosphere of all-pervasive fear, routinely sporting bulletproof vests underneath their pinstriped suits.

Macready was already certain the Castle and every other government department were riddled with spies and informers. Military Intelligence believed these men had set up Assistant Commissioner Redmond after he realised confidential information was leaking to the IRA. 'This probably was the cause of his murder in January 1920 for there is good reason to suppose that Sinn Fein were informed of his movements by his own men.'[71] Basil Thomson heightened official insecurity with regular warnings of supposed IRA plans to attack government buildings. Photographic passes were introduced at the Castle but hastily withdrawn after a British Army officer carrying one was captured by the IRA while strolling in the Dublin hills and executed as a spy.[72]

Fisher's report revealed an Irish administration mired in stagnation, bureaucratic intrigue and sectarian bigotry, whose bunker mentality had completely demoralised the civil service. 'With the notable exception of General Macready who had fortuitously now been imported, the Government of Ireland strikes one as almost woodenly stupid and quite devoid of imagination.'[73] While clearing Under-Secretary MacMahon of disloyalty, Fisher damned him for weakly abdicating his authority to the almost universally loathed Assistant Secretary Sir John Taylor. He recommended pensioning Taylor off immediately, whether he retired voluntarily or not. Fisher's assistant, 'Andy' Cope, a former Customs and Excise detective close to Lloyd George, had conducted a parallel inquiry into the police, rapidly concluding that Inspector-General Smith was 'not equal to the responsibilities of his post. He looked haggard and tired out with worry and his nerve appears to be giving way.'[74] Smith and the DMP's Edgeworth-Johnstone were disturbingly isolated, living cooped up in the Castle and rarely venturing outside, except in armoured cars with an armed escort, 'a phenomenon not unnoticed by, and not without effect upon, the officers and rank and file of the two forces'.[75] Like French two years earlier and in almost identical terms, Cope also attacked the confusion and inefficiency of five different, overlapping and competing intelligence systems.

In the short term Fisher recommended overhauling the government machinery and the police and intelligence systems while giving better protection to life and property. But in the course of diagnosing Ireland's underlying problems, he also clinically dismantled the entire foundations of

British government policy. Fisher contemptuously dismissed the Castle's small Ascendancy clique as completely unrepresentative and denounced Sinn Fein's banning as an 'indescribable folly'[76] that tarred every republican indiscriminately with membership of the 'murder gang'.[77] He attributed most violence to harsh and arbitrary security measures ('a tremendous weapon of oppression'[78]), especially police and army raids based on faulty intelligence that scooped up many innocent individuals and alienated a moderate nationalist majority. British government policy was continually expanding the area of conflict and making universal martial law inevitable – 'a counsel of despair'.[79] A new outlook and major initiatives were needed to win the hearts and minds of an 'apathetic, cowed, sullen'[80] population and by degrees 'isolate the murder gang'. Somewhat condescendingly, Fisher argued that treating the Irish like children had made them mischievous children who needed time to develop a sense of responsibility. But for a senior civil servant he had displayed impressive open-mindedness, imagination and even daring. Fisher accepted that, while extreme republicans did not fully represent Sinn Fein, they were 'inspired by a fierce and fanatical patriotism',[81] and banning Sinn Fein simply because it wanted ultimate separation from Britain was ludicrous. 'It is a political party, however much people may dislike it; and if the test of whether or no a political party is to be recognised is that its programme shall contain nothing anathema to people of different political complexion, then I can't imagine any party which ever could be recognised.'[82] Fisher recommended lifting the ban on Sinn Fein and declaring publicly that people could legitimately vote for it without being labelled murderers.

Fisher even warmly endorsed Sinn Fein's land courts for preventing anarchy in disturbed rural areas – though his proposal to convert the IRA into an Irish militia was clearly a dozen bridges too far. He also wanted to end police and army indiscipline and reprisals against political opponents, recommending a symbolic break with the past by abolishing the post of Viceroy and its unpopular 'atmosphere of pinchbeck royalty'.[83] As a civil servant Fisher's radical analysis could not directly influence British Government policy, but it was designed to open up a debate within the small political circle formulating Irish policy – a process from which Lloyd George had deliberately excluded most government ministers. Incredibly, the Cabinet never received a single situation report on Ireland from either the Chief Secretary or the Commander-in-Chief between January 1919 and December 1920. Fisher hoped that over time his policy alternatives would eventually culminate in peace feelers and negotiations with Sinn Fein, and, if and when that happened, he intended Dublin Castle to be ready.

Fisher now installed in the Irish administration a dozen young, intelligent civil service high-flyers whose star performer, Sir John Anderson, was a tall, glacial, prodigiously intelligent 38-year-old Scot, widely regarded as the most brilliant public servant of his day.[84] As Joint Under-Secretary, Anderson immediately discovered that civil administration had become 'practically non-existent'.[85] The prison service was under intolerable strain, the army was below strength, most of the population outside Ulster was hostile to British rule and the RIC, according to Inspector-General Smith, stood on the brink of collapse. To tackle this crisis, Anderson relied especially on Cope, who remained as Assistant Under-Secretary, and Mark Sturgis, a sardonic 36-year-old Oxford graduate who was married to an aristocrat's daughter.[86] Since the trio favoured conciliation and negotiations leading to Dominion Home Rule, Lloyd George had shrewdly left himself the option of an eventual compromise peace.

Anderson's strategy was to bide his time until the government realised military victory was unattainable and he could then reach out to Sinn Fein. Playing this long game, Anderson's team immediately began identifying and cultivating potential intermediaries and even kept the discredited MacMahon on because of his potentially valuable contacts with the Roman Catholic hierarchy and Sinn Fein. Sturgis recorded that 'the PM is peeved with MacMahon and doesn't quite see why he shouldn't go – but he is irreplaceable as a link with the Church'[87] – a judgement that would ultimately be triumphantly vindicated.

But, if Lloyd George had placed doves in the Irish administration, he balanced them by appointing some prominent hawks, including the new Chief Secretary. Greenwood was prepared to allow the Castle's 'peace party' considerable latitude, partly because he too had been shocked by a 'sloppiness in administration and a lack of cohesion in the protective forces that is amazing. The Army and Police are immobile, and therefore glued to the ground. The police in Dublin and many of the RIC are shakey [sic]. The civil service is nervous and everybody more or less scared.'[88] Nonetheless, he did not believe a negotiated compromise was attainable or desirable. Greenwood bubbled with invincible optimism, and his constant assertions that the tide had turned and victory was inevitable soon made Pollyana look like a manic depressive. He assured Bonar Law that 'the hostiles are growing frightened and . . . the mass of Irishmen are losing faith in Sinn Fein as a winning side'.[89] The new Chief Secretary also won a power struggle with French, whose pessimism over the situation contrasted starkly with his own attitude. The Viceroy described the Irish situation as worse than he had ever known, and submitted memoranda to a new Irish Situation committee established by Lloyd George. Greenwood effectively threatened to resign if his authority over the Viceroy was not recognised.[90] Increasingly, French became a marginalised, almost forgotten figure as the locus of British political power in Ireland shifted back to Dublin Castle.

With a new civil administration in place, Macready now concentrated on reforming a 'hopelessly out of date'[91] police system. He regarded Chief Commissioner Edgeworth-Johnstone as charming but ineffective, while Inspector-General Smith seemed physically and emotionally exhausted. 'As regards the RIC we are sitting on a volcano.'[92] Since the start of April 1920, 142 officers had resigned and another 105 had retired as medically unfit. The situation had made Fisher so 'very apprehensive as to the fate of the force'[93] that he had warned about the possibility of wholesale resignations and policemen retaliating for the murder of their colleagues. Macready planned to win popular support by boldly merging the RIC and DMP into a single force under a Catholic Irishman, but his old friend Sir Edward Bulfin declined the post of head of police. When resistance surfaced within the RIC and DMP to this shotgun marriage, Macready settled for a new Police Adviser who would coordinate both forces and resuscitate their intelligence systems. On Churchill's recommendation he chose 50-year-old General Hugh Tudor, the War Secretary's friend since their Indian Army days. Tudor had proved himself a brave, innovative artillery commander on the Western Front and he recruited his staff from an old boys' network of Royal Artillery officers. His former aide, William Darling, gave up the joys of insurance ('a blissful field of travelling and selling and canvassing and sightseeing'[94]) to become Tudor's secretary. His Deputy Chief of Police and Director of Intelligence, Colonel Ormonde Winter, was a 45-year-old Londoner and lifelong adventurer who had served with the British Army in India, at Gallipoli and on the Western Front and who willingly abandoned a well-paid but undemanding appointment as League of Nations Boundary Commissioner in Schleswig-Holstein.[95] Although Winter had no professional intelligence experience, Tudor placed greater value on someone's professional and social background and personal qualities.

As 'O', Winter became a legendary figure in Ireland, a cloak-and-dagger man of mystery with black greased hair and monocle, a taste for fine food, wines and attractive women and a proficiency in French, Russian and Urdu. Aggressive and utterly fearless, he had had an acquittal in his late twenties for the manslaughter of a boy who had stoned his boat on a river. In adulthood he still thrived on quarrels and stormy relationships and for a spymaster could be remarkably unsubtle. In Winter's mental universe there existed only black and white, right and wrong, heroes and villains, us and them, an unwavering friend but an unforgiving foe. This attitude extended to colleagues as well as enemies. Winter's military and political attitudes were representative of Tudor's inner circle, which quickly emerged as the reconstructed administration's 'super-hawks'. These former artillery officers had spent four years dropping huge shells on German lines and believed that the surest route to victory was by literally flattening the enemy and then hammering him into the ground.

The new Castle administration's honeymoon period with press and public lasted only six weeks. Initially Anderson noted improving relations with the Catholic hierarchy and a decline in IRA attacks that suggested Sinn Fein moderates were reining in republican extremists. But a more human face and some worthy administrative reforms hardly changed the fundamental Irish situation, and in late July a more downbeat Anderson warned Greenwood that 'the tide has set in the opposite direction. A critical situation has unquestionably arisen.'[96] Nationalist hopes of a fresh start were evaporating amid a welter of newspaper complaints that the new team's conciliatory approach was at odds with a rapid military and police build-up that pointed to a British quest for military victory.

In fact the new security chiefs were divided over goals and methods, in the same way that Dublin Castle was split between hawks and doves. Macready never intended to reconquer Ireland. Although he believed universal martial law might theoretically cow the population, 'a good deal of blood would have to be spilt in the process'[97] – but this was something the government had no appetite for, and the British public would not tolerate. Besides, he had insufficient troops for such a move. While Macready would hold the line in Ireland, this moderate conciliator favoured political compromise and he regularly urged the government to make an imaginative gesture to Sinn Fein. But the pugnacious Tudor believed only in a political settlement dictated by a victorious British side in the same way that a beaten Germany had been forced to sign a 'Diktat' in Paris. He told a police audience that defeating the IRA was an essential precondition for a durable peace, asserting, according to one listener, that '"This country is ruled by gunmen and they must be put down." He talked about giving home rule to Ireland, and he said home rule could not be given until all of these gunmen were put down and he called on the RIC to put them down.'[98] Tudor's advisers comprised, in effect, a war party bent on reviving RIC morale, re-equipping it with modern weaponry, rebuilding its intelligence system and then grinding down the IRA, as the British Army had worn down the Germans in a war of attrition.

Tudor's entourage were civilised men who considered the IRA's guerrilla tactics war crimes deserving of ruthless counter-measures. But they always doubted the willpower of British politicians, most of whom they regarded as unprincipled appeasers. Winter thought Lloyd George especially duplicitous, 'hitting the insurrection on the head by means of Tudor and Macready and offering its leaders a bouquet by the underground methods of Cope'.[99] Tudor's team was equally unflattering about the Irish people, about whom they knew little and cared less. Winter had served in Ireland twenty years earlier but had seemingly acquired his opinions mostly from the vantage point of a foxhunter's saddle. 'The Irishman, without any insult being intended, somewhat resembles a dog, and understands firm treatment, but like a dog, he cannot understand being cajoled with a piece of sugar.'[100] However, nobody doubted the new police leadership's courage and commitment. Unlike Smith and Edgeworth-Johnstone, Tudor ventured out frequently among his men, while Winter revelled in dashing across country in his fast American car or swooping dramatically down from the skies in a two-seater aeroplane.

By mid-July 1920 police reform had become critically urgent. Inspector-General Smith was in daily fear of mass resignations or his men running amok, especially when, after a brief lull, fifteen RIC officers were killed in the five weeks up to the end of July, a threefold increase in the death rate. The highest-ranking casualty was Divisional Commissioner Gerard Smyth, an aggressive wartime colleague of Tudor, who had appointed him in June to reinvigorate the Munster police. Tudor was actually present at Listowel barracks on 19 June 1920 when Smyth notoriously reassured an audience that 'you may make mistakes occasionally, and innocent persons may be shot, but that cannot be helped. No policeman will get into trouble for shooting any man.'[101] IRA retribution was swift. Smyth regularly visited Cork's County Club, favoured by landed families and high-ranking military officers. But one waiter was an IRA spy, and, when Smyth arrived unexpectedly on the evening of 17 July, a hastily assembled six-man Volunteer squad shot him dead as he relaxed in the smoking lounge.[102]

Increasingly the police were hitting back and a deadly cycle of assassination and instant retaliation became a feature of the Anglo-Irish War. After two policemen were killed in Tuam, County Galway, on 20 July 1920, colleagues rampaged through the town threatening to shoot inhabitants, smashing windows, hurling grenades and setting fire to businesses. Afterwards an English reporter compared Tuam to the devastated wartime towns of Belgium and France. Although every policeman at Tuam was Irish, many reprisals were attributed to the English ex-soldiers increasingly filling the RIC's depleted ranks. After a few weeks' training in Dublin they were posted throughout Ireland, where, because of a shortage of uniforms, they sported military khaki and dark police green, a combination that soon had them nicknamed 'Black and Tans', after a well-known Co. Galway pack of foxhounds. Despite republican propaganda depicting them as gangsters for hire or convicts released from prison to terrorise Ireland, one historian insists that

> British recruits for the RIC were fairly ordinary men. The typical Black and Tan was a small fellow and young. He was an unmarried Protestant from London or the Home Counties, and had fought in the Army during the Great War. He was a working-class man with few skills, who joined the RIC because the pay was good. A few of his comrades might have spent a few days in jail, but the typical Black and Tan had no criminal record and a good reference from the Army.[103]

Conditions in Ireland undoubtedly encouraged some Black and Tan criminality, but Tudor and Winter admired their courage and ruthlessness and rapidly accelerated recruitment from May onwards. By the end of the war almost 10,000 had served for a time in Ireland.

On the same day that Tuam burned, Anderson announced that 'the position throughout Ireland is worse than in 1916'.[104] The British Government faced a straight choice between conciliation and massive force, though even a military dictatorship could not guarantee success, especially as it would have to rely on a demoralised civil service and police. Anderson urged instead an immediate offer of Dominion Home Rule with protection for Ulster. But two days later the Cabinet's Irish committee recommended immediate martial law – though a top-level conference between the Cabinet and the Irish Executive at Downing Street on 23 July failed to agree a policy initiative.[105] After an inconclusive debate between doves like Curzon, Macready and Anderson and hawks such as Churchill, Long, Birkenhead and Tudor, Lloyd George held his counsel, apparently adopting a policy of pursuing the military option while leaving the door open to an eventual compromise with Sinn Fein. At the meeting Tudor announced his intention of recruiting 500 British ex-army officers to support the police, and the Auxiliary Division of the RIC was established on 27 July 1920. Within days their distinctive uniform of khaki and Glengarry cap had appeared on the streets of Dublin.

By then the Castle was in the throes of another crisis. On 20 May 1920 Irish dockers had embargoed British 'war materials' and railway workers refused to carry troops and munitions, precipitating the most serious industrial dispute since the Dublin Lockout of 1913. It was just as bitter and almost as protracted as the earlier strike. It seriously impeded the British military build-up, and the Castle put pressure on railway companies to dismiss thousands of employees refusing to cooperate. On 30 July Collins intervened by making 'non-combatant' supporters of the British Government's hardline policy 'legitimate targets'.[106] Frank Brooke, chairman of the Dublin and South Eastern Railway, had known for some time that his life was in danger. In February 1919 Robert Barton, the Dail's Minister of Agriculture, had declared that an appropriate reprisal for the death of one of his election workers on hunger strike would be the lives of Lord French and Brooke, who was also a Unionist member of the Viceroy's Advisory Committee.[107] For this Barton was arrested but escaped from prison a month later, only to be caught again in January 1920 when he was sentenced to three years' penal servitude. Brooke compounded his crimes, in republican eyes, by approving the suppression of Dail Eireann, Sinn Fein and the Irish Volunteers in September 1919. He began carrying a revolver and, except when chairing board meetings at Westland Row Station, rarely ventured out of 'Coolattin', his County Wicklow estate. Tobin dispatched Keogh, Slattery and Vinnie Byrne to eliminate Brooke there. Byrne reported that they scouted the estate

unarmed so that, if we were challenged, we were just having a spin. There was a kind of a public road running through the demesne and we cycled through it. As we went along, you would not know where an RIC man would appear out of the bushes. There was nothing doing here. We were only back a day or two when information was received that Brooke would be at a certain office in Westland Row.[108]

On 30 July Brooke chaired a board meeting at Westland Row station before retiring at noon to his private office. As he and fellow director Arthur Cotton relaxed, Jim Slattery and three other Squad members entered the building and made their way upstairs. When Cotton saw the intruders entering the inner sanctum, he dived under a table while Brooke leapt from his fireside chair and tried to run for it. But, according to Slattery,

> we immediately opened fire on him and he fell. As we were going down the stairs again Daly said to me, 'Are you sure we got him?' I said I was not sure, and Daly said, 'What about going back and making sure?' Keogh and myself went back. When I went into the room I saw a man standing at the left of the door and I fired a shot in his direction, at the same time looking across at Brooke on the floor. I fired a couple of shots at Brooke and satisfied myself that he was dead. Although I did not wound the other man who was in the room, I was informed afterwards that it would have been a good job if he had been shot, as he too was making himself a nuisance.[109]

Brooke, who was shot through the heart and lungs, reeled across the room and fell dying near the fireplace, just as an incoming train muffled the sound of gunfire. Newspapers noted the 'amazing precision and coolness'[110] of the unmasked assassins, and hinted at an inside job: 'The murder must have been carefully planned and it is evident that those who carried it out had made themselves thoroughly familiar with the surroundings of the station and the location of the rooms.'[111] Brooke's death, like that of Redmond six months before, was a deadly warning to hardline supporters of British Government policy, but it also struck hard at his close friend the Viceroy.

Brooke's killing helped create an enduring myth about the Squad's lethal omniscience, though the humdrum reality was one of seemingly interminable, unproductive patrolling, punctuated occasionally by bursts of violence. Bill Stapleton recalled that 'in spite of the excellent intelligence section there were many weary days without any action. This inaction took all our courage and faith in Michael Collins to keep us going. Many were the times that for days we tramped the streets of Dublin looking for our target and waiting for the signal of our intelligence officers.'[112] The monotony was compounded by living in drab and austere safe houses and a bleak social life in which restaurants and cafés were out of bounds and meals restricted to an early breakfast and late supper.

Many targets evaded assassination through luck, cunning or favourable circumstances. After the Squad had shot Detective Sergeant Richard Revell seven times, Paddy Daly was amazed to read an evening newspaper interview in which the policeman recounted lying still on the roadside and feigning death.[113] When Vinnie Byrne's unit arrived in the early morning intent on ambushing Detective Sergeant Coffey near his North Circular Road residence, he stationed two men who had not 'very long to wait when Coffey and his escort appeared, coming down Kenmare Parade. As the man on the corner was about to open fire, two women came over, stood very close to them and asked them something about the Salvation Army. In the meantime, Coffey and his escort got away up the N.C. Road. It was a very near thing for him.'[114] Because the ever-alert Detective Sergeant Bruton was vulnerable only while attending Mass, an exasperated Tom Keogh eventually decided to sit beside Bruton in church and 'give him his pass-out checks'.[115] But Collins vetoed his plan because of the outrage that would have been aroused by a church killing. The Squad was also expected to avoid endangering bystanders, as on 22 June 1920, when it went after Albert Roberts, the RIC's Assistant Inspector-General. His chauffeur-driven car passed regularly through Beresford Place, where grenades could have disabled it but would also have caused havoc among the crowds and horse-drawn vehicles – as well as starting an animal stampede. Instead, Paddy Daly reluctantly settled for a volley of shots that shattered the car windows but only wounded Roberts, whose driver zigzagged rapidly through the traffic to Dublin Castle.[116]

Because the Squad shunned disguises, its members risked recognition by onlookers, though this happened surprisingly rarely, and a death warning invariably guaranteed silence. Sometimes an eyewitness was very close to home. After Vinnie Byrne had helped kill three policemen in Exchequer Street, his father confronted him; angry not at his son's involvement but at Vinnie's failure to warn him to avoid the area when the attack occurred.[117] Sometimes incriminating evidence was left behind at the scene. When Pat McCrae dropped a collar with a traceable laundry mark, he alerted Paddy Daly, who raided the laundry with the Squad, seized every file and customer list and warned the manager that he would be shot if he assisted the British authorities.[118]

The Squad endured prolonged separation from home and family. Daly, a widower, rarely saw his three young children, who were left in the care of friends. Bachelors put their relationships with girlfriends on hold or avoided them entirely. But, despite the pressures and dangers, nobody defected or resigned, and their morale proved impervious to British propaganda depicting them as cowards and psychopathic gangsters. The Squad regarded themselves as soldiers carrying out government orders and executing legitimate targets. They also depersonalised victims, about whom they knew little more than a name, and almost never discovered the reason for their execution. Even Paddy Daly was rarely taken into Collins's confidence. 'When Alan Bell was shot I did not know why he was listed as a man to be eliminated. We knew in some cases, but in others we did not know. We were soldiers carrying out orders and we did not ask any questions.'[119] Some members felt a certain compassion, and Jim Slattery always said a prayer for the souls of the dead, but Joe Leonard retained a lifelong hatred for men to whom he gladly dispensed 'vouchers for angel's wings'.[120] None, though, was haunted in later life by terrible memories or remorse.

Chapter 4

DUEL

THE STRUGGLE BETWEEN THE BRITISH AND IRA INTELLIGENCE, JULY–NOVEMBER 1920

L
ate July and early August 1920 were a dismal time for the Castle administration. Sturgis feared that Brooke's killing had been instigated by 'the gun man element'[1] to precipitate martial law and scupper any possibility of Dominion Home Rule. The Restoration of Order in Ireland Act's draconian powers of curfew, arrest, internment and court martial ushered in the bloodiest phase of the conflict and abruptly terminated the brief political honeymoon enjoyed by Sturgis and his colleagues. Since arriving in Ireland, they had lived openly and uneventfully at Kingstown's Royal Marine Hotel, travelling daily into Dublin by car and enjoying a relaxed social life of golf, restaurants, horse racing and visits to the theatre. But now, Fisher warned the British Cabinet, they must either return to London or risk administrative paralysis by transferring permanently into Dublin Castle.[2] As the government needed a credible Irish administration, it instructed Anderson's men on 12 August to abandon the Royal Marine and move *en masse* into the Castle, which was to be their home until the end of the Anglo-Irish War.

Soon afterwards David Neligan rejoined G Division's remnants in the Castle, where the 'situation grew worse as time went on, for hordes of officials lived in terror of their lives and had to be accommodated there, never leaving the place day or night'.[3] But, although the Castle's three gates were under constant IRA surveillance, Anderson's team could still move around in cars registered under fictitious names. Cope even appropriated and secretly garaged a new police vehicle in which he took colleagues for spins around the Dublin countryside. Even so, a surfeit of bridge, amateur musical nights and shop talk soon had Sturgis bemoaning 'this accursed Castle' and venting his frustration on the local population: 'I almost begin to believe that these mean, dishonest, insufferably conceited Irishmen are an inferior race and are only sufferable when they are whipped – like the Jews.'[4] When visiting the Castle, Macready encountered officials in 'a state of nerves that it was pitiful to behold'.[5] Greenwood never visited his Phoenix Park lodge, while French's world shrank dramatically after the Ashtown ambush, following what was to be his last train journey in Ireland. The Viceroy drastically reduced his public appearances and spent long periods in Phoenix Park, where, as Macready noticed, 'many persons like the Lord Mayor were not over anxious to be seen visiting the Lodge for fear they might be marked out by the gunmen as upholders of the government'.[6] The GOC was himself a prime IRA target and always carried an automatic on his knee when driving or in a coat pocket while strolling through Phoenix Park. An armoured car accompanied him everywhere.[7]

The IRA also tried to kill Major Hill Dillon, Macready's Chief Intelligence Officer at GHQ, after discovering both his North Circular Road residence and his passion for horses. But it abandoned two assassination attempts at race meetings, first when a party of Black and Tans suddenly arrived and then after Hill Dillon failed to show up at Punchestown.[8] The most endangered British soldier in Ireland was General Strickland, commander of 6th Division in Cork. The IRA tried capturing him in September 1920 as a bargaining chip for better treatment of jailed Volunteers, but the unit lying in wait for his car on the Quays missed a scout's signal and opened fire too late.[9] Strickland's chief intelligence officer, Colonel Kelly, also evaded a trap by spotting an IRA scout and accelerating out of danger before the attackers could hurl their grenades.[10]

British newcomers underwent a crash course in the new realities of Irish life, which, according to Tudor's secretary William Darling, 'was for many of us nasty, brutish and short'.[11] Major-General Douglas Wimberley became 'ever vigilant of all local Irish, and all were our enemy unless we knew them to be otherwise'.[12] A British army officer's wife who arrived in Dublin during the summer of 1920 discovered that she had exchanged her genteel London tea parties and literary soirées for an armed escort to social engagements. At a general's dinner party she was amused by an officer's agitation over a noise on the landing until on entering 'the dining room I found a revolver laid beside each plate – knives, spoons, forks and revolvers, in fact. The General who had taken me into dinner said, conversationally, "This is just the sort of night they would come." I said nothing, but looked around to see where, if "they" came, I could take cover.'[13]

By 18 August 1920 Sturgis believed 'Tudor, Winter and Co. must come into the Castle both to live and work'.[14] Since May they had stayed at Park Lodge, a heavily protected building close to army headquarters in Phoenix

Park. Surrounded by armed sentries and rings of barbed wire, they dined amid the gloom with their loaded revolvers resting on tables, served by RIC constables and a depressive mess steward who eventually blew his brains out. Because of an accommodation shortage in the Castle, which forced Winter to use an office borrowed from the Director of Naval Intelligence, they actually remained at the Lodge until early October. But the delay allowed Winter to study the Irish situation, Sinn Fein and the IRA, tour police stations and establish good relations with Basil Thomson and Hill Dillon. Winter quickly realised that he faced a massive task resuscitating police intelligence. 'The morale of the RIC was at a low ebb, whilst the DMP, for political purposes, had practically ceased to function.'[15] Collins's decimation of G Division had eliminated detectives who could recognise those IRA leaders who now 'stalked the city with impunity'. Furthermore, the failure to convict

> one single murderer, the exasperating delays of the civil courts in these cases where criminals were arrested, coupled with the systematic boycott of the Police and their families, had led to a large number of resignations. The men were immobilised behind their then ill-fortified barracks, and served but little practical use except in providing the personnel for their defence. This had a far reaching effect on the supply of Intelligence.[16]

Although Winter knew the well of police intelligence had run dry, discovering the causes proved more difficult. He tended to blame a morally deficient population of whose history and way of life he knew little, whose psychology he could not fathom and who seemed as inscrutable as any oriental. In this war both sides stared at each other across a chasm of mutual incomprehension. Most British intelligence officers regarded the Irish as coarse and uncivilised: fluent liars, congenital lawbreakers, instinctively violent and insatiably greedy. But, sadly, avarice had given way to a craven desire to stay alive, and even large rewards for the killers of Redmond and Bell and the capture of Breen and Treacy went unclaimed. Winter's colleagues also accused the Irish of duplicity and treachery, skilfully ingratiating themselves with people while simultaneously arranging their executions: 'There were spies everywhere; and a very large percentage of the population was ready to act as extra eyes and ears for Sinn Fein and for the IRA even if they were not prepared to fight for them.'[17] Yet neither the British Army nor the police ever established a proper counter-intelligence system.

Whatever Winter's opinions of the Irish, he realised the government's muddled and inconsistent policy seriously discouraged informers because, while the IRA was openly at war, the British Cabinet peddled a fiction that it was simply suppressing political crime through the due process of law. Even then it always acted tardily and usually in response to IRA actions. The Restoration of Order in Ireland Act came almost a year after the shooting war had begun, and mass arrests, internment, deportations, courts martial, curfews and executions were implemented piecemeal and only as the military situation deteriorated. Furthermore, the British Government oscillated constantly between coercion and concession, first resisting and then capitulating to hunger strikers, refusing to speak to terrorists and then putting out peace feelers and conducting secret negotiations. This vacillation only confused and demoralised the army and police, and Military Intelligence became increasingly exasperated by a policy of 'stroke and slap' and 'a state of affairs which was neither war nor peace' that only 'resulted in mystifying and misleading every single party in Ireland'.[18] For their part, many Volunteers became blasé about a cycle of arrest, release and re-arrest, certain that an amnesty was inevitable after the British Government cut a deal with Sinn Fein.

Traditionally, Southern Irish Unionists at least could always be relied on to supply intelligence, but by 1920 they were a demoralised, powerless rump caught on the 'wrong' side of a revolution and routinely subjected to boycott, intimidation and violence. Some also ended up dead by a roadside wearing the notice 'a warning to spies'. Winter claimed most victims had not informed and were simply killed to stop them doing so in the future. But he knew that public uncertainty about someone's 'guilt' or 'innocence' endowed the IRA with seemingly 'miraculous faculties for tracing a betrayer. To speak to a policeman was attended with grave risks; for it to be known that information had been given meant death.'[19] The IRA identified and executed a few elderly loyalists who did help the British. In March 1921 they kidnapped 70-year-old Mrs Lindsay of Coachford, County Cork, after she had reported Volunteers preparing an ambush, and killed her when Macready ruled out exchanging her for the lives of five condemned Cork Volunteers. Winter's limited resources forced him to reject numerous appeals for protection, but he was still shaken to discover that many loyalists (including some of his closest friends) were paying the IRA 'protection money'.[20]

When Winter began creating a new intelligence system, he was the sole employee, and his Central Office had no premises. But he was not unduly concerned:

> The building of an efficient Intelligence Service is not a task that can be accomplished in a day, a week or a month. The ramifications of the Sinn Fein organisation were multiple, and widespread, and to create a service to counter these require an intimate knowledge of their constitutions, methods and resources, which can only be obtained by experience and a prolonged study of the pamphlets and documentary evidence available.[21]

Winter also had to recruit 150 staff, a time-consuming process that involved checking the antecedents and references of every clerical worker, all of them females of English extraction. He then had to train them before they could even start work. Winter's male employees were former army and naval officers, his secretary, L.K. Lockhart, yet another member of the Royal Artillery fraternity.

Starting from scratch at least meant that Winter expected recruits to do things his way, especially as Tudor had promised him complete operational independence. Intelligence was to be Winter's show, and his management style was emphatically hands-on. But an inability to delegate or share power and his demand for unquestioning loyalty caused considerable tensions, which Winter attributed to petty-minded ambition and jealousy on the part of 'disruptive elements'. He cashiered one intelligence officer, who then threatened him with 'offensive action'.[22] Lloyd George also infuriated Winter by recruiting for him a chief assistant: Charles Tegart, an Irish graduate of Trinity College Dublin and the Empire's leading counter-insurgency expert.[23]

Tegart had succeeded in defeating a serious pre-war rebellion in Bengal, and the prime minister clearly hoped that he possessed the magic formula for a quick victory in Ireland. But Winter resented having this stranger foisted on him. Soon after Tegart had started work in London on 17 July 1920, Winter berated Malcolm Seton, the Permanent Head of the India Office, who had arranged Tegart's transfer. Seton was not impressed by Winter and saw trouble ahead, warning Anderson that he was

> borrowing one of the most expert criminal investigation officers in the British Empire to work under an officer who, as I gathered from my

conversation with him, knows nothing of the country or people and has never done investigative CID work. I am not criticising that officer but it is certain that the professional may not always see eye to eye with the amateur as to the best way of doing things and the latter may find the former too slow in his methods.[24]

The unsuspecting Tegart had been pitched into a struggle with an enemy who, unfortunately for him, was not Michael Collins but Winter, bristling at this donnish, pipe-smoking, tweed-jacketed newcomer. Tegart's deliberate manner and careful weighing of evidence placed him bang in the sights of someone whose appetite for battle was undiminished. Soon their relationship, devoid of personal chemistry, disintegrated entirely after a lengthy memorandum from Tegart dashed any hope of an 'Open Sesame' solution in Ireland. He reminded Winter that his own Bengal victory had taken 'five years plodding and patient investigation, assisted by a large and highly trained office in which all information was carefully and systematically indexed, collected and pieced together'.[25] Tegart predicted a long haul in Ireland, for which he intended gearing up slowly and methodically. He would do this by establishing his London office, recruiting talented staff, studying every relevant report from Dublin Castle, the Irish police, Scotland House and MI5, creating a card index system and meeting secretly in London with key individuals to identify the IRA's structure and ways of undermining it. This would all take time, though he sensed that politicians wanted someone 'who would strike immediately. I can see no hope of this succeeding unless the person selected has all the details at his fingertips.'[26]

Winter exploded at what he believed was a professorial Tegart tutoring him in the basic principles of intelligence; he also had no patience with Tegart's pessimistic acceptance of a long war. Determined to arrange this colonial interloper's return passage to India, Winter was supported by Basil Thomson, who resented another – potentially rival – intelligence presence in London. On 18 August 1920 they carved up Irish intelligence. Thomson assumed responsibility for England and America, Winter looked after Ireland and Tegart was relegated to a nebulous link role between them. Even then Thomson would deal with him only through a liaison officer,[27] though he disingenuously protested to Macready his hurt that 'apparently someone has been spreading the impression that I was jealous of any other organisation working in London, whereas all I wanted was to relieve myself of work'.

Oozing insincerity, Thomson was breezily confident about the new arrangements' eventual success: 'Winter's men here are a little cold about the feet but they may be all right when they get to know more about the job.'[28]

Instead, Winter piled the pressure on Tegart by instigating an absurd dispute about his office accommodation. By now, Tegart was vulnerable, having lost Lloyd George's support after the 'Welsh Wizard' had discovered that he was not after all a fellow member of the magic circle. Tegart's posting was terminated on 30 September 1920 in well under 100 days and soon he was where Winter wanted him – half-way across the world in India. Winter then converted the London office into a training establishment for secret service agents run by his best friend, Major Cecil Cameron, a brittle individual married to a drug-addicted fantasist. Cameron's appointment said more about Winter's loyalty than his judgement. Four years later Cameron became yet another associate of Winter to commit suicide. Winter compounded his prickly inability to delegate by compulsively involving himself in operational matters. He was always happiest in the thick of things and regarded being turned down by the Staff College as the luckiest break of his life: 'When the Great War came in 1914 I certainly preferred the active and more exciting life of a gunner in the front line to the sedentary work I might have had to perform as a staff officer.'[29]

It was hardly ideal training for establishing and running a large organisation, but Winter's personality quirks do not adequately explain the British intelligence failure. The problem went much deeper, to the very heart of a fatally flawed government policy. In the early summer of 1920 intelligence primacy still lay with the army, and, as a result of increasing IRA attacks on soldiers, many officers volunteered for intelligence duty. Dublin Military District's intelligence branch was reorganised and a plain-clothes section known as Special Branch Dublin District created to collect military and political information in the capital. Its headquarters were in the Castle offices of General Boyd, who commanded the Dublin District. But Special Branch's leader was Lieutenant-Colonel Walter Wilson, a dashing General Staff officer and former English rugby international without professional intelligence experience but whose aggression had impressed his superiors. Wilson's original nucleus of intelligence officers consisted of Major Carew, Captains H.F. Boddington, P. Carpenter and A. Thorpe, and Lieutenants W. Noble, P. Atwood and P. Hyem. As Wilson's organisation expanded, Hyem and Thorpe became responsible for office administration under Captain F. Harper-Shore.[30]

Initially Macready regarded this dual system of army and police intelligence as a temporary expedient, but it bedevilled the British war effort to the very end. Macready knew that every successful intelligence system rested on two interdependent principles – organisational coherence and political certainty – but neither existed in Ireland when he arrived and none materialised thereafter. Instead, a dual police and army system ('a hermaphrodite intelligence service'[31]) prevented unified control at the top and, by encouraging inter-service rivalry, spawned what Military Intelligence admitted was 'duplication, jealousy, expense and leakage of information'.[32] But, although Macready realised reform was imperative, its shape depended on the political context, which in 1920 was the British Government's flagship Government of Ireland Act. This envisaged a Home Rule government for Southern Ireland weaning nationalists off violence and the rebellion gradually fading away, and, since this devolved government would also control the RIC and DMP, Macready anticipated the police resuming its traditional intelligence primacy. This would allow him effectively to wind up the military system. On the other hand, if the conflict intensified and universal martial law ensued, he intended merging police and military intelligence under a British GHQ Director of Intelligence.[33]

Everything depended on the British Government clarifying its objectives in Ireland, and Macready longed for it to decide on a course of action and adhere to it, come what may. But, although Lloyd George had assured him in March 1920 that Sinn Fein's continued obduracy would result in draconian repression, Macready saw not fixity of purpose, only endless equivocation: 'The great handicap to the creation of a sound Intelligence system was the feeling of uncertainty in regard to the policy of the Government, alternating as it did between coercion and conciliation.'[34] This ambivalence forced Macready to temporise and keep his intelligence options open; afterwards he regretted not immediately establishing a purely military organisation.

But at least Winter got on well with Wilson – a fellow adventurer, decorated war hero and 'a distinguished officer of not only exceptional ability but also outstanding courage'.[35] Both men were determined to turn the tide of the intelligence war by importing English agents to pressurise Volunteer GHQ and the IRA's Dublin Brigade. Initially they planned to flood Ireland with spies but soon scaled this back to concentrate on Dublin. Even here, the new intelligence offensive was dogged from the very start by an inter-service rivalry that the army denounced as 'the vicious plan of allowing parallel systems of secret service to work simultaneously in the same area'.[36] Wilson's spies, who began arriving in the summer of 1920, were mainly ex-army officers recruited by the War Office and dispatched to Ireland after a short course at a school of instruction in Hounslow. Posing initially as Royal Engineers, they soon adopted civilian covers such as shop assistants, garage hands, workers on cross-channel ferries and railways, journalists, farmers and even tramps, all of which facilitated direct contact with likely sources of information. According to British Intelligence, they 'made friends with Dublin citizens of every class and both sexes, they mixed with crowds and they were arrested with officers and men of the IRA'.[37] Many lived undercover in the hotels, boarding houses and flats of the Georgian area south of the Liffey close to Stephen's Green. Winter's agents were more often civilians, although the War Office recruited his Auxiliary intelligence officers.

The duties of British agents varied considerably. Auxiliary and military intelligence officers accompanied raiding parties, analysed captured documents, maps and photographs and interrogated suspects. Others, posing as prison warders, monitored conversations, visitors and letters as well as cultivating the more gullible detainees. Michael Noyk frequently visited Kilmainham to warn republican prisoners that governor Maye was a suspected British spy.[38] British agents also operated undercover amongst the civilian population. Wilson divided the Dublin District into six areas under head agents whose cells of Special Branch officers and civilian informers collected information on IRA personnel, Volunteer arms dumps, operations, safe houses and potential targets as well as reporting on the state of enemy morale. They also tried locating Dail, Volunteer GHQ and Dublin Brigade offices and leading republicans like Collins and Mulcahy. A favourite ruse was knocking on the front door of a suspected safe house late at night, pretending to be a Volunteer caught out by the curfew. The family of Kathleen McKenna, a typist on the Propaganda Department's *Irish Bulletin*, rarely turned strangers away, though eventually she says they became afraid of their own shadows. Once, she and her father heard moaning outside the house and discovered a man wearing felt-soled slippers, lying stretched out on the pavement with his eyes closed. McKenna recalled:

When we drew near the moaning ceased, and was not repeated. He had not an Irish countenance; he was slight, fair – perhaps reddish – he was well-dressed, well groomed; he most certainly was not drunk for there was no odour of stout or whiskey neither was he wounded. 'Get a glass of water, Daddy, to put to his lips; maybe it will bring him round.' Daddy hurried off leaving me alone with this prone figure. Then my eyes fell again on his strange footwear which might suggest to the uninitiated that he had issued from a nearby fireside; but I recalled that the British hired assassins used similar shoes when on their murderous missions. In the silence, in the solitude, I suddenly grew panicky, and rushed up the doorsteps to meet Daddy. Half a minute later when we came down there was neither sight nor light of the playboy.[39]

McKenna never discovered whether the 'playboy' was ill, paralytic or a very sober British agent, but her reaction was typical of a spy mania sweeping Dublin in the summer of 1920. It was a collective paranoia fuelled by speculation and rumours that gripped the population, had neighbour suspecting neighbour of informing and transformed innocent street encounters with strangers into all-pervasive enemy surveillance. A witch-hunt for spies and traitors gathered pace, first enveloping and then sweeping away many innocent people and in this rancid atmosphere made people terrified of being labelled a tout (informer). Most Dubliners came to assume that walls did indeed have ears. Celia Shaw, a UCD student, was afraid to speak openly in college after being warned that speeches at the Literary and Historical Society were being reported to the Castle. 'We were warned over a person in the Ladies' Room who was always to be seen reading a newspaper but never joining in the conversations. I must say I never could decide on that lady as so many did exactly these things.'[40]

* * *

In time British spies would discover that Dublin was a dangerously deceptive battleground where assassinations and heavily armed Auxiliary patrols coexisted with leafy suburbs barely touched by violence. Superficially it resembled many British cities with red pillar boxes and telephone boxes, trams, cinemas and music halls, English newspapers, British cars and tourists, Georgian architecture and grand social events like the Royal Dublin Horse Show. Furthermore, since the British military build-up had overwhelmed existing barracks accommodation, many army officers and their wives lived in the flats and boarding houses on sedate avenues, along which they casually strolled. This unusual situation was possible because of a general understanding that off-duty British soldiers were not legitimate targets. Macready had devised alternative arrangements but was reluctant to restrict his officers' freedom: 'Although here and there officers had been shot at, no dead set had been made against them and as a class it was generally considered that the gunmen were more likely to direct their attentions to senior officers than to the juniors or regimental officers, many of whom continued to live in rooms and houses in Dublin.'[41] Although many Volunteers grumbled, particularly as Irish markets, fairs and social events were being suppressed, the unofficial truce held.

But Volunteer GHQ had stipulated death as the ultimate punishment for communicating information to the enemy. And the executions of Byrnes, Quinlisk and Mulloy had starkly demonstrated the risks of spying for British Intelligence, despite Mulcahy's highly improbable claim that 'none of these people would have been killed if they could have been otherwise effectively disposed of as either direct or indirect murderers and a danger to our whole central organisation'.[42] One British spy paid the ultimate price at Finglas in Dublin's northern hinterland. Hitherto the area had been remarkably dormant because Volunteer GHQ used it as a refuge for hard-pressed city units and Volunteers escaping their British pursuers. But some Finglas Volunteers resented Black and Tans freely using the Gormanston depot and on 20 September 1920 they killed an RIC District Inspector at Balbriggan, about three miles away. Later that night Black and Tans sacked the town, wrecking a factory and thirty shops and houses and shooting two men dead. During the rampage local residents saw Tans being guided by a tramp nicknamed Jack Straw, who had been observed recently in the district. IRA intelligence officers hunted him, but Straw had apparently vanished until a Volunteer officer in Lusk reported him on the outskirts of the town. Straw was picked up by an IRA party in a car, which offered him a lift, but drove him to a nearby mill, where a court martial sentenced him to death as an enemy spy. A Volunteer officer, Joe Lawless, says Straw admitted being a British intelligence agent and that he died bravely: 'He stood erect and folded his arms, replying: "No, when I undertook this mission I was fully aware of what the end might be and now I accept my fate without complaint."'[43]

Besides fearing capture and execution, British agents in Dublin endured loneliness, the necessity of always hiding everything about themselves and an inability ever to relax, be caught off guard or make a slip of the tongue.

Ultimately they could trust only themselves. Their survival depended on considerable inner strength, common sense, swift and sound judgement, shrewdness, a nose for danger and absolute self-control. Courage, strong nerves and physical and emotional stamina were also vital. Paradoxically, although a spy – like an ambassador – is sent abroad to lie for his country, integrity was indispensable, because only the higher goal of defending his country's vital interests could justify the deceit of espionage and allow an agent still to regard himself as an honourable man enjoying his masters' trust. They also had to perfect their covers, merging into everyday jobs and surroundings while simultaneously carrying out their clandestine activities. A good memory was needed to recall suspects' names and descriptions as well as places and passwords, and above all to master a cover story. British spies established lines of communication to their controllers and headquarters, favouring the telephone, post and 'dead drops' such as a cell member's accommodation address, a loose brick in a wall or a hole in a tree hollow. Secrecy was maintained as far as possible by using codes, numbers and invisible ink.

Much intelligence work in Dublin was nocturnal when emptier streets and darkness facilitated searching garages, warehouses and railway sheds for hidden IRA arms dumps as well as surveillance of suspected houses and buildings. There was also a curfew that General Boyd had introduced on 20 February 1920. Initially it lasted from midnight to 5 a.m., though its starting time was advanced regularly during the next eighteen months. Dublin under curfew was not exactly a ghost town. Essential workers like doctors, nurses and dairymen had passes and DMP, Auxiliary and British army curfew patrols frequently encountered homeless men, prostitutes, drunks, people supposedly going to the doctor and even British army deserters. One British soldier challenged a man who claimed he had forgotten to feed his hens and only wanted to see if they were asleep![44] Some Dublin policemen working secretly for the IRA would stop British agents carrying curfew passes and carefully note their personal details.

The quality of British intelligence agents varied enormously. Among the best was Captain Robert Jeune, a decorated British army officer and interpreter who had joined Wilson's Special Branch in London. After attending its Hounslow training school, he transferred straight to Dublin. Here he trailed 'Shinners', hunted information 'which would lead us eventually to stamping out the revolt' and stole documents from Arthur Griffith's house during 'a surreptitious night raid'.[45] But Winter confessed that in Ireland 'the difficulties and risks of getting into contact with suitable persons were serious for those concerned'.[46] Instead, Cameron's London Bureau gave Irishmen recruited in England a crash intelligence course, a suitable cover and invisible ink to communicate via a dead letter drop in London. Many inadequate candidates were discarded and only about sixty agents of variable quality enlisted during a nine-month period. Some proved unreliable, untrustworthy and likely to sell themselves – and their employers and colleagues – to the highest bidder.

The worst agent to slip through the net was Frank Digby Hardy. Winter regarded him as a 'villain of the first water',[47] who caused British Intelligence nothing but mortification and ridicule. This mendacious con artist and career criminal had first been imprisoned in 1886 for forgery and during the next thirty-four years was regularly incarcerated for theft, larceny, embezzlement, fraud, obtaining money by false pretences, bouncing cheques all over the British Isles, neglecting his family – and stealing a bicycle.[48] Hardy's serial ineptitude demonstrated only a gift for staying always one step behind the law, and he accumulated prison sentences totalling twenty-two years. By 1918 he was in Ireland swindling money from customers on the promise of cheap stout, a scam which landed him five years in Maryborough Prison. Hardy's release in August 1919 after only nine months was an extraordinary remission for such a persistent offender and was probably earned by him volunteering for British Intelligence. Certainly within days a Brigadier Linacre was interviewing him in London. To boost his credibility Hardy brought a letter of recommendation from the Leysian Mission, an East End Methodist philanthropic foundation whose wealthy benefactors helped the deserving poor and sinners anxious to repent. They were exactly Hardy's kind of people.

After joining British Intelligence and undergoing the usual crash training course, Hardy was in Dublin by late July 1920. Winter hoped to exploit his talent for deceit and spinning yarns, but Hardy was, in reality, more dangerous to his employers than to the IRA. While many spies stayed loyal to country, employer, colleagues, family or even their own particular vision of honour and decency, Hardy's only allegiance was to himself. He was hardly back in Ireland before he started looking for an escape hatch, applying unsuccessfully to join the Deanery staff of Westminster Abbey. Clearly, having scammed Methodists for a testimonial, Catholics for non-existent alcohol and Anglicans for a job, Hardy was an ecumenist who cared nothing for theological differences: he ripped off people of every denomination.

On 3 September 1920 Sturgis learnt that '"O" is on the trail of Michael'.[49] Basil Thomson and Winter were grooming Hardy for a sting operation designed to ensnare Collins. But the IRA was already on to Hardy, who, sloppy and egotistical as ever, had written three weeks earlier to the Viceroy boasting about his knowledge of Sinn Fein and the location of IRA arms dumps throughout Ireland. When a postal worker passed Hardy's intercepted letter on to the IRA, Tobin told Collins that another Jameson was on the scene.[50] Then in mid-September Robert Brennan of the Dail's Foreign Affairs Department was told by a friend about his encounter with a stocky, husky-voiced, middle-aged Englishman who claimed he was a disillusioned British secret service agent who wanted to meet Sinn Fein leaders and double-cross his paymasters.[51] Brennan arranged a meeting with Hardy, who bragged about being at the centre of British Intelligence, though he was 'practically one of the boys himself',[52] having been on a job in Ulster for which he had spent time in Derry Jail. Although his present intelligence mission was to trap Collins, Hardy offered to lure Basil Thomson to a lonely spot on Dun Laoghaire pier where the IRA could kidnap him. He also wanted to discuss long-term cooperation with republican leaders. Brennan directed Hardy to Great Brunswick Street, where Arthur Griffith, who had refused to go on the run, openly maintained an office. Brennan immediately tipped off Griffith to expect a visit from Hardy, who told him that he had been incarcerated in Derry Jail in December 1918. On Griffith's instructions Brennan researched newspaper files, uncovered Hardy's criminal record and concluded that he had been released for his present mission.

Meanwhile Vinnie Byrne was shadowing Hardy's endless futile meanderings:

I can only tell you I was footsore and weary walking around the city after him. I remember he walked to Westland Row station, turned back, waited outside the Queen's Theatre for a considerable time, then up to Grafton Street, dilly-dallying all the way, and back across town. He went into the Hamman Hotel in O'Connell Street and, as I was about to enter the hotel, he came out again and started walking aimlessly about the town. I was not sorry when I was relieved early that evening.[53]

When Tom Cullen discreetly searched Hardy's hotel room, he discovered personal documents confirming him as an 'ordinary decent criminal' and a completely useless spy. Collins quickly decided that Hardy was more useful alive as propaganda, especially as eliminating the British spy would have involved the moderate Acting President Griffith in an assassination. And Griffith had concocted a delicious sting operation that would humiliate the British secret service. On 16 September 1920 Hardy was suckered into attending a supposedly secret meeting with Griffith and the IRA's inner council. Simultaneously Irish, English and foreign journalists gathered to witness the exposure of a British *agent provocateur*. Offered a scoop, they readily agreed to play walk-on roles in the charade by pretending to be inner council members, though Michael Knightly of the *Irish Independent* needed little persuasion – he was already working undercover for Collins.[54]

The *Freeman's Journal* recorded that, as they sat around a table,

> there was a knock at the door, and the man was ushered in. 'Good evening, Mr Hardy,' Mr Griffith said, cordially. Mr Hardy was a fair-haired, clean-shaven Englishman of about 50 years of age. He had a heavy jowl, and walked quickly towards the seat reserved for him at the Council table. Mr Griffith then introduced the visitor. 'This gentleman', he said, 'is Mr Frank Hardy, who has expressed a desire to meet you in regard to certain matters. He will explain his proposals.' Mr Hardy seemed slightly nervous, and after a quick glance round the table, modestly lowered his eyes. For a few moments he spoke rapidly but soon recovered his sang-froid. The unsuspecting journalists listened attentively and sympathetically while the confessed spy un-bosomed himself. He told the story of his life and how he hoped to help the Sinn Fein movement.[55]

Hardy's suitably embellished career resumé mingled wholesale fabrication with occasional slivers of truth. He described ten years' employment with the Duke of Connaught in North America, a brief return to England and then flight to Ireland to escape conscription. After being arrested for involvement in republican arms raids and sentenced to five years in Maryborough Prison, Hardy claimed his father's powerful Masonic connections had secured his freedom and entry into British intelligence. But Hardy now professed hatred for Basil Thomson as 'the man responsible for all the dirty work in Ireland', offering to deliver him up, procure weapons for the IRA and carry out a shooting to prove his commitment. With the hook in place, he decided it was time to reel Griffith in.

Gaining in confidence, Mr Hardy went a step further. He suggested that it would prevent the Secret Service chiefs from becoming suspicious of him if we would provide him with a certain amount of genuine information which he would delay in reporting. Thus if he could report that Mr Michael Collins was in a certain place on Wednesday and hold back his report until Friday, he would gain the confidence of his superiors and be able further to assist the Sinn Fein movement. 'And, of course,' he added familiarly, 'no harm would come to Mick.' He was a very stupid man.[56]

Armed with Cullen's information and a collection of press cuttings, Griffith then proceeded to demolish Hardy's cover story. Knightly watched as 'Hardy sat up in surprise, while darting his right hand into his pocket where I have no doubt he had a gun. I signalled to Desmond Fitzgerald to watch his hand. The record having been finished, Arthur Griffith said, "Now, Mr Hardy, there is a boat leaving Dun Laoghaire this evening and my advice to you is to take it." Hardy relaxed and the meeting was concluded.'[57] In an adjoining room Robert Brennan watched Tobin and Cullen grinning as they listened to the proceedings. '"I hope you're not going to shoot him, Tom," I said. "No," said Tom, "Griffith said there should be nothing of the kind. I'm here to see that he gets on the boat".'[58]

If Collins preferred Hardy alive, Winter was probably tempted to use his revolver on the spy when he read next day's newspaper headlines about 'an English spy unmasked' and 'treachery at its vilest'. But Hardy had already skipped the country. Winter believed that he had really intended to betray king, country and Thomson, but more probably Hardy was simply scamming Irish republicans as he had scammed everybody else throughout his entire life. As the fiasco reverberated through the Irish and British press, scorn was heaped on British Intelligence for employing such an incorrigible rogue, a scraping of the barrel that lent credence to republican claims that jails were being emptied of criminals to serve in Ireland. Although this was untrue about Auxiliaries and Black and Tans, it was much closer to the mark in the case of Frank Digby Hardy.

Despite the Hardy debacle, Winter was determined to exert maximum pressure on the IRA and especially to stop gunmen like Breen and Treacy swaggering around Dublin. He intended reclaiming the capital's streets through his newly arrived Auxiliaries, ex-army officers recruited and paid by the War Office who brought all their military experience to the Irish war.

Formidable and courageous, they brought an aggressiveness and casual disregard for legality that frightened civilians, the IRA and their own security-force colleagues. Soon, Auxiliary armoured cars, powered by Rolls Royce engines, equipped with revolving machine-gun turrets and steered by utterly reckless drivers, roamed Dublin. And time and again their checkpoints, searches and raids would force the Squad hurriedly to dump its weapons and abandon operations. Although the Auxiliaries' headquarters was Beggar's Bush Barracks, their most feared unit was the Castle's 'F' Company, whose commander, Captain W.L. King, was a former Connaught Ranger. King had resigned from the Canadian North West Mounted Police to fight in Ireland, but he still lived by the Mounties' code – he always got his man.

Republican propaganda depicted the Auxiliaries as drunken, psychopathic murderers, but Collins's RIC mole Peter Forlan regarded them as 'gentlemen officers of high rank. There were ten of them working with me, and at all times they behaved as gentlemen and most of them were very friendly towards Ireland. Two became Catholics while in Dublin. They married Irish typists who had come from London to work in the Castle.'[59] They behaved better in Dublin than outside, partly because of the capital's large contingent of British and foreign journalists, and some even made quixotic gestures like protecting suspects from beatings by angry British soldiers. What the Auxiliaries lacked in Ireland was not fighting spirit but ideological conviction and emotional commitment. Most were already contemplating their next war zone and fortunately for them Palestine, then under British mandate but simmering with unrest between Jews and Arabs, was looking a likely candidate.

The Dublin IRA's response to the Auxiliaries was singularly ineffective. McKee's poorly armed Brigade did not manage a single attack on them until the end of 1920. Even the Squad settled for pinpricks such as hijacking a large consignment of wines, whiskey and brandy on its way to Beggar's Bush. Everyone assumed that Auxiliaries were likely summarily to execute anyone caught carrying arms. When Paddy Daly ran into one of their motorised patrols while shifting a small weapons cache, he slipped into a pub where the Volunteer barman concealed his incriminating parcel under cellar floorboards. 'No sooner had I got to the counter than he plonked down a bottle of stout in front of me. I never drank a bottle of stout before, or since, and said to him, "I don't know what will happen if I drink this." He said to me, "Drink it and be damned with you".'[60] Suddenly, the Auxiliaries swept inside, but the barman diverted them from a search by dispensing free and liberal hospitality. After swiftly downing a succession of pints and exchanging banter the intruders left.

Winter had fifty Auxiliary intelligence officers, but it was 'F' Company's legendary Captain Jocelyn Hardy whom Dublin Volunteers hated and feared most. This former Connaught Ranger had spent most of the First World War in German captivity, where his dozen escape attempts made him expert in forgery and disguises like a feigned limp. Hardy finally escaped in March 1918 and returned to the lines in France, where 'the Germans had the last word'.[61] Just five weeks before the end of the war a serious injury meant Hardy no longer needed to simulate a limp, because he wore an artificial replacement for the real leg left behind on the battlefield. In Dublin he tried disguising his physical handicap with a rapid gait; it only made him instantly recognisable as 'Hoppy' Hardy.

Hardy's hair-trigger temper convinced David Neligan that he 'had a slate off'[62] and made his interrogations chilling affairs, especially when he worked in tandem with his best friend Captain King. Detainees were first softened up under the Castle's old medieval tower in five windowless dungeon-like holding cells only twenty feet square with bare stone walls, an iron bed, a mattress and two blankets, kitchen chair, tin chamber pot and a small table. The heavy oak door's peephole was covered by a strong plate of glass through which prisoners could peer into a passage lit by a single weak electric bulb, making it impossible, one suspect recalled, 'to know at any time if it were day or night, especially if the prisoners had no watch – disorientating. The whole chamber was permanently plunged in gloom and it was difficult to see at all in its more remote corners.'[63] The lucky ones got half an hour's exercise in a small yard, the base of whose high walls were ringed with barbed wire.

Hardy and King conducted their questioning in the Auxiliaries' Intelligence Office, which bruised Volunteers had ruefully nicknamed 'The Knocking Shop'. Ernie O'Malley, a leading IRA officer, was brought here after being arrested for possessing a gun and incriminating documents, though he tried passing himself off as a dim Kilkenny farmer. O'Malley recalled:

There were two men in the room; one was in civilians, the other in khaki. The man in the uniform of the Connaught Rangers was medium-sized and slight in build. He walked with a limp. His face was pale, the pupils of his eyes were large and black, around them was a thin rim of blue. He worked his lower lip. The other man was over six feet; well built, with an air of command, the lines on his forehead were drawn together when he spoke. He was Major King; the other Captain Hardy.[64]

This formidable double act occasionally operated as good cop, bad cop, but they really preferred bad cop, bad cop: it brought out the best in them. Hardy, a future dramatist, had probably scripted this little morality play, refined over numerous performances, but ultimately he was less concerned with abstract notions of truth and justice than pounding a suspect into submission.

Hardy immediately smashed O'Malley's face and forced him to the ground, where another blow produced blood and excruciating pain. His continued denials only brought a pulveriser from King which sent him flying against a wall. After Hardy had failed to break him with either threats to his mother or an offer of freedom if he cooperated, Hardy approached with a glowing poker. It made O'Malley's eyes burn, singed his eyebrows, curled his eyelashes and triggered a coughing fit. Disorientated, he recalled King furiously raining blows on him and then rising with swollen eyes, blood choking his throat, his nose knocked askew and the room a distorted jumble of red and blue. Screaming, Hardy grabbed O'Malley's throat, almost strangling him. As he gulped for breath, O'Malley saw King grabbing a revolver from a desk drawer. O'Malley recalled the following exchange:

'Do you know what this is?' I nodded.

'Now watch.' He broke the action and spun round the cylinder on either side, showing me the lead points and the base of the cartridges. 'You see, it's loaded.' I watched the six cartridges. 'Get up against the wall.' I backed until I was touching the wall.

'I am going to give you three chances; if after the third you don't answer your brains will be on that wall.' He spoke slowly. 'Who gave you the automatic? . . . One . . .'

No answer.

'Two . . .'

He slowly cocked the hammer. I looked along the bluish barrel, my legs twitched in shivers at the thighs. I brought my heels together with a snap.

'Three . . .'

I stood stiff. He pressed the trigger. There was a bang. He had used a blank cartridge.[65]

Mock threats of summary execution happened frequently and sometimes went as far as the commanding British officer of supposed military firing squads asking for a blindfolded prisoner's last statement.

* * *

British efforts to regain the intelligence initiative were often surprisingly innovative and resourceful. Thomson and Hill Dillon's primitive 'confidential hotline' enabled informers to send letters anonymously to a safe London address; predictably most were from practical jokers and republicans making false accusations against well-known loyalists. Some, though, came from IRA officers anxious to get out of the war but saving their face by having themselves arrested.[66] Winter, a keen foxhunter, imported fifty bloodhounds to track IRA suspects. However, Volunteers quickly discovered that spraying their trousers and boots with disinfectant literally threw the dogs off the scent. The animals were even less successful in big towns. When British soldiers raided an empty flat in South Frederick Street and stumbled on Mulcahy's papers, they also found a pair of kilts – theatrical costumes belonging to the actor house owner but which they assumed belonged to the Volunteer Chief of Staff. After the bloodhounds had had a sniff, everyone took off on a futile rooftop search – which Mulcahy watched from among a crowd of spectators on the ground.[67] Eventually Winter pensioned the dogs off to a hunt, with which they presumably enjoyed a happier and more productive life chasing foxes over the English countryside.

British Intelligence's holy grail was capturing or eliminating Collins, the most wanted man in Ireland. But reliable information on him proved elusive, and most of the scraps that came Winter's way proved fanciful or salacious. As an officer and gentleman he shielded his chaste female shorthand writer from a report about Collins sleeping once a week with a girlfriend, sparing her blushes by passing the juicy item directly to Greenwood and Anderson.[68] Time and again, Winter's hopes of bagging Collins rose and then fizzled out. Instead, Collins circulated easily around his favourite haunts and Irish government and Volunteer offices, with a freedom of movement that was possible only because of the virtually complete collapse of British Intelligence. The lack of success in tracking down Collins is often attributed to British ignorance about Collins's appearance, but they knew very well what he looked like. Winter had Collins's photograph, and it was also posted on the wall of 'F' Company's interrogation office and produced in *Hue and Cry*, a photographic compilation of IRA suspects issued to RIC officers. In fact, Collins's immunity derived more from the fact that he had the luck to live in an era before saturation media coverage could ensure that his face became instantly recognisable to British forces. One British Army officer who served in Dublin in 1920 and 1921 explained this

> slowness or inability to recognise well-known people; of course you recognise them when you go to some function on purpose to see them or see their pictures. When you see them in real life where you would not expect them it is entirely a different matter, these 'picture' people have to come to life in your brain. Very few people and possibly no one would recognise the Queen if she was going round a supermarket wheeling a trolley.[69]

Even so, many Dublin policemen knew Collins by sight but did nothing – from either sympathy or fear. One officer amused and bemused Collins by clicking to attention and saluting every time he passed by. Broy also enhanced Collins's security by having him ditch his military-style breeches and leggings in favour of a conventional business suit and merging anonymously into the civilian population. This makeover confounded British expectations of an Irish revolutionary leader and gratified Broy when he saw Collins cycling past in heavy city-centre traffic wearing 'a high quality soft hat, dark grey suit, as usual, neatly shaved and with immaculate collar and tie, as always, seeming to be ready for the photographer. His bicycle was of first-class quality and fitted with a lamp and many other accessories. He looked like a bank clerk or stockbroker or "something in the city" and cycled as if he owned the street.'[70]

Realising that anyone behaving nervously or timorously was more likely to attract enemy suspicions, Collins acted naturally whenever he was in danger. When a British military patrol once stopped his car in Capel Street, the driver, Joe Hyland, heard a rear door open and close, and assumed that his boss had hightailed it up a side street. To his astonishment, Collins was actually standing nonchalantly beside the vehicle, allowing himself to be searched. 'I said to Collins when I reached the destination that it was a very narrow escape. He said, "little does that officer know what he has let slip through his fingers".'[71] Sometimes Collins brazened his way out of difficulty. At the Gresham Hotel in 1920 during his Christmas lunch with Tobin, Cullen and Thornton an Auxiliary raiding party scrutinised and searched every diner. Thornton says that, although they did not identify anyone, 'the one man they came back to time after time was Michael Collins. Whether it was his defiant attitude that attracted more attention to him than anybody else, the fact remains that they seemed to concentrate on him. They finally left without recognising him. Needless to remark we had a hectic Christmas Eve after that escape.'[72]

Collins frequently rode or simply walked through enemy lines. Neligan once saw him cycling down Grafton Street with his coat flying. '"Where are you going for?" say I. "I'm going over to Batt O'Connor's to sleep," he says. "There's about a thousand Tans and British tommies around Parnell Square with rolls of barbed wire colonnading off the whole bloody place." They were closing in and he'd walked right through the middle of them.'[73] Collins's operational style disconcerted provincial Volunteers like Tom Barry, who habitually took painstaking precautions and was surprised in Dublin by the sight of salaried republican leaders carrying briefcases to their offices. One night he was in Collins's entourage when it ran straight into about fifty Auxiliaries. Barry recalled:

I didn't know what the hell was going to happen, I thought we were all for it, and Collins just leaned over before we got out of the car and said, 'Act drunk.' He put on this extraordinary performance then, joking with them and falling about the place, and in no time they were in very good humour with us. When we got back I gave out to him, I told him the least he could do was put up some kind of advance guard for him and us. So he just laughed and said I was a 'windy west Cork beggar'. I wasn't feeling in such good humour about it and I persisted, but he explained to me then that this was the only way they could survive in the city. He was right, of course.[74]

Collins was bold, not reckless; a calculated gambler who always left himself an escape route by having GHQ Engineering construct secret receptacles in the office walls, floors and cupboards of any premises that he used regularly.

While Collins was very careful about his own security he remained vulnerable to the negligence and even folly of others. Incredibly, one Abbey Street businessman sent Collins a letter with his name on the envelope to Vaughan's Hotel requesting him to intercede in a planning dispute. Instead, in a blistering rebuke, Collins told the offender that he 'was amazed at this monstrous indiscretion. For three years previously the British authorities have spared no effort to locate me, yet a letter can be sent to me at an address which at one time I used, disclosing more to the enemy than with all his organisation he has been able to find out in the time mentioned.'[75]

Unable to pinpoint Collins's movements, the British hoped for a lucky checkpoint stop or raid on a pub, hotel, office or safe house. But, although Collins did not have an official bodyguard, help was never far away. When Auxiliaries raided Kirwan's pub while Collins and Thornton were meeting a police mole, he moved casually around the bar until the intruders had gone. He knew that the barman, a Volunteer like the other staff, had a fully loaded revolver nestling under the counter.[76] Even so, Collins assumed that if the British caught him they would quickly eliminate him and he instructed Broy to smuggle in a gun and bombs with which he could fight his way out. Broy was less pessimistic. He believed the British would relish making Collins suffer at length by exiling him to some remote island like St Helena.[77]

By making Collins the most wanted man in Ireland, British Intelligence transformed him in popular consciousness into the embodiment of the revolution. Its pursuit only heightened public fascination with this Irish Scarlet Pimpernel who continually bamboozled those seeking him here, there and everywhere. Often Collins's capture seemed imminent, but it never happened. One British soldier recorded that, 'night after night we have been told Michael Collins has been located, he was imprisoned, the CID had surrounded such and such a house and all sorts of rumours. At the time of writing he is still at large. The population of Dublin are too loyal to give him away.'[78] Sturgis reported many near misses and supposed arrests. On 4 November 1920, 'Tudor tells me they have caught at Longford a man they think is Michael Collins and have ciphered for a strong body to come from Dublin to identify him. Sounds too good to be true.' It was. Next day Sturgis learnt that 'they have not caught Michael Collins at Longford'.[79]

The numerous alleged sightings of Collins enhanced his almost mythical status, and rumours abounded that he cruised by British soldiers and Auxiliaries, sometimes in drag or disguised as a priest, and supposedly traversed Ireland by train – hidden inside a packing case. Collins also fascinated his hunters, whose unavailing pursuit of their quarry helped swell his reputation, since many of them could only ascribe their failure to catch him to his brilliant talent for avoiding detection. While many British officials regarded Collins as public enemy number one, others like Macready and Sturgis grudgingly respected someone they called 'Michael', and many had their own Collins story. One, Douglas Duff, had left an English monastery to join the Black and Tans. Having travelled from Galway in civilian clothes to deliver dispatches to Dublin Castle, Duff had a few hours to kill before returning. He and an Auxiliary Cadet were crossing O'Connell Street on their way to a cinema when Duff's companion caught his arm.

'Good Lord, man', he said, 'look at that chap over there! I'll swear it's Michael Collins.' Startled and thrilled, I looked and saw that it really was the man whose description hung on every Police Barrack wall in Ireland. Excitedly I agreed with my companion. 'Ten thousand shining simoleoans,' he muttered in a dazed manner. I was thinking of the renown and promotion that we should get if we captured him. 'Come on, we'll nab him,' he said. We closed in on him and my companion took hold of his shoulder. He wheeled at once and stood facing us, a good-natured smile playing around his lips, and before we had any time to speak, he said: 'Peelers, I suppose? What do you chaps want?' 'You're Michael Collins,' said the Auxiliary Cadet, 'I'm sure of it.' 'And supposing I am, what is it you will be wanting with me?' he answered. 'You are under arrest and will be taken to the Castle for identification,' I snapped. 'Listen, boy,' he answered. 'Do you think I am fool enough to walk about the streets of Dublin in broad daylight without an escort? Look around you. Do you see those three men near the hoardings there?', pointing to men who were looking intently at us. 'Do you notice that couple on the edge of the pavement? Can you see those four men talking together just in front and that couple who are pretending to be interested in the shop window?' Everywhere we looked we stared at men who looked unwinkingly at us, and all of whom had their hands in their pockets, a sure sign that they carried a gun. 'If I raise my hand they will shoot the pair of you, and we shall be clear away long before anyone dares to even try helping you. Now take my advice, my brave Peelers, and go quietly, there has been enough blood shed in Ireland without wasting yours.' We decided that discretion was the better part of valour and wisely moved away, whilst Michael Collins waved a gay farewell, saying 'Good-bye, boys' as he went.[80]

Collins also established himself in popular imagination by astutely manipulating the Irish newspapers like the *Irish Independent* and *Freeman's Journal*. Collins was, in effect, his own spin doctor, using friendly journalists to stimulate dramatic headlines and foster his image as a glamorous revolutionary leader exuding excitement and danger. And, although a fugitive and man of mystery, Collins was simultaneously perceived as the revolution's omniscient guardian, ever watchful and certain to unmask and punish its enemies. Collins was clearly an adept self-promoter and he was very sensitive about anything – or anyone – tarnishing his carefully constructed heroic self-image. Three days after Bloody Sunday, for instance, he wrote to Eamon Duggan protesting about newspapers like the *Freeman's Journal* describing him as 'one of the murder gang'. Intent on retaliation, he proposed, in all seriousness, that Duggan's firm of solicitors threaten to sue the papers for criminal libel.[81]

A fascinating portrait of Collins at full throttle is that of Liam Deasy, an IRA officer from west Cork, whom Volunteer GHQ summoned to Dublin in early 1921 after the death of his Brigadier. Deasy and a fellow officer, Tadhg O'Sullivan, were dining at Devlin's pub when Collins suddenly breezed in, summoned a taxi and led them outside to begin an exhilarating three-day magical mystery tour. Deasy recalled:

> Tadhg turned to me and asked, 'Where are we?' 'I think this is Phoenix Park racecourse,' I replied. 'Good God,' he said, 'these fellows are mad, boy!' Collins looked back smilingly from the front. Then jumping out of the taxi, he led us into the racecourse. Nothing would do him now but to bring us into the reserved stand where we stood shoulder to shoulder with the enemy.[82]

Afterwards and somewhat poorer, they hurtled back to Devlin's, where Collins vanished briefly on sensitive business. Then, shepherding them to Vaughan's Hotel, he airily dismissed the owner's warning about an imminent curfew and insisted on meeting a contact upstairs, so that by the time the party finally left the premises Deasy could hear enemy lorries rumbling down the far side of a deserted Parnell Square.

Next morning after breakfast Collins and Deasy surreptitiously met Detective MacNamara at Jury's Hotel in Dame Street. Afterwards, strolling through a maze of side streets to Collins's Harcourt Street office, they discussed the war in west Cork, Collins firing 'a fusillade of questions regarding details of the situation and the possibilities of future development. Collins's immediate grasp of military detail, as was evidenced by his relevant and piercing questions, was astonishing and impressed me in a singular way.'[83] After Collins had spent half an hour working through reports and accounts, they met Tahdg O'Sullivan at Devlin's, having arranged to drive to

Rathgar for lunch. When a British military and police patrol stopped their taxi and ordered them out, Deasy saw

> one of the plain-clothes policemen approach Collins and run his hand through his hair to have a good look at him. I felt that it would need something more than an alibi to save me from imprisonment and something worse. I held my breath and waited for the inevitable. It is more than possible that the policeman did not recognise his man, but not less likely that he realised that Collins's arrest would be equivalent to the signing of his own death warrant. Whatever the reason, he allowed us all to pass.[84]

Over lunch Collins playfully teased Deasy and O'Sullivan about Cork men being out of their depth in the big city, vowing to show 'these bloody country fellows, what a grand place Dublin really is'.[85] Collins's party descended on a Sandyford pub, where they sang songs and swapped stories in the crowded bar before ending up at a house in Palmerston Park (a bastion of Unionist respectability). Here Collins presided over an IRB meeting. But even after most of the exhausted party had retired for the night, he 'was now relaxing and in turn went to every room and started a pillow fight. By four o'clock when the last dropped off from sheer exhaustion there was nothing to be seen in any bedroom but feathers from floor to ceiling.'[86] On Deasy's third day in Dublin he was finally summoned to a formal meeting with Collins and Mulcahy, who appointed him the west Cork IRA's Brigadier.

Collins's *tour de force* was a consummate actor's performance, a skilfully honed presentation of spontaneity, friendliness and cavalier disregard for his own safety. But, in reality, his every move during the three-day encounter with Deasy had been calculated for maximum effect. By cultivating Deasy, Collins fostered good relations between GHQ and an effective but wayward west Cork Brigade as well as ensuring that, when he returned to Cork, Deasy would disseminate favourable reports about him on the revolutionary grapevine. Furthermore, Collins had taken the opportunity to scrutinise Deasy's character, views on war strategy and ability to work harmoniously with GHQ. The west Cork brigade was vital to the IRA campaign, and he needed to have full confidence in its commander. Although Deasy professed surprise at his appointment, Collins had clearly used their time together as an extended job interview. Deasy always regarded Collins as 'the greatest leader of our generation',[87] even though eighteen months later they parted over the

Treaty. On 22 August 1922 Deasy and Tahdg O'Sullivan were only a few hundred yards away when they heard the gun battle in which their Irregular unit ambushed and killed Collins at Beal na Blath crossroad.

Despite Collins's frenetic lifestyle, his inner circle utterly dismissed any suggestion that he binged on alcohol and cigarettes. Thornton insisted that, 'as one who was very closely associated with him during those strenuous days, I can say that Collins rarely took anything and when he did it was a small sherry. Drinking was naturally discouraged everywhere those days because of the necessity of keeping a cool head under the very strenuous circumstances.'[88] Instead, Collins alleviated stress through innocent, somewhat juvenile high jinks. Broy recalled guests at a GHQ dinner lavishing huge dollops of rather queasy hero worship on Collins:

> Apples and oranges were laid on a table to make the letters 'IRA' and we all enjoyed ourselves for that evening as if we owned Dublin. Tom Cullen spoke there and said that we could all die for Mick Collins, 'not because of Mick Collins, but because of what he stands for'. Mick was persuaded to recite 'The Lisht', which he did with his own inimitable accent. When he was finished, there was a rush for him by everybody in the place to seize him. I was very proud of the fact that he fell into my arms.[89]

Broy hero-worshipped Collins with such quasi-religious devotion that he never went full tilt at him during their wrestling bouts in case he inflicted injury on his leader's sacred personage. But others were silently sceptical, their simmering resentment stoked by Collins's mercurial temperament, aggressiveness and coarse language. Although Tom Barry regarded Collins as good-hearted and generous, he could see that 'he was also a man who could easily be disliked. He was very domineering.'[90] While the Collins cult attracted many followers, others remained agnostic, longing for him to experience a great fall from his pedestal of uncritical adulation.

Although capturing Collins would have been the glittering prize, the British hunted other IRA leaders like Mulcahy, whose nomadic existence entailed twenty-two different hideouts during eighteen months on the run.[91] He rarely used an office, preferring a safe house, in which he worked alone on documents that he carried around in two attaché cases. Twice, this extraordinarily risky *modus operandi* allowed the British to seize important Volunteer GHQ material. British Intelligence also tried pinpointing important

IRA locations, and, although unaware of Crow Street's existence, it knew about a Dublin Brigade headquarters. Until December 1920 this was situated in Lower Gardiner Street, about 400 yards from O'Connell Street, hidden deep inside the Dublin Typographical Society. This busy trade-union building had many legitimate visitors, who provided ideal cover for a constant stream of Volunteer traffic. McKee's Brigade council met here, provincial emissaries were vetted before meeting Dail ministers and GHQ Directors, and the headquarters also hosted important meetings like that of March 1918 which established Volunteer GHQ. Its survival was crucial to the IRA's Dublin campaign and security precautions included having scouts on the pavement outside, secret hideouts in the office walls where important papers could be hurriedly concealed and an electric push button in the hallway for the porter to warn of a British raid.[92]

As the war intensified during the summer of 1920 with a daily round of ambushes, bombings, assassinations and reprisals, a lengthy drama riveted the Irish and British publics and raised political bitterness to heights unknown since the death of Ashe. Unsurprisingly, it was another hunger strike. On 12 August, Terence MacSwiney, Lord Mayor of Cork and Commandant of its 1st IRA Brigade, was caught with a police cipher, court-martialled four days later and sentenced to two years' imprisonment. He immediately began a hunger strike, apparently on his own initiative, intending to pit his willingness to die against that of the British Government to let him. After being transferred to Brixton Prison in London on 18 August, MacSwiney deliberately conserved his strength, buying time either for the British Government to release him or for a wave of sympathy to develop at home and abroad.

The British Cabinet had surrendered to April's Mountjoy hunger strike and initially it wobbled again under tremendous pressure from nationalist Ireland, the Roman Catholic Church, the British press, American public opinion and even Southern Unionists. But the earlier capitulation had devastated police and army morale. Tudor and Winter regarded MacSwiney as a supremely dangerous opponent, a leading Volunteer and Sinn Feiner as well as a ruthless advocate of killing policemen. They warned that another cave-in might trigger mutinies. Winter thought anyway that the prisoner was bluffing, surviving on nutrients smuggled into Brixton inside the voluminous beard of his spiritual adviser, Father Dominic.[93] By now even Sturgis was heartily sick of the 'hunger cult' and agreed that this time the government had to show it meant business.[94]

Although Collins opposed hunger strikes, he understood their propaganda value, especially as MacSwiney's dragged on seemingly endlessly after everyone had assumed that he would die within a fortnight. As week followed week and family and visitors reported graphically on his physical disintegration, Ireland was transfixed by the whole grisly business, in which both sides seemed prepared to go literally to the death. Collins deliberately exploited such episodes to reinforce the symbolic link between individual resistance and the national struggle. During April's hunger strike at Mountjoy prison he got the Squad to kill Detective Kells and now Collins had it prepare to eliminate the remnants of G Division. But, although the Squad shadowed Detectives Bruton, Coffey and Revell every Sunday on their way to Mass near the Castle, Collins would not sanction their execution as long as MacSwiney remained alive. He did not want to destroy MacSwiney's chances of a last-minute release or give the British Government an opportunity to justify its hardline stance. However, Collins's restraint risked the Squad being sucked into the same kind of routine that had doomed many of its victims, and once, when Coffey suddenly bolted back into the Castle, Daly thought the Squad's surveillance had been blown. 'How every member of the Squad was not known to the Castle authorities I do not know. I often thought it was a mad idea, turning up there every Sunday.' So did the newsboys, who chorused 'Misters! They're not here today!'[95]

MacSwiney finally died on 25 October after seventy-four days. But, although the British Government had held the line and forced republicans to abandon hunger-striking, it was a pyrrhic victory that alienated huge swathes of nationalist Ireland. A week later a 19-year-old medical student, Kevin Barry, was hanged at Mountjoy, the first official British execution of the war. Many people regarded the death of someone still legally a youth in the first political hanging since 1798 as part of a deliberate British policy to return the country to an earlier barbarism.

* * *

As the conflict got dirtier, so did the intelligence war. Both sides assumed the worst of the enemy. In April 1921 Volunteer GHQ ordered an investigation into 'all cases of persons killed by the British and marked by them as spies "executed by the IRA"'.[96] Some dirty tricks were relatively harmless scams, like the time Winter suddenly materialised in the Castle wearing a wig, dark glasses, chestnut moustache, trench coat, flannel trousers and a bowler hat, and gleefully informed the government's bemused legal adviser, William Wylie, that he planned to commit a criminal offence. Posing as a chartered accountant, he intended removing £2,000 from a recently discovered Collins bank account. When Wylie patiently explained that the bank would still be liable for the money, the stone-faced Director of Intelligence simply ignored such pettifogging legalism. 'Off he set with a party of policemen, insisted on the production of the books and drew, in notes, the exact amount standing to Collins's credit. Of course inside a week the amount had to be handed back again as no government could possibly stand over that sort of illegality. That gives you an idea, however, of how things were run in those hectic days.'[97]

Winter also went after the *Irish Bulletin*, a free republican newssheet produced by the Dail's Propaganda Department. Despite its small staff and shoestring budget, the *Bulletin* was read avidly by foreign journalists for its leaked Castle documents, mail intercepts and eyewitness accounts. An irritated Winter decided to shut the *Bulletin* up – or down – for good. After several attempts to find its secret office, a British raiding party finally captured its typewriters, duplicator, documents, newspaper files and circulation list. Winter then organised a disinformation operation involving a counterfeit *Bulletin*, whose skilfully slanted contents confused regular readers about republican policies and actions. When the genuine article began using a distinguishing stamp, Winter simply came up with another expert forgery.[98]

Fleecing Collins and embarrassing a republican newspaper was good dirty fun, but other dirty tricks were potentially lethal. Colonel Kelly, the British 6th Division's intelligence officer in Cork, was an Irishman with a cunning and labyrinthine mind, a ruthless will to win and a prodigious capacity for spinning webs. Kelly was made for espionage. His agents masqueraded as civilians to rob post-office mail, and they also secured the evidence which convicted MacSwiney. After MacSwiney died, Kelly was very interested in who would be elected his successor as commandant of Cork's 1st Brigade. He discovered that the two leading candidates were Sean Hegarty, a suspect in the killing of Mrs Lindsay, and Donal O'Callaghan, suspected of involvement in Strickland's attempted abduction. Kelly rooted for an ineffective Hegarty as the person least likely to damage British forces, appointed himself his unofficial campaign manager and swung the election by the machiavellian ruse of distributing a forged letter in which O'Callaghan seemingly claimed a British reward for information. After O'Callaghan had fled the country, Hegarty became a shoo-in as the new commandant, an appointment that delighted the British army because it 'suited the Crown forces exceedingly well – they could not have a nominated a better man for the position from their point of view'.[99]

O'Callaghan escaped with his life, but Kelly's murderous duplicity fatally ensnared another IRA leader. He tested one intelligence officer's new maid by leaving sabotaged bullets lying casually around the house, and she repeatedly took the bait and the ammunition. Eventually the maid returned from leave in mourning, claiming her brother had died accidentally. But Kelly knew him as a leading IRA officer in Kerry who had been killed by the defective bullets exploding in his revolver as he tried to assassinate a resident magistrate. Kelly's successful ploy also stopped thefts of ammunition from army barracks in the 6th Division area, forcing the IRA to dump sacks of perfectly good bullets.[100] Far from being a rogue operation, Kelly's was part of a coordinated sting organised from British Army GHQ by Hill Dillon, who distributed the defective ammunition to every Divisional staff. After discovering that IRA sympathisers were stealing ammunition from army stores in Dublin and corrupt British soldiers selling weapons, Hill Dillon had secret service agents offload TNT-filled bullets in public houses. Eventually the IRA realised what was happening, though the Dublin Brigade's munitions factory still had laboriously to check every new piece of ammunition. General Boyd resisted such methods and told GHQ in late April 1920 that he 'had always been opposed to such a policy as being un-British and likely to lead to reprisals', and would not cooperate any longer without an assurance that Macready had sanctioned it.[101]

A British raiding party discovered the war's dirtiest trick in November 1920 when it captured Mulcahy's attaché cases at a flat in Longwood Avenue, off the South Circular Road. Dublin Castle quickly claimed that documents proved Mulcahy had planned to infect British troops with typhoid in contaminated milk and spread glanders among cavalry horses through infected oats. Although republicans ridiculed this as British black propaganda, Sturgis enthused over 'evidence of the most thorough and complete plot to murder individuals, poison troops, horses, etc. – to blow up the Manchester Ship Canal, etc. etc. This will look very good in "Print." The papers collected in the Mulcahy raid are absolutely smashing and should practically kill the English support of SF.'[102]

The one person who was not talking was Mulcahy, who in a forty-year career and a historical record stretching to millions of words never once mentioned the affair – not even to repudiate British accusations. He could not, because they were true. Mulcahy's lifelong interest in science had equipped him – or so he believed – with the necessary technical expertise. After the Rising he had enrolled as a medical student at University College Dublin, and as Chief of Staff he retained an office in its Chemistry Department. Furthermore, his friend and Volunteer colleague Jack Plunkett confirmed Mulcahy's authorship of the plans, though dismissing them as typical of a 'First Medical'.[103] But Mulcahy was clearly given specialised assistance and detailed guidance on growing the typhoid bacillus, disseminating it without endangering either the perpetrators or civilians, and destroying instruments and clothing afterwards. Although Mulcahy's captured papers were destroyed by a German air raid in 1940, the British Army's Director of Publicity had retained a copy of the typhoid plans. These show that Mulcahy was aware of the danger of British retaliation but beguiled by the possibility that 'a couple of thousand horses infected would make a sensation. Saddles etc. would have to he burned and stables disinfected.'[104] And Mulcahy had a very personal knowledge of typhoid's devastating effects on human beings, because twenty years earlier the disease had killed his own mother. His pioneering work in the field of germ warfare sits uneasily with Mulcahy's carefully cultivated image of stern moral rectitude and left him teetering on the brink of a war crime comparable with the poison gas attacks in the First World War.[105]

* * *

Many supposed spies died simply because they were in the wrong place at the wrong time, especially social outcasts like tramps. One, David Walsh, was seized by the Cork IRA and interrogated round the clock for two days. Walsh's repeated denials of espionage only convinced his captors that he had a trained agent's ability to resist pressure and they finally took him to a lonely mountainous area where a parish priest and an empty grave awaited. But they promised that if he confessed everything they would give him his freedom and a passage to Australia. Terrified, isolated, gullible and eager to seize the chance not just of life but a new one on the other side of the world, Walsh concocted a bogus story about having informed on an IRA camp. Flushed with their success at finally eliciting the 'truth' from such a dangerous adversary, his captors hurriedly court-martialled and convicted Walsh. Like many tramps in this war he died as he had lived – alone.[106]

Because Dublin swirled with suspicion, it was dangerous to be seen regularly outside or behaving furtively near a secret location like a Dail department or an IRA arms dump. In late 1920 IRA scouts outside Brigade headquarters in Lower Gardiner Street reported a suspected enemy spy constantly scrutinising pedestrians.[107] They bundled the man into a taxi and interrogated him in a nearby storeroom, but he refused to answer any questions, even when his captors ordered him to kneel and prepare for his execution. Only when his request for a priest was turned down and death seemed imminent did the suspect crack and confess – not to spying for the British but to pimping for a Gardiner Street brothel. Brigade Headquarters was situated near what was reputedly Europe's largest red-light district and he had been drumming up business for the oldest profession, not the second oldest. In another case, Laurence Nugent, in whose Upper Mount Street home the *Irish Bulletin* was produced, spotted a stranger hanging around outside for days on end. After Nugent's wife gave the person's description to Collins, 'the man was not seen around again, but we asked no questions'.[108]

Physically resembling an enemy agent or informer was also dangerous. When the IRA raided an Inchicore laundry to destroy an Auxiliary clothes consignment, the manager slipped across nearby fields and warned British soldiers in Richmond Barracks. After five Volunteers had been captured, the Dublin Brigade sentenced the manager to death and dispatched a unit to his golf club. Seizing a man with a limp who matched their target's description, they were parading him on the links prior to execution when club members convinced them in the nick of time that he was the wrong person. The manager had already fled to Belfast.[109]

Even loyal IRA intelligence officers came under suspicion, especially as gathering information or recruiting double agents sometimes involved contact with the enemy. The intelligence world has been described, memorably, as a wilderness of mirrors in which nothing is what it seems; apparently trustworthy men defect, uncertainty about a colleague's ultimate loyalty breeds suspicion and consorting with the other side is easily misconstrued as treachery. Dan McDonnell, a Volunteer GHQ Intelligence officer, was almost killed by his own side after David Neligan had introduced him casually to a couple of British agents as an ordinary Dublin civilian. Crow Street ordered him to cultivate the pair, and their superficial friendship provided ideal cover for McDonnell's own espionage. As both British spies were harmless, Collins and Tobin decided to keep them in place, especially as eliminating them might bring in more effective replacements. Indeed, Crow Street enhanced their credibility with British Intelligence by having McDonnell feed them titbits of information. It was a dangerous association, but luckily for McDonnell he discovered just in time that 'some of us had been followed and were under observation to be shot by local IRA companies in Dublin because of our mixing around with the British forces'.[110]

Florrie O'Donoghue, a Cork Brigade Intelligence Officer, was once mistaken as an enemy spy. When a company intelligence officer learnt about a new resident regularly leaving his house early and returning late, he shadowed the suspect to the main police barracks and decided he must be a detective. He also saw a stranger visiting the house and departing in darkness just before curfew – when he could not be identified or followed to his own home. A few weeks later O'Donoghue was asked to ratify both men's execution. To his relief correct procedures had been followed because he himself was the suspicious visitor whose death warrant he was being urged to sign.[111] The other person was the RIC county inspector's clerk whom O'Donoghue had recruited as a double agent. Jim Dalton, intelligence officer of Limerick's 1st City Battalion, was not so lucky. 2nd Battalion shot him dead in March 1920, ostensibly because he had been spotted meeting British intelligence agents – even though such contact was authorised as a way of turning enemy spies. But Dalton's death was the byproduct of a bitter internal Brigade feud over 1st Battalion's failure to turn out during the Easter Rising. His alleged collaboration was a convenient excuse for settling old scores.[112]

* * *

British Intelligence was obsessed with the idea of the IRA as a political 'Murder Incorporated', dispatching its specialist hit men throughout Ireland to eliminate dangerous opponents. At the end of May 1920 Greenwood assured the Cabinet that the killers were handsomely rewarded from American funds channelled to Sinn Fein and issued as cheques from Collins. The bagmen distributing these to the killers in Dublin pubs were none other than Sinn Fein's trustees, Arthur Griffith and Michael Fogarty, Bishop of Killaloe.[113]

Topping Winter's list of 'contract killers' were Liam Lynch, leader of Cork's ruthless 3rd Brigade, and Dan Breen and Sean Treacy. Lynch had organised the Fermoy ambush of September 1919, and the British believed he was masterminding every major IRA operation in Cork and Munster in general.

They were especially incensed by an IRA attack on 28 May 1920 in Kilmallock, County Limerick, close to Lynch's home village, which destroyed the police barracks and killed two RIC officers. In August and September 1920 two different Lynches died violently, apparently after being mistaken for Liam. In the first killing, at Hospital, County Limerick, a British raiding party summoned James Lynch outside and shot him dead nearby. Next was John Lynch, a Limerick county councillor and Sinn Fein election agent from Kilmallock, where the RIC station still lay in ruins. He was in Dublin delivering money for the Dail Loan, but nearing the end of a week's stay. His hotel, the Royal Exchange, was situated 100 yards from the Castle and kept under British surveillance because rural Volunteers were collecting boxes of arms and ammunition there.

Just after 2 a.m. on 22 September a senior officer from the RIC depot arrived at the Castle and told the regular army officer on duty, Captain G.T. Baggallay, that a man called Lynch, whom he believed had shot policemen in Limerick, was staying at the Royal Exchange. Baggallay directed the police officer to Dublin District Special Branch's office in Lower Castle Yard, where Captain Harper-Shore provided a dozen agents to surround the hotel and occupy the reception area while a police party raided Lynch's third-floor room. At the hotel the Special Branch officers heard shots being fired in quick succession after which the RIC men came down with papers which they had taken from the room. Upstairs Lynch's bullet-riddled body lay stretched out on a bed with – according to the police – a discharged revolver lying by his side. Initially the British announced triumphantly that they had killed Liam Lynch after he had fired first. But after realising that the forty-year-old corpse was almost certainly not that of a 27-year-old guerrilla leader, they hastily banned an inquest and public funeral. Republicans insisted that a British 'murder gang' was operating its own lynch law, a shoot-to-kill policy, and, when Neligan discovered Captain Baggallay's role in the affair, Collins added the officer's name to his death list.[114]

The British were also on the trail of Breen and Treacy, whom they mistakenly believed had killed Divisional Commissioner Smyth in Cork. After spending a year in Dublin, the pair had returned to Tipperary in April 1920 and carried out attacks on police barracks in the south-west of Ireland. But by August Breen was back for an operation to remove grenade splinters from his legs. So was his inseparable companion. They quickly discovered a very different Dublin crawling with British intelligence agents, troops, Auxiliaries and civilian spotters anxious to collect on the large reward for their capture. Breen and Treacy began carrying weapons strapped to their wrists. Although the brutally unappealing and thick-skinned Breen loved city life and withstood the pressure well, it began to wear down Treacy, a quintessential country boy. Soon they were living hand-to-mouth, broke, frequently hungry and sleeping in the open air. Their friendship with McKee, Clancy, Crow Street and the Squad did not do them much good; the republican movement was chronically short of funds.

Winter knew Breen and Treacy were back in Dublin and was 'very anxious to make the acquaintance of both these men'.[115] So was Major G. Smyth, a brother of the late Divisional Commissioner. He had been serving in Egypt with the artillery when he persuaded the military authorities to send him on extended leave in Ireland, where Winter got him into Dublin District Special Branch. Smyth's highly personal but very dangerous mission to neutralise his brother's supposed killers was very dangerous because even Winter accepted the Tipperary pair were 'brave and fearless gunmen'.[116] After Breen's operation, Crow Street asked him and Treacy to stay on for an important assignment – almost certainly Bloody Sunday – although by now Breen was 'obsessed with the idea that if I remained in Dublin my days were numbered'.[117] With the city centre increasingly dangerous territory, Breen and Treacy fled Kirwan's pub on 10 October after an employee had reported enemy spotters in the street outside. They sought refuge with the Flemings, a Tipperary family who then lived above their shop on the Drumcondra Road in north Dublin.

As committed republicans, Michael Fleming, his brother James and children Peter, Kay and Dot suspected they were under enemy surveillance and they thought it safer to lodge Breen and Treacy with their friend, Professor Carolan. He taught at the nearby St Patrick's Teachers' Training College, next door to his home, 'Fernside', where he gave them an upstairs bedroom and a key so they could come and go freely. Carolan also pointed out a low wall at the bottom of the back garden as the best escape route in the event of a British raid.[118]

On the evening of 11 October Breen and Treacy bumped into the Fleming sisters at a newly opened cinema in O'Connell Street. Kay thought that a furtive bow-tied civilian was following them but, fearing she had succumbed to spy mania, kept her suspicions to herself. But after inviting the starving pair back for a meal she again spotted 'bow tie' outside the cinema. When the party returned, Michael Fleming reported seeing the spotter loitering outside.

Despite the curfew drawing near, Breen and Treacy thought it safer to slip out of the back door and return to Fernside, quietly making their way upstairs in darkness to the room where they shared a bed. Breen placed a loaded revolver on a chair while Treacy slipped his weapon under the pillow, alongside a crucifix and rosary beads. After chatting for a while they dozed off. Soon afterwards an armoured car and lorries carrying British soldiers and military intelligence officers pulled up outside. The convoy included Major Smyth and Captain Robert Jeune, who later claimed they had only gone 'on chance to Professor Carolan's house'[119] after drawing a blank at a house in Dun Laoghaire. But even if the raid was not based on a specific tip-off, Carolan and Fernside were clearly high on the British suspect list – and not by chance.

Hearing running engines, Carolan hurriedly tapped a warning on the upstairs bedroom door before returning to the hallway, where an impatient raiding party had already smashed in the front door's glass panels. Breen and Treacy heard voices demanding men's names and a noise from the back garden where Jeune's men had taken up position. A dazzling searchlight beam trained on the bedroom momentarily disoriented Breen, though he still registered the single peal of a nearby church bell. The sound of footsteps on the stairs caused him and Treacy to leap out of bed, hurriedly don socks, shirts and trousers and grab their weapons. When the locked door handle began turning slowly, Treacy whispered, 'Good-bye, Dan, until we meet above'.[120] Suddenly two bullets ripped through the door panel. Breen shot back, firing almost literally blind in the darkened house and guided to the attackers' location by their English voices on the stairs:

> Bullets were flying from every direction, and our door had been pushed partly open. I blazed away on to the landing. Blood was streaming from my right thumb but I felt no pain. I heard a thud on the landing as if somebody had fallen. Sean could not find his glasses. This was a severe handicap to him as he was very short-sighted. Worse, still, his gun had jammed. I shouted to him to get back to the window. He stepped back, just as another bullet buried itself in the wardrobe. I felt a sharp pain in the region of my spine. Feeling certain that my days were numbered I told him to make his escape and that I would join him when I had fought my way through.[121]

As Breen raked the landing, he heard retreating footsteps on the stairs, but soon electric torch beams appeared followed by gunfire which hit his forehead, thigh, both legs and a lung. Breen expected to die at any moment but was determined to go down shooting. Reloading, he fired until the soldiers retreated and in the ensuing lull he heard occasional cries, groans and the wailing of Carolan's young son.

Once again, the British attackers regrouped and crept back upstairs. Once again, Breen emptied his gun before retreating to the bedroom, stepping over the bodies of an officer, a soldier writhing in agony and Smyth – who ironically had died at the hands of someone he had mistakenly blamed for killing his beloved brother. In the bedroom, Breen was surprised to find that Treacy had disappeared. He assumed his partner had fled through the half-open window, believing Breen to be dead on the landing. Breen decided to leave the same way and, luckily for him, Jeune and most of his men had raced to the front when the gun battle erupted.[122] After crashing through the glass conservatory roof, Breen dangled from a beam, bleeding from head to foot and firing at glittering steel helmets. He then groped his way to the low wall at the bottom of the garden, climbed over, crossed neighbours' gardens and eventually stumbled on to the main Drumcondra road. Realising that he would soon encounter another British party, Breen scaled the high wall of St Patrick's Training College. With blood flowing from his forehead and drifting in and out of consciousness, he crossed the college grounds and exited over walls at the other side. After wading the river Tolka, Breen stood on the opposite bank, lost, shivering and at the end of his endurance. Deciding to throw himself on the kindness of strangers, he knocked on a door. 'I realised well enough what a spectacle I must have presented at such an unearthly hour, half-clad, dishevelled and bloodstained. For the second time I knocked. A man opened the door. My appearance was sufficient explanation. I mumbled that I needed shelter, and instantly swooned. As though from far away I heard his words, 'I do not approve of gunmen, I shall call the military.' A woman's voice reprimanded him: 'If you do, I'll report you to Michael Collins.'[123]

The man, Mr Holmes, was a retired policeman and a Unionist. But, despite the curfew, his wife summoned a neighbour, Nurse Long, to staunch Breen's bleeding wounds.

Although Breen believed that Treacy was dead, he too had crashed through the conservatory and made it over the low garden wall. Bleeding from hands and knees and clad only in shirt, trousers and socks, Treacy pushed northwards to a friend's Finglas home, where, in the early morning hours, he at last fell asleep.

At Fernside, Jeune's search party stood amidst the debris of what he acknowledged had been a 'disastrous raid'.[124] A couple of IRA gunmen had killed two British officers and broken through a supposedly impenetrable cordon, leaving only the badly wounded Carolan in custody. Winter claimed that the raiders found Breen and Treacy's overcoats in the hallway, which, if true, can only have heightened their fury at the hapless professor. Subsequently, a British military inquiry decided he had been hit in the crossfire, probably by Breen and Treacy. But Carolan lingered on in hospital for another fortnight and swore in a dying declaration that a British officer had ordered him to face a wall before shooting him in the back. His claim was effectively corroborated by Robert Jeune, who was still cursing himself for not staying at the rear of the house when 'from the garden, I heard a single shot – which made one think that there might be a gunman in the house. But far from that it was a most unfortunate accident – which involved Professor Carolan being shot by mistake while being questioned.'[125] By now a cynical public was accustomed to controversial deaths occurring while someone supposedly 'resisted arrest' or 'attempted to escape', but shot while trying to answer questions was a startling addition to the official lexicon.

The British intelligence officers clearly knew about Carolan's connection to the Flemings, on whose home they soon descended. While they searched, Nurse Long arrived, ostensibly to get brandy for a difficult patient, but really to say that Breen was alive and in need of clothes and medical assistance. The raiders eventually left, taking Michael and James Fleming, who refused under questioning to give up Breen and Treacy. James's interrogator at Mountjoy, an intelligence officer called Captain Donald McLean, was added to Crow Street's assassination list.[126]

Nurse Long contacted a Volunteer officer, Joe Lawless, who arrived to take Breen to hospital. He found Breen lying on a mattress, semi-conscious and in excruciating pain.[127] Collins and McKee had already arranged his admission to the Mater, which treated wounded Volunteers off the books – something that Winter had long suspected. As the hospital was situated only a mile from Fernside, he wanted to search it for Breen and Treacy. But Anderson was afraid of a patient dying if his bandages were removed and took three days getting Cabinet approval,[128] a delay that allowed Breen to be spirited inside. As his car waited in a nearby garage while the Eccles Street entrance was checked, Treacy arrived for an emotional reunion. When the all-clear came, he helped carry Breen's stretcher inside, shook his hand and left. They never saw each other again. On the morning of Thursday 14 October, Winter was finally allowed to enter the Mater but when the raiding party arrived Breen was hurriedly concealed in the Maternity Home. Eventually the searchers gave up and left.

When Paddy Daly visited Treacy's safe house at Inchicore, he found him lying on a sofa, weary, despondent and clearly lost without Breen. But Treacy was adamant about keeping an appointment with Dick McKee at the Republican Outfitters in Talbot Street, a shop which Breen acknowledged was 'so closely watched that it was never advisable to remain there for long'.[129] And on that particular day there was a large military presence on the streets for the funeral of the British officers killed at Fernside. McKee and Clancy were already at the Republican Outfitters discussing with Brigade officers and GHQ Intelligence leaders plans to attack Greenwood, Tudor and others in the funeral procession. But when Tobin, Cullen and Thornton learnt that the targets would be staying away, they left the premises. Outside they passed Treacy, who was on his way to the shop.[130]

Soon afterwards, Clancy left the Republican Outfitters on other business just as an armoured car and a lorry carrying British soldiers and intelligence officers turned the corner into Talbot Street. McKee was chatting with Treacy, three Volunteers and an assistant when he heard the vehicles some distance away, looked out and shouted a warning to flee. McKee got away just before the convoy, by chance or design, stopped outside the shop.[131] While the others hesitated Treacy walked out, ignoring the raiders as they leapt down on to the pavement. Treacy then jumped on a bicycle that someone had left standing on the pavement. But it was much too big for him, and, while Treacy manoeuvred it, a British intelligence officer called Christian recognised him and ran forward shouting 'This is Treacy!' Treacy shot Christian and wrestled him to the ground, where they struggled violently. Treacy got a few more shots off, which held the other British officers at bay, and tried turning his weapon inwards against the more powerful but visibly weakening Christian. But, when Christian's colleagues saw Treacy about to break free, they fired on him, and the armoured car crew joined in with machine-gun bursts. When the firing ceased, Treacy and Christian were lying dead on the pavement while nearby another British agent called Price lay fatally wounded. Two civilians had also been killed.

When Treacy's body reached the Castle, Winter compared its 'white and pallid face'[132] with a captured photograph and closed his voluminous file on the Tipperary man. But it was not over for Crow Street and the Squad, which both thirsted for vengeance. On Saturday 16 October two Tipperary policemen, Sergeant Roche and Constable Fitzmaurice, arrived to identify a mangled body lying in the Mater that the Castle hoped was Breen's, but when Neligan took them to the hospital Roche exclaimed in disappointment, 'That's not Dan Breen. I'd know Dan Breen's ugly mug anywhere.'[133] The dead man was a Dublin Volunteer who had accidentally blown himself up. Neligan then arranged to show the visitors around the city next day, an arrangement he casually mentioned to Tobin later that evening. On Sunday afternoon Neligan was waiting for Roche and Fitzmaurice outside the Ormond Hotel when four Squad members suddenly arrived to assassinate them. Neligan had not remotely considered this a possibility, in the light of the Tipperary policemen's marginal involvement with Breen and Treacy. Neligan initially pleaded for their lives, but when he saw Roche and Fitzmaurice strolling along the Quays he reluctantly acquiesced to their execution. After briefly chatting with the policemen Neligan made an excuse and left, discreetly waving a handkerchief in their direction as a signal to Joe Dolan and Frank Thornton, the designated gunmen. The Squad joined in as well, killing Roche instantly. Fitzmaurice was wounded and pursued up Capel Street but still escaped through the cordon.

Neligan regarded this as the most terrible episode of his life. At the Castle afterwards he was immediately summoned to meet the RIC's top brass and a shaken Fitzmaurice, who claimed he had seen Neligan talking to Roche's killers. Somehow Neligan kept his head and bluffed his way out by reminding Fitzmaurice that he had mentioned his Dublin trip to a lady at Limerick Junction station. Incredibly, when the woman was arrested, she turned out to be an IRA intelligence officer. This was the closest call of Neligan's espionage career.

Seven months later Crow Street identified 'bow tie', the suspected betrayer of Breen and Treacy, as Robert Pike, a former soldier who lived in a cottage near the Flemings' back gate. Shortly after leaving a pub at closing time, Pike was shot on his way home when a member of the Squad dismounted from a bicycle near the Tolka bridge, fired three times and rode away.[134]

* * *

High on the IRA's hate list were 'Hoppy' Hardy and Major Percival, the British officer commanding west Cork. Hardy was difficult to get at in Dublin because of his heavy escort, but he was vulnerable on leave in England. When Detective MacNamara told Crow Street that Hardy was going on leave, it arranged for Joe Dolan to shadow him on the boat and then on the train to London. There Hardy 'got off the train slowly at Euston – his wooden leg was a handicap. But once on the platform he bobbed off to a waiting taxi faster than I ever saw him go before. He must have felt he was being followed. He was gone like a flash and there wasn't a taxi near enough for me to chase him.'[135] Dolan watched the railway station for days until Hardy finally reappeared, whereupon he sent a coded telegram to Vaughan's Hotel. Tobin dispatched the Squad to get Hardy at Dun Laoghaire, but it could only watch helplessly from a distance as a double-turreted armoured car collected him safely.

Collins took a close personal interest in Percival, whose ruthlessness made him feared and hated in Collins's own home area of west Cork. In July 1920 Percival led a party of soldiers and police which caught Tom Hales, commandant of 3rd Cork Brigade, and a Volunteer, Tom Harte, in a farmhouse near Bandon. Hales claimed that Percival and Colonel Kelly, General Strickland's chief intelligence officer, planted bullets on him and that he and Harte were bound with leather straps, punched in the face, beaten with a revolver butt and prodded with bayonets. At Bandon military barracks they were placed in front of a firing squad and put through a mock execution photographed by a British officer, by which time Harte had gone insane. Later, Hales was brought before a group of officers and accused of organising every murder in the area. He claimed he was hit forty times, lost four teeth, was hurled to the ground and had pliers used on his hands. An automatic pistol was placed against his temple and he was warned that if he did not give up the names of battalion commanders he would be shot. Hales said he kept silent and the officer finally left the room. According to Hales he was then put in a hospital ward along with a dozen wounded policemen who shouted for his blood day and night. On 20 August a court martial sentenced him to two years' hard labour in prison. There he was contacted by Collins, who had been in Frongoch with his brother Sean and had chaired the 3rd Brigade's inaugural meeting in January 1919 when Tom had been elected OC. Hales sent graphic descriptions of his treatment, which made a deep impression on Collins. Broy recorded that when describing Hales's treatment 'the impression he created was as vivid as if one actually saw the pliers being used to tear the flesh of the victim'.[136]

But Winter claimed – without producing any corroborative evidence – that Hales had voluntarily given up the names of many Volunteer officers and only invented a cover story to protect himself from IRA retribution.[137] Hales gave Collins the names of his interrogators while Florrie O'Donoghue, the Cork IRA's chief intelligence officer, got Kelly's maid to steal his photograph and that of the mock execution. He also told Collins that Percival was vacationing in London and at Dovercourt on the south-east coast. Collins dispatched Frank Thornton to England with an assassination unit. Although Percival was safely ensconced inside Dovercourt's military barracks, Thornton discovered that he was returning to Ireland through London's Liverpool Street station. Thornton's team was in place a quarter of an hour before Percival's anticipated arrival when at the last moment Collins's man in London, Sam Maguire, suddenly arrived. A Scotland Yard contact had tipped him off that the CID had spotted Thornton's men and were preparing to surround the station. They escaped just before a military and police cordon was thrown around Liverpool Street.[138]

Crow Street and the Squad also wanted to kill John Ellis and Thomas Pierrepont, the official hangmen whom Dublin Castle imported from England. Of these experienced executioners, Ellis had a more celebrated client list that included Dr Crippen and Sir Roger Casement, but Pierrepont outdid him in sheer dogged productivity. By the time Pierrepont finally hung up his rope after forty years' service, this equal-opportunities executioner had dispatched over 300 men and women. Crow Street had tremendous difficulty in getting at Ellis and Pierrepont because of the security blackout which always shrouded their movements in Dublin. Once Tobin believed they were travelling through Kingstown (Dun Laoghaire) and ordered the Squad to scrutinise disembarking ferry passengers, but in fact Ellis and Pierrepont always arrived a few days early to be driven to Mountjoy in an armoured car. One warder suggested to Collins that he substitute a bottle of poison for the five noggins of whiskey stipulated in Pierrepont's contract, only to be told very firmly, 'This isn't war.'[139] Another time Ben Byrne recalled the Squad assembling for an attack on Pierrepont at the Gresham Hotel but 'unfortunately, the British were not quite as simple as we had led ourselves to believe, and the Gresham Hotel story would appear to have been sent out merely as a red herring. Pierrepont did not stay in a hotel during his visit here, and was, in fact here two or three days prior to the executions. He stayed in Mountjoy all the time.'[140]

* * *

In early October 1920 Tudor and Winter finally moved into the Castle, where they managed a semblance of a social life as Tudor played golf under heavy escort and Winter attended race meetings and the Royal Dublin Horse Show. But their presence only heightened the Castle's already febrile atmosphere. Anderson's team was united by a common purpose and mutual respect but their personalities often grated on each other. Sturgis was exasperated by the neurasthenic Cope's threats of resignation and frequent retirements to bed with exhaustion. Tudor's former soldiers kept their distance from the civil servants; yet another clique in a nest of cliques. But Sturgis was able to observe Winter close up with appalled fascination: 'a marvel – he looks like a wicked white snake and can do everything . . . a super sleuth and a most amazing original.'[141] Sturgis's doubts about Winter multiplied as he watched him in action and listened to his constant complaints about colleagues. Senior civil servants were soon manoeuvring to sideline Winter. In mid-November 1920 Sturgis reported him 'struggling against a rising tide of overwork and insufficient – (or inefficient, perhaps both) staff. The great Andy is to thoroughly overhaul, advise and get going the organisation.'[142]

But, while his detractors carped or tried to marginalise him, Winter was there for the duration, protected by Tudor and Greenwood. Whatever Sturgis's occasional fantasies about Cope as Chief of Police, the various Castle factions were stuck with each other. Not that it bothered Winter, who by mid-October 1920 believed he had the Dublin IRA on the run. However, Collins already had plans in the pipeline to jolt his burgeoning optimism.

Chapter 5

SEEKING A KNOCKOUT BLOW

COLLINS AND BLOODY SUNDAY, 21 NOVEMBER 1920

By late 1920 the British resurgence in Dublin had forced both Volunteer GHQ and McKee's Brigade on to the defensive as a sustained military build-up, and the newly arrived Auxiliaries seemingly wrested the initiative from the IRA. McKee's Brigade appeared to be unable to prevent the enemy achieving a psychological ascendancy in the capital, and between July and Bloody Sunday it could not mount a single attack on the Auxiliaries or kill a single British soldier. Paradoxically, although McKee was a dynamic Brigadier revered by his own men, he had spread himself too thinly by serving also as GHQ Director of Training and producing the IRA newspaper *An t-Oglac*. He had even allowed his Vice-Brigadier, Peadar Clancy, to run a draper's shop, which the British kept under constant surveillance. Most crucially of all, McKee had neglected to create an active service unit to wage a full-blown military campaign in Dublin. While the British poured in reinforcements, most Dublin Volunteers remained in full-time civilian employment, even though a curfew had restricted opportunities for night-time attacks. All this meant that until the end of 1920 the Squad was effectively the IRA's Dublin campaign. This lacklustre performance began to produce muffled frustration with McKee at Volunteer GHQ, but McKee's standing with the rank and file and a strong relationship with Collins and Mulcahy stymied change until after his death.

By late 1920 there was a real British belief that the summer's administrative and personnel changes and the commitment of military and police resources were beginning to tell and would eventually grind down the IRA in a war of attrition. For the first time in many months optimism surged not just in the Castle but in Downing Street, Scotland House and even British Army GHQ in Dublin. On 25 September Greenwood told Law euphorically that 'the tide has turned . . . Today a fellow came from Dail Eireann. I said

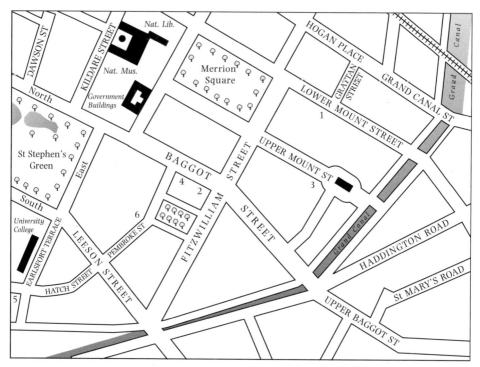

Map 3. Bloody Sunday: Main assassination area, south central Dublin

1 Lieutenant McMahon (killed)
2 Captain Newbury (killed)
3 Lieutenant Bennett (killed)
   Lieutenant Ames (killed)
4 Captain Baggallay (killed)
5 Captain Fitzgerald (killed)
6 Lieutenant-Colonel Woodcock (wounded)
   Colonel Montgomery (fatally wounded)
   Captain Keenlyside (wounded)
   Lieutenant Murray (wounded)
   Major Dowling (killed)
   Captain Price (killed)

Also

117 Morehampton Road
   Captain McClean (killed)
   Thomas Smith (killed)
   John Cadlow (wounded)

Gresham Hotel
   Captain McCormack (killed)
   Lieutenant Wilde (killed)

Griffiths [*sic*] the Vice president must come out in the open publicly. It's the first feeler. Let 'em feel a bit more!'[1] Next day Macready told the Cabinet that the military situation was improving with Volunteer casualties increasing and army and police morale rising, especially after its stand against MacSwiney's hunger strike. He warned, however, that 'the effect of this on the extremists is to make them desperate – they feel that they have their backs to the wall and that desperate measures are necessary. We may therefore expect to see a temporary increase of murder and outrage.'[2] On 13 November Macready reported continued progress. Rebel attacks were down, and, although men on the run were supposedly being organised into flying columns, he believed they really wanted to stay in hiding. Moderate nationalists were openly asserting themselves and previously ardent supporters of rebellion were wavering, all of which tended 'greatly to the disorganisation and depression of the rebel forces and their leaders'.[3] On 29 October Basil Thomson had reported that police recruitment was up, and the belief 'that Sinn Fein is going to get the worst of the struggle seems to be growing'.[4] Such optimism proved infectious, and in a speech at the Guildhall on 9 November Lloyd George boasted that he now had 'murder by the throat'.[5] Winter, too, had a spring in his step as his agents and Wilson's Special Branch appeared to be getting the upper hand in the intelligence war. Notice had been served on Liam Lynch, Dan Breen was temporarily inactive and Sean Treacy had been rendered permanently inactive. A widespread belief that the British were operating a shoot-to-kill policy was proving a decidedly effective weapon in Winter's campaign to reclaim the streets of Dublin. His mounting conviction that he had the IRA on the run was strengthened by the behaviour of the highly visible Auxiliaries. Unlike G Division, they were not holed up in the Castle; they now literally swaggered through the streets of Dublin with their holsters slung around their hips, ready to use their revolvers at the slightest provocation.

Only one Cabinet member, the Secretary of State for India, Edwin Montague, dissented from the prevailing optimism. On 10 November 1920 he requested a discussion of the Irish situation, frustrated that, like most of his colleagues, he had been excluded not just from policy formation but even from access to reliable information. All he had to rely on was the newspapers and they were telling a very different story. 'I read with a glow of hope the Chief Secretary's assurances that things are improving. Am I wrong in thinking that his splendid optimism must sometimes be daunted by what appears to be the increasing frequency of murder on the one hand or the other?'[6] Montague was deeply anxious that 'terror is answered by terror, crime by crime, blood by blood. I feel a growing conviction that even if the murder gang in Ireland can be destroyed by this process – which I doubt – the younger generation in Ireland is being educated in murderous thought.' Keeping Ireland inside the British imperial system by such methods was counter-productive, because a Carthaginian peace would leave a permanently embittered population. 'We have got to live with these men, or rather the survivors. The Prime Minister yesterday described the situation as one of war. Does it not follow that we should consider the termination of the war?'[7]

On the Irish side, Crow Street believed the new British intelligence offensive in Dublin was intended to decapitate Volunteer GHQ. Thornton felt the enemy had 'built up quite a formidable organisation and were without doubt securing quite a lot of very valuable information',[8] while Mulcahy admitted that 'the pressure on us was very great; we were being made to feel that they were very close on the heels of some of us'.[9] In September and November 1920 Mulcahy devised proposals to disrupt British intelligence-gathering in the capital by having unarmed enemy officers stopped unexpectedly in the streets, reducing their interaction with the population and forcing them to move around in armed parties. He also recommended confronting them in hotels, restaurants and theatres and confiscating any concealed weapons, papers and identity cards. Mulcahy thought these counter-measures 'would have the effect of throwing the English troops on the defensive. Especially it would interfere with their facilities for securing knowledge from police and civilian sources.'[10]

In September the British resurgence caused a reorganisation of Volunteer GHQ. Peadar Clancy became GHQ's Director of Munitions and Frank Henderson, 2nd Battalion commandant, joined the Department of Organisation while Oscar Traynor succeeded Clancy as McKee's deputy.[11] Soon afterwards the British captured 4th Battalion's commandant with a list of his most active Volunteers, many of whom were quickly arrested. Second Battalion also suffered losses. It blamed these on a local military policeman, John Ryan, but McKee vetoed his execution because of insufficient evidence.[12] A Brigade officer noted a corrosive impact 'on the morale of the men, particularly as the Auxiliaries were now so much in evidence everywhere and we seemed to have withdrawn completely from the fight. We agreed that some action would have to be taken to counteract this influence.'[13] Second Battalion officers recommended a lightning trawl of its area and executing any armed stranger. Again, McKee turned them down, but he intimated that this time it was only because something much bigger was brewing.

Collins believed the British threat to the IRA's position in Dublin demanded dramatic action, and he planned to eliminate many enemy intelligence agents in one massive swoop. It was the gamble of all gambles. But to have done nothing, allowing the situation to deteriorate and watch the British tighten their grip on Dublin, simply was not an option. Collins had invested too much time and effort – as well as reputation – in the struggle for the capital simply to let it slip away. Although the war had spread to many parts of Ireland, the two crucial areas were Dublin and Cork. Defeat in either city would have imperilled the entire revolution. In politics and war Collins's guiding principle was always to get his retaliation in first. Undoubtedly, taking on British intelligence agents in one coordinated operation was enormously risky. By committing the cream of the Dublin Brigade, the Squad and Volunteer GHQ Intelligence, Collins was in a sense putting almost every chip he had into the pot and staking everything on one spin of the wheel. But that was his style, because, once he had decided that the dangers of inaction far outweighed those of action, Collins was never going to walk away from the table. This calculated gambler had done his homework and weighed the odds. Once he had made the decision in principle, all that remained was the question of timing.

Success depended on absolute secrecy, meticulous planning and ruthless execution, both metaphorically and literally. Collins began by compiling dossiers on the new British spies operating in the capital. Normally Tobin would have supervised this, but he had recently suffered a nervous breakdown,[14] and, since Cullen was away on other business, Collins used Thornton and Charlie Dalton.[15] They spent six weeks exploiting every Intelligence Department source in Dublin, while Joseph Griffin, the Dublin Brigade's Intelligence Director, passed on information from his 4th Battalion intelligence officers. Thirty policemen reported nocturnal encounters with people carrying curfew passes and any houses lit up well into the early morning hours. One constable, Patrick Mannix, soon identified suspects living in Upper Mount Street, Shelbourne Road and Morehampton Road.[16] Intelligence also came from Neligan, MacNamara and Mernin at the Castle, while Crow Street's own intelligence officers intercepted letters, shadowed informers and interrogated waiters, footmen, maids and porters. 'Maudie', a maid at 28 Upper Pembroke Street, told Dalton about certain residents acting strangely, following no regular occupation and working mostly from their flats. When she handed over the contents of their waste-paper baskets, Dalton discovered photographs of wanted Volunteers and documents on their movements and associations.[17] Information was also provided by neighbours. Sean Hyde, a veterinary student living in digs in Lower Mount Street, reported that two residents of a furnished lodging house were British intelligence officers using the pseudonyms Peel and McMahon and that McMahon had been out after curfew on the night John Lynch had been killed at the Exchange Hotel. There was even a source in the Auxiliaries' 'F' Company where Sergeant Reynolds topped up his already generous wages by selling information to the IRA.[18]

British carelessness also facilitated IRA intelligence-gathering, because, instead of spies being dispersed throughout the city, some units had been concentrated in private flats and boarding houses. One group shared 28 Upper Pembroke Street with Colonel Woodcock, CO of the 1st Lancashire Fusiliers, his wife Caroline and adjutant Captain Keenlyside. Woodcock certainly knew about the undercover unit, because his wife was aware of residents whom she referred to as the 'Hush Hush Men' who 'came in and went out at odd hours'.[19] One of these intelligence officers, Captain Robert Jeune, had participated in the Fernside raid. He belonged to Wilson's Special Branch, like his flatmate Lieutenant Murray, a close friend 'Chummy' Dowling, Peter Ames, George Bennett and Leonard Price.[20] Such concentration no doubt facilitated the pooling of information, and it was probably assumed that so many agents were proof against IRA ambush. The agents also congregated in city centre haunts such as the Café Cairo and Kidd's Buffet in Grafton Street.

Thornton brought some Crow Street colleagues incognito to these places, where he was amused by the agents' assumption that he, too, was English:

'Cor blimey, how did you learn the Irish brogue! We're here in Dublin for the last twelve months and we can't pick up any of it, yet you fellows seem to have perfected it.' Of course, naturally we told them that there was an art in these matters, and just passed it over. Naturally men of this kind were very little use to the British but they didn't realise that until it was too late.[21]

Thornton and others were introduced

in the ordinary way as touts and eventually became great friends of men like Major Bennett, Colonel Ames and other prominent Secret Service officers. Naturally Collins and all his staff and the whole activities of the organisation were discussed there daily. On one day, one of these officers turned suddenly to Tom Cullen and said, 'Surely you fellows know these men – Liam Tobin, Tom Cullen and Frank Thornton, these are Collins's three officers and if you can get these fellows we would locate Collins himself.' Needless to remark, if the ground opened and swallowed us we could not have been more surprised, and for the moment we felt we had walked into a trap, but that wasn't so at all. It was a genuine query.[22]

But, although Wilson's Special Branch was making progress in identifying its enemy counterparts, inter-service rivalry meant it was keeping this information to itself. Thornton also claimed that in one location the IRA managed to get a member appointed hall porter and that gradually others were infiltrated into the staff of various houses. They collected valuable information about British agents and purloined keys for the hall door and individual rooms. According to Thornton, 'we tracked down and got a complete detailed report on every individual'.[23]

Eventually, Thornton and Dalton recommended executing nearly sixty British intelligence officers at twenty locations.[24] But trying to kill so many enemy agents piecemeal over time was clearly futile and so Collins decided to risk a coordinated pre-emptive strike, a concept which must also have appealed to his sense of the dramatic and his willingness to play for the highest stakes. Collins's conviction that only decisive action could prevent enemy mastery of Dublin was shared by McKee, whose Brigade guarded the national institutions and leadership. Mulcahy too thought it 'a question of time only until a well-organised series of British raids would act against the Dail, GHQ and brigade offices, with a gang in the background to shoot dangerous men'.[25]

Massacring enemy agents also risked provoking large British troop reinforcements, internment and deportations, army and Auxiliary rampages and further executions. For months Macready had warned about the consequences of high-profile IRA assassinations. Strickland's death in September, he claimed, would have turned Cork into another Sodom and Gomorrah, while 'if they killed Tudor there would hardly be a village within ten miles of a Black and Tans detachment that would not be in flames within 24 hours'.[26] In early October Macready told a Downing Street security conference that if General Boyd 'got killed the best part of Dublin would be in flames and I told them quite straight that I should make no attempt whatever to stop it because I was quite convinced that it would be useless to do so'. [27] On 27 September 1920 a Head Constable was shot dead in a public house near Balbriggan in north County Dublin. Within hours the town was sacked by lorryloads of Black and Tans from the Gormanston depot, who burned down a woollen mill, thirty shops and houses, fired indiscriminately at terrified inhabitants and killed two men at random.[28]

While the Irish administration generally sympathised with the Black and Tans, it knew that this time they had gone too far. Sturgis would have accepted the 'dignified shooting' of two men whom he believed, wrongly, were prominent Sinn Feiners, but 'the burning spoilt the whole thing. Still, worse things can happen than the firing up of a sink like Balbriggan and surely the people who say "Stop the murders before all our homes go up in smoke" must increase.'[29] By now Macready hated Ireland, longed for 'somebody to sink it under the seas'[30] and considered that if the Black and Tans had eliminated only 'well known members of the Murder Gang when their own officers and comrades are murdered I should remain silent. But this wholesale burning not only does no good, or at least very little, that I am afraid they will get so out of hand that it will require half the British army to get rid of them.'[31]

Gormanston was about half an hour's drive from Dublin and wiping out British intelligence officers risked precipitating an even bigger Balbriggan, especially if Auxiliaries in the capital also ran amok. Collins also had to consider public reaction to a massacre, especially in the event of serious British retaliation. While IRA leaders would hide in safe houses, Collins could do nothing to protect the civilian population: the ordinary Dubliners were on their own.

Because of the scale of the proposed operation, Collins needed the top-level approval of a Dail government that normally distanced itself from IRA actions. At a unique joint session of the Cabinet and Volunteer GHQ Thornton argued 'that each and every man on my list was an accredited secret service man of the British government'.[32] Even so, Brugha still removed some names because of insufficient evidence. Despite a contemporary British assertion, endorsed by some later historians, that provincial Volunteers perpetrated Bloody Sunday, Collins delegated operational responsibility to the Dublin Brigade. McKee, in turn, entrusted detailed planning to Sean Russell, the 27-year-old commandant of 2nd Battalion, who shared his Brigadier's organising brilliance and an anti-English fanaticism that survived into the 1930s, when he controlled an IRA bombing campaign in British cities and only ceased with his death in 1940 on board a Nazi submarine. Russell's contribution to Bloody Sunday has never been remotely recognised, yet, while Collins devised and produced this savage drama, he was its unacknowledged director.

Russell planned Bloody Sunday at Dublin Brigade headquarters in Lower Gardiner Street. For three weeks, he and McKee met battalion commandants, Squad leaders and Intelligence Department representatives, outlining details, distributing names and addresses of enemy agents and identifying Volunteers needed for an operation encompassing every battalion area. Since British spies were predominantly nocturnal creatures, spending much of their free time indoors, Russell believed they were most vulnerable on Sunday mornings, when people slept late and relaxed and assassination units were most likely to surprise armed and experienced enemy officers. Dublin's suffocating inertia disgusted one British intelligence agent: 'No one is ever astir before ten o'clock, and the vast army of R.I. constables, D.M. Police, ex-officers, servants and lady clerks which had been assembled in the Castle to put down the Sinn Fein Rebellion did not take long to capture the careless rapture of Irish slothfulness, and used to remain abed until the sun had warmed the day.'[33] Russell had learnt from 1916, when the Military Council used the Easter holidays as a smokescreen to start the Rising. On Sunday 21 November, a major GAA match scheduled for Croke Park would have the city in similarly festive mood and lull the British authorities into a false sense of security. Russell planned simultaneous attacks, otherwise British agents at some locations would have time for defensive measures. The attacks would have to be brief so that Volunteers could escape over the Liffey before the British closed its bridges and swamped Dublin with troops.[34]

Russell estimated that this commando-style operation required well over 100 men, far beyond the Squad's resources and requiring many inexperienced Volunteers, whose appetite and aptitude for close-order killings was uncertain. One, Todd Andrews, believed

the prospect of killing a man in cold blood was alien to our ideas of how war should be conducted. We were apprehensive, too, because it could be a very dangerous operation. We were already being affected psychologically by the terror of the Tans. I had increasing fears that we might be surprised by the Tans. If that happened and we were captured, we would have been shot or hanged. It is not an agreeable prospect for a nineteen-year-old psychologically unattuned to assassination.[35]

Russell took care to reassure his apprehensive novices and minimised their chances of being recognised by rotating the assassination units around the city's battalion areas. Members of the 1st and 2nd Battalions north of the Liffey would strike in the southern side of the city and 3rd and 4th Battalions north of the river, except for the Gresham Hotel in Upper O'Connell Street, which Russell assigned to 2nd Battalion.

During the final week Russell accelerated preparations dramatically. He allocated targets to senior battalion officers, whom he ordered to reconnoitre locations and choose their men from approved lists. Russell reduced the risk of leaks and the time for doubts by telling rank and file Volunteers about the operation only in the last few days. Assassination units were to consist of at least eight men, almost all led by a Squad member and a GHQ intelligence officer, who were to exercise tight control over their untested subordinates. Because even the Squad specialised in outdoor assassination of individuals and not indoor battles with trained gunmen, Russell wanted to catch enemy agents literally napping and unable to use their personal weapons. Unit leaders were to station guards in hallways, on pavements and behind houses to deal with awkward civilians and cut off escapers. While some brought sledgehammers, these were to smash down locked doors – not, as the British subsequently alleged, to crush victims' skulls. GHQ intelligence officers would accompany every unit to seize papers, maps and documents.

Every unit was to agree an assembly point to which most men would come on foot just before the synchronised start at nine o'clock, allowing time for a final reconnaissance. But some Volunteers would use cars for a quick escape or to smuggle weapons away. In some cases, though, the guns were to be handed over to female civilians. Russell also arranged for units to return safely to their own battalion areas. Some Squad members living on the southern side were to go straight home. But others, including unit leaders reporting to Russell's command post in a North Richmond Street house, had to cross the Liffey. Just in case the British quickly closed its bridges, a commandeered ferry would operate between the North and South Wall quays. Volunteers could also use safe houses at Ashbourne on the city outskirts.

A final complication that last weekend was British raids and searches for 200 Volunteers listed in Mulcahy's captured papers. On Friday 19 November, Sturgis gleefully recorded troops 'raiding tonight for these beauties and will have them on the run anyway if they've taken fright and bolted'.[36] Saturday 20 November was for last-minute meetings at Brigade Headquarters. McKee and Russell checked that unit leaders had reconnoitred targets and briefed their men about the Liffey ferry crossing. Russell also made the Squad's Paddy Daly responsible for first aid at North Richmond Street headquarters, a deliberate sidelining which Daly bitterly resented.[37] To avoid forewarning the British, Russell did not stand down Volunteers who were due to steward the GAA game at Croke Park on Sunday afternoon. He intended to avoid trouble at the ground by withdrawing them late on Sunday morning.[38] Russell and McKee also met car drivers and ordered intelligence officers to deliver any confiscated intelligence papers to North Richmond Street.

Repeatedly on Saturday, the IRA leadership felt it necessary to stiffen Volunteers' resolve. Joe Leonard recalled McKee warning

all those present of the gravity of the action to be taken on the next morning, Sunday. He explained that it was of vital importance to exterminate enemy intelligence officers who were residing in hotels and boarding houses in the centre of the city and who had become a terrible menace to our organisation and said further that he was conscious of the enormous dangers the men would encounter in dealing such a crushing blow to the enemy, and that the moral effect produced would be worth any sacrifice sustained by us.[39]

Collins, Mulcahy and Brugha also turned up to give high-level and visible support, but wavering in the ranks persisted to the very end. Simon Donnelly, 4th Battalion's deputy commandant, warned McKee that he was having tremendous difficulty persuading men to volunteer. 'He understood and realised it was not our usual mode of warfare. "Well, Simon", said he, "do your best. If we don't get them, they will get us".'[40] Captain Paddy Flanagan, leader of the Upper Pembroke Street unit, harangued thirty members of 3rd Battalion, but one man still backed out.[41] In the final hours Russell met a succession of 2nd Battalion units and emphasised that 'the men to be shot were members of a new secret service which the enemy had brought in to the country; that many of them had great reputations as secret servicemen working for England during the recent war; that it was vitally necessary for the success of our fight that they be removed; that no country had scruples about shooting enemy spies in wartime'.[42] There was a last-minute emergency when 'Maudie', the maid at 28 Upper Pembroke Street, tipped off Dalton that Lieutenants Ames and Bennett had just shifted to new lodgings in

Upper Mount Street. Russell hastily assembled a scratch unit under the Squad's Vinnie Byrne.[43]

Finally, late on Saturday night, the IRA leaders retired to Vaughan's Hotel to unwind, but also to steel themselves for momentous events. As the midnight curfew drew near, they began dispersing to safe houses. Brugha and Mulcahy went to a small cottage in the grounds of the Children's Hospital at Temple Street,[44] while McKee and Clancy accepted an offer of accommodation at the nearby Gloucester Street home of an auctioneer called Fitzpatrick. When a trusted porter sensed an imminent raid, Collins, Gearoid O'Sullivan, Diarmuid O'Hegarty and Rory O'Connor slipped across Parnell Square to a top-floor flat, from which soon afterwards Collins watched 'Hoppy' Hardy and King's Auxiliary search party enter Vaughan's. Inside, three of Collins's party, Sean O'Connell, Joseph Kavanagh and Piaras Beaslai, were chatting with Conor Clune, the head clerk of Raheen Rural Industries in Clare, who was in Dublin with his boss, Edward MacLysaght, for an annual audit.[45] Clune knew nothing about Sunday's operations, and only after he and MacLysaght had parted for their separate lodgings did Clune decide to meet up with O'Connell, a fellow Irish-language enthusiast. When Beaslai and O'Connell heard a commotion in the front hall, they fled through the back and climbed a wall into an adjoining garden, where they hid until dawn. Kavanagh had nothing incriminating on him and decided to brazen it out along with Clune, who was shouting histrionically that 'we can die for Ireland as well as anybody else'.[46] When Hardy questioned him, Clune misguidedly claimed he was a guest, even though his name was not in the hotel register. After searching him, Hardy bellowed 'this bloody fellow hasn't even got a toothbrush on him'[47] and arrested Clune.

Some time after midnight Hardy's and King's lorry stopped at Fitzpatrick's house in Gloucester Street, a decaying Georgian thoroughfare in the city's red-light district close to O'Connell Street. When they banged on the door, McKee and Clancy began burning incriminating papers about Sunday's plans, a delay which prompted the Auxiliaries to smash their way inside, arrest both men and Fitzpatrick, and try unsuccessfully to rescue the documents in the fireplace. Why Fitzpatrick's house was raided is still uncertain. Oscar Traynor thought McKee was careless about his personal security and that he and Clancy had been shadowed from Vaughan's,[48] while McKee's sister Moira said 'Collins was very doubtful of Fitzpatrick',[49] whose adopted daughter associated with Auxiliaries and later decamped to England. Collins's former secretary Eithne Lawless, who had entered a Gloucester Street convent, claimed that before the raid she saw a white piece of paper pinned to Fitzpatrick's door and that it was subsequently removed. This, she deduced, was a signal to the Auxiliaries.[50] But intense British army and police activity was occurring that weekend and quite possibly the Auxiliaries were only checking out a house which two strangers had been seen entering just before curfew. That the raiders knocked and waited hardly suggests a swoop on known, dangerous, high-ranking IRA officers. With its three detainees, the Auxiliary patrol headed back to the Castle, collecting Clune from Vaughan's on the way.

As the curfew took hold, Captain Robert Jeune slipped out of 28 Upper Pembroke Street to lead a search for IRA arms at Inchicore railway yards. His fellow intelligence officers had Saturday night off and were dining with Ames and Bennett before they transferred to new lodgings in Upper Mount Street. The American consul was another guest, but he declined an invitation to stay overnight. Jeune remembered morale was high as 'information was coming in well and we were beginning to get on top of the IRA who were becoming desperate. I happened to receive information from three different sources to the effect that something was going to happen, but there was nothing definite.'[51] After a couple of hours unsuccessfully trawling the railway yards Jeune decided against returning to his lodgings and handing over to Dowling. Instead, he bedded down for the night in a railway carriage.

Unlike most Dubliners, Volunteers on duty that Sunday morning rose early and some even attended Mass before heading off to prearranged meeting places. Tom Keogh and Jim Slattery's Lower Mount Street unit consisted of two intelligence officers and seven 2nd Battalion Volunteers: Frank Teeling, Billy McLean, Sean Smith, Jim Dempsey, Andy Monaghan, Denis Begley and Dinny O'Driscoll.[52] Lower Mount Street ran from Merrion Square to the Grand Canal and was part commercial and part residential in character, with a sprinkling of offices and nursing homes. Number 22 was a furnished lodging house, and, when the unit assembled, Keogh and Slattery went over the operational details once again before posting McLean outside as a scout.[53] Soon afterwards a maid answered a knock on the front door and a stranger stepped inside, asking to see Mr McMahon, for whom he had a letter. Just as the maid was telling him she did not know if McMahon was in, another man entered looking for Mr Peel and 'he then produced a revolver and said, "Come along show us the rooms. None of your nonsense."'[54] After the main group of Volunteers had rushed in, the maid followed Keogh and Slattery upstairs, shouting, possibly as a warning, 'Mr McMahon, quick, there are some men here.'[55] On the first-floor landing the maid was forced to point out McMahon's unlocked door to the right and call out for him.[56] She heard McMahon shouting 'What's up?', whereupon Keogh went inside, followed by Monaghan and Begley. Begley recalled that

> the first thing Tom Keogh said was 'Where are your guns, Mac?' There were two men in bed and one answered that he had no guns, only a couple of souvenirs. Tom Keogh said, 'Well, Mac, I must get them whatever they are,' and he walked over to the chest of drawers, opened the top drawer, and took out two guns, one of which was a Colt Automatic, and a smaller gun. Andy Monaghan and myself were at the end of the bed keeping the two men covered with revolvers. When Tom Keogh got the guns he just turned to us and said, 'Carry on, lads', giving us definite instructions that the man named Mac was to be executed; the other man was not to be interfered with.[57]

Begley says that the other man, the 'famous Mr C lay in bed with his eyes closed and his hands over his head; he never spoke'.[58] When they shot McMahon, 'Mr C' supposedly rolled out of bed and hid underneath. In 'Mr C's' version he was sharing a bed with McMahon when they were awakened by shouts of 'Hands up!' and he saw five men at the foot of the bed covering them with revolvers. The leader searched the room, took McMahon's wallet from his coat and then asked where the weapons were kept. After McMahon indicated a bag in the corner, the leader broke it open, removed three revolvers and put them in his pockets. 'Mr C' then heard shooting in the hallway and when someone shouted that the house was being surrounded, the five intruders turned as if to rush out. But the leader raised his revolver and fired at the bed. Begley recalled:

> I saw McMahon raise his arm to cover his face and at the same time I threw myself out of the bed on to the floor practically simultaneously. I heard other shots ring out from the other room. Just as the first shot was fired McMahon gave a yell and I saw him leap up out of the bed. After the men had gone I went round and found McMahon lying under the bed with just his legs sticking out.[59]

Begley then hid under the bed when he heard more firing, fearing that the attackers would return.

The model of a revolutionary chief executive: Michael Collins, Director of Intelligence, Irish Volunteers GHQ.

The leader at play after the cessation of hostilities. Collins (left) relaxes during the interval of a hurling match at Croke Park in September 1921.

Richard Mulcahy, Chief of Staff, Irish Volunteers GHQ, was Collins's nominal superior but also his indispensable ally and protector.

Tom Cullen, Assistant Director of Intelligence, Irish Volunteers GHQ.

Below, left: Frank Thornton, Deputy Assistant Director of Intelligence, Irish Volunteers GHQ.

Below, right: Liam Tobin, Collins's Number Two as Deputy Director of Intelligence, Irish Volunteers GHQ.

Dublin Brigadier Dick McKee (second from right) during his arrest by British troops at a Dail office in Harcourt Street in late 1919. McKee habitually wore a distinctive dark overcoat.

Peadar Clancy, McKee's best friend, closest associate and Deputy Brigadier.

Collins's G Division mole Eamon ('Ned') Broy in his later manifestation as Garda Chief Commissioner.

The Spy in the Castle: Sergeant David Neligan, Dublin Metropolitan Police.

A contemporary group photograph of five members of Collins's Squad. From left to right: Mick McDonnell, Tom Keogh, Vinnie Byrne, Paddy Daly and Jim Slattery.

Assistant Commissioner W.C.F. Redmond, DMP, assassinated on Collins's orders on 21 January 1920. The other officer is T.J. Smyth, Belfast Commissioner, RIC, and soon promoted to Inspector General.

Left: Jack Byrnes ('Jameson'), the British spy who, fatally for himself, got too close to Collins.

Below: Two of the British officers who died on Bloody Sunday, 21 November 1920. Left: Captain G.T Baggallay; right: Major Dowling.

Henry Quinlisk (extreme right), ever the dandy in his Irish Brigade uniform. Unmasked as a British spy while attempting to compromise Collins, he was executed in Cork on 18 February 1920. *(Copyright Jim Herlihy)*

Alan Bell, the high-ranking British security official who was on the trail of the republican movement's finances and paid the price.

The scene of Bell's death in Dublin on 26 March 1920 showing the tram from which he was dragged to his death. The cross marks the spot where he fell, and the arrow points to the pavement to which his body was carried.

The Viceroy Lord French (left) with the new British Army GOC, Sir Nevil Macready.

The Chief Secretary for Ireland 1920–21 Sir Hamar Greenwood seated at his desk.

The new team installed in Dublin Castle in 1920. 'Andy' Cope is seated second from the left. Sir John Anderson is seated third from the left and Mark Sturgis is seated on the extreme right.

Right: Colonel Ormonde de l'Epee Winter, Chief of British Intelligence in Ireland, 1920–1.

Far right: Basil Thomson, Head of the Directorate of Intelligence, London, 1919–2.

All together: 'F' Company Auxiliaries pose for a group photograph in Dublin Castle.

A group of the Tipperary Volunteer leaders. Sean Treacy is second from left seated beside a standing moustached Dan Breen.

Above: Winter's protégé Eugene Igoe posing in Dublin Castle.

Above, right: Captain Jocelyn ('Hoppy') Hardy, the dreaded 'F' Company intelligence officer.

Right: Hervey de Montmorency, 'F' Company intelligence officer.

British soldiers on high security alert outside Mountjoy Gaol during the emotive hunger strike of April 1920.

Some of the English bloodhounds that Winter imported to run fleeing Irish Volunteers to earth.

"Escape'. Using stand-ins, the British staged the alleged attempt by McKee and Clancy to escape from Dublin Castle on Bloody Sunday. Above: the two men with Conor Clure relaxing in humane captivity after their arrest. Below: the scene when the volunteer leaders 'attempt to escape'.

British troops apprehend Volunteer suspects in May 1921 outside the burning Custom House.

Right: Auxiliary guardsmen arrested after the Custom House attack.

Below, left: Two Auxiliaries collect weapons thrown away by Volunteers trying to evade capture as they fled the Custom House.

Below, right: Men detained after the attack await screening by Auxiliaries. Many Volunteers were caught because their hands smelt of paraffin.

The disabled Molly Childers enjoys a brief moment of domestic tranquillity at the family's Bushy Park residence with her son Erskine. (*Reproduced with the kind permission of The Board of Trinity College Dublin*)

Across the landing Slattery had quietly ordered the maid to shout 'Mr Peel, quick, there are some gentlemen here',[60] but the only sound from inside was that of a heavy object being dragged across the floor. Slattery tried to smash his way inside and fired several shots at the door lock, but even after his men had broken the panel, they had to fire blind, as Peel had barricaded the room. Suddenly, shooting erupted downstairs where the housekeeper had spotted a passing Auxiliary patrol and screamed 'Murder!' As Auxiliaries chased McLean into the building, they shot him in the ankle, though he managed to shut the door and return fire through a letterbox. An Auxiliary doing likewise wounded McLean's right hand.[61] After the entire IRA unit had assembled in the hallway, Slattery, Dempsey, Teeling and Begley decided to escape through the rear of the house. They squeezed through a small bathroom window into the back yard, where Slattery and Dempsey jumped a back wall. But Begley was called back inside because of shooting from British intelligence officers living in nearby houses, and Teeling, wounded in the stomach, hid in bushes. At the front, Keogh's group decided to take its chances in the open, and, under Keogh's covering fire, Begley, Monaghan and O'Driscoll dashed outside, followed eventually by Keogh himself. They all managed to reach the Liffey ferry, half a mile away.[62]

In the back garden Auxiliaries discovered the wounded Teeling and gave him ten seconds to reveal his comrades' names. As they counted slowly, their commander, Brigadier-General F.P. Crozier, arrived from Beggar's Bush. Crozier was fully in favour of hanging Volunteers, but only after a fair trial, and he halted the summary execution just in time. The Auxiliaries had also lost two men: Cadets Garnin and Morris. They had been dispatched to speed up reinforcements from Beggar's Bush but had been cornered at Mount Street Bridge by IRA men, who shot them dead in a nearby garden.

Captain Newbury and his pregnant wife lived in a flat at No. 92 Lower Baggot Street, a broad Georgian thoroughfare close to St Stephen's Green. Joe Leonard and Bill Stapleton arrived there with a ten-man unit and, after a last-minute reconnaissance, they rang the doorbell at 9 a.m. Leonard said the housekeeper, Mrs Stack, 'by dumb show pointed out the officer's quarters'[63] in the hall, and he and Stapleton knocked on the front parlour door. Receiving no response, they tried the back parlour door, which a clearly suspicious Newbury opened slightly. Before he could slam it shut, Leonard and Stapleton burst in and pursued him through folding doors into the apartment's front room. Still in his pyjamas, Newbury tried escaping through the window. He did not make it. Leonard and Stapleton hit him with a volley of shots while a guard posted in the street outside also joined in. Stapleton recalled that 'the man's wife was standing in a corner of the room and was in a terrified and hysterical condition'.[64] But Mrs Newbury recalled her dying husband lying slumped over the window ledge, as one killer harangued him about the location of his intelligence papers. After leaving, Leonard counted his men and discovered one missing. He had to get Mrs Stack to open the front door again and race upstairs to retrieve the stranded Volunteer. Mrs Newbury meanwhile had thrown a blanket over her husband's corpse. Soon afterwards she gave birth to a stillborn baby. A few days later she herself died.

Late on Saturday Lieutenants Bennett and Ames had transferred to their new lodgings at 38 Upper Mount Street, where they spent a first and last night. On Sunday morning, Vinnie Byrne's scratch unit assembled in Westland Row at eight o'clock and with time to spare ambled through Merrion Square, arriving just before nine o'clock. Byrne posted five guards outside, rang the bell and jammed his foot in the front door when it was opened by a servant girl, Catherine Farrell.[65] After she had indicated the British officers' bedrooms, Byrne sent some men to the back of the house to deal with Ames. He then gently tried Bennett's front parlour door. It was locked, but Farrell showed him another way in through the back parlour. Byrne and Sean Doyle burst through its folding doors just as Bennett went for his pistol under a pillow. While GHQ intelligence officer Frank Saurin searched for intelligence papers, they trained their weapons on Bennett, who seemed to believe the intruders were engaged on an arms raid. When he asked them what was going to happen, Byrne replied reassuringly

'Ah, nothing.' I then ordered him to march in front of me. As we were entering the back of the hall, I heard the hell of a row going on somewhere outside – very heavy revolver fire. My next surprise was hearing a ring on the door. The man covering the door looked at me, but did not speak a word. I said to him: 'Open the door', and in walked a British Tommy, a dispatch rider. Ordering him to put up his hands, which he did, I left him under guard in the hall. I marched my officer down to the back room where the other officer was. He was standing up in the bed, facing the wall. I ordered mine to do likewise. When the two of them were together, I said to myself 'The Lord have mercy on your souls!' I then opened fire with my Peter. They both fell dead.[66]

As Byrne tried to calm an hysterical Farrell, gunfire erupted outside between another IRA unit and British officers living in the street as well as a passing Auxiliary patrol. Byrne hesitated before deciding to spare the life of the British soldier in the hallway: he was, after all, simply in the wrong place at the wrong time. As Byrne's men left, they were fired on by Major Carew, a Dublin Special Branch intelligence officer who lived nearby, and shots were exchanged all the way down Mount Street. Here, too, the IRA unit had left someone behind, because Saurin was still inside searching for intelligence papers. Tom Ennis covered Saurin's exit by forcing Carew back, allowing them both to escape to the Liffey ferry. Instead of going to Russell's headquarters, Saurin walked home to Clontarf, his pockets stuffed with captured papers. These included Ames's notebook detailing British agents, informers and spotters working O'Connell Street and Parnell Square and proved to Saurin's satisfaction that the dead men had indeed been dangerous British intelligence officers.[67]

Todd Andrews's 4th Battalion unit had been assigned to 7 Ranelagh Road, a private home in which lodged Lieutenant W. Noble of Dublin District Special Branch. His boss, Wilson, regarded him as 'possibly, unostentatiously, the bravest of all'.[68] When the landlord's 15-year-old daughter opened the door, IRA Captain F.X. Coughlan jammed it with a stick. Volunteers made their way inside and raced upstairs to Noble's bedroom. Andrews remembered cocking his revolver, ready to shoot the spy on sight, but instead

> found the room empty except for a half-naked woman who sat up in bed looking terror stricken. She did not scream or say a word. I was very excited but, even so, I felt a sense of shame and embarrassment for the woman's sake. I was glad to get out quickly and moved to the next room where there was a man shaving. He was literally petrified with fear. His safety razor froze in mid-air. Thinking he was Nobel [*sic*], I was going to pull the trigger of my .45 when Coughlan shouted, 'He's all right'. He was a lodger in the house and was apparently one of our intelligence sources.[69]

Descending, Andrews saw the hall guards talking to two armed strangers, who turned out to be Joe Dolan and Dan McDonnell. These GHQ intelligence officers were to seize Noble's intelligence papers and kill his female companion, supposedly another British agent. But Noble had gone out hours earlier, leaving her in the house. The woman ended up being shot, along with Noble.[70] Furthermore, Dolan and McDonnell couldn't find any papers despite a furious rampage in which they, either accidentally or deliberately, set fire to a room containing children. Coughlan had to usher them to safety and form a bucket chain to extinguish the flames. Afterwards, his men dumped their weapons into a waiting taxi and fled on foot. On their way back Dolan and McDonnell encountered Tom Keogh coming off the Lower Mount Street operation with a wounded MacLean. They helped Keogh get to North Richmond Street, where he received medical treatment.

The target at 119 Lower Baggot Street was Captain Baggallay, a GHQ officer who had lost a leg in the First World War. At five minutes to nine, Pat McCrae arrived with the Squad's Jimmy Griffin and Ben Byrne and parked his car behind a house opposite.[71] The IRA unit included Sean Lemass, a future Irish Taoiseach. When a maid opened the door, Griffin and Byrne told her they had a Castle wire for Baggallay. Although one Volunteer, Matty MacDonald, had brought a sledgehammer to break into the officer's bedroom, the door was unlocked. MacDonald recalled Baggallay lying in bed in pyjamas. They had a brief conversation in which he toyed with the British officer.

Captain Baggally?' [sic]
  'That's my name.'
  'I suppose you know what we came for? We came for you.'
  'I suppose you've come for my gun.'
  'Oh, Yes.'[72]

When Baggallay made to hand over his weapon, he was shot twice in the heart. Downstairs, maids began screaming. Another man in pyjamas emerged from his room and ran straight into the hallway guards, who initially mistook him for a lodger. But even after discovering that he was another British officer, they let him go because there were no orders to eliminate him. A few minutes later the IRA unit had disappeared. By the time police arrived, every other resident had gone too. McCrae collected Griffin and Byrne then drove down Merrion Square and Westland Row, picking up other Squad members coming off Upper Mount Street. He took them to the Squad's Great Charles Street arms dump. After they had returned their weapons and McCrae had hidden the car, everyone quickly vanished.

At the Gresham Hotel in Upper O'Connell Street the two British targets were Captain Patrick McCormack, a 45-year-old member of the Royal Army Veterinary Corps, and 30-year-old Lieutenant L.E. Wilde. At nine o'clock an unmasked IRA unit walked into the busy reception area and ordered everyone, guests and staff alike, to raise their hands and stand still. They then marched the hall porter upstairs at pistol point and forced him to identify the officers' rooms. Soon afterwards the hotel manager, James Doyle, was awakened by a muffled noise that reminded him of a carpet being beaten. By the time the hall porter rushed in to alert him, the armed intruders had gone, McCormack lay dead in a nearby room and the body of Wilde, still in his pyjamas, was stretched out at his bedroom door. When Doyle telephoned the Castle, General Boyd told him that similar killings were occurring all across the city.[73]

Another hotel attacked that morning was the Eastwood in Leeson Street, where a ten-man unit from 4th Battalion under Captain Christy Byrne arrived to eliminate Lieutenant-Colonel Jennings.[74] Byrne ordered two men to cover the rear and led the main group inside, where they cut telephone wires and asked the receptionist for Jennings's room number. But the manager insisted that Jennings had not stayed the night. Byrne says that, after he had checked the officer's room, 'the boots evidently got into a state of panic and told them that there were twelve flying officers staying there and that if we wanted them he would direct us to their rooms. By this time the remainder of our party had withdrawn and we consulted amongst ourselves as to what we should do. We decided we had no instructions regarding procedure and we all withdrew.'[75]

Captain Paddy Flanagan, a ruthless psychopath, was an inspired choice for turning No. 28 Upper Pembroke Street into a slaughterhouse. This boarding house and the adjoining building had been converted into a single residence with a connecting ground-floor archway. Here lived Colonel Woodcock and his wife Caroline, Woodcock's adjutant Captain Keenlyside and Robert Jeune's Dublin District Special Branch unit. After his twenty-two men had assembled at 8.55 a.m., Flanagan quickly went over the arrangements one last time, reminded them that his approval was necessary before any killing and then ordered a number of Volunteers to cover the rear. Charlie Dalton, who anticipated discovering a treasure trove of intelligence papers,[76] recalled that 'at the zero hour of 9 a.m., the hall door was open and the porter was shaking mats on the step. There were separate staircases in this double-house and a party proceeded up either staircase.'[77]

Standing inside at her third-floor bedroom window, Mrs Woodcock spotted a man clambering over the side garden wall at the back.[78] She initially assumed he had an assignation with a maid, but then she saw the intruder produce a revolver from his coat pocket, creep towards stone steps leading to the basement and point it at the back door. Mrs Woodcock alerted her husband, who was on his way to breakfast. After instructing her to stay inside the room, Colonel Woodcock rushed downstairs, intending to warn Colonel Montgomery in his ground-floor flat and then bolt the front door. He was too late. Three men with revolvers were in the hallway – Flanagan, Dalton and another Volunteer. Beside them stood Greene the porter. Flanagan ordered Woodcock to raise his hands. 'At the same time the younger man who was closest to me backed away from me. He said "What is your name?" I said "Woodcock." He said "Are you sure?" I said "Yes" and added "Do not forget there are women in the house." The other man said, "We know it." The younger man said, "Turn around." I did so.'[79] Just then Woodcock heard Montgomery's door handle turning and shouted 'Look out!' But as one intruder forced Montgomery to raise his hands, Woodcock heard two shots from elsewhere in the house, whereupon his captors opened fire. Woodcock saw Montgomery hit in the chest and shoulder and fall forward at the foot of the stairs, fatally wounded. Woodcock was shot in the chest and shoulder and a final time in a hand as he scrambled upstairs. With blood flowing from his wounds, he plunged into his bedroom, threw himself on the bed and lost consciousness.

After shooting Woodcock and Montgomery, Flanagan and Dalton headed upstairs to the third floor on the other side of the house where 'Maudie', the maid, had identified Dowling's and Price's bedroom. They knocked on the door, entered and saw the two officers dressed in pyjamas sitting up in bed. Flanagan ordered them both to get up, and Dalton never forgot their startled looks as they complied. While he searched for their intelligence papers, Dalton heard Flanagan open fire and saw both men falling. Flanagan seemed irritated by Dalton's performance, ordering him to 'Get the hell out of this'.[80] In another room loud knocking on their door awakened Keenlyside and his wife. A large group of armed men filed inside, ordered the captain out of bed and hustled him downstairs in his pyjamas. When Mrs Keenlyside begged them not to hurt her husband, they pushed her roughly back inside. But she followed them downstairs, on the way encountering more armed strangers who were descending with Lieutenant Murray, whose hands were raised. A maid was pleading with his captors, 'Don't shoot my Murray!'[81] One Volunteer thought that if Murray had shown any initiative he could have jumped them.[82] In the hall Keenlyside and Murray were asked to confirm their names, placed side by side against a wall and shot, Murray in the back and Keenlyside in the jaw and arms. But neither was fatally wounded. The inexperienced and nervous gunmen were not up to the job. The hand of one shook so violently that a colleague snatched his revolver away, while another needed to support a trembling weapon on his left arm.[83]

After the killers had fled, Mrs Keenlyside helped her husband to their bedroom and bandaged him as best she could until doctors and nurses arrived. In the hallway Mrs Woodcock saw 'great splashes of blood on the walls, floor, and stairs, bits of plaster were lying about, and on the walls were the marks of innumerable bullets'.[84] She had heard only half a dozen shots but calculated that about fifty had actually been fired – not one by a British officer. Remarkably calm, she rang the barracks for help and fetched rugs and hot water bottles for her wounded husband. But Mrs Woodcock also 'literally shook with mixed feelings of pity and passionate anger'[85] and she especially swore vengeance on Greene the porter. From the bedroom window she had first watched about fifteen attackers running down the lane at the side of the house before the gunman in the back garden tried unsuccessfully to scale back up and over its high wall. But after Greene had emerged from the basement, he opened the garage door through which the stranger escaped. Mrs Woodcock kept her eyes on Greene until British soldiers arrived and then accused him of being an accessory to the killings. 'He said, "How could I help? Was I not threatened with a revolver or words to that effect?" I said, "You are lying, you were not threatened".'[86] She then handed Greene over to the officer in charge.

As Dalton escaped he heard shooting in Upper Mount Street and saw residents peering through windows, but he and Saurin caught the Liffey ferry safely, dumped their weapons in a safe house and reported to Russell in North Richmond Street. Across the city in Inchicore, Captain Jeune awakened after his night's sleep in a railway carriage and telephoned the Castle to finalise his hand-over to Dowling. Only then did he learn from the adjutant that

'there have been some raids by the "Shinners" and I am afraid that they have got some of our fellows.' On getting back there I found a very distressing scene. In the flat next to Murray's and mine, I saw the body of my friend 'Chummy' Dowling, a grand ex-Guardee, wounded three times in the war, lying full length on the floor. As he was to have relieved me he was in uniform and had obviously been shot through the heart, probably by a small Sinn Feiner, because there was a bullet hole in one corner of the ceiling. In the doorway of the bathroom was Price's body. Murray had already been taken to hospital.[87]

The targets at 'Brianna', 117 Morehampton Road, were 31-year-old Captain Donald McLean, his 23-year-old brother-in-law John Caldow and Thomas Smith, the landlord. When Smith's 10-year-old son opened the door, an IRA unit rushed upstairs, forced McLean into an upper room and turned away his pleading wife. She heard one intruder demand McLean's name, another say 'That's good enough' and then a burst of gunfire. After they had left she entered the room and saw her dead husband sitting by the fireplace. Smith had also been killed, but a seriously wounded Caldow survived.[88]

The IRA's next target was Captain Fitzgerald, who lived in Earlsfort Terrace and whom GHQ Intelligence believed was attached to the Auxiliaries. While serving in Clare as an RIC barracks defence officer, he had been kidnapped and shot before escaping over a wall. A servant girl, Kathleen Hayes, admitted the Volunteer unit that arrived to finish the job and they forced her at revolver point to lead them to Fitzgerald's room. Two men entered and soon afterwards Hayes heard the captain scream, followed immediately by four shots. The attackers fled immediately, leaving Fitzgerald's body lying on the bed with bullets to the heart and forehead.[89]

Other British army officers had close calls that morning. Just after 9 a.m. an IRA unit entered a flat in Fitzwilliam Square that was occupied by Major Crawford, who commanded the Royal Army Service Corps's motor repair depot. Crawford was sitting in his dressing room as his wife slept. He heard a knock on the door and, thinking it was some of his own men calling, he shouted 'come in'. When there was no response, Crawford opened the door to three men holding Webley revolvers who ordered him to raise his hands. At first Crawford thought it was a practical joke until a fourth intruder poked a weapon into his stomach and forced him back inside. When they asked him if he was Major O'Callaghan, he replied that a Mr O'Callaghan who was totally unconnected to the British Army lived on the floor above. As the IRA men searched his flat, Crawford denied he was a British secret service agent and showed them his identity papers. After scrutinising these and his driver's licence, they ordered him to bed while they examined other documents. Eventually they got Crawford out of bed and when they began shouting abuse he told them, 'My wife is not very well and if you are going to shoot me please take me downstairs, as it would be unpleasant for my wife to see'.[90] But instead they left, after ordering him to leave the country within twenty-four hours.

At North Richmond Street Russell was relieved that every casualty had been British, except for the wounded McLean and Teeling in custody. But, as news of the killings spread, Dublin trembled at the prospect of British soldiers and Auxiliaries going on the rampage. The Gresham's manager immediately rang General Boyd to beg for protection. After receiving an anonymous tip that Larry O'Neill, the pro-Sinn Fein Lord Mayor, was to be killed, his chaplain appealed to the Castle. Ironically it sent Auxiliaries to guard O'Neill in the Mansion House, where they occupied an office that Collins used frequently, shocking visitors every time they opened the door.[91] Leading republicans lay low in safe houses, alert for British Army lorries and raiding parties. At the Children's Hospital Brugha and Mulcahy stayed indoors until mid-afternoon, when shooting erupted not far away at Croke Park. Brugha was ready to go out in a blaze of glory. Opening a window, he brought the chair up, took off his boots and set two guns down beside him. Mulcahy would have liked to slip out the back door but he 'had to follow Cathal's mood, so I sat on his bed with my gun while he sat on his chair alongside the window with his two guns alongside him on the bed, and we waited and waited until some time after five o'clock the all-clear message came in some way or another. Immediately the situation cleared I left and made for the south side.'[92]

Cope, who was on duty during Greenwood's absence in London, telephoned Anderson and Sturgis as they relaxed in Phoenix Park's viceregal garden. Both men reeled at the news of killings, which Sturgis believed were an expression of republican desperation and 'the forlorn hope of striking at the Military ring which is closing on them'.[93] At a mid-afternoon conference in the Castle Anderson met Cope, Sturgis, Tudor, Boyd, Wilson and Winter (whom Sturgis thought 'distinctly nervy and overwrought'[94]). Colonel Brind was also present as acting GOC during Macready's leave in France. Incredibly, the GOC learnt about events in Dublin only from his hotel's Monday's newspapers.[95] To avoid retaliation the conference decided to keep soldiers and Auxiliaries busy. Certainly their already considerable anger was stoked by rumours that Mrs Newbury had gone mad after seeing her husband killed and that some of the British victims had been hammered to death. One army officer recalled:

The troops were burning to get out and take affairs into their own hands. In fact the men of one regiment, which had lost two officers in the murders, paraded on their own with no higher ranks than corporal with the intention of marching out of barracks. They were stopped just in time. At that time all barracks gates were locked and a quarter guard mounted. The Staff were afraid of reprisals by the troops. They were right.[96]

Dublin Castle worked flat out to prevent troops and Auxiliaries retaliating; searching departing trains, traffic on all roads out of Dublin and the Kingstown–Holyhead steamers. As far as possible military officers were to be withdrawn from flats and boarding houses and relocated into commandeered hotels. The army also occupied City Hall – something which Sturgis believed was long overdue because of its proximity to the Castle and its use by Sinn Fein as virtually a rival seat of government. Finally, known IRA officers and gunmen were to be arrested and interned in special detention camps, a measure that Macready had unsuccessfully recommended to the government only weeks before.[97] But Bloody Sunday had changed everything.

While the Castle conference continued, it was being overtaken by events at Croke Park. After the morning's shootings, Russell stood down Volunteer stewards, though the GAA match was still scheduled to go ahead. But when Russell learnt after lunch that Auxiliaries and soldiers were on their way to the ground, he went there and appealed for officials to shut the gates, turn away queues and evacuate spectators.[98] But they feared that a late cancellation would precipitate a stampede and cause the very deaths which Russell was anxious to prevent. Still insisting that the match be rearranged, Russell departed, only to return when an IRA officer reminded him that the GAA had no stewards to implement his instructions. Russell decided to organise an evacuation himself. Initially one turnstile attendant agreed to stop admissions but while he sought higher approval a large, impatient crowd of 10,000 people built up. When the attendant returned he reopened the gate and the game commenced at 2.45 p.m. Russell left in despair and this time he did not come back.

The British authorities believed that after the morning's shootings IRA killers had melted into the crowds at Croke Park. At 1.30 p.m. Major Mills, the Adjutant of the Auxiliary Division at Beggar's Bush, was ordered to lead a mixed force of Auxiliaries and RIC to the ground, split up his men and post parties at each of the four gates. The crowd would then be ordered to leave Croke Park with all men stopped and searched for weapons. Subsequently, a

British military inquiry decided that the search party was fired on by spectators and that RIC members returned fire, some shooting over the heads of the crowd and others at civilians attempting to evade arrest, creating a stampede. When the firing ceased, fourteen civilians had been fatally injured in what nationalist Ireland believed was a direct reprisal for the morning's assassinations. One long-suppressed document takes us as close as we are likely to get to the truth about the affair. This is a letter written the day after Bloody Sunday but withheld from the military inquiry in which Mills protested to his superiors, effectively blaming the RIC contingent for a massacre. He claimed that he had been travelling in a car in the rear of RIC vehicles and as they approached a railway bridge near the south-west corner of the ground he saw RIC men in front trying to get out of their tender, agitated and shouting about an ambush. Mills wrote that 'at this moment I heard a considerable amount of rifle fire, as no shots were coming from the football field and all the RIC Constables seemed excited and out of hand'. Having got the firing outside the ground stopped, Mills heard shooting continuing inside, ran down into the ground, eventually got the firing stopped and organised the crowd to file out. When he went round the ground, Mills found two children being carried out, apparently dead, a woman and man who had both been trampled to death and got ambulances for the wounded. 'We found no arms on any of the people attending the match. I did not see any need for any firing at all and the indiscriminate firing absolutely spoilt any chance of getting hold of any people in possession of arms.'[99]

Unavoidably absent from Croke Park were thirteen men detained by 'F' Company Auxiliaries at Dublin Castle. Because of a shortage of accommodation, they were being held in a room of the Old Detective Office. Conditions were surprisingly relaxed with only a few guards on duty, boxes of hand grenades and ammunition strewn around and the prisoners free to move about – though some preferred chatting in front of an open fire. Eventually a lorry deposited another four captives – McKee, Clancy, Fitzpatrick and Clune. The two IRA leaders were clearly intent on blending in inconspicuously because, when a 19-year-old Volunteer, Patrick Young, approached his Brigadier,

Dick McKee just looked at me as if I were a complete stranger and turned away from me. I didn't know Clancy well enough to talk to, which was just as well, as he turned away and started talking to Dick McKee. I made my way back to my own party, full of resentment at the attitude of McKee and

Clancy. I had been talking to McKee only a few days before this. Not being able to understand their attitude I kept looking over at them and I suppose Dick McKee must have noticed me as he made a signal to me which I took to mean not to worry. I was very relieved at this. Later on I did get talking to McKee for a minute while there was no sentry in the room. He said it would be better for me if the 'Auxies' did not know I knew him as they might try to get information from me about him and their methods of getting information were not recommended.[100]

As news of the morning's assassinations filtered through, agitated Auxiliary guards briefly disappeared while Young and other prisoners pondered a break-out. 'It looked easy enough to blast the window and make a run for it.'[101] But the guards soon returned. After the Croke Park shootings, Young broached the possibility of escaping with McKee, but the Brigadier had spotted Auxiliaries with machine guns on top of a wall of sandbags separating them from the guardroom. 'We all kept far away from the stuff lying around after that.'[102]

Outside, Collins was trying frantically to rescue McKee and Clancy. He summoned Traynor and Russell to 46 Parnell Square, where they waited until a British military lorry parked outside drove away. Inside they found only a single occupant – a young boy crying for his arrested father. Thereafter they could not re-establish contact with Collins.[103] McKee and Clancy were on their own. At about 5.30 p.m. Hardy and King arrived to transfer prisoners to Beggar's Bush, and, when they isolated McKee and Clancy from the main group it was clear that their efforts at concealment had failed. Ironically this was not because of McKee, since the British still did not know that he was the IRA's Dublin Brigadier. But they knew Clancy very well indeed. His shop, the Republican Outfitters, and his leadership of April's Mountjoy hunger strike had made Clancy a marked man. Young also saw Captain King and another Auxiliary trying to identify the person arrested with McKee and Clancy:

When they came to Clune and Fitzpatrick they were not sure what to do. One said that's him and the other said no it's him. My belief is that they were looking for Fitzpatrick as the others were arrested in his house. Both Fitzpatrick and Clune were similar in build and were wearing brown suits. In the end one of them said 'Oh you'll do', sending Clune over to McKee and Clancy.[104]

As the main group prepared to set off for Beggar's Bush, Young was searching for his cap when McKee 'took his off and gave it to me, saying "I don't think I will want this any more".'[105]

Later, Winter received a telephone call in his Castle office about three dead prisoners in the guardroom. The officer in charge said that, after he and his men had gone for a meal, the trio had suddenly attacked a sentry. One had thrown a couple of grenades which did not explode because the detonators had not been primed; he then dived behind a pile of mattresses after the guard had opened fire. Another prisoner had seized a rifle and shot at other guards, while the third swung a spade at Auxiliaries who were crouching behind an overturned table. The officer in charge and his men had rushed back in and opened fire, creating a diversion that allowed their colleagues to shoot the attackers dead. Winter saw one of them lying on his back clutching a grenade, with the others slumped nearby. He noted a deep spade mark in a wooden bench and extracted a bullet from the door. 'I had but little sympathy with two of the dead men, by name Dick McKee and Peter Clancy, both of whom would probably have been hanged. The third man I could not identify, but he subsequently turned out to be a notorious gunman named Clune.'[106]

Neligan recalled that on Monday 22 November 'the atmosphere in Dublin . . . was electric with tension and fear. Death stalked the streets.'[107] The British authorities had isolated the capital while troops and Auxiliaries searched for the killers. The post was still delivered but no mail was forwarded to the rest of Ireland. British forces occupied bridges, barbed wire was stretched across main roads, civilians were not allowed to congregate, armoured cars patrolled the city, no phone calls could be made to the outside world and many cinema and theatre performances were cancelled.

Collins still believed that McKee and Clancy might be alive and in the morning had Neligan meet Tobin and half a dozen Squad members in a backstreet church near the Castle. Tobin said he was to search the Bridewell for McKee and Clancy, and, if his cover were blown, Collins would have him smuggled to America. But, if both prisoners were there, then the Squad would attempt a rescue. At the Bridewell Neligan scrutinised every prisoner through cell peepholes before returning to the church. 'I told Tobin they were not there. He asked me where I thought they were and knowing that they had been arrested by the Castle Auxiliaries, I answered: "Probably dead."'[108]

Nationalist Ireland derided an official British account of the three men's deaths, certain they had been tortured, mutilated and finally murdered.

Young, too, could not believe they had attempted to escape, especially after McKee had earlier rejected a break-out when he had seventeen men available.[109] But quite possibly McKee and Clancy, at least, had decided that their situation had changed for the worse after Hardy and King had singled them out – particularly as their captors would soon realise the significance of the burnt papers found at Fitzpatrick's house. They would not have gone meekly, especially as their chances of escaping had actually risen because most Auxiliaries were out patrolling the city. Freedom was tantalisingly close because their holding room faced almost directly onto Dame Street. Once outside, they could run through Crane Lane directly opposite, and disappear into a network of narrow commercial streets. It must have been a tempting gamble, and, if it failed, then these two friends who together had grown up, fought and conspired would at least die together. It is more difficult to speculate whether Clune would have joined an attempted break-out or was sucked into yet another of the misadventures which in twenty-four hours had taken him from rural Clare to Dublin and then, via Vaughan's, to this almost final resting place. Of all Bloody Sunday's victims, Clune was surely the unluckiest: the wrong man in the wrong place no fewer than three times. What is certain is that, contrary to legend, none of the three men was tortured or mutilated. MacLysaght collected Clune's body from the King George V Hospital and examined those of McKee and Clancy as well. The claim 'that their faces were so battered about as to be unrecognisable and horrible to look at is quite untrue. I remember those pale dead faces as if I had looked at them yesterday. They were not disfigured.'[110]

On 25 November 1920 the funeral procession of the dead British officers wound its way through the city to a destroyer waiting at the North Wall. It was a massive and sombre affair. Shops and businesses closed, Union Jacks flew at half-mast, six aeroplanes hovered overhead and large crowds lined the route with Auxiliaries sometimes enforcing respect by throwing men's caps into the Liffey. Resting on horse-drawn gun carriages, the Union Jack-draped coffins were followed by representatives of Army GHQ, the heads of the police and 1,000 soldiers and police slow-marching to the solemn music of military bands. At the docks the Last Post was sounded as the remains were carried on board. Around the same time, Captain McCormack and Lieutenant Wilde were being buried with due honours in the city's Glasnevin Cemetery, where without public ceremony six of the Croke Park victims were also laid to rest on this day.[111]

The same air of solemnity prevailed in London, where the coffins were escorted to Westminster Abbey or Westminster Cathedral by the Household Cavalry and bands of the Brigade of Guards. The spectacle heightened emotions in Britain, and there was a public outcry for the killers' apprehension and punishment. Dublin Castle hoped that eyewitnesses would identify them in line-ups of numerous Volunteer suspects and then have them fast tracked in courts martial. Mrs Woodcock helped by returning from her English refuge and, with a police escort, trawling the city's jails. 'We started off as usual in a closed car, at a great pace, followed by more cars full of detectives, every man with his hand in his right-hand pocket. I realised now very well what that meant. I sat buried in a fur coat, another fur up to my eyes. I did not like it a bit.'[112] In a small hut partitioned by a window covered with felt out of which a narrow slit had been cut, Mrs Woodcock peered through to the other side, where numbered prisoners paraded. So did a forlorn band of 'soldiers, detectives, one or two other women, and a little boy, whose father had been murdered before his eyes, and who had said he thought he could recognise "the man who killed daddy"'.[113] By now she considered any shifty Irishman guilty – but of which particular crime?

> They all seemed absolutely terror-stricken; they were shaking and gibbering with fright. They were not there to be shot, they were only there to be looked at, and yet they looked, I imagine, as a coward would look when facing a firing party. One or two nervously sucked cigarettes. I do not know why they were allowed to smoke at all. As each batch went away unrecognised by anyone, some of them sang in a quavering voice a sort of song of triumph – or possibly relief. The noise was stupid and irritating. It was the most extraordinary feeling to meet all those pairs of eyes. The prisoners had to look straight in front of them at the hut, and they stood there, licking their pallid lips, with quavering faces and shaking hands.[114]

Yet she did not recognise a single face out of the 200 men who shuffled before her gaze. 'I know that some of them must have the blood of my friends on their hands. Some looked capable of any crime.'[115] But she resisted the temptation to finger anyone.

Ultimately only eight men stood trial, seven of them low-level Volunteers whose defence was organised by Michael Noyk. He visited Kilmainham regularly, always checking for hidden recording devices and warning the accused against loose talk.[116] James Boyce, indicted for murdering Baggallay, could clearly look after himself, but his co-defendant Thomas Whelan was a naive and talkative country boy oozing child-like delight about his caring new friend, governor Maye, whom Noyk believed was a British intelligence agent.

> I said to Whelan: 'Have you been talking to this man?' 'Yes', he said, 'he was speaking to me'. I said: 'What did he say to you?' He answered: 'He said: I admire you as one soldier to another and am interested to know what battalion you belong to.' Whelan excitedly and proudly replied: 'I belong to C Company of the 3rd Battalion, Dublin Brigade.' A sudden fear came over me, as I knew that meant Whelan was doomed. He had fallen into the trap. Boyce, on the contrary, with typical Dublin astuteness, said nothing.[117]

Noyk also learnt about another inmate, James Greene, the elderly hall porter who was charged with Montgomery's murder in Upper Pembroke Street. Yet this frail septuagenarian was actually innocent of assisting the IRA before or on Bloody Sunday. He was in legal freefall because Mrs Woodcock's restricted view from the back bedroom window had prevented her seeing Greene being coerced into opening the rear gate. When Noyk told Collins that Greene's friends and employers had abandoned him, he ordered Noyk to defend the porter 'as fully as if he had been one of our own men'.[118] But finding a defence team was tremendously difficult. Many Dublin lawyers suddenly became unavailable for such controversial – and potentially career threatening – briefs. Three leading barristers who declined were later reincarnated as the Irish Free State's Governor-General, Attorney General and Chief Justice respectively. Noyk finally secured two Nationalists, Charles Bewley and Charles Wyse-Power, and James Williamson, a Unionist QC who worked tirelessly for the republican accused. The prosecution team was led by Sir Roland Oliver and Travers Humphreys, whom Winter regarded as 'the most deadly cross-examiner I have ever known'.[119]

Three months after Bloody Sunday, courts martial commenced in the council chamber of a fortified City Hall. Its usual entrance was closed for security reasons and admission was through the Lower Castle Yard after a rigorous Auxiliary search. According to Noyk, the court consisted of 'five high-ranking officers and a Judge Advocate, all of whom sat at a long table with a revolver in front of them. The room was filled with Secret Service men. One could hardly raise one's eyes without being aware of someone's scrutiny, and the names of the various witnesses on behalf of the Crown were not disclosed.'[120] Mrs Woodcock sank Greene immediately with her confident, moving and apparently irrefutable testimony about having 'carefully watched the accused in the garden and at no time did he appear to be intimidated or threatened by the other man; in fact he was talking to him for some seconds in a perfectly natural manner'.[121] Her husband insisted that Greene had not seemed afraid on Bloody Sunday and, like his wife, made the – no doubt rehearsed – point that he did not have his hands up either, apparently clinching proof of complicity. Greene testified that he was extremely frightened at the time. He said that after the hallway shootings he had gone into the back yard, where, out of fear, he had helped the gunman escape. But his own testimony carried little weight against the Woodcocks' apparently damning evidence, and Greene was lucky to receive only ten years.[122]

Noyk was hardly surprised by Teeling's conviction for killing McMahon in Lower Mount Street, because he had been 'caught red-handed when he was escaping over a garden wall, so there could be no real defence for him'.[123] But, although a resident had identified both Boyce and Whelan as hallway guards during Baggallay's assassination, Boyce was acquitted while Whelan was sentenced to death. Noyk was most hopeful for Paddy Moran, who stood accused of murdering Ames and Bennett. His was the only case 'in which we could put up a watertight defence'.[124] The star witness, Major Carew, was distinctly shaky in his identification, while a queue of people alibied Moran, including his housekeeper, church worshippers, a tram conductor, former British soldiers, a policeman, a Scotswoman, a Jew and the daughter of a British officer. A devotee of amateur dramatics, Winter hugely enjoyed their impassioned descriptions of Moran's probity, religiosity and filial devotion and their multiple sightings of him miles away from Upper Mount Street. But Humphreys exposed numerous contradictions in their testimony and produced a damaging photograph of Moran in Volunteer uniform brandishing a revolver. After Moran's conviction, Winter could not resist buttonholing Williamson, who complained sardonically that 'Dublin solicitors get up their cases so badly'.[125]

Noyk was devastated by the guilty verdict on Moran, whose innocence he protested for the rest of his life. When Moran had been charged, he himself had stated that 'I was not in Upper Mount Street on that morning'.[126] Moran's carefully crafted denial was undoubtedly true, and he was certainly executed for a crime which he did not and could not possibly have committed, because, ironically, on Bloody Sunday morning, he was at the Gresham executing two completely different British officers. On Saturday night, 20 November, Paddy Daly had seen Sean Russell putting Moran 'in charge of the Gresham Hotel. Paddy Moran was not a member of the Squad, but he volunteered for the work. He was Captain of "D" Company of the 2nd Battalion, and on that account Sean Russell did not put a member of the Squad in charge of the Gresham Hotel operation, knowing that he could not improve on Paddy.'[127] Ultimately, Moran's trial was a futile riot of perjury, something which Noyk must have known. His indignation at the verdict and Moran's execution rested on narrowly legalistic grounds – that his client was being hanged for killing the 'wrong' people.

Teeling evaded execution after the IRA arranged for two friendly British soldiers at Kilmainham to smuggle in bolt cutters for an escape on 14 February 1921. Moran, whose trial had just ended, was offered a place in the escape party but refused, as he expected to be acquitted. Whelan was not included, but he bore no grudges. He and Moran were executed on 14 March at Mountjoy. Winter commended the hangman's technical excellence and 'the rapidity with which a man leaving the condemned cell ended his life with the pulling of a lever'.[128]

On 22 November GHQ Intelligence assembled in Crow Street for its own post-mortem on what that morning's *Freeman's Journal* first described as 'Ireland's Bloody Sunday'.[129] According to Dan McDonnell, they 'were disappointed with the result',[130] and especially at the wide discrepancy between the Intelligence Department's original projections and the final tally. Some targets had been away unexpectedly on Sunday morning. Noble had left his Ranelagh Road lodgings, Jennings had not slept at his hotel and many occupants of a house in East Road close to the docklands had departed on Saturday. But other planned actions had simply failed to materialise, through either incompetence or sabotage by unenthusiastic Volunteers. GHQ was particularly dissatisfied by 4th Battalion's failure to attack many places on the North Circular Road and avenues close to Phoenix Park, and Collins soon squeezed out its commandant, Christy Byrne.[131]

Many targets at a hotel in Exchequer Street also escaped because, although the IRA unit knew their names, their room numbers were unlisted in the register and the porter refused to cooperate. The unit left without firing a shot because the only way it could have made certain of eliminating the targets was by killing every male resident.[132] Laurence Nugent of 3rd Battalion admitted that his men did not relish Bloody Sunday and, although most obeyed orders, they did not want to discuss the episode afterwards.[133] Three 4th Battalion Volunteers never returned to duty and another was court-martialled for missing the Baggot Street action.[134] Clearly many men were quietly relieved or ambivalent when their operations were aborted. Todd Andrews recalled that, 'As I went back to Terenure through quiet suburban roads and lanes well known to me I wondered whether I was glad or sorry that Nobel [*sic*] had not been at home. I would certainly have felt no remorse at having shot him but I found it hard to get the memory of the terrified woman or indeed the equally terrified lodger from my mind.'[135]

Some Volunteers' families disapproved of their participation in Bloody Sunday. The Squad's driver, Pat McCrae, had excused his early morning departure as a fishing trip with friends. But on his return he was flummoxed when his wife asked him where the catch was. After a late breakfast McCrae was asleep on a couch when she

> came into the room crying with a 'Stop Press' in her hand. I woke up and asked her what was the matter. Before speaking she handed me the 'Stop Press' and wanted to know was this the fishing expedition I had been on. Seeing that there was no use in concealing things any longer from her, I said: 'Yes, and don't you see we had a good catch' or words to that effect. She then said: 'I don't care what you think about it, I think it is murder.' I said: 'No, that is nonsense; I'd feel like going to the altar after that job this morning.' After this I tried to calm her. I don't think she put out any lights in the house during the following winter. I did not stay at home then for about a week. That Sunday night I slept in a grove in the demesne known as St Anne's which was nearby.[136]

Ever since 1920 the exact number of British intelligence officers killed and wounded on Bloody Sunday has been intensely, if inconclusively, debated. While the British Government did not admit to any, then or since, the British Army conceded privately soon afterwards that 'a large number of British Court-Martial and Intelligence Officers were killed in their bed'.[137] Winter, however, insisted that only two were involved in court-martial work and none, as the IRA claimed, in the trial of Kevin Barry. It is now possible to establish most victims' status, although a definitive verdict remains impossible until every relevant official British document becomes available. Of the fifteen British dead and four wounded, the two executed Auxiliaries can be discounted immediately. They were simply in the wrong place at the wrong time. Woodcock and Keenlyside were regular army officers but they knew they were sharing the house with and giving cover to a British intelligence unit – something which the IRA would have considered made them legitimate targets.[138] Robert Jeune has verified that Dowling, Price, Montgomery, Ames and Bennett as well as the wounded Murray were all intelligence agents belonging to Wilson's Special Branch. Captain McLean was one of Winter's men, attached to the Intelligence Department Headquarters staff, Dublin Castle,[139] but uncertainty remains concerning his wounded brother-in-law and dead landlord. McMahon and Peel were the pseudonyms presumably of two undercover British intelligence officers. McMahon was actually Lieutenant H. Angliss of the Royal Inniskilling Fusiliers. The exact status of Newbury and Fitzgerald remains uncertain, though the presence of Newbury's pregnant wife must raise profound doubts that he was involved in intelligence work in Dublin. Baggallay was not an intelligence agent. The IRA had misinterpreted his involvement in the raid that killed John Lynch at the Royal Exchange Hotel.

Of the two Gresham dead, McCormack's lifestyle during his three-month stay in Dublin was hardly that of a spy. According to the hotel manager,

> while he was here I never saw him receiving any guests. He slept well into the afternoon and only got up early when a race meeting was on. When I found him shot in his room, 'Irish Field' was lying beside him. I mentioned to Collins after the Truce that there was a grave doubt as to Captain McCormick [sic] being a British agent. He said that he would make inquiries into the matter, but after this the matter was never referred to again.[140]

However, in March 1922 Collins delved into McCormack's death after receiving a letter from the dead officer's mother, an Irishwoman who was a sister of the late Bishop of Galway. She insisted that her son was 'thoroughly Irish in his education and upbringing' and would never have become involved in anything so 'discreditable' as espionage.[141] A former captain in the Veterinary Corps, McCormack had been demobilised about a year earlier and was in Ireland purchasing horses for his new employers, the Alexandria Turf Club of Egypt. He should have returned to Egypt in mid-October but stayed on to arrange travel for his wife and children. Mrs McCormack thought her son was killed in mistake for a Captain McCormick whom she believed had served on Kevin Barry's court martial. On 7 April 1922 Collins conceded to Mulcahy that McCormack's death had been a mistake – and not the only one:

> We had no evidence that he was a Secret Service Agent. You will also remember that several of the 21 November cases were just regular officers. Some of the names were put on by the Dublin Brigade. So far as I remember McCormick's [sic] name was one of these. In my opinion it would be as well to tell Mrs McCormick [sic] that there was no particular charge against her son, but just that he was an enemy soldier.[142]

As for the killing of Wilde at the Gresham, it seems that he was a former RAF officer and an Irishman who had become politically involved with the British Labour Party. A few days before his death Wilde had written to party leader Arthur Henderson offering to put his knowledge of Irish history and his close contacts with the Catholic Church to his service to help shape policy on Ireland.[143] A couple of months later the Gresham's manager mentioned Wilde's death to the Australian Archbishop Clune during his peace mission to Ireland. After speaking to Collins, Clune told the manager that Wilde had been well known in Spain as a British intelligence agent. But that hardly constitutes definitive proof – or even comes close to it.[144]

Bloody Sunday is often presented as an unqualified triumph for Collins and a devastating blow against British intelligence that decisively influenced the course of the entire war. In his convoluted prose Mulcahy insisted that

> There is no doubt that the killing of these spy murderers completely saved the situation in Dublin as far as retaining Dublin as the seat where there was being sustained a group who were a representative government and a group who were a guiding military authority representing the Irish stand. Coming on top of this the Kilmichael ambush must have been, in the eyes of the British political authority, a very damaging blow to their confidence in their military policy in Ireland. It must have been an understanding of this that drove the British forces in Ireland to burn Cork on the 11th December.[145]

Traynor claimed that the effect of Bloody Sunday 'was to paralyse completely the British Military Intelligence system in Dublin'.[146] Thornton went even further by asserting that 'the British Secret Service was wiped out on the 21st November 1920'.[147] But Collins knew the operation had fallen far short of his vaulting ambitions and that its achievements were counter-balanced by the tragedy at Croke Park and the deaths of McKee and Clancy, which Beaslai regarded as 'the greatest blow we had yet received – perhaps the biggest blow the IRA received in the whole war'.[148] Mulcahy recognised it also as an immense personal blow to Collins because in McKee and Clancy 'he had two men who fully understood the inside of Collins's work and mind and who were ready and able to link up the resources of the Dublin Brigade to any work that Collins had in hand and to do so promptly, effectively and sympathetically'.[149]

Oscar Traynor, the new Dublin Brigadier, did not revive the Collins–McKee axis, and Mulcahy suspected him of deliberately hindering Volunteer GHQ by ignoring its requests for increased activity and then 'fretting to do all kinds of things'[150] when told to stay quiescent. McKee's and Clancy's deaths also occurred when de Valera was preparing to return from America and Brugha's antipathy to Collins was becoming apparent. Mulcahy confessed that both he and Collins failed to realise that Brugha was 'taking a greater interest as to how he could affect the GHQ Staff without knowing exactly what he wanted to do with or through the GHQ staff except weaken Collins's position there'.[151] Mulcahy thought Brugha's new assertiveness encouraged Traynor in an anti-Collins direction. McKee's death also weakened Collins by removing McKee's considerable influence over the Cork IRA, which later came out against both Collins and the Treaty. Finally, Collins's political position was eroded by Griffith's imprisonment from Bloody Sunday until the Truce. A mutual respect had developed between them and if Griffith had remained free he would have been an important counterweight to the de Valera–Brugha axis in the Dail cabinet.

Nor did Bloody Sunday decisively affect the intelligence struggle or the overall course of the war – if anything the reverse was true. Many British intelligence agents had escaped and were now on their guard, making a repetition of Bloody Sunday impossible. Moreover, Robert Jeune did not consider it a significant setback for Special Branch and by the end of his tour of duty a few months later he believed the IRA in Dublin was being ground down by Macready's intensified campaign of massive searches and widespread arrests.[152] But even after every qualification, Bloody Sunday remains a remarkable achievement by Collins. It sent a seismic wave through the British political system, shaking public faith in the government's assurances that its Irish policy was succeeding. After 21 November 1921 the credibility gap was just too wide between a claim that it had murder by the throat and the fact that the rebels had been able to plan and execute a city-wide operation without being detected in advance and getting away almost completely unscathed. The shock forced Lloyd George to begin reassessing his policy and goals in Ireland. Shortly afterwards the first peace feelers went out to Sinn Féin and so, in that sense, Bloody Sunday was indeed the tipping point of the war.

Chapter 6

SLUGGING IT OUT

BLOODY SUNDAY TO MARCH 1921

Far from deciding the battle for Dublin, Bloody Sunday ushered in a new phase of heightened struggle. One inhabitant recalled war amid all the outward trappings of peace.

Men and women went about their daily lives to the accompaniment of grenade explosions and small-arms fire. Through all this the shops were open, business went on, men worked and played, made money and lost it, women went shopping, children played, young people made love and danced and went to the pictures while terror walked beside them. Soldiers in full war kit patrolled the streets. The unseen army of the Republic walked the streets, too, and the first warning of its presence was the crash of bombs and revolver fire. After such an ambush whole blocks of buildings in the city would be cordoned off and every occupant searched. Trams would be held up by trigger-happy Auxiliaries and all men passengers taken off for questioning and searching. The gates of St Stephen's Green . . . would close and everyone found inside would be subjected to interrogation and search. . . . if there were no women searchers about many a woman found herself the custodian of a revolver surreptitiously slipped to her by the stranger sitting beside her, and many a man, already searched, found himself the temporary possessor of highly dangerous documents.[1]

On 22 November the Volunteer Executive made Oscar Traynor Dublin Brigadier, a full-time appointment on an annual salary, and ordered him to intensify the IRA campaign.[2] But he immediately lost his first Vice-Brigadier, Sean Russell, who succeeded Clancy as GHQ Director of Munitions. Many Brigade officers were under arrest and most of Traynor's 1,500 Volunteers were in hiding. Though Quartermaster McGurk was still at liberty, he could not be found. When Traynor finally tracked him down a week later, he proved so useless that Traynor quickly dismissed him, along with two battalion commanders.[3]

The Brigade was also flat broke, and Traynor rescued it only with an emergency collection of £500. Suspecting the British were closing in on Brigade headquarters, he shifted it from Lower Gardiner Street to the former Plaza Hotel in nearby Gardiner's Row. Its new owners, the Irish Engineering Union, leased Traynor an office suite in an isolated part of the building that could be reached only by a separate staircase. Here, Brigade staff posed as a branch of the Irish Clerical Workers' Union in rooms with secret hideouts for confidential documents. Here too there was a hallway buzzer for the caretaker to warn of a British raid. But the British never located this new HQ. Luck and tight security played a part, but Traynor still believed that 'the fact that Brigade Headquarters survived the whole period of the intensive campaign against the British is extraordinary'.[4]

Just before he died, McKee had planned to ambush Auxiliaries conveying mail from Beggar's Bush to Ballsbridge post office, but the plan was never carried out. At Traynor's insistence this operation finally went ahead on 14 December 1920, the first IRA attack on Auxiliaries in Dublin and almost six months after their arrival in the city. Traynor would have liked this to be the start of daily attacks on the police and army which would generate a relentless momentum. But this was completely unrealistic as long as most Dublin Volunteers remained in full-time civilian employment, meaning that 'very often our excuses for leaving in a hurry aroused unnecessary suspicions in the minds of our fellow workers, to say nothing of our employers'.[5] Only a full-time active service unit (ASU) could effectively take on a British garrison of thousands of policemen, soldiers and Auxiliaries, and during December 1920 Traynor organised 100 Volunteers into an ASU. Composed of four sections, one in each battalion area, its mission was to conduct ambushes and arms raids and generally make 'war at all times of the day or night'.[6] Traynor appointed Captain Paddy Flanagan as leader because of the absolute ruthlessness that he had demonstrated on Bloody Sunday. His men were paid £4 10s a week, just like the Squad, with which they were to work closely. The ASU commenced operations on 12 January 1921, when Flanagan led a daylight attack on a British army lorry.

GHQ intelligence officers also felt the heat after Bloody Sunday, when two British secret servicemen arrested Joe Guilfoyle on suspicion of being an IRA member and deposited him at the Bridewell to await an Auxiliary escort. Fearing summary execution, he risked confiding in a policeman, Maurice Aherne, who, luckily for him, was secretly working for Collins.[7] When

Guilfoyle's escort arrived, he was shocked to see it led by 'Hoppy' Hardy, who immediately roughed him up in the doctor's room before announcing that he was removing the battered prisoner for further interrogation. But Aherne warned Hardy to return with Guilfoyle or he would prefer charges, and though the Auxiliary left in a fury he came back a couple of hours later after putting Guilfoyle through a mock execution on a nearby golf course. Guilfoyle was briefly interned but then resumed his intelligence activities.

Although the Squad was not officially on the run after Bloody Sunday, it still risked being flushed out of hiding by massive British Army and Auxiliary dragnets, like that of late November 1920 in which Paddy Daly was mistaken for the house owner giving him sanctuary and interned until February 1921.[8] One group – Joe Leonard, Jimmy Conroy and Charlie Dalton of GHQ Intelligence – shared cold, depressing, unfurnished rooms at the Summerhill Dispensary, a large complex close to Mountjoy Square containing a Registry of births, deaths and marriages, a chemist's and housing for medical staff. Dalton recalled a bedroom 'illuminated only by the rays of light from the street lamps. From our beds we could see the curfew patrols passing along the thoroughfare outside. We slept lightly, waking often with a start to hear a lorry pulling up outside. There was a building opposite which was often raided. Even in our slumbers the sense of danger was always near us.'[9] British searches also lapped around the Squad's headquarters in Upper Abbey Street, and in early 1921 Vinnie Byrne investigated a burst of grenade and revolver fire nearby:

> I threw off my jacket, tucked up my shirt sleeves and with my overalls on me, I looked the real hard-working fellow. I proceeded to the gate and opened the wicket. Standing outside was a British Tommy. I popped my head out and asked what was all the shooting. He replied: 'Those bloody Shinners ambushed us.' I said to him: 'That's terrible' and then I remarked: 'I had better be getting back to my job, in case the boss is looking for me.' Closing the wicket, I went back to the lads and told them what had happened. Later, we learned that the ASU had attacked the lorry at the corner of Swift's Row and Ormond Quay.[10]

Geo. Moreland, the sham cabinet-makers that served as a cover for the Squad's headquarters, was never raided.

Despite the increased activity on the part of the British, the Squad was still active, and just before Christmas 1920 it killed Detective Inspector Philip

O'Sullivan, a 23-year-old bachelor, decorated war hero and expert decoder. Crow Street believed that he was close to locating Collins's Henry Street office and had an intelligence officer shadow him for a week.[11] In the early evening of 17 December, when O'Sullivan met his fiancée as usual, two gunmen opened fire on him. While O'Sullivan's girlfriend grappled with one shooter, the other pumped bullets into his prone body. As O'Sullivan lay dying, Joe Leonard noticed an old flower-seller who had 'lifted O'Sullivan's head on to her lap and was saying, "My poor boy, they have shot you", and then sensed there was a strange atmosphere around her – dropping his head on the pavement she waddled away, not praying'.[12]

The Squad also eliminated William Doran, the 45-year-old head porter at the Wicklow Hotel, where Collins dined frequently. After a fellow employee had reported Doran as a British informer, Tobin ordered his execution. On 28 January 1921 the Squad and GHQ intelligence officers waited outside the hotel where Doran usually dusted mats between 8.30 and 9 a.m. When he appeared on the pavement, an inside contact raised the restaurant blind to confirm his identity and Doran was immediately shot dead. Without any IRA claim of responsibility, Doran's widow believed that British forces had killed her husband. When she asked for Collins's help, he did not have the heart to tell her the truth and authorised financial assistance to the family.[13]

In early February 1921 the Squad finally avenged McKee's and Clancy's deaths, responsibility for which Crow Street attributed to John Ryan, the former British military policeman whose execution McKee had vetoed. Ryan was further compromised in IRA eyes by his sister, who had a shebeen, close to the Gloucester Street house where McKee and Clancy had been captured, that was frequented by British troops and Auxiliaries. Ryan's daily routine invariably began around midday at his local pub. On 5 February 1921, the Squad's Tom Keogh and Ben Byrne made their way there accompanied by Jim Slattery, Vinnie and Eddie Byrne, Frank Bolster, Jimmy Conroy, Joe Leonard, Mick O'Reilly, Bill Stapleton and Mick Kennedy of GHQ Intelligence. As they passed a funeral cortège, a taxi driver, scenting business, asked them if they, too, were going to the burial. Keogh replied, 'No, but I'm going to arrange for one'.[14] Keogh and Ben Byrne entered the pub by a side door, ordered a couple of drinks and chatted casually while scrutinising customers. Eventually Byrne noticed one man immersed in a racing paper. Although his face was not clearly visible, he fitted Ryan's general description. Byrne recalled that

Keogh nudged me to make a move, and I, taking the hint, approached the man and asked him what they were tipping for some particular race, the three o'clock or the 3.30. This brought about the desired result because he had of necessity to lower the paper. Immediately he did so we knew our search was over. Without any hesitation or delay Keogh fired on him, I doing likewise. We made no delay, nor did we make any further examination of our victim, because we were perfectly satisfied from our previous experience that Ryan would betray no more members of our organisation.[15]

Collins also carried the intelligence war to England in early 1921 after Auxiliaries began carrying handcuffed IRA suspects in their vehicles as hostages against IRA attacks. There was some IRA pressure for retaliation in Britain, where security gates had been installed at the entrance to Downing Street and armed bodyguards protected Lloyd George. Neligan confirmed that killing the prime minister 'was mooted more than once in high IRA circles, but never sanctioned. One of those who favoured it also thought up a scheme for bombing the crowds leaving the London theatres, but this was turned down as preposterous.'[16] Instead Collins dispatched Frank Thornton to London to coordinate the simultaneous kidnapping of a dozen government ministers and MPs and hold them in safe houses until Auxiliary hostage-taking ended. For a couple of months Thornton shadowed politicians, many of whom seemingly spent a lot more time with their mistresses than their families. Eventually he selected twenty-five targets and had the London IRA ready itself for a swoop. But before Collins could give his final approval, hostage carrying suddenly ended and the operation was abandoned.[17]

* * *

Despite Special Branch's losses on Bloody Sunday, Wilson believed that only a hard core of IRA gunmen remained active, but isolated from a population increasingly sick of the conflict. General Boyd was similarly optimistic, telling Robert Jeune: '"I think we have broken the back of the movement now, don't you?" I replied, "Yes, sir, and I think six months should see it out" to which he answered "Yes, I think you are right. Hamar Greenwood says two months, but I think that is rather optimistic."'[18] Using Mulcahy's captured papers, Macready's deputy Brind rapidly interned over 500 suspects. By the Truce in July 1921 over 4,000 men had been incarcerated. Administering the camps severely drained British troop strength and the army would have liked to relocate them outside Ireland. Macready claimed that 'at one time it was seriously suggested that the internees should be sent to St Helena but unfortunately the proposal never materialised'.[19]

On 10 December 1920 the British Cabinet authorised martial law in Counties Cork, Limerick, Tipperary and Kerry. When Macready finally returned from France on 11 December he approved a two-week weapons' amnesty, after which anyone caught bearing arms or wearing uniform would be executed. Sturgis would have preferred 'to declare war on them and shoot them for being out of uniform, not in it'.[20] Macready also wanted to sideline Winter, hand intelligence entirely over to the military and recall Wilson, whose tour of duty had ended soon after Bloody Sunday.[21] But on 17 December, Anderson persuaded him to retain Winter and in the interests of greater cohesion even give him control of Special Branch.[22] Winter's removal would have antagonised Tudor, increased the army's influence and created an impression that Ireland was being handed over to military rule when Anderson's goal was a politically negotiated settlement. Macready went along with Anderson partly because he believed Wilson's successor as Head of Special Branch was 'no good. He does not like the work, has no heart for it and is anxious to get away.'[23] Reluctantly Macready agreed to try Winter as intelligence supremo for six weeks: if he was still dissatisfied after that time, he would inaugurate full-blown military control.

After taking over Special Branch at the end of December 1920, Winter was promoted to Chief of the Combined Intelligence Services and Director of Intelligence for the Crown Forces. But his detractors at the Castle were still conducting a whispering campaign against him, and Macready was hardly reassured when Winter initiated raids on monasteries supposedly sheltering Collins. On 2 January 1921 the manhunt culminated in fiasco when troops entered a nunnery, provoking Macready's withering remark to Sturgis that 'if "O" doesn't know the difference between a man and a woman I should take time to instruct him. I have heard "O" charged with many crimes but not this one.'[24] General Boyd thought amalgamating a specifically Dublin organisation like Special Branch with Winter's national Central Intelligence Office was 'a grave mistake'.[25] Many Special Branch members resented being subsumed into a larger police organisation, and their primary loyalty remained with Boyd.[26] Furthermore, as the general commanding Dublin District, Boyd received secret service information and prior warning of any intelligence operation in the capital, a duplication which caused 'delay in taking action, overlapping in work and a registry created on the lines of compromise and satisfactory to neither military nor police'.[27] Finally, although Winter was nominally the new intelligence supremo in Dublin, Hill Dillon remained Macready's GHQ intelligence officer, leaving intact an inherently inefficient dual military/police system.

Chief Secretary Greenwood was not worried because he thought the war would soon be over anyway. In December 1920 he assured Lloyd George that, 'We are on top, with the House and the Country and I believe most Irishmen wishing us well. Our position and strength is rapidly improving. The S.F. cause and organisation is breaking up. There is no need of hurry in settlement. We can in due course and on our own fair terms settle this Irish Question.'[28] Warren Fisher did not share Greenwood's confidence because on a return visit to Dublin in early February 1921 he found 'no grounds for optimism at all'.[29] Although forty killings occurred during his stay, the Chief Secretary still radiated optimism, despite having to 'live immured in his Lodge, his visitors restricted to the Officers of Government (and possibly stray members of the non-representative clique known as the old Ascendancy party) and necessarily out of direct (or, I imagine, any other sort of touch) with the ordinary people of Ireland and their currents of thought'.[30] Fisher emphasised that the Government of Ireland Act was not a panacea because few independent candidates would stand in elections for the new Southern Parliament, which anyway could only be held with 'Black and Tans in and about the polling booths'.[31] And Sinn Fein had the political power and popular support to render futile any new political arrangements which the British Government devised. Fisher was extremely depressed at the contrast between a united republican organisation operating under a single direction and an Irish administration fragmented between politicians, police and army, all apparently incapable of cooperating effectively. The police seemed out of political control, and the idea that they were capable of 'thinking out and organising some concerted plan of campaign is a proposition which even an ostrich could hardly entertain'.[32] The need for unified control was undeniable, but the administrative machine's innate conservatism smothered reform. Sturgis pined for 'a virtual dictator – to be obeyed by everyone, military, police, civil servants etc. As it is we are a great sprawling hydra-headed monster spending much of its time using one of its heads to abuse one or other of the others by letter, telegram and word of mouth.'[33]

While Winter reorganised British Intelligence at the start of 1921, he still wanted to avenge Bloody Sunday. 'The leaders of Sinn Fein stalked the city with impunity and in order to circumvent this condition I asked Tudor for permission to form an "Intelligence Squad" under the leadership of a reliable Head Constable. These men were either old members of the Special Branch or experienced members of the local police. Their duties were to wander about the streets in twos or threes attired in plain clothes.'[34] Their leader was Eugene Igoe, a Catholic from a Mayo farming family who, although still in his early thirties, was already an RIC legend because of his eagerness to hit back at the IRA. In June 1920 he had warned that 'if the Sinn Fein organisation think that they will terrorise the police force in carrying out their duties they are making a very big mistake. On the contrary, they are making them more determined every day to carry out their duties.'[35] In January 1921 Winter made Igoe a temporary Head Constable and transferred him to Dublin with a commission to go after IRA leaders and those provincial Volunteers gravitating to the capital.[36]

Igoe recruited a group of RIC officers driven out of the provinces who, according to the Squad's Bill Stapleton, 'wore civilian clothes and were always elegantly attired. The appearance of this unit in Dublin greatly increased the work of the Squad and also made it more perilous.'[37] Dublin Volunteers came to know them as the Igoe Gang, but Anderson nicknamed them Tudor's Tigers.[38] In Dublin their ruthlessness and combative mentality inspired fear among Volunteers. An evocative photograph shows them armed to the teeth, smiling and relaxing in an open-topped car, eerily reminiscent of Western desperadoes. And indeed they regarded Ireland as England's Wild West, a land where rough frontier justice prevailed. A superior of Igoe's acknowledged that he had a freewheeling attitude to legality since he 'found it necessary to be handier with his gun than the gunmen were with theirs. Hence his extreme unpopularity. There is no doubt that, whilst the Police Officers in Dublin are filled with the utmost admiration for Igoe, he is regarded by the IRA as a murderer and that his life will be in danger wherever he goes.'[39]

Operating out of the Castle, the Igoe Gang concentrated on railway stations, scrutinising passengers and shadowing suspects, some of whom (according to Traynor) they killed.[40] Heavily armed, they also circulated constantly around the city centre, where, Stapleton recalled, their *modus operandi* was to stroll along the streets, drop into shops, pubs and restaurants, theatres, attend on the fringes of football matches, etc, always on the look-out for country members of the Volunteers and on one being recognised the well-dressed members of the Murder Gang would quietly move around the individual or individuals and smilingly chat and talking quietly force him into a secluded spot and there, while still chatting and smiling, would interrogate him. Rarely, if ever, did they produce guns. Somewhere within 100 yards or so of the Igoe Gang there was invariably an Army motor van and when the Gang decided to arrest an individual a whistle was blown or a signal was given and the waiting van would arrive and take away the prisoner.

It is not to be thought that the Igoe Gang was always courteous and polite. The procedure just described was simply their method of working which enabled them to effect arrests and interrogation without creating any excitement or drawing attention to themselves whatever. They did on occasions, but particularly at night time when darkness helped them somewhat, indeed act very brutally and commit a number of murders.[41]

Collins wanted the Igoe Gang destroyed but even he could not glean much information on it. Time and again GHQ intelligence officers picked up the trail only for the Squad to arrive too late. Eventually Tobin decided to import a Galway Volunteer, Tom ('Sweeney') Newell, who knew Igoe. Constantly shadowed by Stapleton, carrying two revolvers, spare ammunition and hand grenades, he combed the city centre.[42] At last, Newell spotted Igoe in Grafton Street heading towards St Stephen's Green, where Tobin ordered him and Charlie Dalton to rendezvous with the Squad. As he made his way to the Green, Vinnie Byrne 'noticed a group of men standing along a wall and speaking to two of them was Charlie Dalton. I did not know any of the other men and I thought to myself that the group was probably the south side ASU. I carried on up Dame Street. As I was passing Charlie I gave a slight nod of my head towards him. He did not recognise me. I thought it was strange.'[43]

Byrne was right. Igoe had recognised Newell, turned suddenly and cornered him and Dalton, who remembered that the manoeuvre 'was carried out so quietly and neatly that the pedestrians did not notice anything amiss. I could see that we were covered from their pockets and looking around I saw that we were surrounded. The Gang were standing about in groups of two and three on the footpath.'[44] Mentally reciting acts of contrition, Dalton was put up against a wall, where he claimed to be simply a solicitor's clerk innocently giving a stranger directions. But Newell knew that Igoe had trapped him and was openly defiant. Eventually Igoe ordered Dalton to leave, keep walking and not look back. His knees knocking as two men followed him, Dalton was certain he was about to be shot 'while attempting to escape'. 'The agony was to keep walking. I wanted to tear through the streets away from those footsteps pacing behind me. That was what they wanted too.'[45] But Dalton got away in Wicklow Street by slipping through the doorway of his father's office and dashing upstairs.

Newell was not so fortunate. Igoe walked him to the Four Courts and genially bade him farewell, but soon afterwards Newell was shot from behind and badly wounded in the hips and legs. Perhaps on a whim, Igoe had his police car carry Newell to hospital, and the evening headlines reported the shooting of a well-known rebel fugitive when he went for his weapon after Crown forces had recognised him. Newell's injuries were very serious. Even when Collins got him released after the Truce, he was hospitalised for another two years before being discharged a cripple for life.

But the duel between the Squad and Igoe had its comic aspects. Like two lumbering heavyweight boxers, they circled each other, staring meaningfully, making occasional feints but throwing remarkably few punches and inflicting little or no damage. On one occasion the Squad was lined up on the north side of the Liffey ready to gun down Igoe's men, who then drove along on the opposite side. Next time the Squad positioned itself on the southern side and again could only watch helplessly as Igoe's cars raced along the other bank. Finally both sides retired to their respective corners, unbloodied and unbowed. On the day of the Truce, 11 July 1921, Winter promoted Igoe permanently to Head Constable in recognition of his Dublin service, but after the Treaty he and his wife had to leave Ireland forever.[46]

* * *

In the weeks after Bloody Sunday Collins's power rose to its zenith. Basking in republican admiration, he was also acting President for a month between Griffith's arrest on 26 November and de Valera's return from his prolonged American tour. But pressure was mounting on him. Already shaken by losing McKee and Clancy, Collins was deprived of a valuable cabinet ally during Griffith's lengthy imprisonment. Furthermore, Mulcahy claimed that Brugha was 'developing a very active antipathy to Collins. With Dev's return Cathal was encouraged and was given an opening of being more active [sic] in influencing the atmosphere of the Cabinet.'[47] Mulcahy admitted that, because Brugha had conceded day-to-day control of the Volunteers to himself and Collins, they hadn't realised his slow-burning resentment at Collins's fame and adulation. Brugha 'was apparently, without our realising it at that time, probably taking a greater interest as to how he could affect the GHQ staff without knowing exactly what he wanted to do with or through the GHQ Staff except weaken Collins's position there.'[48]

By January 1921 Brugha was starting to reassert his authority over Collins by chairing weekly meetings of an Army Council at which every GHQ Director had to deliver a report. During one session Brugha castigated Collins's performance as Director of Intelligence, complaining that no proper documentation of his department's expenses existed.

Mulcahy also believed that Brugha was influencing Traynor while he, in turn, was being used by de Valera to destabilise Collins. When de Valera returned from America on Christmas Eve morning 1920 he had immediately berated Mulcahy: 'You are going too fast. This odd shooting of a policeman here and there is having a very bad effect, from the propaganda point of view, on us in America. What we want is one good battle about once a month with about 500 men on each side.'[49] At the time Mulcahy regarded this as the off-the-cuff remark of someone out of touch with Ireland and fatigued by a tiring trans-Atlantic journey. But at an Army Council meeting a few weeks later de Valera dismissed the publicity value of provincial ambushes and proposed a headline-grabbing action in Dublin. He suggested capturing Beggar's Bush Barracks or destroying inland revenue and local government records in the Custom House. De Valera and Brugha instructed Collins to have GHQ Intelligence look into a possible attack on Beggar's Bush while Traynor reconnoitred the Custom House.[50] Despite their misgivings about occupying large British government buildings, Collins and Mulcahy did not resist, especially since, as heroes of the Rising, de Valera and Brugha carried considerable authority in military matters.

By the end of 1920 Collins's G Division sources had also become wasting assets. Joe Kavanagh had died in September after an appendix operation, by which time most political work was already concentrated in the Castle. Left behind at Great Brunswick Street in charge of office duties, Broy provided increasingly meagre information even before his world fell apart, literally overnight. On New Year's Eve 1920 Auxiliaries raided the Dawson Street flat of Collins's secretary Eileen McGrane, where Tom Cullen had been storing intelligence material.[51] There was so much information that a van was required to convey it to the Castle. The documents included Broy's copies of G Division reports which were well over a year old and should have been destroyed. Depositing them with McGrane was doubly absurd because she lived opposite – and frequently and incautiously visited – the secret headquarters of the Cumann na mBan (the women's IRA).[52] Soon afterwards this too was captured.

Within hours Collins warned Broy to prepare for the inevitable fallout. Every remaining vestige of G Division's political work was transferred immediately to the Castle. Broy's responsibility for the office in which the captured documents had been typed made him the prime suspect, ending his residual usefulness to Collins.[53] Throughout January 1921 Broy lived from day to day, sleeping fitfully and dragging himself to work, where, as rumours swirled around him, he continued to protest his innocence. When a colleague identified him as having typed two captured reports, Broy claimed that he had been sucked into a nightmare of coincidence and circumstantial evidence. If his superiors hoped that by leaving him twisting slowly in the wind they would get him to confess, they had picked the wrong man. Broy was cool and tough, and as a policeman he more than anyone knew how to play out that particular waiting game. The end finally came on 17 February 1921 after Superintendent Purcell brought Broy to the Castle. There, Broy and an inspector waited outside the Chief Commissioner's office until Purcell finally re-emerged 'trembling and with his face as white as a sheet. In a quivering voice, he told me that I was to be arrested for giving out the documents to Sinn Feiners. The Inspector, although a loyalist, was also shocked and rendered speechless. I, of course, was not surprised, although I had to express indignation to the best of my ability.'[54]

Broy could have knocked out both Purcell and the inspector and tried bluffing his way past Auxiliary sentries, or even shooting his way out. But that was as good as a signed confession. Instead he had his pistol removed and after being searched was taken in a police van to Arbour Hill Military Prison. But despite his predicament, a great weight of uncertainty had finally been lifted off Broy and after months of mental torture he once again enjoyed a good night's rest. However, he was in deep trouble, because 21 November 1920 had changed everything. One British soldier noted that 'in Dublin time is now reckoned as since or before Bloody Sunday', while Neligan heard fellow detectives speculating 'that Broy was to be executed. In the temper of the time, it was a distinct possibility.'[55]

Collins remained secretly in touch with Broy through a sympathetic prison chaplain and a solicitor who told him Collins was planning to send the Squad into Arbour Hill prison in a captured British vehicle, disguised as soldiers and carrying forged release papers for Broy.[56] But Broy demurred. He was reluctant to risk Volunteers' lives. He still hoped to extricate himself by protesting his innocence and emphasising the improbability of the automatic prime suspect actually leaking intelligence to the enemy. Neligan also pointed out the dangers of a rescue attempt. The prison had four machine-gun nests, vigilant army guards, 10 feet-high walls topped by barbed wire, an alarm system that could be heard for miles and two military garrisons nearby. Instead, he suggested frightening off Detective Chief Inspector Supple, who was assembling the evidence against Broy. Soon afterwards, a fellow-worshipper at Mass quietly warned Supple to go very slowly.[57]

Ironically, another disgraced policeman was also a guest of His Majesty. Captain King of 'F' Company was charged with murdering two republicans whom he had taken out of the Castle for 'a bit of shooting'[58] and whose bullet-riddled bodies were discovered in Drumcondra soon afterwards with tin cans forced over their heads. But one survived long enough to make a statement. As policemen, King and Broy exercised separately from other prisoners, and, like two old lags, they lapped the main courtyard, proclaiming their innocence and bemoaning their fate. 'Major [sic] King was full of his own grievances for being arrested and, of course, I duly enlarged on mine. He said, "All Governments are the same. They utilise the services of people like you and me and are then quite prepared to hang us if it suits their purpose." He appeared to be afraid that the "politicians" would hang him just to show how "fair-minded" they were.'[59] But King had not been entirely abandoned. The prison's military staff told Broy that Greenwood had subscribed £500 to King's defence, while Tudor and Winter regarded every accusation against the Auxiliaries as republican black propaganda. Sturgis also reported that 'Hoppy' Hardy was strenuously intimidating witnesses,[60] as well as testifying at the court martial that King had been elsewhere with him when the two men had been shot. It all helped. On 15 April 1921 King was acquitted.[61]

After weeks of inaction, charges amounting to high treason were laid against Broy in early April 1921. But he was fortunate because a Detective Sergeant McCarthy, who had resigned a year earlier to move to London, had also done some office typing. Since McCarthy was mildly sympathetic to Sinn Fein and none of the captured documents had been typed after his departure, he made an ideal fall guy. So when the prosecution decided to have McCarthy testify at the court martial, Collins smuggled him to New York. After McCarthy's disappearance, Broy's solicitor cheekily requested a speedy trial for his client, who was anxious to get back to work![62] Bereft of a key witness, the prosecution stalled continuously without ever divulging the reason for McCarthy's non-appearance. Broy stayed in prison until shortly after the Truce, when Collins insisted on his release.

One reason for Broy's refusal to run was his anxiety to avoid pointing the finger at his close friend Detective Sergeant McNamara, who was still the Assistant Commissioner's confidential clerk. Yet, while Broy was in prison, McNamara, too, was brought down after Collins had leaked to Sinn Fein's Publicity Bureau a British Government letter accusing American sailors of supplying weapons to the IRA. Inexplicably, Collins had sacrificed McNamara for the short-term advantage of instigating a diplomatic row between Washington and London.[63] Although McNamara was the main suspect, he was not formally accused, and instead Edgeworth-Johnstone dismissed him. When Neligan met him coming down the stairs afterwards, he warned McNamara to be careful, especially about the Auxiliaries' 'F' Company. Subsequently, McNamara went on the run, operating on the fringes of the Squad.[64]

McNamara's removal left Neligan dangerously isolated and very depressed: 'I missed him terribly; we were great friends and now I was alone in the Castle. It set me wondering when my number would come up!'[65] But instead of resigning Neligan ingeniously burrowed even deeper into British Intelligence by joining the secret service. In May 1921 Cope interviewed him and passed Neligan on to a British intelligence officer who gave him his cover as an insurance agent, a curfew pass, an automatic pistol, ammunition and instructions about secret signs and inks. He then sent him undercover in Kingstown (Dun Laoghaire).[66]

Collins was delighted at Neligan's audacity and his access to British intelligence reports about IRA personnel and activities in the Kingstown area. Collins would cycle out to meet Neligan in a pub opposite Blackrock College, often waving en route to passing Auxiliary patrols. Together they

concocted a report for the British and laughed heartily at its contents. We said that arms were pouring into Ireland daily for the rebels, hundreds of Volunteers offered themselves for flying columns in a desire to immolate themselves on the altar of freedom. The ordinary people were prepared to fight to the last man, millions of cash were being sent from the USA; the morale of the Volunteers was buoyant. I gave the courier this gem. The secret service must have needed a headache powder having read it.[67]

But Collins was also experiencing problems with the Squad. Far from being a band of brothers, it often experienced tensions between its strong-willed members. Slattery never acknowledged Paddy Daly as his leader and regarded the Squad more as a loose confederation than a tight unit with one commander: 'I received my orders through Mick McDonnell. I looked upon him as the officer in charge of the section to which I was attached. There was another section under the command of Paddy Daly.'[68] Daly, on the other hand, always insisted that he was the commander of a single, disciplined unit, dismissing McDonnell as a marginal figure who was always 'butting in, and on account of that he often did damage because he was too eager. He was not a member of the Squad.'[69] But Vinnie Byrne partially corroborated Slattery, arguing that after July 1919 Mick McDonnell had led an unofficial, part-time Squad of six to eight men and only in early March 1920 was an official, full-time Squad created. Even then, Byrne, Keogh and Slattery never looked to Daly and considered themselves 'McDonnell's trio'.[70] Frank Thornton, too, regarded McDonnell as the first Squad leader.[71]

While the Squad's structural incoherence suited Collins's distaste for clear chains of command and his obsessive need for control, it often left subordinates operating with incomplete knowledge. This could be very dangerous. Vinnie Byrne recalled that on 29 November 1919 he, McDonnell, Keogh and Slattery were shadowing Detective Sergeant John Barton in Grafton Street. Suddenly Daly, Leonard and Ben Barrett appeared

on the same errand as we were. Now it was a race to see whose party would get Barton first. As one party would pass out the other to have a go, people would come in between us and our quarry. Barton got as far as the Crampton monument and was in the act of stepping off the path to cross over to the police station in Brunswick St. when fire was opened on him. He went down on his side, falling to the right slightly. Then he turned towards the left and raised himself a little on his right knee and said: 'Oh, God, what did I do to deserve this?' With that, he pulled his gun and fired up College St.[72]

In his account, Byrne was deliberately imprecise about which group fired first, because this was a 'friendly fire' incident. To Leonard's astonishment there was 'a heavy fusillade of firing at us from an unexpected place in the opposite direction from us. It was explained to us later when we had all decamped and on meeting Mick McDonald [sic] he told us that he had an independent squad out to do the same job.'[73]

Although Daly claimed that between his arrest after Bloody Sunday and his release in February 1921 Joe Leonard acted as Squad leader, most members clearly looked to Tom Keogh. George White, a well-informed ASU member, says that under Keogh the Squad became increasingly undisciplined and fuelled on alcohol, causing an unhappy Collins virtually to provoke a mutiny after Daly's release by telling

> Keogh that he intended to put Daly in charge of the Squad, Keogh refused to hand over to Daly and the majority of the Squad backed Keogh and threatened all kinds of reprisals. In fact, at a meeting in Gardiner St. which was presided over by Oscar Traynor and attended by the Squad and members of the ASU at which I was present, the attitude of the HQ Squad was definitely disobedient and they cut up rather rough. This trouble resolved itself at the burning of the Custom House when Keogh and the majority of the Squad were arrested; Daly assumed command automatically.[74]

Ben Byrne supported White's account:

> When Daly was arrested and interned in Ballykinlar, Tom Keogh became OC with Slattery second in command. On Daly's release he was not able to oust Keogh from the position Keogh had held during his, Daly's, internment. It was only after the Custom House when the Squad as such had ceased to exist that Daly and Leonard, by virtue mainly of the fact that they were probably the only members of the Squad free at that time, became accepted as persons fitted to fill the vacancies.[75]

Vinnie Byrne was dismissive of Daly: 'It is my honest opinion that Keogh was in charge of the group. I was out umpteen times and Daly was never with us.

He might have been out an odd time but I know that Keogh and Slattery went to Crow Street for information from the Intelligence and we got no information from Daly or Joe Leonard.'[76]

* * *

Even after Winter's promotion in December 1920 the British Intelligence system remained dysfunctional. Winter's own empire, officially designated 'D' Branch, Chief of Police, controlled the RIC, DMP, the Auxiliary Division, Crimes Branch Special, Dublin District Special Branch and Cameron's secret service agents. Its Central Office collated its information as well as that of Military Intelligence, Scotland House, informers and captured documents. Its officers also interrogated IRA suspects and made recommendations for their release, internment or trial. But Macready's dream of an integrated intelligence system remained as elusive as ever. Military Intelligence regarded 'D' Branch as 'a peculiar organisation' run by an 'enthusiastic amateur',[77] and Special Branch officers never reconciled themselves to Winter's leadership. Moreover, Basil Thomson's agents still operated in Dublin – presumably with Winter's permission – despite their agreement of August 1920. And the RIC's Crimes Branch Special still functioned outside the capital alongside Military Intelligence in an inefficient parallel system.

Winter's major initiative was to establish Local Centres throughout Ireland under Divisional RIC Commissioners responsible for coordinating police and military intelligence.[78] But staff recruitment was slow because few junior police officers were trained in intelligence duties and new entrants spent a month studying Central Office's organisation and methods. Although the Belfast Centre opened in January 1921, those at Cork, Limerick, Kildare, Athlone, Galway and Dundalk began operating only during March and April. Clonmel's did not start until June – only a month before the Truce. Military Intelligence doubted the value of these centres and excoriated the Divisional Commissioners' understanding of intelligence.[79] Winter also created a Raid Bureau to examine, summarise and distribute copies of captured documents as well as a Registry with a card index system and files on enemy organisations such as Sinn Fein and the Republican Police. A Photographic Section had snaps of every detainee, making it easier to arrest re-offenders. It also duplicated photographs found during raids.

Because of diminishing returns, Winter relied less on secret servicemen and informers, especially during the last six months of the war, when, as

Military Intelligence acknowledged, the population 'was in a state of open rebellion or was in sympathy with such rebellion'.[80] Rewards and bribes became totally ineffective because 'the bulk of the people were our enemies and were therefore far more incorruptible than has been the case in former Irish movements'.[81] Winter lamented that 'there was not a nibble at the bait'.[82] But the army was reluctant to accept that nobody would bite, and in early March 1921 Macready urged Anderson to authorise £10,000 for capturing Collins, Brugha and Mulcahy.[83] Anderson was sceptical about rewards, which he thought demoralised government supporters – 'such as they are'[84] – by casting doubt on the security forces' ability to catch wanted men. They also made rebels like Breen and Treacy into even greater popular heroes. The British Cabinet agreed and turned Macready down, leaving Collins (contrary to legend) without a price on his head.

Winter's interrogators frequently but unsuccessfully tried bribing detainees. Christy Harte, a Vaughan's Hotel porter completely trusted by Collins, was arrested on 31 December 1920 and told after a routine softening-up in the Castle that he had been seen carrying Collins's bicycle down the hotel steps. His interrogators offered him £10,000 if he simply telephoned a coded message the next time Collins visited Vaughan's. Harte was released but never made the call.[85] Reluctantly Winter acknowledged that IRA terror was more effective than the lure of money, citing two passengers on Alan Bell's final tram journey who had told him they had not claimed the reward because they knew they would not live a day to enjoy it. After Bloody Sunday Winter kept two witnesses – a man and his sister – under protection in Scotland, but they refused to testify at the courts martial, pleading, 'We want to live until we die.'[86] The best informers who acted voluntarily were clergymen, bank managers, shop owners and employees of military contractors, farmers and civilians employed by the British Army and police. 'Women were particularly useful, but their employment sometimes involved relations that were more than friendly. This was occasionally inconvenient.'[87]

Military Intelligence admitted that 'Secret Service was on the whole a failure in Ireland',[88] where strangers, especially those with English accents, were regarded warily. Deep penetration of the enemy was impossible unless agents displayed absolute commitment and ruthlessness – 'in which case they ran a reasonably good prospect of being shot at any moment by the Crown Forces'.[89] Furthermore, 'if a man was suspected he was given false information; if this was acted on by the Crown Forces suspicion became a certainty'.[90] So, although initially Winter and Wilson had intended to flood Ireland, they scaled their ambitions down primarily to Dublin. Even there, the intelligence offensive was undermined by 'the vicious plan of allowing parallel systems of secret service to work simultaneously in the same area'.[91]

Increasingly, Winter relied for intelligence on raids and searches. He believed that the Irish 'had an irresistible habit of keeping documents. They would hide them in the most unexpected places, but they seldom evaded discovery by the trained sleuth; and by this time the Dublin District Intelligence Service men had become outstanding experts.'[92] Although Winter's day usually started in mid-morning, he was still there at 11 p.m. to see the raiding parties off and then welcome them back in the early hours. Frequently he retired to bed only at 4 a.m. Raids scooped up suspects and enemy documents, allowed questioning of the families of Volunteers on the run and provided cover for meeting informers. Most raids resulted from definite information or surveillance, but some were conducted on the off-chance of netting a returning fugitive. Because in daylight IRA scouts often spotted uniformed parties before they reached their destination, plain-clothes units in motor cars would arrive unexpectedly and leave before anyone could intervene.

The raiding strategy's vital breakthrough was capturing Mulcahy's papers in November 1920.[93] His lists of Volunteers' names and addresses started a snowball process in which finds in one house initiated further raids and more discoveries of documents and suspects. By the Truce of July 1921, 6,311 raids had been carried out in the Dublin District. Yet Mulcahy seemed incapable of learning. On 21 January 1921, when British search parties appeared nearby, he cycled away from a house on Merrion Road, leaving yet more papers on a table. This time Mulcahy got away with it because when he risked returning that evening they still lay undisturbed.[94] But he was not as lucky a few weeks later when soldiers raided a South Frederick Street flat and seized documents that included a report on a major IRA ambush. Mulcahy's propensity for losing vital information provoked merriment in British Intelligence, where a monocled officer languidly told Michael Noyk that 'this Chief of Staff of yours ought to be scrapped; he is always losing his papers'.[95]

But Mulcahy was not the only person feeling the heat. The British almost stumbled on Brigade Headquarters in Gardiner's Row while Oscar Traynor was meeting his Adjutant, Kit O'Malley, and Emmet Dalton, GHQ's Assistant Director of Training. Dalton was a former British Army officer who still looked the part with his debonair toothbrush moustache and cultured accent.

Suddenly the hall porter's buzzer warned them of a British search party that was sealing off the entire block and Brigade papers were hurriedly concealed in secret cabinets. Although the soldiers missed the Brigade office, they remained in the hallway until Dalton suggested going downstairs and brazening it out. There he exchanged a few quiet words with a soldier, who saluted him and fetched an officer to whom Dalton quietly confided that he, too, was a British officer on a highly secret mission. Then, after snapping, 'Come along, men', he led Traynor and O'Malley away to safety.[96]

There was a successful raid near the Castle gates on the solicitor's office of Eamon Duggan, Collins's predecessor as Director of Intelligence.[97] When Auxiliaries arrived on 26 November 1920 Duggan nonchalantly granted permission for a search of his room, whose shelves were bulging with hundreds of clients' files. After combing the lower rows unsuccessfully, a detective climbed a ladder and found files covered in years of dust containing Duggan's entire collection of intelligence reports. Winter regarded this concealment as a cunning ploy, but it was incredibly naive of Duggan to retain such redundant material and then permit a search of his legal papers. The security-conscious Noyk destroyed every incriminating document in his solicitor's office, including numerous communications from Collins and Griffith.[98] One British raid on 26 May 1921 finally located Collins's Finance Office in Mary Street, though Collins was in a city-centre pub at the time. Frank Thornton witnessed the raid and warned Collins to stay away.[99] When Mulcahy met him soon afterwards, he noticed Collins's disquiet that the British had got so close.[100]

Not every raid went smoothly. Sometimes Volunteers fled in advance after tip-offs from IRA agents like William Beaumont. This former Dublin Fusilier cultivated the Auxiliaries 'F' Company and became their drinking buddy in hotels, pubs and, after curfew, at the Castle.[101] An armoured car always delivered him home safely in the early hours. The IRA also tried luring raiding parties into ambushes. In early February 1921 a Volunteer GHQ intelligence officer spotted an enemy agent conducting surveillance in Seville Place, close to the O'Toole Gaelic Football Club whose rooms were used by many nationalist societies. After Crow Street had got the Club to organise a continuous flow of visitors to attract the British spy's attention, the Squad and the ASU positioned themselves in Amiens Street and Portland Row. Tom Cullen and Frank Thornton then detained the British agent, forcing him to reveal both his name and the telephone number of his Dublin Castle controller. Cullen then rang the controller, mimicking the spy's voice, with urgent news of a major republican gathering at the Club. As Cullen and Thornton walked down Talbot Street soon afterwards, a convoy of ten lorries passed them, but when they reached Seville Place there was no sign of the soldiers. Their convoy had simply halted for ten minutes before returning to barracks. Thornton speculated that a suspicious controller had tried unsuccessfully to contact his agent and then put out an alert.[102]

Occasionally, Volunteers resisted British raiding parties. A fifteen-minute gun battle in Great Brunswick Street occurred on 14 March 1921 when armed guards at a republican meeting fought Auxiliaries. By the time the building had been stormed most Volunteers had vanished through the back door – though two were caught with weapons and subsequently executed.

Persistent British raiding and searching forced many Volunteers to go on the run, made travelling with weapons in Dublin very dangerous and resulted in the capture of eight Dail and Volunteer GHQ offices, the Dublin Brigade's main weapons workshop and the Republican Police headquarters.[103] By 1921 the British had also identified nearly every Dublin Brigade officer, many of whom they arrested, imprisoned or interned. They had also established the structure of Volunteer GHQ, its close relationship with the Dublin Brigade and the names and positions of most republican leaders. But constant raiding dramatically increased paperwork at Winter's headquarters, where summaries of captured documents often exceeded 100 pages before they were copied and distributed to politicians, army and police leaders and every intelligence branch. Winter decided personally which detainees to release, intern or prosecute, and with 1,745 arrests in the Dublin District alone during a three-month period he devoted considerable time to 'sorting out the wolves from the lambs'.[104] By the first week of May 1921, besides those in prison, 19 IRA Brigade Commanders, 53 Brigade Staff Officers, 77 Battalion Commanders, 182 Battalion Staff Officers, 1,407 Company Officers and 1,596 other ranks were interned throughout Ireland.[105]

Puzzled and curious about Irish republican mentality, Winter liked to interrogate prominent suspects. Collins's secretary Eileen McGrane was the nearest he came to meeting his enemy counterpart, but disappointingly she remained silently defiant, uttering not a single word in one and a half hours. A colleague of Winter's boasted that he would quickly break her, but he retired defeated after another wordless session.[106] By contrast, Countess Markievicz would not keep quiet after her arrest in September 1920 – for being in a car without a tail light! Although a daughter of the Irish Ascendancy and married to a Polish count, she had become a republican convert who had fought in the Rising before ending up as the Dail government's Minister of Labour. Winter regarded her as a treasonous, caterwauling shrew who was 'hard, unrepentant, but loquacious, and left me in no doubt as to her opinion of the English. She informed me she was proud, proud of having been responsible for the deaths at her hands of eight British soldiers, and hoped she would be responsible for the deaths of more.'[107] But to his satisfaction Markievicz had paid a huge price for her disloyalty because time, 'coupled with her political anxieties, had long since torn any fragments of beauty from her brow'.[108] The Chief Secretary's wife, Margery, was also disappointed by the release of this 'thoroughly bad woman but no charges against her could be proved'. Learning from Macready that Markievicz's estranged Polish husband was a typist at the US embassy in Warsaw, she thought it would be a wonderful idea – 'but hard lines' on him – to deposit Markievicz in Poland.[109]

Winter was especially fascinated by Erskine Childers, the Dail's Director of Publicity. Born in London, raised in County Wicklow and educated at Cambridge, Childers had fought for the British in the Boer War and written a classic espionage novel *The Riddle of the Sands*. Despite espousing Irish nationalism and smuggling of rifles for the Irish Volunteers, Childers had carried out naval intelligence for the Royal Naval Air Service during the First World War. But subsequently his republican sympathies had reasserted themselves and he became Sinn Fein's leading propagandist. After tea, cigarettes and cosy conversation, Winter mischievously provoked this highly intelligent 'English renegade'[110] by subtly shifting to politics. This provoked Childers into a dramatic mood swing as he raged at British Government iniquities, excitedly demanded his papers back and exploded when Winter inquired, deliberately obtusely, about his past. 'I told him I regretted being unable to return the whole of his correspondence, but there was certainly one letter which I felt sure he would like to retain. It was an invitation to his wife to attend Buckingham Palace in order to be decorated with the M.B.E. for her services during the war. At this, his fury knew no bounds.'[111] Finally, a deadpan Winter asked whether Childers wanted the return of a brother's letter accusing him of grotesquely biased propaganda and reminding him to teach his children about their English heritage. 'And so we parted, he taking the documents that I thought were good for him, and I retaining the ones that were not.'[112]

But most prisoners did not enjoy cosy chats over tea. Despite interrogation guidelines recommending friendly small talk, an even temper and the avoidance of brutality, many innocent detainees confessed simply to escape more bullying, threats and beatings. However, British interrogators remained stolidly pedestrian and unimaginative, never employing techniques like electric shock treatment or water torture. One republican said that prisoners were

> brought before a special team consisting of a lawyer, who carried out the 'reasonable' and persuasive approach and a fierce 'Inquisitor' who bullied and threatened. The method generally used was to ring the changes rapidly on these two approaches until the prisoner was first bewildered and then reduced to a condition in which his resistance and caution collapsed and he would give, whether willingly or accidentally, all the information which he had.[113]

Under pressure for quick results, British intelligence officers processing literally thousands of suspects lacked the time for subtly eliciting information or playing mind games with prisoners. Not that many would have conceded that anything as sophisticated as a brain was encased inside the average Volunteer's skull.

Winter's interrogators induced very few Volunteers to cooperate, though he said some made 'voluntary statements' to secure better prison treatment or their release under the cover of ill health. Winter claimed that Sean Hales, the IRA's leader in west Cork, gave up the names of most of his officers before alleging sadistic torture in order to evade retribution from his own side.[114] Another Commandant helped foil an attack on a police barracks with barrels packed with gelignite. Winter also recruited some IRA double agents such as Vincent Fovargue, intelligence officer with the Dublin Brigade's 4th Battalion.[115] He claimed that Fovargue capitulated in Dublin Castle because he was facing a long prison sentence, but the decisive factor was his terror at seeing 'Hoppy' Hardy brutalise other prisoners.

Winter intended using Fovargue to cripple the IRA's campaign in Britain, a plan set in motion on 31 January 1921 when Winter fabricated an ambush of the lorry taking Fovargue to Kilmainham. The next morning's newspapers reported that Fovargue had escaped while his guards pursued their supposed attackers. Fovargue got his battalion commander's permission to take off for England, and fled. But on 3 April the body of a young brown-haired man with a slight moustache, well dressed in a blue serge suit, was discovered on a

Middlesex golf course. Pinned to his chest was a card warning 'Spies and traitors beware'.[116] Soon afterwards, Winter was perusing the corpse's photograph when he recognised Fovargue, whose desolate end he blamed on the dead man's carelessness rather than any negligence on his own part. Winter's only regret about this expendable pawn was losing 'someone who was a potentially good agent'. But in reality Fovargue had been doomed from the start. He had lacked the steely personality and self-control necessary to carry off an intelligence deception and his fellow prisoners at the Castle had quickly become wary of him. They saw Fovargue as excessively talkative, inquisitive and too free with the names of republican leaders. And his 'escape' deceived nobody, including his own battalion commander, who found out about the charade almost immediately.[117] It is hard to believe that Winter really thought the IRA would not discover that the 'ambush' of Fovargue's lorry had not taken place. By the time Fovargue boarded the boat for England, he was already doomed.

The beatings which broke Fovargue were an everyday occurrence. Private J.P. Swindlehurst, who guarded Mountjoy's grilling room in early 1921, heard Auxiliaries 'at it night and day knocking information out of suspects and prisoners alike' before carrying them out 'more dead than alive'.[118] Swindlehurst also protected Jury's Hotel in Dame Street, which Dublin District Special Branch had appropriated after Bloody Sunday. Under the new management Jury's rapidly lost its four-star rating for customer care. An iron gate shielded the entrance and its reception hall served as a guardroom where Swindlehurst and his fellow sentries slept on the marble floor. Constantly admitting secret service men and detectives, Swindlehurst noted that 'the days and nights have been a constant repetition of comings and goings . . . Prisoners were brought in occasionally, a few looked about all in, covered in blood, minus teeth and numerous other injuries. After a grilling in one of the upper rooms we could hear the groans and curses coming down the stairway, a dull thump indicated someone had taken a count. They took them off to Mountjoy Prison.'[119] On 31 January 1921 an actress accompanying Auxiliaries was shot leaving a nearby theatre. 'We heard the shooting and saw people running away. We didn't know until they dragged some of the slayers in, what it was all about. The rest of the night we spent listening to the groans and yells coming from the grilling room.'[120]

During a sombre guided tour one British intelligence officer pointed out rooms in which eleven British agents had supposedly been slaughtered on

Bloody Sunday. Swindlehurst recorded that the rooms were still 'in the same state as they were left that morning, walls and carpets spattered with blood, a ghastly sight'.[121] But the officer was pulling his leg, because Jury's had not been attacked on Bloody Sunday; the blood was of more recent origin and certainly not that of British spies. However, the current residents were in danger, as Swindlehurst noted:

> The nights have been full of alarms, shots and bombs. Early in the morning I was on sentry at the main entrance behind the iron gate when the noise of a motor and running footsteps caused my pal and I to look out for trouble. The runner was a secret serviceman being pursued by Sinn Feiners in a car. They dropped him with a fusillade of shots when he was about two yards from the doorway. His impetuous roll knocked us into the hall; when we were going to reply to them. In a few seconds they were gone leaving a bomb in the roadway which failed to explode. The victim was luckily only slightly wounded, one through the leg and another through his hand. We don't know where he had been but a big party of men moved out armed to the teeth at dawn so he must have got some information which was acted upon.[122]

But some British intelligence officers applied psychological pressure instead of rubber truncheons. Soon after being promoted in early 1921 from Vice-Commandant of 3rd Battalion to Chief of the Republican Police, Simon Donnelly was conducting surveillance of Dublin Castle when five armed men in civilian clothes suddenly frog-marched him inside to the Auxiliaries' Intelligence Office, 'The Knocking Shop'. Photographs of Collins, Mulcahy, Breen and other wanted men plastered its walls. Although Donnelly produced fake identity papers and gave a false name and address, his interrogators already knew his identity and Volunteer rank. Donnelly then admitted to being a junior officer, but when he claimed to know nothing about IRA leaders an

> Auxiliary produced a Webley revolver and asked me if I knew all about it. I said I did. After all a Vice Commandant had to admit to some military knowledge. He placed his elbows on the table, revolver in hand. I sat opposite. It was, at least so I thought, aimed at my heart. He started to press the trigger very slowly. I saw the hammer rising – it seemed an awful long time. I

dropped my eyes to where I thought my heart should be. At this time, to use an old phrase, it was in my mouth. The gun clicked and nothing happened. I was still alive. I came to the conclusion afterwards that it was a trick gun used by them to frighten prisoners and force them to speak.[123]

Since he had not been assaulted, Donnelly assumed that his captors were saving him for prolonged torture. Instead, they gave him a cigarette and chatted convivially. Lowering his guard somewhat, a more relaxed Donnelly was sufficiently emboldened to complain about the British denying IRA prisoners POW status:

One of them asked me, 'Do you want to be treated as a prisoner of war?' I replied, 'Yes'. 'Very well', says he, 'you will get your wish'. I wondered. 'Do you know anything about international laws of war?' I was asked. 'Very little', I replied. 'Well', said he, 'you have been captured in civilian clothes that bear no distinguishing mark. Neither do you wear a uniform. Captured under such circumstances, we can shoot you now without trial.' I was silent. I certainly lost that argument.[124]

Donnelly was then transferred to the guardroom where McKee, Clancy and Clune had died and was soon joined by two other prisoners – one an IRA intelligence officer whose face the Auxiliaries had beaten to pulp. Next morning, in the Intelligence Office 'Hoppy' Hardy produced a pocket containing Donnelly's name and a map of Dublin showing IRA battalion areas and assassination locations. Donnelly recalled:

I began to feel very uncomfortable. He produced a second book from his pocket. He proceeded to read out the names, one by one, of the British agents shot in the 3rd Battalion area, and after each one he looked at me and said very slowly and deliberately, '3rd Battalion area and you are Vice-Commandant'. When he had completed the list of whom I think there were about twelve or fourteen, another Army Officer came in and saluted and said, 'Sir, the prisoner, Donnelly, is to be sent to Kilmainham at once.' I was returned to the guardroom and later on sent under armed escort to Kilmainham.[125]

Donnelly was charged with murder but escaped before his court martial.

Winter also tried bugging prisoners in internment camps by surreptitiously installing microphones and detectaphones, but he claimed these were useless in wooden huts and, bizarrely, that 'a microphone of English manufacture seems ill adapted to the Irish brogue'.[126] But these devices did deter inmates from openly discussing escape plans. Winter's intelligence officers in the camps lacked essential local knowledge but they culled some general information about politics – though not IRA plans – from prisoners' letters. Agents sent inside, apparently after a brutal interrogation, did sometimes establish sufficient rapport with prisoners to build up prosecution cases.

* * *

During early 1921 the Dublin struggle intensified. Flanagan's ASU ambushed British military parties at Rialto and Dolphin's Barn, confiscated messages from dispatch riders and attacked Auxiliaries, though mostly when they were off-duty or on leave. After a tip-off from an Ivanhoe Hotel porter that a Captain Tams and his wife were residents, an assassination unit arrived – only to find the couple had just left for Phoenix Park racecourse.[127] The ASU did kill two men staying at their family homes in Inchicore and Dolphin's Barn.[128] But Auxiliary parties remained too dangerous to confront regularly, especially after they had foiled an ambush near the Tolka bridge in Drumcondra on 21 January and captured three ASU members who were subsequently executed – one of them a brother of the Squad's Sean Doyle. The biggest IRA operation in early 1921 occurred on 11 April with an attack on the London and North Western Hotel, a railway property at the North Wall docks. This was occupied by 100 Auxiliaries, who, instead of fortifying it, relied on keeping civilians at a safe distance. 2nd Battalion's O/C, Tom Ennis, had conducted surveillance of the hotel exterior and organised an attack during curfew hours in order to avoid civilian casualties. Seventy Volunteers, including the Squad and ASU, set the building on fire with grenades, though a mine did not detonate.[129]

One new player in the intelligence war was Hervey de Montmorency, a 52-year-old scion of an old Anglo-Irish family. A born adventurer, he had already fought in the Boer War, mined diamonds in South Africa and hunted for pirates' treasure in South America.[130] A Home Ruler and Irish Volunteer before 1914, he had became disillusioned with Irish nationalism after serving on the Western Front with the Royal Dublin Fusiliers. Shocked by the Easter

Rising, Montmorency then underwent an almost religious conversion to Unionism. During an Irish vacation in January 1920 he could see only a 'witches' cauldron' simmering and suffered 'qualms of conscience for having run guns into the south of Ireland in 1914'.[131] By now he regarded his fellow Irishmen as treacherous, cruel, vain, thriftless, jealous, garrulous, savage, cowardly criminals – and that was only for starters. But at least their punishment would enable him to purge his soul and so shortly after Bloody Sunday the War Office chose Montmorency to replace one of the dead intelligence officers – though to his immense disappointment he eventually found himself reassigned as an Auxiliary intelligence officer with 'F' Company.

From the moment he arrived in late December 1920, Montmorency was sceptical about both Dublin Castle's will to win and the British public's resolution to stay the course in Ireland. Prickly, blunt and easily exasperated, Montmorency saw himself surrounded by the delusions and naivety of people who needed a wake-up call – in more ways than one. On his very first morning as he stood in a deserted Lower Castle Yard wondering when his 'chief and colleagues would have sufficiently recovered from their breakfasts to justify me in presenting myself to them, the swarm of lady clerks burst for the first time upon my astonished gaze; buzzing, chattering and barely stopping to repair their faded complexions by artificial means, they hurried past me through the archway on their way to earn their daily bread'.[132] Montmorency quickly concluded that the DMP was on the enemy's side and that some G Division detectives were actually IRA double agents, 'proof of the incompetence of the English intelligence service in Dublin; for they were continually in our midst, gravely suspected by us of betraying us to the murder-gang while carrying out their constabulary duties'.[133] Army guards were conniving at prison breaks undeterred by any fear of punishment by 'military adventurers' at army headquarters staff, whom he believed were more concerned with attending race meetings than fighting a war. But, in Montmorency's opinion, sloth was not the only deadly sin gripping Dublin Castle because, somewhat censoriously, he saw lust and licentiousness everywhere. The Castle was an Irish Sodom and Gomorrah in which a large contingent of female clerks

used to work in a hall of considerable size, known to ribald young officers as the 'bird-cage'. It defied the wit of man to explain their usefulness, because whoever had engaged them had not troubled to select trained stenographers; so that, in the intervals of philandering and dancing in the throne-room, or Saint Patrick's Hall, they were busily employed sorting card indexes. When our secretary was asked who had engaged them, he used to put his thumb unto his nose and spread his fingers out.[134]

Montmorency knew that many IRA killings succeeded because the victims had ignored elementary security precautions, yet breathtaking acts of folly seemed endemic among the British garrison. One customer instructed a Grafton Street photographer to send prints of himself – in police uniform – to the Black and Tans Bloodhounds Section at Gormanston Camp. Not surprisingly, a postal worker passed the letter to IRA Intelligence.[135] Montmorency himself rarely ventured outside the Castle, having convinced himself that an IRA spotter was shadowing him everywhere. 'It was a horrible feeling to be so hunted; sometimes I contrived to shake off my pursuer, but at other times he stuck to me like a leech. I knew that my follower had no weapon on him, but I also knew that if he could manoeuvre me towards some gunman he only had to make a signal and I should be a dead man.'[136] Frequently overcome by tension, Montmorency would feel the air being literally sucked out of him and would have to back up against a wall until a friend arrived to rescue him. He always carried a cocked revolver at the ready inside his coat pocket, and regularly practised shooting from the hip inside the Castle grounds, not to mention flicking a hat into a killer's face.

And potential killers there were a-plenty. After Volunteer GHQ Intelligence had discovered that three Castle RIC officers dined regularly at the Ormonde Hotel, Jim Slattery cased its restaurant. He eventually recommended a street ambush, because an inside attack would have endangered other customers and might have encountered undercover British intelligence agents. On 23 February 1921 a Squad unit consisting of Jimmy Conroy, Mick O'Reilly and Ben Byrne shot the three policemen. Byrne recalled that

in less time than it takes to relate, two of them were lying on the ground dead. The third man, by some extraordinary strength of will, succeeded in rushing across the road. He had got to the opposite pavement, outside Honan's window, when the three of us fired at him. Some one of us grazed his spine with a bullet, with the result that he catapulted himself clean through the shop window, but was dead when he landed there.[137]

Montmorency was in the vicinity at the time. He knew the three men, plain-clothes orderlies, and had accompanied them through the Castle's Dame Street exit and across the road towards Parliament Street before they parted. Montmorency had turned right to go to a different restaurant and had gone only about ten yards when he heard four or five pistol shots. As a panicked crowd ran past him he whipped out his pistol and ran to the scene but saw only three bodies with their brains blown out.[138] The dead men had made themselves vulnerable by falling into a set routine, though the Castle's cramped conditions also contributed to their demise. Macready complained to Anderson about 'another idiocy. Apparently a notice was put up in the Castle that certain people could not get their lunch in the mess there, and the three men concerned, I understand, habitually took their lunch at the same restaurant, and of course the gunmen were lying up for them.'[139]

Even a British intelligence officer like Captain Cecil Lees was capable of elementary – and fatal – carelessness. The 44-year-old agent was a former Chinese Labour Corps commander whose father had been a British consul in France and whose French fiancée was staying undercover with him at the St Andrew's Hotel at the corner of Exchequer and Wicklow Street. Volunteer GHQ Intelligence got onto the 'Frenchman'[140] after he sent a letter to the War Office which was diverted to the IRA by a postal worker. But when the Squad began familiarising itself with his hotel's layout, Lees suddenly disappeared. Tobin was resigned to losing him,[141] but one Sunday evening Ben Byrne and Tom Keogh were in the Scala cinema's dress circle when, just before the film started, 'a lady and gentleman proceeding to their seats were caught in the beam of the projector'. Byrne recalled: 'Keogh nudged me and said, "I think that is Lees." We decided we would keep a watch on this gentleman, and whether he was Lees or not, find out where he was living. After the show we followed him and found that he was staying in St Andrew's Temperance Hotel in Wicklow Street.'[142] Byrne and Keogh knew that Lees reported regularly and early to the Castle. Shortly after 9 a.m. next morning, 29 March 1921, they were waiting as Lees walked by with his fiancée and shot him dead.

Collins also used the Squad in one of his most complex and dangerous operations. Its origins lay in Cathal Brugha's continued obsession with assassinating the British Cabinet, first contemplated after the 1918 'German Plot' arrests and again following the Dail's suppression in September 1919 when he sent Liam Tobin and Mick McDonnell to London on a fortnight's reconnaissance.[143] Although they reported unfavourably, Brugha just could not get the idea out of his system. In early 1921, behind the backs of Collins and Mulcahy, he persuaded 27-year-old Sean MacEoin to take a hit team of two dozen Volunteers to London. MacEoin had misgivings because as a 'country boy' he could hardly find his way around Dublin, let alone London. Fortuitously, MacEoin then sought out his close friend Collins with whom he sat on the IRB's Supreme Council. Collins was dumbstruck at Brugha's recklessness and manifest distrust of him. He immediately dispatched MacEoin to Mulcahy, who said he 'was surprised and appalled at the idea. I upbraided MacEoin for doing such a thing and said that under no circumstances must he do such a thing as go to London, that he must go back at once to his command area and warned him very severely of the precautions he had to take on the way home.'[144] MacEoin did what he was told. Brugha might have been Collins's titular superior, but the Director of Intelligence held the greater sway with MacEoin, having initiated him into the IRB.

From his Dublin hotel MacEoin dispatched a female messenger to Longford with news of his imminent return. But she told her uncle, a retired police officer, who immediately tipped off the RIC. They arrested MacEoin at Mullingar railway station, shooting and seriously wounding him when he tried to escape. Collins regarded MacEoin's capture as 'simply disastrous'.[145] Fearing that 'Cork will be fighting alone now',[146] he instructed the Longford IRA to prepare for hostage-taking if MacEoin was sentenced to death. Collins also told the Squad to ambush the British military convoy bringing MacEoin to Dublin.[147] On 3 March 1921 the Squad travelled by tram to Lucan, about nine miles west of Dublin, and waited near the Spa Hotel. But after five fruitless hours it gave up, stopped a car and ordered its owner to drive them to Dublin. The driver, an ex-British Army officer, refused to cooperate and dared them to shoot him. Eventually, however, he offered to sit silently if one of them drove and was put in the back between two men. According to Charlie Dalton, none of the unit actually drove a car, but

Ben Byrne said he had a slight knowledge. On hearing this, Tom Keogh said: 'I'm not going to risk my neck. I am going to walk home.' We took his guns and he walked across the fields. We later learned from himself that he walked along the canal into town. The remainder of us started for town in the car. We drove as far as Islandbridge, where we ordered the British army officer to get out, telling him we would leave his car at the Park gate in Parkgate Street, which we did.[148]

When MacEoin eventually reached Mountjoy, Collins wanted Oscar Traynor and Paddy Daly to infiltrate the prison through the female entrance and break MacEoin's fall from a hospital window. But as they were about to set off from a nearby house a friendly warder arrived with news that MacEoin was exhausted from rehearsing the escape.[149]

Still Collins would not give up. He next planned to send the Squad into Mountjoy in an armoured car, disguised as British soldiers and led by two bogus officers carrying forged release papers.[150] Emmet Dalton was made for the lead role, especially as he had kept a couple of British Army uniforms from the war. One was a perfect fit for Joe Leonard, who two years earlier had participated in a spectacular break-out from Mountjoy but whom Collins thought was now unlikely to be recognised in the prison. Collins already knew where he could get an armoured car. McKee's former Vice-Brigadier, Michael Lynch, had seen one outside his home in the grounds of the Dublin Abattoir, protecting two British Army lorries making daily meat collections. Sometimes its bored crew left the vehicle unattended and wandered around.[151] Collins had Charlie Dalton monitor their routine from inside Lynch's house. Simultaneously a Squad member in corporation uniform sketched maps of the abattoir. Within a week, Dalton had confirmed the armoured car crew's casual behaviour, and Pat McCrae assured Collins that he could drive the vehicle to Mountjoy, about a mile away along the North Circular Road.

By 1921 hundreds of troops and Auxiliaries were guarding this maximum-security jail, which was crammed with republican prisoners. Penetrating it challenged even a consummate organiser like Collins. His plan, involving twenty men at two separate locations, relied on detailed information from the Squad, Charlie Dalton, prison warders, inmates and Mountjoy visitors. Although initially Bill Stapleton thought it 'sounded a bit ridiculous to me, I like all of the Squad and GHQ Intelligence had faith in Mick Collins and his planning. He had, by good planning and anticipation of British reaction, piloted us through many a hazardous operation successfully in the past.'[152] Charlie Dalton admired how Collins 'considered every detail, explored every aspect of the job and overlooked no possible flaw'.[153]

Early on Whit Saturday, 14 May, the Squad gathered unobtrusively at the abattoir's iron gates, disguised as cattle market employees. From inside Lynch's house Charlie Dalton had already seen four crewmen leaving the armoured car and stroll off to watch cattle being slaughtered. When the remaining two clambered out ten minutes later for a cigarette, he raised the blind as a signal to the Squad which immediately fanned out through the abattoir, killing a British soldier who tried to reach a telephone. Pat McCrae, Tom Keogh, Bill Stapleton, Peter Gough and John Caffrey then changed into army-style dungarees, climbed inside the heavily armed vehicle and swept out through the gates. At the same time Charlie Dalton brought news of its imminent arrival to a safe house on the North Circular Road. There, his brother and Leonard were waiting, dressed as British officers and with Emmet standing erect, medal-bedecked and radiant. Dalton recalled:

> They came out into the street. At the same moment the car appeared. We saw it turning out of the avenue and coming towards us. I saw Joe and Emmet picked up. And then, the happiest young man in Dublin that morning, I cycled away to the stable in Abbey Street. There I found Michael Collins waiting. His look searched mine for an answer to the question there was no need to ask. He was overjoyed, and my satisfaction was unbounded to be the bearer of good news to him. He was all smiles. 'I hope the second part will be as successful,' he said.[154]

At 10.30 a.m. the armoured car drove up the avenue leading to Mountjoy's main gates, slowing down to avoid booing crowds. Dalton jumped out, rang the look-out warder's bell, imperiously waved official-looking papers and demanded immediate entry for himself and Leonard. Simultaneously, McCrae drove through three successive gates into the prison yard, where he swung around to prevent two inner gates closing. He kept the engine running. A sentry who observed this usual manoeuvre asked McCrae whether he was going out. 'I said yes. At least in my own mind I was hoping I was'.[155] Stapleton thought that the sentry 'was suspicious and sensed that there was something amiss. He was watching the gate intently, just as I in my dungarees and khaki beret, was watching him.'[156] Dalton and Leonard then strode into the main building, where, unexpectedly, a warder immediately recognised Leonard from his time in Mountjoy. 'As the warders were returning from their quarters on duty a warder Kelly was so surprised at seeing me that he said "O Jesus" and then clasping his hand over his mouth dashed upstairs, knocking down all the warders descending.'[157]

Escorted to governor Munro's office, Dalton and Leonard were disconcerted to find him chatting to seven prison officers; they had expected to see MacEoin lodging a complaint of ill-treatment. Instead MacEoin and other prisoners were being inspected by a new commander of the Auxiliary guards, who had insisted on meeting his new charges. Deciding to brazen it out, Dalton presented written authorisation for MacEoin's temporary transfer to the Castle for interrogation. But when Munro started to ring the Castle for confirmation, Leonard hurled the telephone against the wall and Dalton drew his gun to cover the staff, whom they both tied up. However, just as Dalton and Leonard were about to seize the master keys and locate MacEoin, they heard gunfire erupting in the courtyard. Collins's plan had called for the Squad's Frank Bolster and two Volunteers to keep the heavy outer gate open by distracting its guard with wrongly addressed parcels. But the guard was having none of it and locked the gate. Bolster's group overpowered him, seized his keys and reopened it, but a sentry on the roof raised the alarm and opened fire. As pandemonium broke out across the yard, Tom Keogh killed the gate sentry, forcing Dalton and Leonard to flee. Leonard recalled:

It was now or never. On Dalton and myself rushing through the main door I spotted the rifle. Picking it up I ordered the British military back and on their refusal to obey knelt down and threatened to fire on them. They, seeing an officer kneeling in the firing position, broke and retired to their quarters but the police advanced from another position. It was time to jump on the back of the whippet and go, taking the rifle with us. We shouted at Pat to let her rip and Pat McCrae drove down that drive and on to the North Circular Road at a speed that was very satisfactory, seeing that we were exposed to a very heavy fire from the prison.[158]

When the armoured car arrived safely at North Richmond Street Michael Lynch saw Dalton sitting serenely

at the back of the car coolly smoking a cigarette and immaculate in his British uniform. He was completely imperturbable although he had only a few moments before undergone an experience that would have driven most men crazy. Let me say at once that this was no pose, no bravado, but sheer unadulterated nerve. His comrade Leonard was also the essence of coolness, so much indeed that in his retreat from Mountjoy he stooped and picked up the dead soldier's rifle at the gate. He had it in his hand when I saw him.[159]

Joe Hyland drove Leonard and Dalton away in the taxi that was originally supposed to smuggle MacEoin into hiding, dropping them off at Howth, nine miles outside Dublin, after Leonard remembered his sister's friendship with local nuns. At the convent they sipped tea with a sympathetic sister who eventually produced two suits borrowed from a local publican, promising to send their British army uniforms on in case they proved useful again.[160] While Leonard and Dalton returned to Dublin by tram, the armoured car motored north, its crew enveloped in glum silence, except for Lynch, who was revelling in the prospect of battle: 'I told McCrae to be prepared for action as I intended that we should hit up any enemy car that came into sight. This was an opportunity that could not be missed.'[161] However, a malfunctioning radiator overheated, the car spluttered, backfired and eventually shuddered to a halt outside Clontarf Golf Club. Lynch and the others clambered out sweating and gasping for air, stripped the car of weapons and ammunition, ignited petrol flowing from burst fuel pipes and escaped over nearby fields.

Even then Collins didn't give up. A few weeks before MacEoin's court martial at the City Hall he asked Noyk to smuggle weapons inside with which MacEoin could fight his way out and link up with the Squad and ASU.[162] Although the solicitor agreed, he doubted that MacEoin stood a chance, especially as he would be handcuffed, with armed military policemen standing on either side of him. Furthermore, court-martial officers kept their guns on the table in front of them and the room would be filled with secret servicemen. And, even if MacEoin somehow reached the street outside, there were machine-gun nests on the roof of the City Hall and surrounding buildings. Collins dropped the idea. MacEoin remained in prison until the Truce, when Collins warned the British Government that his continued imprisonment imperilled peace negotiations.

* * *

Despite signs that British pressure was wearing the Dublin IRA down, Macready remained dissatisfied. He especially disliked a British Government embargo on de Valera's arrest after he returned from America, a 'protective umbrella' that he claimed endangered morale among soldiers and Winter's intelligence agents, as well as making it 'impossible to carry out a repressive policy if we have one hand tied behind our back'.[163] Macready warned that IRA gunmen were consorting with de Valera in order to evade capture and if a

British raid became unavoidable 'firearms may go off, with disastrous results'. Macready also believed de Valera's immunity had encouraged him to support the 'intensified outrage'[164] which resulted in sixteen IRA attacks in Dublin during the first twenty days of 1921. Predicting a renewed murder campaign, Macready urged Greenwood to warn that the British Government would respond to rising violence by extending martial law to the capital. But nothing happened. Macready blamed the Chief Secretary's 'optimistic frame of mind for which none of us living in Ireland could see any grounds'.[165] Although Macready never considered martial law a panacea, he believed its application in Dublin would end 'the clumsy and unworkable system of divided control'[166] in the rebellion's nerve centre, reduce casualties and shorten the war.

Macready also griped at Winter, whose military subordinates were feeding him damaging allegations about their chief's supposed incompetence and who survived mainly because of the lack of a credible alternative.[167] On 8 April Macready told Anderson that 'everything seems to point to the view that Winter has not got the right method, and we here very much doubt whether he will ever get it. He is, I fancy, a "born sleuth", but I doubt his organising power, and that, as far as I can see, is what is holding up the machine.'[168] Anderson and Cope had also quarrelled with Winter about his organisation's effectiveness and vetoed his gung-ho plan to arrest Sinn Fein leaders at the funeral of the Archbishop of Dublin, William Walsh; as the incredulous Sturgis put it 'to bait the mousetrap with a dead Archbishop and then promote a battle over the corpse'.[169] It did not get any better. Winter's unfortunate tendency to lose subordinates persisted, causing many to consider him jinxed. On 19 May Sturgis noted that 'another poor devil has committed suicide in 'O's office – this is the fifth – there seems a curse on the place'.[170]

But Winter was not the only person whom Macready held in low esteem; he extended this view to just about everybody else in the Irish administration. In his opinion, Tudor was energetic but lightweight and superficial, a 'person who does not go very deeply into the heart of things', while Cope – who was in charge when Anderson was away – was 'quite unfit for Chief Adviser to the Chief Secretary, who is equally unfit to keep a steady head on running a big show'.[171] Macready's ideal intelligence chief was himself, and he constantly proposed new initiatives – like his suggestion in early April 1921 that the directors of large insurance companies in London should encourage their agents in Ireland to pass on information to British Intelligence. A month later he wanted the state to stop subsidising the IRA by stopping unemployment pay to its members.[172] Macready was especially annoyed at the postal service, whose staff the British regarded as 'manifestly corrupt'.[173] His perception of rampant disloyalty was apparently confirmed on 11 April 1921, when he discovered that Mulcahy's brother Paddy worked in the Dublin GPO. Macready derided the Post Office's argument that it had no proof of any connection between Paddy and his brother's activities (Paddy was in fact in the IRA):

> I am bound to say that I think his presence in the GPO is a distinct danger, and even if it is not, he ought to suffer for the sins of his brother. The Almighty has already laid down that the children suffer for the sins of their fathers unto the third and fourth generation and therefore I do not see why brother Mulcahy should not suffer for Richard, and if they do not kick him out of the GPO altogether, he should certainly be moved to some town in the North which has the reputation of being loyal.[174]

Macready did not speculate on how long he expected Paddy Mulcahy to survive in Ulster.

* * *

By May 1921 the Dublin Brigade was ready for its biggest operation since Bloody Sunday. Because Beggar's Bush was too heavily manned and fortified, Traynor decided to attack the Custom House – 'the administrative heart of the British Civil Service machine'.[175] Its four floors contained numerous offices belonging to the Local Government Board and the Inland Revenue with over 100 staff and dozens of telephones including, reputedly, a secret line to the Castle. Until April 1921, British troops had guarded this superb late-eighteenth-century Portland stone edifice, but the only protection now consisted of a few policemen, locked and barricaded doors, sandbag emplacements and rows of barbed wire. Traynor had carried out surveillance by wandering the corridors with an official-looking envelope, noting granite walls but also wooden presses, shelves, substantial bundles of papers and a Will Room on the ground floor that was crammed with documents wrapped in linen folders. Situated under the dome, this room could act as a chimney, making it possible to burn the whole building.

Traynor spent nearly three months continually revising his plans: 'They were in my mind day and night. They were altered dozens of times as weaknesses and better points occurred to me.'[176] He eventually proposed a commando-style operation involving seventy Volunteers. They would overpower guards, isolate the Custom House by disconnecting telegraph and telephone wires and preventing employees leaving, and then set the building alight. Because petrol was too dangerous to handle, paraffin would be raided from an oil depot on the Quays a few hours before the attack, poured into hundreds of tin cans and driven by commandeered lorry to the Custom House. Simultaneously Volunteers would occupy fire brigade stations and immobilise the engines. Deploying so many men in a single place was risky and Traynor allowed only twenty-five minutes for the entire operation so that evacuation would occur before the British were alerted. He also intended delaying enemy forces by ambushing their vehicles and barricading every route between British Army barracks and the Custom House. A dubious Collins believed this would give the impression of a general uprising and made Traynor settle for a much smaller protective circle encompassing Liberty Hall, Lower Abbey Street and Gardiner Street. Collins also vetoed using Crow Street's intelligence officers, whom he could not afford to lose if anything went wrong.[177]

Since the Custom House was in 2nd Battalion's area, Traynor gave operational control to its commandant, Tom Ennis. He intended using only his own men and 2nd Battalion members of the Squad until Paddy Daly protested to Collins that this would divide the Squad. Ennis grudgingly backed down but got his own back by giving the Squad a roving commission on the Custom House's periphery, neutralising guards, acting as look-outs and rounding up civilian visitors.[178] After a final inspection Traynor's adjutant Harry Colley persuaded him to employ 100 men. When Crow Street provided details of the secret telephone line to Dublin Castle, they arranged to have it severed just before the attack.[179] At a final briefing for officers and men, Traynor and Ennis demanded strict adherence to the timetable. After entering the Custom House at 12.55 p.m., a lorry would distribute tins of paraffin which Volunteers would carry to allotted stations on various floors. At 1.00 p.m. sharp, officers would have documents and furniture piled up and by 1.20 p.m. floor officers would blow once on a whistle to signify readiness. Two blasts by Ennis would order ignition and immediate evacuation – all within twenty-five minutes of entry.

Initially the attack on 25 May went to plan. Small groups of Volunteers, many disguised as workmen in dungarees, overcame guards and invaded the

Custom House on time. They rounded up staff and corralled them in an inner quadrangle at the rear. Only the caretaker resisted and he was shot dead. But the lorry carrying tins of paraffin discovered the quayside gate locked and was forced to drive to the Beresford Place entrance, delaying fuel unloading until 1.10 p.m. Then two floor officers blew their whistles almost simultaneously, which many Volunteers mistook as the double blast for evacuation. On the ground floor Ennis drove them back upstairs. Reluctantly calling on the Squad, he sent Vinnie Byrne to the second floor where Byrne piled up ledgers and papers and drenched them in paraffin. Stepping outside, Byrne opened an office door slightly, threw in burning paper and set it ablaze.

Outside, Traynor waited increasingly nervously for the evacuation to begin, five minutes after his stipulated deadline. Nearby Paddy Daly stood forlornly. On Ennis's instructions he had been turned away at every door, like a gate-crasher at some fabulous works party evicted by bouncers on management orders.[180] Suddenly gunfire erupted as Auxiliary tenders roared into Beresford Place. They had been on routine patrol when Volunteer scouts fired on them in the mistaken belief that their convoy was on its way to the Custom House. As the Squad opened fire with high-powered automatic pistols, civilians were caught in crossfire. From Gardiner Street, Colley watched as 'a convoy of the steel trolleys which the Dublin Corporation used in those days to convey the rubbish and which ran on the tram tracks, came round the corner from Talbot Street into Gardiner Street. Immediately they appeared, intensive machine-gun fire was opened on them and I saw the men engaged on them taking what cover they could, and some of them running for their lives across the street.'[181] Traynor and Daly escaped when a teenaged Volunteer hurled a grenade into an Auxiliary lorry and was shot dead. As half a dozen maimed Auxiliaries lay on the ground screaming, Traynor fled through Lower Gardiner Street while Daly ran into Abbey Street.

Inside the Custom House there was pandemonium. The Squad urged men to fight their way through enemy lines, but only a few followed Doyle and Slattery as they dashed outside. Machine-gun fire shattered Slattery's hand and seriously wounded Doyle, who staggered into a car that drove off.[182] Although some Volunteers escaped, dozens dropped their weapons and surrendered. Others mingled with staff trooping out of the burning building, but Auxiliaries segregated them on the quayside. After descending the stairs, Vinnie Byrne fired at an Auxiliary in the doorway and when an armoured car appeared at the entrance he dived behind a sandbag barricade just before a machine-gun burst. With the Custom House well alight he walked out, hoping to sidle away unobtrusively, but an Auxiliary struck his face with a rifle, shouting, 'This bastard came out of the building'.[183] Pretending to be a harmless cabinet-maker on an errand, Byrne had a lucky break when a dead body distracted his captor, allowing him to melt into civilians lining up outside Brooks Thomas, a large building supplier. Shuffling towards a British officer who was checking identities, he rolled cigarettes furiously to mask the smell of petrol on his hands. When his turn came Byrne exuded an aroma of tobacco and a well-practised deference:

> I humbly asked him: 'Could I go home now?' He looked at me and said: 'What are you doing here?' I replied: 'Sir, I was on my way to Brooks Thomas to buy some timber.' He then ran his hands all over me and pulled out a carpenter's rule and a few pieces of paper out of my pocket. The papers showed different sizes of pieces of timber, which I usually carried as a decoy. Handing me back my ruler and paper, the officer said: 'Get to hell out of this.' I said: 'Thank you, sir.' I was once more clear.[184]

Encountering Daly again outside the Abbey Theatre, Traynor learnt from a Volunteer that a lorry had driven the badly wounded Ennis to his Marino home. After making arrangements with a nursing home to have him admitted, Traynor and Daly cycled out to find Ennis lying semi-conscious on a bed, soaked with blood from a large gaping wound to his groin and being nursed by his wife holding an infant. Collins's driver, Joe Hyland, took the three men to the Eccles Street nursing home, where Ennis was carried to the top floor, more dead than alive. Daly and other Squad members then visited Slattery and Doyle in the Mater's 'secret ward' for wounded Volunteers. It was surrounded by other wards and very difficult for strangers to reach – especially policemen and soldiers. Slattery's right hand had been ripped apart and Daly told him to pose as a passer-by who had been accidentally caught up in the fighting.[185] After an amputation, Slattery returned to the Squad as a left-handed gunfighter, but although Doyle was conscious and cheerful he was seriously ill and died two days later.

IRA losses at the Custom House were severe, with five Volunteers dead and eighty-three captured. 2nd Battalion, the operation's spearhead, had lost three men and almost sixty had been taken prisoner. Most of the Squad had also been captured. Colley remembered 'that evening in the Brigade Office there was a great silence. We were thinking that our success in burning the Custom House had been too dearly bought by the large number of our best fighters who had been captured.'[186] Paddy Daly thought it vital to 'conceal our crippled state from the enemy, who might otherwise have taken advantage of it to deal us a decisive blow'.[187] Over the next few days Traynor instructed battalion officers to give the impression of business as usual by having ordinary Volunteers take time off work for daylight attacks. But, although a setback, the Custom House operation was in small scale as significant as the Vietnam War's Tet offensive: a military catastrophe that drained the enemy's commitment to an apparently endless war. And, just as Tet was quickly followed by the Paris Peace negotiations, so the Custom House attack was the prelude to the Truce of 11 July 1921.

Chapter 7

LOOKING FOR A WAY OUT

THE QUEST FOR A TRUCE, MAY–JULY 1921

IRA losses at the Custom House forced Traynor into his second Brigade reorganisation in six months when he amalgamated the ASU and Squad into a single entity known as the Dublin Guard. Collins wanted the compliant Paddy Daly as the Guard's leader, rather than the prickly Flanagan. He got his way when a scandal erupted after Traynor had ordered Flanagan to execute a suspected spy being treated in Jervis Street Hospital. Flanagan's execution unit dragged the patient from his bed and shot him dead in the courtyard, an action that one Volunteer said 'brought down on the unit the wrath of GHQ just as it brought down on GHQ the wrath of the medical fraternity'.[1] The Mater, which secretly treated wounded Volunteers, demanded their removal within twenty-four hours and only relented after Collins placated the hospital management. While Traynor was just as responsible for the fiasco, he let Flanagan take the fall, prompting the resignation of a dozen angry Volunteers.[2] Subsequently, the Dublin Guard proved relatively ineffective because of Daly's inability to impose his authority on a large organisation.

Although the British did not fully realise it, they were finally wearing down a Dublin Brigade, which Thornton admitted was critically short of weapons. The British had seized a considerable amount of arms and ammunition at the Custom House and soon afterwards captured one of the Brigade's munitions workshops as well as a Squad arms dump in Great Charles Street.[3] Dan McDonnell believed 'things were so bad with all the units that it was a question of how long they could last. We had no ammunition; we had a few guns.'[4] Volunteers had been reduced to cutting Winchester rifle ammunition down to fit .45 revolvers, a desperate ploy that seriously injured a number of Volunteers. To get some ammunition McDonnell and Joe Dolan risked summary execution by their own side after raiding an IRA company's underused weapons dump. 'Dolan and I went to Blackhall Street in the middle of the day to this dump and we took every weapon belonging to the company away with us because we decided we had to get to use it. I knew best how to get in this particular dump and pulled out all the stuff. There was not much in it. There was enough to keep us going for another while.'[5]

The Dublin Guard kept the IRA's campaign in the capital going mainly by picking off easy targets, primarily off-duty Auxiliaries. On 26 June 1921 it ambushed a couple at the Mayfair Hotel. The *Freeman's Journal* reported that 'shortly before seven o'clock the two officers arrived at the hotel – where their wives were staying. They went to the dining room and were having tea when a knock came to the door. The maid answered and immediately four or five men rushed through the hallway and dashed into the dining room.'[6] In fact it was the maid who had told the IRA about both men's regular visits, given it their descriptions, admitted the Guard unit on a prearranged ring of the doorbell and pointed to the room in which the men were dining with their wives and children.[7] One Auxiliary was shot in the chest and died immediately, while his companion was seriously wounded in the face. Volunteer Michael Stack remembered that,

> on leaving the dining-room, I was about to re-load my gun and as two rounds had been extracted from it, I remained looking at the empty gun. On seeing me, the section leader said, 'What are you going to do now?' I replied, 'I am after losing two rounds of ammunition.' So he asked me did I want him to find them for me. I said, 'I have only four left now if I lose these two.' So he said that we'd have to lift the sideboard out from the wall to retrieve the two rounds, which we did.[8]

But overall the IRA was effectively beaten in Dublin by late June 1921. Traynor's health had collapsed and his doctor sent him to convalesce in Wales, by which time the republican leadership was receptive to a truce. Thornton conceded that had one 'not taken place we would have found ourselves very hard set to continue the fight with any degree of intensity'.[9]

By early summer 1921 the British Government was also seriously considering a cessation of hostilities. This represented a significant shift from Walter Long's insistence only a year earlier that it 'could not bargain with men who have been guilty of those awful murders. The thing is unthinkable.'[10] Six months later, after spinal arthritis had abruptly terminated Long's career, compromise had indeed become thinkable. In December 1920 Lloyd George met

Archbishop Patrick Clune of Perth, Western Australia, who was on a three-month visit to Britain and Ireland, where he had family ties. The prime minister persuaded Clune to mediate with Sinn Fein leaders in Dublin. The archbishop visited Griffith in prison and met Collins secretly. But genuine republican interest evaporated after Lloyd George suddenly made a truce conditional on an IRA weapons surrender, a hardline approach which probably stemmed from his Coalition Government's dependence on the Conservative Party. But only three months later Anderson reported that the prime minister was much more conciliatory and prepared to make significant concessions, a new flexibility that was possible after Bonar Law resigned in March 1921 because of illness. Basil Thomson might also have unintentionally nudged Lloyd George towards negotiations with a gloomy report on 7 April that

> it cannot be conscientiously said that any headway has been made against the Irish Republican Army and there is a feeling among the people that Sinn Fein will win. This feeling is due to the increased prestige gained by Sinn Fein owing to its success in guerrilla warfare, especially in the martial law areas. The fear of reprisals is not so great now. The country folk who were opposed to the operations of the Irish Republican Army in their localities do not now mind and although they are for the most part against murders of individuals they are in favour of ambushes. They are beginning to be proud of the Irish heroes who have gained such victories over the Crown Forces in spite of all the restrictions imposed by martial law.[11]

Another inexorable pressure on Lloyd George was the Government of Ireland Act's implementation timetable. This stipulated elections on 13 and 14 May 1921 for two new devolved Irish parliaments. While Ulster Unionists would contest and win the Northern elections, it was uncertain whether Sinn Fein would boycott the Southern polls or win a landslide victory and then refuse to take its seats. During April and early May 1921 Lloyd George canvassed opinion about a possible truce during the elections. Christopher Addison, the Minister of Health, strongly supported Britain extricating itself from a mire costing over £20 million annually in security expenditure and fuelling 'a really national antagonism on the part of the Irish people'.[12] He believed a truce would make it harder for republican leaders to resume hostilities and if they rejected one they would be blamed for frustrating peace. Secretary of State for India Edwin Montague also supported a generous truce without an

IRA weapons surrender and urged the prime minister to use it to spell out his eventual peace terms.[13] Macready agreed that a truce was politically attractive but warned that it needed a positive IRA response, especially as intelligence-gathering from raids and searches would peter out.[14]

Dublin Castle was split. Greenwood argued that the 'best and most optimistic plan is to go straight on, and not hesitate at the last gate'.[15] A new and more favourable situation would exist after elections. 'The idea of a truce or cessation *for* or *because of* the elections is not a serious proposition. The Sinn Fein Army is growing smaller, losing heavily and certain to be defeated. A cessation now may mean its recovery. When de Valera is ready to advocate cessation – and he will be soon – then I am for dealing handsomely with him.'[16] But Anderson believed that IRA losses and official executions were forcing republican leaders to contemplate any settlement that a war-weary Southern population was likely to endorse. While not temperamentally inclined towards dramatic gestures, Anderson regarded this as 'an unrivalled opportunity for a beau geste and it would be a thousand pities to let it slip'.[17] Tudor and Winter advised against a truce without a guaranteed republican response – something they thought unlikely and unenforceable if given. Ultimately the British Cabinet rejected a truce by majority vote. As it turned out, except for the four successful independent candidates at Trinity College, there was no need for Southern elections. With no rivals prepared to stand, Sinn Fein took the other 120 seats unopposed. The crucial date now became 14 July 1921. Unless a Southern parliament was functioning by then, the British Cabinet would face an unappetising choice between instituting Crown Colony government and universal martial law in Ireland or opting for a truce and negotiations with Sinn Fein.

With time rapidly running out, Dublin Castle's 'peace party' began urgently enticing Sinn Fein to the conference table. The key British intermediary was Andy Cope. He had spent almost a year preparing for this moment, cultivating prominent moderate nationalists as go-betweens, like, said Sturgis, 'an Octopus grasping everything with its tentacles'.[18] His contacts included Lord Justice O'Connor and Martin Fitzgerald, proprietor of the *Freeman's Journal*. Wylie recalled the moment when Cope, dressed in a natty grey suit and straw boater and swinging a walking stick, said in

> his usual flippant way, 'I am off to contact Michael Collins.' I said 'You are what?' 'I am off to contact Michel Collins,' he said. 'Orders have come

through that the leaders of the movement are to be sounded as to the chances of peace and I believe Collins is the man to contact first so I am going out to look for him.' I thought I knew something about Dublin and I confess I would not have had the slightest idea of what to do or how to look for the leader, as he was then, of Sinn Fein. I also believed and still believe that the chances of survival for any man who tried to do this were very small. It was an interesting sidelight on Andy Cope's character and courage that he was quite gaily walking off into the unknown and terribly dangerous because he believed it was essential that contact should be established and he would not detail anyone to do a job that he was afraid to do himself.[19]

Rather surprisingly, Under-Secretary MacMahon became Cope's chief assistant. An almost forgotten figure since being sidelined in May 1920, he was disinterred from his political crypt in April 1921, reanimated and sent out to exploit his clerical influence with Cardinal Logue and his political contacts with people like de Valera, his contemporary at Blackrock College. Another contemporary, James Dwyer, was now a Dail Deputy and an intelligence officer in the Dublin Brigade's 4th Battalion and he apparently acted as MacMahon's channel to Collins.[20] Cope and MacMahon became an indefatigable double act. Sturgis found it 'most amusing how the personal values change in the Peace Stakes. ANDY [sic] is running good and strong right out in front by himself. MacMahon who was nowhere early on has come through and lies second.'[21]

Cope's shuttle diplomacy depended on his complete discretion and a lack of squeamishness in dealing with men whom many of his colleagues would have gladly hanged. Hervey de Montmorency could not 'understand how anyone could have been induced to undertake such an unpleasant task. Cope must have had tremendous courage, patience and a strong stomach to boot, to hold interviews with the savage, unsavoury human butchers, gloating over their murders of constables and soldiers.' Although Montmorency accepted that Cope displayed 'amazing tact and skill', he was 'universally detested by everyone in the Castle, it being generally supposed that he was going to sell us all to the rebels'.[22]

Cope was undoubtedly putting his life on the line by negotiating with enemy leaders and walking the capital's streets unarmed and unprotected. One Volunteer officer spotted Cope visiting Martin Fitzgerald's 'safe' house in Dundrum and requested permission from Volunteer GHQ to kill him. His request was turned down.[23] But any troops and Auxiliaries stumbling on Cope's clandestine activities might also have eliminated him in a mysterious shooting or an 'accidental' weapon discharge in the Castle grounds. As a former detective, Cope knew about counter-surveillance techniques but he could not cover his tracks completely. British Intelligence picked up his paper trail in September 1920 when Robert Jeune burgled a prominent Sinn Feiner's home in Drumcondra and discovered a letter from Cope promising to send on some papers. 'This was distinctly interesting. After this I made a point of trying to find out more about this individual's doings, and found that he had done some rather strange things, such as arranging for some electricians of known Sinn Fein views to come into the Castle at unusual times. Also he was one of the very few Castle officials who could safely walk about the streets of Dublin. But it was decided that no drastic action could be taken against him, as it turned out that he was a protégé of Lloyd George.'[24]

Cope was found out again after getting Erskine Childers released from Winter's custody in the Castle on 9 May 1921 and giving him documents for the Sinn Fein leadership. Cope was mightily embarrassed when Winter's agents captured the papers during a raid on Collins's finance office in Mary Street and circulated in the Castle a copy of a letter in which Childers told Collins: 'Settlement outlined to me by Cope in the Castle a week ago. He is probably a good actor, but his ostensible attitude was one of almost feverish anxiety to get something done and the business over.'[25] Cope tried to prevent similar embarrassment by asking Winter in the future to have an officer weed out such material and bring it straight to his boss. Winter regarded this as a slur on his organisation's integrity and Cope only just dissuaded him from resigning.[26]

It was an unhappy time for Winter, who knew that the British Government was dabbling with people whom he was simultaneously trying to apprehend. Furthermore, shortly before, Macready had imposed on him a GHQ colonel, Ralph Umbreville, to curb the police indiscipline that he and Tudor argued only existed in republican propaganda.[27] Then soon afterwards the IRA tried to kill him. He was closely guarded not just in Dublin but also in London, where Scotland Yard protected his St James's flat, and Winter was not attacked until June 1921, when he, his assistant Lockhart and an escort were driving to an aerodrome on the outskirts of Dublin. Shortly after leaving the Castle Winter was putting a cigarette in his mouth when a shot hit his hand and firing came from every direction. Luckily for him, most of it was wild and as he and his fellow passengers returned fire their driver accelerated away. Despite bleeding profusely, Winter was not seriously wounded, though if his car had been travelling fractionally faster he would have been shot in the head.[28] Returning to duty, Winter indulged in calculated acts of insubordination towards his political superiors. In late June the Dundalk IRA ambushed a train, killing almost two dozen soldiers and about fifty horses. Soon afterwards seven men, supposedly prominent IRA members, were shot dead in Dublin. When newspapers attributed these shootings to the Igoe Gang, Anderson asked Winter to explain their deaths. 'I told him I had instituted inquiries without result, and could only assume that was due to the Irishman's love for a horse, and that, in a spirit of regret that so many horses had perished by this dastardly deed, they had emulated the practice of the Samurai of old and had committed hari-kiri outside their own doorstep. Certainly no other solution was ever found.'[29]

By late May and early June 1921 Cope's situation was increasingly tense and difficult because, as the July deadline approached, the British Cabinet started formulating a new Irish policy. On 24 May the Irish Situation Committee began studying the implications of extending martial law throughout the whole of Southern Ireland and preparing Dublin Castle for Crown Colony Government. Three days later the committee's chairman Austen Chamberlain (Law's successor as Conservative Party leader) reported that martial law under one supreme authority would improve military and police discipline and disarm the civil population – an essential preliminary to pacifying Ireland. He wanted to heavily reinforce the British Army and ensure that the Navy vigorously deterred the importing of arms.[30] The political tempo increased dramatically on 15 June 1921 when the Situation Committee met again at Downing Street to draw up specific recommendations for the period after 14 July 1921.[31]

Chamberlain, Foreign Secretary Balfour, Secretary of War Worthington-Evans, Home Secretary Shortt, Greenwood, Macready and Anderson attended the conference, but it was Macready who dominated the proceedings. After a year of political prevarication he was determined to spell out the consequences of draconian coercion in Ireland. Macready had already circulated the draft of a statement which he wanted published just before the 14 July deadline. This warned that membership of Dail Eireann, the IRA and IRB was treason for which death was the extreme penalty, that anyone caught with arms, ammunition or explosive would be tried by court martial and liable to be hanged, while those apprehended while using them would be tried by drumhead court martial and executed on the spot. Any damage to government property would be recovered through a levy on the surrounding district. The destruction of roads would result in an area's complete isolation and the seizure of any means of transport. Ports could be closed and an ID card system was to be introduced. Although he believed repression would 'land this country deeper in the mire',[32] Macready was prepared to implement it, provided the government realised that it could 'only succeed by being applied with the utmost thoroughness and that only by so doing can the spirit of the soldiers and police be sustained. Half-hearted coercion made the position of the troops and police farcical.'[33]

When Chamberlain asked him whether he would shoot any arrested Dail member who refused to resign, Macready said he intended concentrating on rebel leaders. The kid-glove treatment of de Valera and Griffith had become a standing joke among the army and police, and Macready was losing both their confidence and his own self-respect. After July, he intended instituting drumhead courts martial to try both men for their lives. The case against them was very strong and the law would have to take its course. Greenwood had no problem with this, arguing that 'the quicker men were executed the more palatable executions were to the Irish and the less trouble they cause in this country'.[34] Macready predicted that after 14 July as many as 100 men a week might be executed and the last thing he wanted was to be told after a week that 'this cannot go on'.[35] If he received such an instruction, then that would be the end of it as far as he was concerned. 'The cabinet must understand that any man found with revolvers or bombs would be shot at once.'[36] When Chamberlain enquired whether, for example, if an IRA column of 1,000 men was rounded up everyone would be shot, Macready indicated that he would execute only the leaders. But the time for illusions and half-measures was over. He wanted to know whether the British Government would 'go through with it? Will they begin to howl when they hear of our shooting a hundred men a week?'[37] It had to be 'all out or get out'.[38]

Assistant Cabinet Secretary Tom Jones sensed great trepidation around the table as committee members realised that implementing Macready's recommendations would send tremors through the entire British political system. Balfour feared that even announcing them in advance would be 'unnecessarily terrifying' and suggested transportation instead of hanging. Macready said it was vital to harden the army and police in advance and to prepare the British and Irish public for what was to happen. 'Chamberlain, who seemed nervous right through as to the Parliamentary reactions of the policy, wished Macready to make the pressure of Martial Law fall on the murderous minority rather than on their intimidated supporters.'[39] Afterwards, Balfour asked Macready if he could see any alternative policy. 'I told him frankly I could not.'[40] Macready also increased pressure on the Cabinet by asking for a decision by 7 July at the latest.

Worthington-Evans had also heightened Cabinet anxiety by circulating a pessimistic report from Colonel Sir Hugh Elles, Commandant of the Tank Corps. Visiting Ireland on 13 and 14 May, he had discovered a situation that was 'Gilbertian with the humour left out'.[41] The British Army was besieged:

Officers must move not only armed and in bodies but with their revolvers very handy; in motor cars they carry them actually in their hands. Troops sleep in defended barracks – behind barbed wire. Communication is becoming increasingly difficult. To go from Dublin to Cork one may fly or one may go very slowly – by armed train. This is a curious situation for a force whose raison d'être in the country is to maintain order.[42]

Pouring in more troops would be futile; simply resulting in more divisions coming under siege over a wider area for years to come. A military solution required strict martial law, identity passes, house-to-house searches, an end to IRA arms importation and the dispatch of every available soldier to Ireland. 'The operation should be complete within 2 years. But with anything short of these extreme measures the present situation might go on for such time that political pressures or political change will cause us to abandon the country and we shall be beaten.'[43]

Anderson knew that a momentous decision, one way or the other, was about to be taken in Ireland. He bluntly warned Greenwood that 'Military action to be effective must be vigorous and ruthless. Dreadful things must happen. Many innocent people must inevitably suffer and the element of human error cannot be eliminated.'[44] Trade between Britain and Ireland would dry up within weeks and public services would grind to a halt throughout the entire South. Even worse, this was a guerrilla war without a battle front or any means of distinguishing between friend and foe and in which every army and police excess agitated public, press and parliament. 'We could not have won the Great War under those conditions.'[45] Embarking on all-out coercion without the full support of parliament and country would be 'the wildest folly', especially as their 'instinctive desire in relation to Ireland is to forget'.[46]

Whether the full British Cabinet would ever have ratified the Irish Situation Committee's recommendations is extremely doubtful. It is clear that, although it endorsed Macready's recommendations, some members knew in their hearts they would arouse international condemnation in the same way that German actions in Belgium in 1914 had evoked comparison with the Huns. Macready's performance had been shock therapy and it soon took effect, re-establishing contact between Cabinet ministers and the real world. But the mere possibility that the British Government might proceed with this policy added urgency to Cope's and MacMahon's mission, as well as giving them extra leverage to exert on republican leaders. Both feared that with time running out, de Valera, Collins and Griffith would procrastinate, spinning the process out past 14 July in the hope of extracting further British concessions. With Anderson's approval and probably that of Lloyd George, Cope tried to bring matters to a head by applying Macready's shock therapy to the Sinn Fein leadership. In an interesting dry run for Lloyd George's dramatic threat of 'immediate and terrible war' in December 1921 to compel the Irish delegation to sign the Anglo-Irish Treaty, the Situation Committee's recommendations were immediately leaked to Sinn Fein leaders. On the following day Collins told de Valera that his man (probably Dwyer) had interviewed a British official (almost certainly MacMahon) who was 'very gloomy about the situation'.[47] If the Southern parliament was not functioning within a fortnight of being summoned on 28 June, then the Viceroy would dissolve it and declare martial law of the utmost vigour in the twenty-six counties. British military strength in Ireland would be trebled with 'intense investment of areas, search and internment. He is in a veritable panic to avert the awful times. He wants to see you as man to man. It is quite possible that this is part of the peace move, although I don't accuse him of being aware of it. Cope I should say would be aware of it. Of course, a measure of martial law for the whole of the 26 counties is not unlikely.'[48]

Already rattled by the the approaching deadline of 14 July, Cope found his brittle nerves strained further by Macready's and Brind's behaviour, even though they generally supported his peace efforts. Anderson said that, when dealing with the British Army GHQ, Cope had to 'fight like a tiger', displaying a 'tact, patience and resourcefulness which would have done credit to an early Christian martyr'.[49] Anderson feared the soldiers would 'upset the apple cart not because they want to but out of a mixture of personal pride, soldierly prejudice and downright stupidity'.[50] He thought that Macready was jealous of Cope and wanted to grab the kudos of bringing peace, saying 'Alone I did it'.[51] Sturgis worried that some incident or outrage would derail Cope's secret diplomacy. On 22 June 1921 British military intelligence officers and soldiers searching a large house in the Dublin suburbs arrested a tall man hurrying from a garden. When his beard was removed at the detention centre, it was discovered that he was de Valera. Cope was terrified that Sinn Fein leaders would interpret their president's capture as enemy duplicity or attempts on the British side to sabotage the peace process. He quickly got Greenwood and Anderson to agree to de Valera's immediate release. Winter was in London when he received a coded message about de Valera's arrest; with Lloyd George away in Liverpool he got Austen Chamberlain's assurance that de Valera would stay in custody. But shortly afterwards he was 'angry and dumbfounded' to learn that de Valera had been set free.[52]

On 24 June, the day after de Valera's release, Cope bypassed a hostile Greenwood and got to address a full Cabinet meeting, where, Sturgis said, he 'harangued His Majesty's Ministers and even on his own showing must have been pretty hysterical – he says the sweat poured off him. He talked failure without an offer and Greenwood told him "to curb his Sinn Fein tendencies". However, they heard him out.'[53] But Cope's intervention had only succeeded because the doubts sown by Macready just over a week earlier had gathered momentum and persuaded a considerable number of ministers to endorse a truce and negotiations. Afterwards Lloyd George publicly invited Sinn Fein representatives to attend a London conference along with the Ulster Unionist leaders, a stunning change of direction executed with remarkable speed. Churchill admitted later that 'no British government in modern times has ever appeared to make so complete and sudden a reversal of policy . . . In May the whole power of the State and all the influence of the Coalition were used to "hunt down the murder gang"; in June, the goal was "a lasting reconciliation with the Irish people".'[54]

But Cope's satisfaction was soon tempered by events in Dublin, where, within hours, the IRA's Dublin Brigade tried to encircle Grafton Street and kill every Auxiliary in the area's pubs and restaurants. For weeks Crow Street intelligence officers, disguised as idle students, had conducted surveillance of Grafton Street for a mass attack at 6 p.m. But a general onslaught was called off at the last moment after two 'F' company Auxiliary officers were shot dead a few minutes early.[55] Such incidents tended to strengthen British cynicism and made Cope fearful that everything was falling apart.

Certainly, if Lloyd George had listened to British Intelligence, he would never have opted for conciliation. Winter and Thomson shared an unwavering scepticism about Sinn Fein's motives as well as its ability to deliver real peace and its long-term intentions. Winter insisted that 'the high hopes that Cope has set his heart upon are but as snow on the dusty desert's face. There will be no peace settlement – of that you may be quite sure – at the present moment. But I hope that the proceedings will not be too long dragged out. It will only offer them more breathing space, and more time to negotiate the purchase of arms.'[56]

Thomson believed that Sinn Fein was split between doves and hawks and that militarists like Collins were cramping a politically moderate de Valera. On 13 May 1921 Thomson reported that the IRA was determined to fight on and repudiate any peace acceptable to Sinn Fein as a whole.[57] At the end of June he said Collins was assembling forty Volunteers for intelligence operations in England, having 'boasted that when he acts the War Office will be in no doubt as to whether England or Ireland will be most in need of troops'.[58] De Valera had supposedly told Sinn Fein's Standing Committee that the Church and foreign opinion were exerting immense pressure for peace and that he had to consider the many young men who were dead or imprisoned. But Thomson argued that, while de Valera wanted a way out, he was having tremendous difficulty keeping his grip on Collins's war party, which was 'dead against a compromise'. He was convinced that 'de Valera has no power over Collins; if he had and is sincere, would he not have ordered the murders to stop at once?' Thomson's most valuable Irish informant was constantly insisting that 'no decent deal' was possible and that it was all 'a game to try and gain time'.[59] On 1 July 1921 Thomson reported that de Valera was speaking about his difficulty in getting IRA leaders to consider any reasonable peace proposals and that he was being allowed to remain in contact with the enemy only in order to discover whether they would accept an independent Irish state. Collins was insisting that British peace feelers were a ploy to stifle the IRA and destroy Volunteer GHQ. According to Thomson's source, 'Collins will have no instructions from de Valera as regards military workings and the Government are only wasting time and prolonging the agony. They must beat him at his own game or lose Ireland.'[60] Collins was supposedly gearing up for an all-out offensive, ordering shipping companies to book no more emigrants because he intended conscripting every available young man into the IRA by summer's end.

Thomson's analysis of Sinn Fein's inner workings relied heavily on British Intelligence's greatest secret of the Irish war, that it had embedded a spy at the very top of Sinn Fein. The long-held belief that the elimination of 'Jameson' and Quinlisk definitely terminated British efforts to penetrate the republican leadership is seriously inaccurate because British Intelligence finally succeeded beyond its wildest dreams. During 1920 and 1921 it had an agent reporting regularly on de Valera, Collins, Griffith and other Sinn Fein luminaries. Although Thomson was prepared to give de Valera the benefit of the doubt, this agent depicted him as 'a red-hot extremist' who wanted to assassinate George V during his visit to Belfast in June to open the Northern Ireland parliament. On learning that Lloyd George was not accompanying the King, de Valera had supposedly 'burst out saying they would have a go at him where and when he did visit Ireland. I believe he meant it too.'[61] Consistently deriding peace feelers and negotiations as a waste of time, Thomson's agent insisted that 'any thought of compromise or conciliation with SF is absolutely unthinkable and moreover is impossible'.

Sinn Fein leaders were privately scoffing at Cope's manoeuvrings, convinced they had the British Government on its knees, and only brute force would bring it to its senses. 'Let us put some ginger into it, and get 'em really on the run. It is the only thing that they understand; you must "treat 'em rough".' Continued IRA atrocities were 'fit replies to the policy of conciliation and the lunatic release of de Valera'. This British spy was clearly privy to sensitive information, having learnt quickly about de Valera's arrest at Blackrock on 22 June and his rapid release – despite an official news blackout on both events. The source also knew about Cope's intervention to free de Valera: 'They say here that he was primarily responsible for DV's release and that Boyd was all for keeping him.' The spy also reported correctly the Sinn Fein leadership's decision to go public with a communiqué about the affair.

What do we know about this British spy? Greenwood, who was privy to the secret, titillated Lloyd George's mistress Frances Stevenson by sending her a copy of one of the agent's reports. He hinted at an Irish Mata Hari, whose information was 'straight from the cow'.[62] Certainly she was a forceful personality with strong nerves who knew she was in considerable jeopardy. 'I am risking my sanguinary neck every day, and all day; I wouldn't get ten minutes' grace if they had the slightest suspicion.' She was also extremely close to one Sinn Fein leader whom she called 'Bob' and who kept her informed about political events such as de Valera's arrest: 'Bob told me the news and he had the wind up to a degree. He thought this would have a very bad effect on their show. I have never seen Bob quite so exasperated over anything before.' But she was also accumulating intelligence at informal gatherings where Sinn Fein leaders like de Valera spoke freely, often indiscreetly and perhaps not always entirely seriously. Most unusually for a supposed republican she had not only participated in the British war effort between 1914 and 1918 but retained fond memories of the national unity it had engendered: 'The war was a pleasure to this, and one always felt that everyone was out to win.' Only one prominent female Sinn Feiner fitted this profile, and that was Erskine Childers's wife Molly.

The daughter of a prominent, wealthy Boston doctor, Molly Osgood had met her future husband during his British Army unit's American tour. After a whirlwind courtship they married in January 1904 when she was 25 years old and Childers 33.[63] She had been crippled in a childhood skating accident and, despite regaining the use of her legs, remained permanently disabled. But her battle against ill health had demonstrated Molly's considerable willpower and self-reliance. Intelligent, well read and politically aware, Molly shared her parents' distaste for aristocracy, imperialism and England, though clearly in Childers's case love conquered all. After settling in London, where Erskine was a House of Commons clerk, Molly discovered that she had really married into two families, the Childers and that of Robert Barton, the best man at her wedding. After the early death of Erskine's English father Robert and his Irish mother Anna's confinement in a sanatorium, Anna's brother Charles Barton and Robert's sister Agnes (who had married each other) raised Erskine, his elder brother and three sisters.

The Bartons were a wealthy Anglo-Irish family living on their Glendalough estate in County Wicklow, where their son Robert became very close to Erskine. After an education at Haileybury and Trinity College Cambridge, Childers became a conventional English gentleman, politically liberal and so committed to the Empire that he volunteered for the British Army during the Boer War. His involvement in Irish affairs evolved only gradually from interest to active participation and finally obsession and death. For some years after marrying, Childers returned only a few times a year to Glendalough – stays during which Molly also formed a lifelong friendship with 'Bob' Barton. On a motoring tour of Ireland in 1908 both Childers and Barton were converted to Home Rule, though only in July 1914 did Erskine directly assist Irish nationalists by using his yacht to smuggle in weapons for the Irish Volunteers.

At this stage Childers was committed to a devolved Irish parliament within the United Kingdom, not republicanism and revolution, and when the First World War began he unhesitatingly joined the Royal Naval Air Service. Barton enlisted in the British Army, though his experiences in Dublin after the Rising left him so disillusioned that after his discharge in May 1918 he became a Sinn Fein politician. On the home front Molly became secretary of a welfare committee for Belgian refugees, something about which she was immensely proud and that contributed to her growing affection for England. She had grown to love London, admired the country's wartime national unity and was delighted when King George V awarded her the CBE at Buckingham Palace in recognition of her refugee work.

For the first three years of the war Erskine and Molly's attitudes remained harmonious and both saw the Easter Rising as a pro-German stab in the back. But in the summer of 1917 Erskine's old friend Sir Horace Plunkett got him appointed assistant secretary of the Irish Convention which Lloyd George had established in Dublin so that Irish representatives could agree a political settlement. But Sinn Fein boycotted the Convention and during his nine months in the capital, Childers's beliefs were radically transformed as he observed the party's remarkable rise and listened to Barton expound its ideas at Glendalough. Fascinatingly, both Erskine and Molly were simultaneously undergoing very different crises of loyalty. While he increasingly pitted himself against his homeland, she was becoming progressively attached to her adopted country, a process no doubt accelerated by America's entry into the war on the side of England in May 1917.

Molly was distressed by Childers's emerging vision of his future lying in Ireland, especially as she believed his obligation to England should take priority over his emotional support for Irish republicanism. She did not want to leave England, particularly as it would disrupt their children's education and part her from her English friends. Having given up America for him, she now felt that he owed her a sacrifice. Molly's obvious reluctance to shift to Ireland and her appeals to Childers to reconsider his new mission and his increasingly strident endorsement of Sinn Fein placed considerable strain on their marriage. After the armistice in November 1918, she used her ongoing refugee work as a delaying tactic to stay in England, while his commitment to Irish republicanism was sealed by his membership of the Sinn Fein delegation at the Paris Peace Conference.

In the summer of 1919 Molly made a last-ditch attempt to change Erskine's mind, but he remained adamant about going to Ireland. According to his official biographer, 'Molly ceased resisting there and then'[64] and she and the children finally arrived in Ireland just before Christmas 1919. If she was indeed the important British spy, then it must have been in the critical months before her departure from England when her ambivalence about the direction the whole family's lives were taking and her husband's new political allies caused her to volunteer for British Intelligence. The agent told her controller that 'you know why I took this job on, not for cash but to feel that I was really doing something to help'.[65] Clearly deeply emotionally involved in her mission, she confessed that 'I feel very strongly indeed on this subject and I must let off steam or "bust"'.[66] Making contact with British Intelligence would have caused no problems for Molly Childers. Intelligence officers interrogated her Belgian refugees and she had available her husband's high-level contacts in the Admiralty and the House of Commons. In Dublin, Molly Childers certainly had continuous access to both Sinn Fein's senior men and high-grade political information. As the Dail government's Director of Publicity and later a Dail deputy, Erskine was close to both de Valera and Collins, who made Molly a trustee of the Dail Loan. At their Bushy Park Road home in the south Dublin suburb of Terenure, Molly also ran a press cuttings and reference service and established a political salon. As the hostess she provided hospitality and attentiveness while Sinn Fein leaders relaxed, socialised, gossiped and spoke more candidly than perhaps was wise.

But if Molly Childers was indeed spying for the British, then who was the leading Sinn Fein politician 'Bob' who unsuspectingly relayed so much confidential information? An obvious candidate was her relative by marriage, Robert ('Bob') Barton. As the Dail government's Minister of Agriculture he was in Sinn Fein's upper echelons and served as a key Truce negotiator. But the British released Barton from Portland Gaol in England only on 1 July 1921 in order to facilitate the Truce negotiations, while it was on 25 June that the female spy had submitted her lengthy report about 'Bob's' exasperated reaction to de Valera's arrest. However, there was another Robert in Sinn Fein's leadership, a highly strung individual who was also involved in the Truce negotiations and whose increasing bouts of exasperation she had witnessed at first hand – her own husband, Robert Erskine Childers. Although her report mentioned de Valera and Collins by name, she hid the identities of other Sinn Fein leaders, referring to 1, 3 and 4: clearly a trio from a more extended list. Using her husband's lesser-known forename as a means of identification was hardly a giant leap of imagination in the game of espionage.

That Molly Childers had the qualities to carry off such a dangerous role is not in doubt because throughout her life this remarkable woman had consistently displayed intelligence, courage, decisiveness and single-minded determination. Her inner fortitude had enabled her to triumph over literally crippling physical tribulations which had perhaps trained her for the solitariness of espionage. And by shifting from America to England and finally Ireland she had demonstrated that ability to adapt to different customs, social settings and political attitudes – to fit seamlessly into whatever circumstances she found herself in – that is indispensable in any successful spy. Moreover, Molly's forceful personality idiom and her American-sounding turn of phrase were consistent with someone urging her employers to 'get 'em really on the run'.

If Molly Childers was the 'cow', then it was a secret that she – and everyone else who knew – took to their graves. She stood by her husband to the end and after Erskine's execution during the Irish Civil War became the keeper of his memory.

* * *

Occasionally in the final push to effect a truce Cope went behind his sceptical Chief Secretary's back or else blindsided him with a *fait accompli*. Right to the end Greenwood remained impervious to the desirability of a truce, having assured Lloyd George in early May that 'the inside news is that the Murder Gang are getting worried, and they want a way out. In my opinion de Valera will carry the leaders of the IRA but there will be sporadic outrages by the ruffians still at large even after peace.'[67] Two months later Greenwood boasted that 'we're pressing on after the IRA. I know we're defeating them, though we're bound to lose brave men. . . . The RC Church is coming out more and more on side of police because the rebellion has failed.'[68] So when de Valera hinted that releasing Griffith, MacNeill, Duggan and Barton would speed negotiations, Cope bypassed Greenwood on 30 June and got Anderson's approval, citing the Chief Secretary's absence in London as the reason.

Despite their personal differences, Macready supported Cope's efforts to secure a Truce. On 5 July 1921 his deputy Colonel Brind welcomed the release of Griffith, Duggan and Barton because 'although all these individuals are extremists they are men of some education and may during their imprisonment have developed the sense to see that their claim to a republic will never be granted'.[69] Brind believed that the Catholic Church and Irish newspapers would pressurise Sinn Fein to meet Lloyd George, though the success of any conference depended on republican leaders realising that they were bound to be beaten and 'nothing will ever induce the British nation to allow them to secede'.[70] As yet he had seen little evidence of moderation in captured correspondence, 'official communiqués' or republican journals, and every previous British peace feeler had been misinterpreted as proof that the IRA was on the brink of victory. The best hope was that the 'dreamers and agitators' could no longer deny mounting IRA losses, British military reinforcements, public opinion in Ireland, Britain and America, imminent and universal martial law and the knowledge that this was absolutely the final chance of a peaceful settlement. 'On the surface the outlook is not hopeful – but there is just a chance that the Sinn Fein leaders may at last see reason, and risk the displeasure of their more fanatical followers.'[71]

On the same day as Brind's memorandum the South African prime minister Jan Smuts arrived in Dublin to throw his weight behind a truce. As a former Boer guerrilla leader who had made peace with the British and had arrived in June to attend a Commonwealth conference, he was in the unusual position of being trusted by both sides. Smuts had contributed to King George V's emotional plea for peace when he opened the Northern Ireland parliament on 22 June and now he persuaded Sinn Fein leaders to accept Lloyd George's invitation to a London conference.

With the decision made in principle, it required only the practical arrangements of a truce to be finalised. On 8 July Macready met General Boyd, Tudor and Cope at Parkgate, where it was agreed that, in the event of a truce, raiding and searching would stop; the army would confine itself to supporting the police and lift the curfew. On the morning of Saturday 9 July, Barton and Duggan met Cope and McMahon at Dublin Castle prior to a conference with Macready and Brind at British Army GHQ.[72] The weather was sunny and Cope was wearing a blue blazer and straw hat. Anxious to prevent anything going wrong at the last moment, he advised the Irish representatives to act in measured terms, saying Brind was 'a very dangerous man'. MacMahon reminded them they were dealing with military men who were going to lose their jobs in the event of peace. Barton and Duggan refused Cope's offer of a lift in his private car to Parkgate, and so the party took a tram, with the Irish pair riding on top. Cope, who remained downstairs, paid the fares when they alighted at Parkgate and ushered them anonymously through the sentry gate as his 'friends'. Inside, the terms for a truce beginning on 11 July were clinched.

At the last moment, there almost occurred one of those incidents which Sturgis had feared would derail the entire process. In the first week of July, while Traynor was convalescing, Volunteer GHQ ordered acting Brigadier Sean Mooney to commit his every available Volunteer to wipe out Auxiliaries parading with their girlfriends in O'Connell, Grafton and Nassau streets. The operation was timed to commence at 7 p.m., and battalion units had assembled and were about to move when they were informed that GHQ had called the attack off because a truce had been agreed.[73]

Why Collins and Volunteer GHQ allowed this operation to go so close to the wire with its potentially catastrophic consequences for the Truce is a mystery. It certainly puzzled 2nd Battalion's commandant, Frank Henderson:

> We were taken entirely by surprise. I could never understand why GHQ had allowed our preparations to go so far practically up to the moment that the attack was launched. A delay in the communicating of the order from GHQ or the accidental arriving of a group in O'Connell Street a few moments before zero hour might have created a difficult situation. It is also to be noted no Auxiliaries appeared in O'Connell Street on the night arranged for the attack. Perhaps they had received a cancelling order also.[74]

The operation also carried enormous risks for the Dublin Brigade because, although the ever-loyal Paddy Daly claimed its cancellation thwarted a major IRA victory, Joe Leonard was secretly relieved at the cancellation, admitting candidly: 'We had not enough ammunition to fill our guns and would of necessity have all been wiped out by their fire. But for the job being called off at the last minute there would have been no Truce.'[75]

During the Truce negotiations one of Collins's British pursuers had finally come face to face with him and lived to tell the tale. Tudor's secretary William Darling says that one night he was summoned to accompany a senior Castle official to Newry, where a police car had collided with another vehicle carrying three civilians. Since he was to escort them to Dublin, Darling sensed that one or more of the trio warranted special treatment. But he did not recognise any of the men for certain until one man in the back suddenly asked him, '"Do you know me?" To this I replied: "No." I said: "I think I know your friends, but I don't know you." There was a further period of silence, then speaking in the dark, he said quite simply and very agreeably: "I am Michael Collins."'[76]

When they finally arrived at a Dublin hotel, Collins invited Darling to join him inside. 'It was well past midnight, and in a room on the left where there was attendance he and I had a couple of bottles of stout together. He was an interesting, indeed a fascinating man. He was unarmed and at his request I put my little pistol on the bar counter.'[77] They talked through the night and Darling was especially intrigued by three books of which Collins spoke highly, a German general's account of the South-West African guerrilla campaign, Walt Whitman's *Leaves of Grass* and, surprisingly, G.K. Chesterton's *Napoleon of Notting Hill*. Collins 'knew it not as a casual reader, I felt, but almost as a political testament, or at least, a text book. He was, I fancy, in his own imagination Adam Wayne, its hero, and he would without difficulty, I thought, find himself speaking as Adam Wayne spoke.'[78]

Darling's encounter with Collins was an indication that the conflict was gradually winding down and the worst was over. Finally, at noon on 11 July 1921, peace of a kind broke out in Ireland. In Dublin harbour numerous ships sounded their sirens while a large crowd at the Castle waited expectantly for a formal Truce announcement that never actually materialised. Years of tension and fear subsided as people celebrated in the summer heat. In O'Connell Street exuberant tricolour-waving crowds sang rebel songs and danced along behind marching bands, wanted men walked the streets unhindered, British Army lorries moved around with their machine guns wrapped in canvas, while Auxiliaries carrying towels and bathing costumes headed for nearby seaside resorts. The *Irish Times* reported an overwhelming sense of release 'after a year and half of imprisonment by curfew'.[79] Shops, cinemas and theatres stayed open far into the night, trams ran late and pub customers partied till the early morning hours. At one party in Vaughan's Hotel, Michael Noyk recalled joining Collins,

Gearoid O'Sullivan, Diarmuid O'Hegarty, Liam Mellows, Liam Tobin, Rory O'Connor, Frank Thornton, Colonel Broy, Detective Sergeant McNamara who was working for Mick Collins, Sean Etchingham of Wexford and many others. It was a joyous occasion and Mick Collins recited, 'Kelly, Burke and Shea', and Liam Mellows sang 'McDonnell of the Glens' – an old Scottish song. Little did we think that night of the events that were in store before another year had passed. It is well for mortal man that he cannot see into the future.[80]

CONCLUSIONS

After the Treaty Collins wrote that he had created Volunteer GHQ Intelligence and the Squad because to paralyse the British machine it was necessary to strike at individuals. Without her spies England was helpless. It was only by means of this accumulated knowledge that the British machine could operate. Without their police throughout the country how could they find the men they 'wanted'? Without their criminal agents in the capital how could they carry out that 'removal' of the leaders that they considered essential to their victory? Spies are not so ready to step into the shoes of their departed confederates as are soldiers to fill up the front in honourable battle. And even when the new spy stepped into the shoes of the old one, he could not step into the old one's knowledge.[1]

Collins was also motivated by the unequal nature of the Irish war in which he sought not an unattainable military victory but a dignified British withdrawal. This, he believed, could be realised by crippling the British intelligence system and compensating, in large part, for the IRA's military inferiority. Decimating G Division eliminated the best G-men along with their knowledge, expertise and contacts and forced Winter to start all over again in 1920. And frightening off informers also stemmed the flow of information to the enemy.

Furthermore, the fear inspired by the Squad permeated every branch of the Irish administration right up to the highest levels in Dublin Castle. Among its residents was Assistant Under-Secretary Taylor, who on police advice moved inside in December 1919 in order to 'outwit the designs of the gang of assassins who have murdered other public officials in Dublin'.[2] He was still there in April 1920, complaining that 'for four months I have not been able to walk outside the precincts'.[3] The abnormal security in which Collins enveloped the British elite in Ireland, the psychological pressures they suffered and the transparent nonsense of any British claims about restoring normality undoubtedly contributed to the Truce of July 1921.

As was the case with G Division itself, which Collins emulated and finally superseded, his organisation far exceeded its limited resources in its power and impact on the enemy. But he never penetrated the higher echelons of the British political, military and police system in Ireland. IRA agents like Broy, Neligan, McNamara and Mernin were junior figures in the bureaucratic hierarchy whose main value lay in their access to confidential documents and information about their colleagues and superiors. As far as we know, Collins never recruited a single important member of the Irish administration, political, military or police. And that was quite apart from the apex of British power in London, about whose policy-making in Downing Street and the Cabinet he knew nothing and which he never attempted to penetrate. Collins's only insights came to him courtesy of the British Government when it deliberately leaked information. When it let him know the decisions of the Irish Situation Committee it was Collins who was being manipulated either by exerting pressure on him or giving him the means, should he choose to use them, to persuade his Dail cabinet and Volunteer GHQ colleagues to accept a truce.

Collins's intelligence system was most useful then on the tactical rather than the strategic level. In Ireland it frequently kept the enemy on the defensive or outwitted him either by frustrating his planned operations and raids or facilitating daring operations such as that on Bloody Sunday and the Custom House. While in purely military power and resources the British were infinitely superior in the intelligence field, the position for most of the war was substantially reversed and British military superiority neutralised. But that was not in itself a decisive factor in the military conflict. By the Truce of July 1921, the IRA was effectively beaten in Dublin, while in Cork the situation had reached stalemate. But the political and propaganda impact of events like Bloody Sunday and that of Collins's intelligence system in general had proved enormous. While the myth far outstripped the reality, the myth itself became Collins's most powerful political weapon.

Afterwards, the British admitted serious and ultimately insuperable intelligence problems in Ireland. According to Winter it was a case of operating

in a completely terrorized, and to a great extent hostile, country. The Rebel Intelligence Service, on the other hand, had the advantage of working amidst a population the greater portion of which was friendly, and even when persons were not, information could often be obtained as the purchase of their immunity. Hotel waiters, tramway conductors, bus drivers, tap-room loafers and members of the Cumann na mBan were all willing agents.[4]

The difficulties were compounded by employing the local population in Irish government departments. Winter acknowledged that it was comparatively easy for the enemy to infiltrate the civil service and police while 'the postal services were corrupt and the telephone services equally so'.[5] The British made their own contribution by allowing wives and families to join army officers, facilitating the unintentional leaking of information to the IRA.

British attempts to create an effective intelligence system were also hampered by institutional troubles, especially overlapping and competing organisations. Even when Winter assumed responsibility for Dublin District Special Branch, its members' allegiance remained with General Boyd. The army conceded that 'parallel systems are invariably vicious. They lead to duplication, jealousy and leakage of information.'[6] At the very time a unified effort was essential army–police relations were poisoned by mutual suspicion, while both were frequently at odds with the civil authorities, justifying Keith Jeffery's assertion that 'the British intelligence effort in Ireland from 1919 to 1921 was crippled by a lack of coherence and centralized direction'.[7]

But British Intelligence in Ireland did learn some valuable lessons about guerrilla warfare, a phenomenon confronted only rarely before in the Empire, as in pre-war Bengal. The trouble was they had little or no time to apply them because, unlike the modern concept of a long war – a protracted conflict which saps the enemy's political will over many years and even decades – the shooting war in Ireland was remarkably brief. Effectively it lasted only from January 1920 to the Truce of July 1921, just over eighteen months, making the British learning curve a very steep one indeed. Consequently, the lessons were really digested only after the British Army had evacuated Ireland, in official reports on the British intelligence campaign by Winter and Military Intelligence, in Staff College lectures, army seminars and military journals. And only in later imperial conflicts in places like Palestine and Malaya could the British apply the lessons of Ireland with varying degrees of success.

One crucial lesson – now an intelligence cliché – was the necessity of winning the local population's hearts and minds through effective propaganda and using minimum force. British Intelligence subsequently admitted that Auxiliary and Black and Tan misbehaviour had seriously alienated popular support. But even more importantly, the battle for hearts and minds must be fought when the possibility of victory still exists. It is arguable that by 1919 that moment had passed in Ireland. Although the general election of December 1918 had not endorsed another insurrection, it had installed a new national political leadership and created a radical new political dispensation with which the British offer to tinker with the status quo simply could not compete. Furthermore, to the fury of many British politicians, soldiers and policemen, the population always distinguished between their excesses and those of the IRA, condemning the latter less – or not at all. The British discovered that they were carrying a burden of history under which they ultimately buckled.

Given the republicans' political, intelligence and psychological advantages and their overwhelming public support, most British Army commanders reluctantly concluded that only draconian repression could have succeeded. Colonel Elles's report of May 1921 had soberly outlined what this would involve, while Macready did so more graphically a month later in front of the Irish Situation Committee. But Macready's shock therapy had been deliberately designed to appal his audience and effect a change – a somersault – in government policy. He knew that British democracy limited what a government could do before provoking domestic and international outrage, public disorder and major political upheaval. Macready had privately argued: 'The obvious course would be to at once arrest the principal members of the IRA in a town or village and give them twenty-four hours to produce the murderers on pain of being shot. I doubt, however, whether even in the state in which Ireland is at the present moment it would be possible for Government to sanction such measures without actually declaring a state of war.'[8] But if this frustrated British Intelligence it accepted this situation; whatever dirty tricks it perpetrated in Ireland, it never ran out of control or challenged its political superiors. However frustrated Tudor's inner circle may have been, his secretary William Darling accepted that 'when we make war we make war, if war is the policy of the Government, but when the policy of the Government is to make peace, we make peace'.[9]

And whatever excesses British forces committed there were certain things which leading British figures would not countenance. Winter recorded his irritation that when Anderson heard of the deaths of McKee, Clancy and Clune in the Castle on Bloody Sunday he was 'somewhat dubious about the accuracy of my information'.[10] Anderson insisted on accompanying Winter to the guardroom, where he listened to statements by Auxiliaries and challenged Winter to show him 'ocular and tangible proof.'[11] Probably the mounting disquiet and shame felt by Anderson and others – their belief that what was being done was destroying Britain's moral justification for ruling Ireland – contributed to their acceptance that battling on was too high a price to pay.

But, if operating in an open society constrained the British, then on the Irish side too democratic values, public opinion and common decency also confined Collins's intelligence system. Just as he refused to allow a church killing and the poisoning of the British hangman, so Collins rejected a scheme dreamt up by Mrs Gavan Duffy of the Cumann na mBan executive. When the RIC held incommunicado a 12-year-old boy whom it considered an eyewitness to the Soloheadbeg ambush, she proposed kidnapping Chief Secretary Macpherson's son and holding him hostage in her County Donegal cottage. According to the Cumann na mBan's secretary, Mrs Wyse-Power, 'She pointed out that such a young child would not suffer at all, but that its parents would – which she considered quite fitting. Collins, however, vetoed the project absolutely, thinking apparently that it would be too unpopular.'[12]

Perhaps the greatest lesson was that intelligence is not a magic elixir, that, as Winter stressed, it 'alone cannot win a war. It is merely an aid to force and it is only by action that the desired end can be obtained.'[13] However, as events in Ireland demonstrated, intelligence can go a long way to denying victory. Ultimately the fault on the British side lay not in a dysfunctional and muddled intelligence system or personal inadequacies but with the politicians at the top. Indeed, the politicians caused many of the problems with which British intelligence officers had to grapple. Throughout the conflict the British Cabinet never formulated, enunciated and adhered to a clear policy, and the only constant was vacillation. British Intelligence concluded that the central problem was 'doubt as to what was the real policy of the Government, while the Government probably found it difficult to define their policy owing to the lack of information as to what was really happening and as to the trend of events. The result was a compromise between conciliation and coercion and a state of affairs that was neither peace nor war.'[14]

Subsequently British Military Intelligence stressed the necessity of an intelligence system that enabled government advisers to place reliable information before the Cabinet. Only when government ministers fully appreciated a situation could they frame an appropriate policy and present arguments with which to persuade public opinion. Yet a damning Fifth Division report argued that the British Government had never realised the true state of affairs in Ireland until it was too late:

> The entire absence of any established system on intelligence precluded political optimism from being exposed and sounder judgments formed. The result was that we were never fully prepared for the next rebel move and that while they were progressing from sporadic murder and intimidation to a well organized guerilla campaign, supported and shielded by systematic frightfulness, our measures always fell short of what the situation demanded; they had been designed to deal with a situation that had passed.[15]

But, if the British Government lacked information as to what was really happening in Ireland, then that was a situation for which it bore responsibility and which it could have remedied. Instead, Cabinet ministers like Montague who craved information were denied it while those best positioned to utilise it neglected to do so. Leading figures like Lloyd George, Bonar Law, Curzon and Balfour did not even visit Ireland between 1919 and 1921.[16] For extensive periods, the prime minister delegated Irish affairs to Walter Long. But Long's tours of Ireland were anything but fact-finding missions; his invisible shield deflected anything that unsettled his own deep-seated prejudices. Yet anyone with an open mind – like Fisher, Anderson and Elles – immediately uncovered an appalling situation which induced shock and incredulity. Only someone like the invincibly optimistic Greenwood failed that particular reality test. Furthermore, instead of creating an effective intelligence system, the British Government passed the buck to Macready, who rapidly passed it on to Tudor and Winter. For most of the war Lloyd George and his inner Cabinet circle preferred comforting illusion to unpalatable truth. When Charles Tegart's analysis, for instance, challenged Lloyd George's requirement for a speedy victory, he was quickly jettisoned.

Instead of accepting that a major rebellion in Ireland enjoyed overwhelming political support, the British Government, as Military Intelligence asserted, 'clung to the idea that what they had to deal with and suppress was political crime'.[17] The Black and Tan Douglas Duff expressed the same point more colourfully, complaining about rank and file frustration:

Our greatest difficulty were our own authorities who were bound to a shilly-shally course of conduct by the pusillanimity of the nabobs of Whitehall. Given a free hand we could have restored order in Ireland in a month, even if it had been a Peace of the Roman style, the kind that required the making of a desolation. But egged on to be brutal and tyrannizing one day imprisoned and dismissed the service the next if we dared to speak roughly to our enemies, it is no wonder that the heart was taken out of the men and that most of us merely soldiered for our pay. We were merely the catspaws of a political junta in London. They even persisted in treating this armed and widespread rebellion as though it were an exceptional crime wave.[18]

The Anglo-Irish War's enduring lesson was that, if a government wants reliable intelligence about a country or a situation, then it must put in place the personnel, organisation and resources to garner such information, analyse it dispassionately and tell the government what it needs to know rather than what it wants to hear. This was true in the years 1919 to 1921; it remains true today.

NOTES

Abbreviations
TNA: PRO The National Archives: Public Record Office
WS   Witness Statement, Bureau of Military History

Prologue
1. Joe Good, *Enchanted by Dreams: The Journals of a Revolutionary* (Brandon Books, Dingle, 1996), p. 75.
2. Liam Tobin WS 1753.
3. Volunteer Joseph Sweeney in Kenneth Griffith and Timothy O'Grady, *Curious Journey: An Oral History of Ireland's Unfinished Revolution* (London, Hutchinson, 1982), p. 79.
4. 'Miss Julia Grennan's Story of the Surrender', *Catholic Bulletin* (June 1917).
5. Tobin WS.
6. Good, *Enchanted by Dreams*, p. 76.
7. *Ibid*.
8. There are full accounts of Wilson's killing in both the *Irish Times* and *Freeman's Journal* of 16 June 1920.
9. Volunteer Joseph Sweeney in Griffith and O'Grady, *Curious Journey*, p. 79.

Chapter One
1. There is a plethora of Collins biographies. They include Piaras Beaslai's pioneering but somewhat unreliable *Michael Collins and the Making of a New Ireland*, 2 vols (London, Harrap, 1926), Frank O'Connor, *The Big Fellow: A Life of Michael Collins* (London, Nelson, 1937), Rex Taylor, *Michael Collins* (London, Four Square, 1958), Margery Forester, *Michael Collins:*

The Lost Leader (Dublin, Gill & Macmillan, 1971), and Tim Pat Coogan, *Michael Collins: A Biography* (London, Roberts Rinehart, 1990). Other useful works are T. Ryle Dwyer, *Michael Collins: The Man who Won the War* (Cork, Mercier, 1990), and Gabriel Doherty (ed.), *Michael Collins and the Making of the Irish Free State* (Cork, Mercier, 1998).
2. Richard Mulcahy, Talk on Michael Collins given by General Mulcahy to Members of the Donegalmen's Association. UCD, Mulcahy Papers, P7/b/180.
3. Kathleen Clarke, *Revolutionary Woman: An Autobiography* (Dublin, O'Brien Press, 1991), p. 138.
4. Michael Hayes, 'Michael Collins', *Capuchin Annual* (1972), p. 253.
5. Florence O'Donoghue, 'Reorganisation of the Irish Volunteers 1916–1917', *Capuchin Annual* (1967), p. 383.
6. For this, see Sean O'Mahony, *Frongoch: University of Revolution* (Dublin, FDR Teoranta, 1987). O'Mahony cites Tim Healy MP as saying that Frongoch was the Irish Volunteers' Sandhurst (p. 58).
7. Mulcahy Lecture at the Grosvenor Hotel, 29 October 1963. Mulcahy Papers, P/D/66.
8. Richard Mulcahy's lengthy two-part critique of Piaras Beaslai's two-

volume life of Collins, part 2, p. 45. Mulcahy Papers, P7/D/66. Hereafter Beaslai Critique.

9. T.E. Lawrence, *Seven Pillars of Wisdom* (London, 1939), p. 23.

10. Eamon Broy WS 1280.

11. *Ibid.*

12. Eamon Broy WS 1285.

13. Beaslai Critique, part 2, p. 45.

14. Lecture at the Grosvenor Hotel, 29 October 1963. Mulcahy Papers, P/D/66.

15. Broy WS 1280.

16. For French, see Richard Holmes, *The Little Field-Marshal: Sir John French* (London, Jonathan Cape, 1981).

17. Long to Lloyd George, 7 May 1918. House of Lords Record Office, Lloyd George Papers, F 32/5/33.

18. Basil Thomson, *The Scene Changes* (London, Collins, 1939), p. 367.

19. *Ibid.*

20. Cited in John Kendle, *Walter Long, Ireland and the Union 1905–1920* (Montreal, Glendale Publishing, 1992), p. 166.

21. Thomson, *The Scene Changes*, p. 367.

22. Wiltshire Record Office, Long Papers, 947/672.

23. Broy WS 1280.

24. Long, 18 May 1918. Long Papers, 947/354.

25. Thomson, *The Scene Changes*, p. 371.

26. Transcript of Mulcahy in conversation with Broy, 1 December 1964. Mulcahy Papers, P/7b/184.

27. *Ibid.*

28. Richard Mulcahy, Talk on Michael Collins given by General Mulcahy to Members of the Donegalmen's Association, p. 3. Mulcahy Papers, P7/b/180.

29. Mulcahy, 'Chief of Staff', *Capuchin Annual* (1969), p. 344.

30. *Ibid.*

31. French to Long, 12 September 1918. Long Papers, 947/332.

32. French to Churchill, 10 April 1919. Imperial War Museum, French Papers, JD FF 8/10.

33. Maryann Valiulis, *Portrait of a Revolutionary: General Richard Mulcahy and the Founding of the Irish Free State* (Dublin, Irish Academic Press, 1992), p. 40.

34. Frank Henderson WS 821.

35. Dan Breen, *My Fight for Irish Freedom*, p. 32.

36. Mulcahy says that 'I had no personal use for Dan Breen or for Treacy' (Beaslai Critique, part 2, p. 34) – though he marginally preferred Treacy to Breen. Mulcahy says that Soloheadbeg 'had many negative and unwarranted features. It took place on the day the Dail was being assembled for the first time and a Dail government was established. With the initiative in the hands of the Volunteers themselves, bloodshed should have been unnecessary in the light of the type of episode it was. It completely disturbed the general public situation in the area and it pushed rather turbulent spirits such as Breen and Treacy into the Dublin area from time to time where their services were not required and their presence was often awkward' (*ibid.*, p. 91).

37. Seamus Robinson, Statement, National Library of Ireland MS 21265. The question of to what extent Collins had encouraged the Tipperary Volunteer leaders clearly weighed on Mulcahy. He considered they were more concerned with killing the policemen than capturing the gelignite – which was not actually used until 18 January 1920 in an attack on Dromobane RIC Barracks. Mulcahy believed that 'it might be found that the boisterous element of Collins' companionship was an encouragement to them, if not before Soloheadbeg then after Soloheadbeg at any rate'.

38. Joe Lawless WS 1043.

39. The classic description by the late Professor F.X. Martin, the doyen of Rising historians whose thesis was

enunciated in 'Myth, Fact and Mystery', *Studia Hibernica*, 7 (1967), and 'The 1916 Rising – a Coup d'Etat or a "Bloody Protest"', *Studia Hibernica*, 8 (1968).

40. Broy WS 1280.
41. *Ibid.*
42. *Ibid.*
43. Richard Mulcahy, 'Chief of Staff', *Capuchin Annual* (1969), pp. 346–7.
44. Mulcahy Lecture at the Grosvenor Hotel, 29 October 1963. Mulcahy Papers, P/D/66.
45. Richard Mulcahy, 'Conscription and the General Headquarters Staff', *Capuchin Annual* (1967), p. 386.
46. Mick McDonnell WS 225.
47. Henderson WS.
48. Broy WS 1280.
49. Mulcahy wrote that 'from the setting up of the full Cabinet on the 2nd April 1919 the positions occupied by Collins were Minister for Finance as a member of the Cabinet, D/Intelligence as a member of the GHQ Staff', as well as D/Organisation and Adjutant General and one of the Vice-Presidents of Sinn Fein. In *Further Notes on the Collins Microfilm in the National Library* Neg. 545 Pos. 919, Mulcahy took Beaslai to task for saying in his biography that Collins was officially D/Intelligence June–August 1919: 'He had in fact been D/I for months past.' Reference to Brugha in Beaslai Critique, part 1, p. 52. Richard Walsh, a member of the Volunteer Executive, claimed that 'one night at an executive meeting in Parnell Square, Collins surprised many of us be resigning his position as A.G. [Adjutant-General] and asking that he be appointed as Director of Intelligence. Certainly a lot of us were astounded that he should wish to relinquish his position as AG and take over the position of DI. I failed to see why he should resign the AG-

ship and I could not see much importance in the position of DI. Apparently C. Brugha seemed quite pleased with Collins's idea and offered no objection' (Richard Walsh WS 400).
50. Henderson WS.
51. *Ibid.*
52. Broy WS 1280.
53. Broy WS 1285.
54. French to Long, 19 May 1919. House of Lords Record Office, Bonar Law Papers, 97/3/28.
55. Bonar Law to Lloyd George, 18 May 1920. Lloyd George Papers, F/30/3/63, Macpherson himself wrote to French that Law and Long 'think that meanwhile we should not take the action contemplated in the minute which I gave you on Saturday. It is foolish in Ireland to attempt to take action unless and until everything is complete to ensure its success. We are agreed it may be necessary for us to proclaim the so-called Parliament (Dail Eirlane [*sic*]) and if need be the Irish Volunteers. This we can do, I am told quite effectively. The police service and prison service need to be overhauled.'
56. 21 May 1919. Bonar Law Papers, 98/3/29.
57. Long to Lloyd George, 21 May 1919. Lloyd George Papers, F/33/2/45.
58. *Ibid.*
59. *Ibid.*
60. *Ibid.*
61. Transcript of Mulcahy in conversation with Broy, 1 December 1964. Mulcahy Papers, P/7b/184.
62. Mulcahy Lecture at the Grosvenor Hotel, 29 October 1963, Mulcahy Papers, P/D/66.
63. Broy WS 1280.
64. Lawless WS.
65. Vinnie Byrne WS 493.
66. Lawless WS. More senior republicans shared the lack of revulsion displayed by Lawless and Connolly. Robert Barton, the Dail Minister of

Agriculture, wrote soon afterwards: 'The shooting of Sergeant Smith, the Dublin G man had a good effect and even Macpherson who has a bodyguard of about 40 and his retainers are so strung up nervously that one of them fired at his private detective the other day thinking him a SF or Volunteer or something. The aim was bad unfortunately' (Trinity College Dublin, Erskine Childers Papers 7833/18).

67. Macpherson to Bonar Law, 13 September 1919. Bonar Law Papers, 98/2/12.
68. French to Law, 13 September 1919. Bonar Law Papers, 98/2/11.
69. TNA: PRO CO CAB 24/78 C.P. 7277.
70. TNA: PRO CAB 24/80 C.P. 7367.
71. TNA: PRO CAB 24/87 C.P. 8082.
72. Lord Stamfordham on behalf of King George V to Bonar Law, 11 September 1919. Bonar Law Papers, 98/2/8.
73. French to Bonar Law, 13 September 1919. Bonar Law Papers, 98/2/11.
74. Macpherson writing to Bonar Law from Marine Hotel North Berwick. Bonar Law Papers, 98/2/12.
75. Beaslai Critique, part 1, p. 89.
76. James Slattery WS 445.
77. Richard Mulcahy, Talk given to Members of the 1916–21 Club, Jury's Hotel, 20 February 1964. Mulcahy Papers, P7/D/66.
78. Mulcahy Lecture at the Grosvenor Hotel, 29 October 1963. Mulcahy Papers, P/D/66.
79. Ibid.
80. Paddy Daly WS 814.
81. Thomson. TNA: PRO CAB 24/120 CP 8227.
82. French and Macpherson memorandum to the Cabinet, 25 September 1919. TNA: PRO CAB 24/88, CO 8227.
83. French, 11 December 1919. Bodleian Library, Macpherson Papers, MS Eng. Hist. C. 940.
84. French in a memorandum drawn up in January 1920. French Papers, JD FF8/10.

85. French to Macpherson, 10 December 1919. Macpherson Papers.
86. French, 3 January 1920. French Papers, JD F8.
87. Ibid.
88. French to Macpherson, 10 December 1919. Macpherson Papers.
89. French, 3 January 1920. French Papers, JD F8.
90. Mick McDonnell WS.
91. Vinnie Byrne WS.
92. Daly WS.
93. Broy, Daly and Vinnie Byrne all claimed in their witness statements to have received the tip-off.
94. Daly WS.
95. Vinnie Byrne WS.
96. Transcript of Mulcahy in conversation with Daly. Mulcahy Papers, P/b/178.

Chapter Two

1. Michael Noyk WS 707.
2. For this cover, see Frank Thornton WS 615, Charles Dalton WS 434 and Dan McDonnell WS 486.
3. Ronald Seth, Anatomy of Spying (New York, Dutton, 1963), p. 198.
4. Seth's Anatomy of Spying is a masterly historical account of various outstanding spymasters.
5. Richard Mulcahy, Talk on Michael Collins given by General Mulcahy to Members of the Donegalmen's Association, p. 18. Mulcahy Papers, P7/b/180.
6. Hayes, 'Michael Collins', Capuchin Annual, p. 254.
7. Mulcahy in his Conclusion to a Talk on Michael Collins at the Grosvenor Hotel, 29 October 1963. Mulcahy Papers, P7/D/66.
8. Professor Liam O'Brian in a typed summary of a talk on Collins. Mulcahy Papers, P7/D/66.
9. Noyk WS.
10. Richard Mulcahy, Talk on Michael Collins given by General Mulcahy to Members of the Donegalmen's

Association. Mulcahy Papers, P7/b/180.

11. Mulcahy wrestled long – but inconclusively – in his attempt to establish exactly when in 1920 Collins resigned the two posts. Beaslai Critique, part 1, 98–100.

12. Beaslai Critique, part 1, p. 81.

13. *Ibid.*, p. 15.

14. Thornton WS.

15. Sean Kavanagh, 'The Irish Volunteers' Intelligence Organisation', *Capuchin Annual* (1969), p. 357.

16. Thornton WS.

17. Broy WS 1280.

18. *Ibid.*

19. Dalton WS.

20. David Neligan, *The Spy in the Castle* (London, MacGibbon & Kee, 1968), p. 71.

21. Tobin's WS does not even mention Collins. For Tobin's appointment as Dublin Brigade Intelligence Officer, see Kavanagh, 'The Irish Volunteers' Intelligence Organisation', *Capuchin Annual* (1969), p. 355.

22. Thornton WS.

23. *Ibid.*

24. *Ibid.*

25. Michael Lynch. National Library of Ireland MS 22117 (1).

26. Dalton WS.

27. Dalton WS, Thornton WS and Dan McDonnell WS.

28. Dalton WS.

29. Thornton WS.

30. Dalton WS.

31. Thornton WS.

32. Dan McDonnell WS.

33. Thornton WS.

34. Neligan, *The Spy in the Castle*, p. 78.

35. Thornton WS.

36. Neligan, *The Spy in the Castle*, p. 60.

37. J.N. (Sean) Beaumont WS 709.

38. Thornton WS.

39. Robert Brennan, *Allegiance* (Dublin, Brown & Nolan, 1950), p. 267.

40. E.C. Foster, *Let the Boy Win his Spurs: An Autobiography* (London, 1976), p. 216.

41. Saurin WS.

42. Mernin WS.

43. *Ibid.*

44. Bernard Golden WS 281.

45. Patrick Mannix WS 502.

46. Peter Forlan WS 316.

47. *Ibid.*

48. *Ibid.*

49. Thornton WS.

50. Dan McDonnell WS.

51. Diarmuid O'Sullivan WS 375.

52. *Ibid.*

53. Charles McQuaile WS 276.

54. Liam Archer WS 819.

55. *Ibid.*

56. Saurin WS.

57. Neligan, *The Spy in the Castle*, p. 118.

58. Saurin WS.

59. Dalton WS.

60. Vinnie Byrne WS.

61. *Ibid.*

62. Bernard Byrne WS 631.

63. There are good descriptions of Moreland in William J. Stapleton, 'Michael Collins's Squad', *Capuchin Annual* (1970), pp. 369–70, Daly WS and Vinnie Byrne WS.

64. Daly WS.

65. Charles Dalton, *With the Dublin Brigade 1917–1921* (London, Peter Davies, 1929), p. 62.

66. *Ibid.*

67. Florence O'Donoghue, 'Lecture on Intelligence in the Black and Tan Days'. National Library of Ireland, MS 31443.

68. Dolan WS.

69. Vinnie Byrne WS.

70. *Ibid.*

71. Matty McDonald interview in O'Malley Notebooks. UCD Archives, Ernie O'Malley Papers, IE UCDAD P17. Hereafter O'Malley Notebooks.

72. Vinnie Byrne WS.

73. Recounted by Richard Mulcahy in a Talk on Michael Collins to Members of the Donegalmen's Association, pp. 16B–16C. Mulcahy Papers, P7/6/180.

74. Vinnie Byrne WS.

75. Slattery WS.
76. *Ibid.*
77. Daly WS.
78. Stapleton, 'Michael Collins's Squad', *Capuchin Annual* (1970), p. 371.
79. *Ibid.*
80. Stapleton WS and Vinnie Byrne WS.
81. The report from which the quotations in this paragraph are taken is in the French Papers, Report of the Committee of Inquiry, 7 December 1919.
82. Quoted in Eunan O'Halpin, *The Decline of the Union: British Government in Ireland, 1892–1920* (Dublin and Syracuse, Gill & Macmillan/Syracuse University Press, 1987), p. 199.
83. Neligan, *The Spy in the Castle*, p. 64.
84. Thornton WS.
85. Vinnie Byrne describing his Squad career on tapes privately held by Dan Moore, who generously loaned them to me for use in this book.
86. Long, 'Report on Visit to Ireland, January 1920', submitted to the Cabinet Committee on Ireland. TNA: PRO CA 27/69/C.I.58.
87. For Redmond's assassination, see the next day's reports in the *Irish Times*, *Freeman's Journal* and *Belfast Telegraph*, Daly WS, and Joe Dolan's article in the *Sunday Press*, 16 July 1961.
88. Neligan, *The Spy in the Castle*.
89. Ben Byrne WS confirms that the term Twelve Apostles was used contemporaneously.

Chapter Three
1. Report on the Detective Branch. TNA: PRO CO 904/24/5.
2. Neligan, *The Spy in the Castle*, p. 44.
3. Broy WS 1280.
4. Neligan, *The Spy in the Castle*, p. 59.
5. Report on the Detective Branch. TNA: PRO CO 904/24/5.
6. *Ibid.*
7. 'A Record of the Rebellion in Ireland in 1920–1921 and the Part Played by the Army in dealing with it (Intelligence)'. TNA: PRO WO 141/93. Hereafter Record of the Rebellion/Intelligence.
8. Broy WS 1280.
9. *Ibid.*
10. *Ibid.*
11. Record of the Rebellion/Intelligence.
12. *Ibid.*
13. Loch Papers 71/12/9. Imperial War Museum.
14. Record of the Rebellion/Intelligence.
15. The Irish Rebellion in the Sixth Divisional Area.
16. Record of the Rebellion/Intelligence.
17. For Thomson's background, see his autobiography *The Scene Changes*.
18. *Ibid.*
19. For Special Branch, see Bernard Porter, *The Vigilant State: The London Metropolitan Police Special Branch before the First World War* (London, Weidenfeld & Nicolson, 1987).
20. Nicholas Hiley, 'Counter-Espionage and Security in Great Britain during the First World War', *English Historical Review*, 101 (1986), p. 836.
21. *Ibid.*, p. 861.
22. Long Papers, 947/672.
23. Record of the Rebellion/Intelligence.
24. Basil Thomson, *Queer People* (London, Hodder & Stoughton, 1922), p. 292.
25. Coogan, *Michael Collins: A Biography*, pp. 127–8.
26. Julian Putkowski, 'The Best Secret Service Man We Had', *Lobster*, 28 (1995).
27. *Ibid.*
28. *Ibid.*
29. Thomson, *The Scene Changes*, p. 389.
30. Putkowski, 'The Best Secret Service Man We Had'.
31. Beaslai Critique, part 1, p. 127, and Mulcahy, Talk on Michael Collins given to Members of the Donegalmen's Association. The meeting place was actually the Home Farm Produce Shop in Camden Street owned by Mrs Wyse-Power.
32. Putkowski, 'The Best Secret Service Man We Had'.

33. *Ibid.*
34. Thomson to French and Macpherson, 19 December 1919. Macpherson Papers, MS Eng. Hist. C. 940.
35. Putkowski, 'The Best Secret Service Man We Had'.
36. Thornton WS.
37. Coogan, *Michael Collins: A Biography*, p. 128. Coogan even claims that Collins 'had penetrated right to the heart of the British Secret Service'.
38. Thornton WS.
39. Putkowski, 'The Best Secret Service Man We Had'.
40. *Sunday Press*, 16 July 1961.
41. Daly WS.
42. Putkowski, 'The Best Secret Service Man We Had'.
43. Long to the Cabinet on 31 May 1920 as recorded by Tom Jones, *Whitehall Diary*, vol. 3, *Ireland 1918–1925*, ed. Keith Middlemas (London, 1971), p. 19.
44. *Irish Times*, 19 February 1920.
45. Michael Knightley WS 835.
46. For Brennan and Quinlisk, see Brennan's autobiography, *Allegiance* (Dublin, 1950), pp. 258–60.
47. *Ibid.*, p. 259.
48. Broy provided a copy of the letter to Collins. Transcript of Mulcahy in conversation with Broy, 1 December 1964. Mulcahy Papers. P/7b/184.
49. Brennan, *Allegiance*, p. 259.
50. Archer WS.
51. Florence O'Donoghue has described the Cork end of the Quinlisk story in his interview in the O'Malley Notebooks.
52. Vinnie Byrne WS. The fact that Mulloy was buried in Grangegorman cemetery in Dublin indicates that he might have been Irish. His funeral procession from Merciers Hospital to the cemetery a week after his death was an impressive one for a supposedly lowly Pay Corps Sergeant. He had an escort of the Company of the Warwickshire Regiment, led by the Warwickshire's Band, the coffin draped in the Union Flag was carried on a gun carriage with a Royal Field Artillery escort, followed by an escort from the Royal Army Service Corps.
53. 'Deep Throat's' legendary advice to the *Washington Post* journalists Bob Woodward and Carl Bernstein during the Watergate scandal which led to President Richard Nixon's resignation. The Viceroy's Military Secretary referred to Bell as having the rank of Chief Commissioner, 29 December 1919. TNA: PRO CO 904/188. Neligan says that 'Collins was not the man to allow his war-chest which had been so painfully gathered to be taken from under his nose' (*The Spy in the Castle*, pp. 77–8).
54. Michael Knightley WS.
55. McDonnell WS.
56. Daly WS and Vinnie Byrne WS.
57. Daly WS. Daly almost certainly meant Ailesbury Road, which preceded Simmonscourt Road, rather than Anglesea Road.
58. *Sunday Press*, 23 July 1961.
59. Daly WS.
60. For Macready, see his *Annals of an Active Life* (London, 1924), vols 1 and 2.
61. Macready to Frances Stevenson, 25 May 1920. Lloyd George Papers, F/36/2/14.
62. At this time it was still a legal requirement for any MP who took an office of profit under the Crown as a Cabinet minister to offer himself for re-election by his constituents.
63. Daly WS.
64. Bonar Law Papers, 103/2/1.
65. *Ibid.*
66. French to Long. 1 July 1920. French Papers.
67. Long to Law, 20 April 1920. Bonar Law Papers, 103/5/2.
68. For Fisher, see Eunan O'Halpin's definitive biography *Head of the Civil Service: A Study of Sir Warren Fisher* (London, Routledge, 1989).

69. *Ibid.*, p. 7.
70. Fisher's Report, which includes a supplementary submission by himself and Cope's addendum on the police, is in the Lloyd George Papers, F/31/1/32–3. Hereafter Fisher Report. Fisher submitted the report initially to his political head, the Chancellor of the Exchequer Austen Chamberlain. Chamberlain had been prepared for an unsatisfactory account but confessed that it disclosed 'a condition both of administration and staff which is worse than I have anticipated'. Law then passed it on to Lloyd George with the advice that he read everything. Lloyd George Papers, F/31/1/32.
71. Record of the Rebellion/Intelligence.
72. Memoir of G.C. Duggan. National Library of Ireland MS 31689.
73. Fisher Report.
74. *Ibid.*
75. *Ibid.*
76. *Ibid.*
77. *Ibid.*
78. *Ibid.*
79. *Ibid.*
80. *Ibid.*
81. *Ibid.*
82. *Ibid.*
83. *Ibid.*
84. For Anderson, see Sir John Wheeler-Bennett, *John Anderson, Viscount Waverley* (London, Macmillan, 1962).
85. Anderson to Greenwood, 20 July 1920. TNA: PRO CO 904/188.
86. For Sturgis, see Michael Hopkinson (ed.), *The Last Days of Dublin Castle: The Diaries of Mark Sturgis* (Dublin, Irish Academic Press, 1999).
87. *Ibid.*, p. 59.
88. Greenwood to Bonar Law, 8 May 1920. Bonar Law Papers, 103/3/1. Greenwood even complained: 'I've not even got a car for a police escort for myself and I ought to have two.'
89. Greenwood to Bonar Law, 25 September 1920. Bonar Law Papers, 103/3/24.
90. Greenwood's threat to Long on 5 July 1920. Long Papers, 947/373.
91. Macready to Long, 23 April and 1 May 1920. Lloyd George Papers, F/34/1/19–20.
92. *Ibid.*
93. Fisher to Bonar Law, 9 May 1920. Bonar Law Papers, 102/5/19.
94. William Darling, *So it Looks to Me* (London, 1952), p. 205.
95. Sir Ormonde Winter, *Winter's Tale: An Autobiography* (London, 1955), pp. 288–9.
96. Anderson to Greenwood, 20 July 1920. TNA: PRO CO 904/188.
97. Macready to Greenwood, 17 July 1920. Lloyd George Papers, F/19/2/12.
98. David Leeson, 'The "Scum of London's Underworld"? British Recruits for the Royal Irish Constabulary, 1920–21', *Contemporary British History*, 17/1 (Spring 2003), p. 30.
99. Winter, *Winter's Tale*, p. 309.
100. A Report on the Intelligence Branch of the Chief of Police from May 1920 to July 1921, p. 70. TNA: PRO WO 35/124. Hereafter Report on the Intelligence Branch.
101. There is a detailed insider account of the Listowel incident by two police constables who led a protest against Smyth. National Library of Ireland N6312 P7153.
102. For the killing of Smyth, see Con Casey, 'Divisional Commissioner Smyth Caused RIC to Mutiny in Kerry, and was shot dead in the County Club, Cork', in *The Kerryman, Cork's Fighting Story* (Tralee, 1949), pp. 77–80.
103. Leeson, 'The "Scum of London's Underworld"?', p. 2.
104. Anderson to Greenwood, 20 July 1920. TNA: PRO CO 904/188.
105. For this conference, see Charles Townshend, *The British Campaign in Ireland 1919–1921* (London, 1975), pp. 101–3.
106. For the dispute, see Charles Townshend, 'The Irish Railway Strike

of 1920: Industrial Action and Civil Resistance in the Struggle for Independence', *Irish Historical Studies*, 21 (1978–9).

107. Robert Barton WS 979.
108. Vinnie Byrne WS.
109. Slattery WS. Slattery may have been mistaken about Daly being a member of the Squad unit which killed Brooke. In Daly's own WS he specifically denies being present.
110. *Irish Times*, 31 July 1920.
111. *Ibid.*
112. William J. Stapleton, 'Michael Collins's Squad', *Capuchin Annual* (1970), p. 371.
113. Daly WS.
114. Vinnie Byrne WS.
115. Ben Byrne WS.
116. Daly WS.
117. Vinnie Byrne WS.
118. Daly WS.
119. *Ibid.*
120. Leonard WS.

Chapter Four

1. Sturgis, *Diaries*, p. 15.
2. Fisher Memorandum, 7 August 1920. TNA: PRO CO904/188.
3. Neligan, *The Spy in the Castle*.
4. Sturgis, 3 September 1920, *Diaries*, p. 35.
5. Macready, *Annals of an Active Life*, vol. 2, p. 470.
6. *Ibid.*, p. 451.
7. *Ibid.*, p. 469.
8. Liam Tobin interview, O'Malley Notebooks.
9. Macready, *Annals of an Active Life*, vol. 2, pp. 499–500.
10. Florence O'Donoghue interview, O'Malley Notebooks.
11. Darling, *So it Looks to Me*, p. 209.
12. Memoirs of Major General Douglas Wimberley. Imperial War Museum PP/MCR/182.
13. Mrs Caroline Woodcock, *An Officer's Wife in Ireland* (Dublin, 1994), p. 34.
14. Sturgis, 18 August 1920, *Diaries*, p. 23.
15. Report on the Intelligence Branch, p. 9.
16. Record of the Rebellion/Intelligence.
17. *Ibid.*
18. *Ibid.*
19. Report on the Intelligence Branch, pp. 23–4.
20. Winter, *Winter's Tale*, pp. 299–300.
21. Report on the Intelligence Branch, p. 64.
22. Winter, *Winter's Tale*, p. 303.
23. For Tegart, see Michael Silvestri, 'Sir Charles Tegart and Revolutionary Terrorism in Bengal', *History Ireland* (Winter 2000).
24. TNA: PRO CO 904/108.
25. *Ibid.*
26. *Ibid.*
27. *Ibid.*
28. *Ibid.*
29. Winter, *Winter's Tale*, p. 101.
30. TNA: PRO WO 35/180 C.
31. Record of the Rebellion/Intelligence.
32. *Ibid.*
33. Macready, *Annals of an Active Life*, vol. 2, p. 462.
34. *Ibid.*, p. 463.
35. Winter, *Winter's Tale*, p. 294.
36. Record of the Rebellion/Intelligence.
37. *Ibid.*
38. Noyk WS.
39. Kathleen McKenna, 'The Irish Bulletin', *Capuchin Annual* (1970), p. 521.
40. Celia Shaw Diary. National Library of Ireland, MS 23409.
41. Macready, *Annals of an Active Life*, p. 507.
42. Beaslai Critique, part 2, p. 46.
43. Lawless WS.
44. J.P. Swindlehurst Diary. Imperial War Museum.
45. Captain Robert Jeune. Memoir on his secret service career in Dublin, 1920–1. Imperial War Museum 76/1/71/1. Hereafter Jeune Memoir.
46. Report on the Intelligence Branch, p. 34.
47. *Ibid.*, p. 36.
48. Digby Hardy's criminal background was detailed in papers captured by

the IRA. National Library of Ireland, Beaslai Papers, MS 33912 (26).

49. Sturgis, *Diaries*, p. 35.
50. National Library of Ireland, Collins Papers, NEG 545 POS 919.
51. Robert Brennan, *Allegiance*, p. 276.
52. *Ibid.*
53. Vinnie Byrne WS.
54. Knightley WS.
55. *Freeman's Journal*, 17 September 1920.
56. *Ibid.*
57. Knightley WS. For details of Hardy's criminal career, see Beaslai Papers, MS 33912 (6). Digby Hardy appears to have been another pseudonym of this inveterate confidence trickster. He also used the names J.L. Gooding and Frank Harling, under which he had been sentenced in December 1918.
58. Robert Brennan, *Allegiance*, p. 283.
59. Forlan WS.
60. Daly WS.
61. J.L. Hardy, *I Escape!* (London, Cherry Tree Books, 1938), p. 256.
62. Neligan, *The Spy in the Castle*, p. 88.
63. D.A. MacManus, *Life in Ireland during her Final Fight for Freedom: A Personal Episode*. Mulcahy Papers P7/D/52.
64. Ernie O'Malley, *On Another Man's Wound* (Dublin, Anvil, 1990), p. 273.
65. *Ibid.*, pp. 278–9.
66. Report on the Intelligence Branch, p. 14.
67. Mulcahy, Beaslai Critique, part 1, p. 29.
68. Sturgis, *Diaries*, p. 35
69. Foster, *Let the Boy Win his Spurs*, p. 220. Collins's Hue and Cry photograph is reproduced in J. Herlihy, *Royal Irish Constabulary: A Short History and Genealogical Guide* (Dublin, 1997), p. 149.
70. Broy WS 1285.
71. Hyland WS.
72. Thornton WS.
73. Neligan, *The Spy in the Castle*, p. 88.
74. Tom Barry in Griffith (ed.), *Curious Journey*, p. 169.
75. Collins letter, 19 July 1921. Liddell Hart Archive, Foulkes Papers, 7/24.
76. Thornton WS.
77. Broy WS 1285.
78. J.P. Swindlehurst, Diary. Imperial War Museum. Winter himself wrote that 'I do not withhold a certain respect for the bravery displayed by many of the leaders among whom Michael Collins stands out pre-eminent. Actuated by an intense patriotism, he combined the characteristics of a Robin Hood with those of an elusive Pimpernel. His many narrow escapes when he managed to elude almost certain arrest, shrouded him in a cloak of historical romance, and he will forever be held in respectful remembrance by the Irish.' Winter, *Winter's Tale*, p. 345.
79. Sturgis, *Diaries*, p. 66.
80. Douglas V. Duff, *Sword for Hire* (London, 1934), p. 80.
81. Foulkes Papers, 7/24.
82. Liam Deasy, *Towards Ireland Free* (Cork, 1973), p. 256.
83. *Ibid.*, p. 257.
84. *Ibid.*, p. 258.
85. *Ibid.*
86. Richard Mulcahy in a Talk on Michael Collins at the Grosvenor Hotel on 29 October 1963. Mulcahy Papers, P7/D/66.
87. Liam Deasy, *Brother against Brother* (Dublin, 1982), p. 81.
88. Thornton WS.
89. Broy WS 1285.
90. Barry in Griffith and O'Grady, *Curious Journey*, pp. 169–70.
91. Mulcahy provides a list of the locations in Beaslai Critique, part 2, p. 43.
92. Oscar Traynor WS 340.
93. Winter, *Winter's Tale*, p. 292.
94. Sturgis, *Diaries*, p. 36.
95. Neligan, *The Spy in the Castle*, p. 107.
96. Volunteer GHQ, General Orders – No. 20, 20 April 1921. Mulcahy Papers P7/A/45.
97. Wylie. TNA: PRO CO 904/177/2.
98. The story of the counterfeit Irish Bulletin is described in Winter, *Winter's Tale*, p. 307, Mrs Stuart

Menzies, *As Others See Us* (London, 1924), pp. 107–8.

99. The Irish Rebellion in the Sixth Divisional Area from after the 1916 Rebellion to December 1921. Imperial War Museum.
100. *Ibid.*
101. TNA: PRO WO 35/180C.
102. Sturgis, *Diaries*, pp. 74–5.
103. John Plunkett WS 65.
104. Foulkes Papers, 7/43. Winter (*Winter's Tale*, p. 325) alleged that the handwritten notes and questions on Mulcahy's typhoid proposal were made by Collins, but they are clearly the work of a medical specialist coaching Mulcahy. A more likely suspect was Professor Hayes of University College Dublin.
105. Valiulis in her biography of Mulcahy mentions the raid but not the typhoid. Risteard Mulcahy mentions neither in his life of his father.
106. Report on the Intelligence Branch, p. 63.
107. Traynor interview, O'Malley Notebooks.
108. Laurence Nugent WS 907.
109. George White WS 956.
110. Dan McDonnell WS.
111. Florence O'Donoghue, 'Lecture on Intelligence in the Black and Tan Day'. National Library of Ireland MS 31443.
112. Thornton WS.
113. Tom Jones, *Whitehall Diary*, p. 17.
114. Neligan recorded that 'Collins was furious. Next day I received a note asking me urgently to make enquiries as to the killers.' He went to the College Street police station in whose B Division the Exchange Hotel was situated and read Baggallay's telephoned account of the shooting (*The Spy in the Castle*, pp. 105–6).
115. Winter, *Winter's Tale*, p. 317.
116. *Ibid.*, p. 319.
117. Dan Breen, *My Fight for Irish Freedom* (Dublin, Poolbeg, 1989), p. 130.

118. When Mulcahy heard that Breen and Treacy were back in Dublin and staying at Fernside, he protested strongly to Collins, urging him to make the Tipperary pair leave Carolan's house. Beaslai Critique, part 2, p. 34.
119. Jeune Memoir.
120. Breen, *My Fight for Irish Freedom*, p. 140.
121. *Ibid.*, pp. 141–2.
122. Jeune Memoir.
123. Breen, *My Fight for Irish Freedom*, p. 157.
124. Jeune Memoir.
125. *Ibid.*
126. Desmond Ryan, 'Fight at Fernside', in *Dublin's Fighting Story* (Tralee, The Kerryman, 1949), p. 140.
127. Lawless WS.
128. Winter, *Winter's Tale*, p. 317.
129. Breen, *My Fight for Irish Freedom*, p. 153.
130. Thornton WS.
131. For the events at the Republican Outfitters, see McKee's own hand-written statement validated by his sister Moira. Collins Papers, NEG 545 POS 919. Also Plunkett WS and Daly WS.
132. Winter, *Winter's Tale*, p. 319.
133. Neligan, *The Spy in the Castle*, pp. 130–1.
134. For Pike's killing, see Dalton WS, Lawless WS and *Freeman's Journal*, 20 June 1921.
135. Joe Dolan WS and his article in the *Sunday Press*, 30 July 1961.
136. Broy WS 1285.
137. Report on the Intelligence Branch, p. 42.
138. Thornton WS.
139. Warder Garmon interview, O'Malley Notebooks.
140. Ben Byrne WS.
141. Sturgis, *Diaries*, p. 32.
142. *Ibid.*, pp. 75–6.

Chapter Five
1. Greenwood to Law, 25 September 1920. Bonar Law Papers, 103/3/1.

2. Macready, *Military Appreciation of the Situation in Ireland*, 26.9.1920. Bonar Law Papers, 103/3/26.
3. Macready to the Irish Situation Committee. Lloyd George Papers, F/180/5/14.
4. TNA: PRO CAB 24/114 C.P. 2027.
5. Lloyd George in a speech at the Mansion House in London.
6. TNA: PRO CAB 24/114 OP 2084.
7. *Ibid.*
8. Thornton WS.
9. Beaslai Critique, part 2, p. 31.
10. A memorandum by Mulcahy captured by British Intelligence. TNA: PRO WO 45/10974/484819.
11. Henderson WS.
12. Ernie O'Malley, 'Bloody Sunday', *Dublin's Fighting Story*, p. 151.
13. Harry Colley WS 1687.
14. Charlie Dalton disclosed Tobin's breakdown in his interview in the O'Malley Notebooks.
15. Thornton WS and Dalton WS.
16. Patrick Mannix WS.
17. Dalton WS.
18. Thornton WS and Reynolds's interview in the Collins Papers, NEG 545 POS 918.
19. Mrs Woodcock, *An Officer's Wife in Ireland*, p. 20. She also said there 'were four Secret Service men living in the house, and two others came in for meals, and I did wonder sometimes if it was safe for them and for us' (p. 60).
20. Jeune Memoir.
21. Thornton WS.
22. *Ibid.*
23. *Ibid.*
24. Thornton WS and Dalton WS.
25. Beaslai Critique, part 2, p. 31.
26. Macready to Sir Henry Wilson, 25 September 1920. Imperial War Museum. Wilson Papers, Macready correspondence. Hereafter Macready–Wilson correspondence.
27. *Ibid.*, 4 October 1920.
28. For a description, see Lawless WS.
29. Sturgis, *Diaries*, p. 43.
30. Macready, 25 September 1920. Macready–Wilson correspondence.
31. *Ibid.*, 24 September 1920.
32. Thornton WS.
33. Hervey De Montmorency, *Sword and Stirrup* (London, 1936), p. 348.
34. Macready–Wilson correspondence.
35. C.S. Andrews, *Dublin Made Me: An Autobiography* (Dublin, Mercier, 1979), p. 152.
36. Sturgis, *Diaries*, p. 76.
37. Daly WS.
38. Colley WS and interview in O'Malley Notebooks.
39. Leonard WS.
40. Donnelly WS.
41. Volunteer Gaughan in his interview with O'Malley, O'Malley Notebooks.
42. Colley WS.
43. Vinnie Byrne WS.
44. Beaslai Critique, part 2, p. 47.
45. For Clune in Dublin, see Edward MacLysaght's unpublished autobiography 'Master of None'. National Library of Ireland MS 4750.
46. Sean Kavanagh, 'The Irish Volunteers' Intelligence Organisation', *Capuchin Annual* (1969), p. 361.
47. *Ibid.*, p. 362.
48. Traynor WS.
49. Moira McKee in her interview in the O'Malley Notebooks.
50. Eithne Lawless WS.
51. Jeune Memoir.
52. Denis Begley, Statement in Collins Papers, NEG 545 POS 915.
53. *Ibid.*
54. Slattery WS.
55. Maid's court-martial testimony. National Library of Ireland, Michael Noyk Papers, Manuscript Collection 103.
56. *Ibid.*
57. Begley Statement.
58. *Ibid.*
59. Noyk Papers, Collection 106, MS 36222.
60. Slattery WS.
61. *Ibid.*

62. Begley Statement.
63. Leonard WS.
64. Stapleton WS.
65. Vinnie Byrne WS.
66. Ibid.
67. Saurin WS.
68. TNA: PRO WO 35/180C.
69. Andrews, *Dublin Made Me*, p. 153.
70. Dan McDonnell WS and Dolan WS.
71. McCrae WS.
72. Matty McDonald in his interview in the O'Malley Notebooks.
73. James Doyle WS 771.
74. Christopher Byrne WS 642.
75. Ibid.
76. Dalton WS.
77. Ibid.
78. Mrs Woodcock, *An Officer's Wife in Ireland*, p. 62.
79. Woodcock testifying against Greene at his court martial. For this, see Noyk Papers, Collection 103.
80. Dalton WS.
81. A. Rutherford in his interview with O'Malley. O'Malley Notebooks.
82. Ibid.
83. Ibid.
84. Mrs Woodcock, *An Officer's Wife in Ireland*, p. 66.
85. Ibid.
86. Ibid.
87. Jeune Memoir.
88. The events at 'Brianna' were reconstructed from DMP reports and witness statements, TNA: PRO CO 904/168/1, and the reports in the *Irish Times* and *Freeman's Journal*, 22 November 1920.
89. Fitzgerald's killing was reconstructed from DMP reports and witness statements, TNA: PRO CO 904/168/1, and the reports in the *Irish Times* and *Freeman's Journal*, 22 November 1920.
90. There is a detailed account of Crawford's experience in the *Belfast Telegraph*, 22 November 1920.
91. O'Malley Notebooks.
92. Beaslai Critique, part 2, p. 48.
93. Sturgis, *Diaries*, p. 76.
94. *Ibid.*, p. 78.
95. Macready–Wilson correspondence. Macready's account of Bloody Sunday in his autobiography is extremely disingenuous. It conveys the undoubtedly intended impression that he was present in Dublin and that he rather than his deputy Brind was responsible for the British military response to the killings. A similar absence from the Irish capital in 1916 had ruined the Commander-in-Chief General Friend. Nor did Macready hurry back; he arrived in London only on 11 December 1920.
96. Foster, *Let the Boy Win his Spurs*, p. 205.
97. Macready, *Annals of an Active Life*, vol. 2, pp. 501–2.
98. Colley WS.
99. TNA: PRO WO 35/88B/1. For a judicious survey of the events at Croke Park and the subsequent British inquiry, see Tim Carey and Marcus de Burca, 'Bloody Sunday: New Evidence', *History Ireland* (Summer 2003).
100. Patrick Young, 'Bloody Sunday'. National Library of Ireland, Beaslai Papers, Collection List 44, MS 33949 (4).
101. Ibid.
102. Ibid.
103. Traynor WS.
104. Young, 'Bloody Sunday'.
105. Ibid.
106. Winter, *Winter's Tale*, p. 323.
107. Neligan, *The Spy in the Castle*, p. 124.
108. Ibid.
109. Young, 'Bloody Sunday'.
110. MacLysaght, 'Master of None'. See also MacLysaght's deposition on the official inquiry into Clune's death, National Library of Ireland, MS 5368.
111. For the funerals, see the accounts in *The Times* and the *Irish Times*, 26 November 1920.
112. Mrs Woodcock, *An Officer's Wife in Ireland*, p. 82.

113. *Ibid.*, p. 83.
114. *Ibid.*, pp. 83–4.
115. *Ibid.*, p. 84.
116. Noyk WS.
117. *Ibid.*
118. *Ibid.* Greene had once been coachman to Sir Hawtry Benson – a leading Dublin doctor who refused to testify on his behalf.
119. Winter, *Winter's Tale*, p. 324.
120. Noyk WS.
121. Mrs Woodcock testifying against Greene at his court martial. Noyk Papers.
122. Greene's eventual fate is unclear. Noyk believed that he died in prison, but George White in his WS 956 asserted that he died in the Workhouse.
123. Noyk WS.
124. *Ibid.*
125. Winter, *Winter's Tale*, p. 324.
126. Noyk WS.
127. Daly WS.
128. Winter, *Winter's Tale*, pp. 324–5.
129. *Freeman's Journal*, 22 November 1921. The *Belfast Telegraph*, 22 November 1921, called it Red Sabbath, Winter described it as Black Sunday in *Winter's Tale*, p. 334, while Mrs Woodcock referred to it as Red Sunday in *An Officer's Wife in Ireland*.
130. Dan McDonnell WS.
131. Christopher Byrne WS.
132. Nugent WS.
133. *Ibid.*
134. Christopher Byrne WS.
135. Andrews, *Dublin Made Me*, p. 153.
136. McCrae WS.
137. Record of the Rebellion/Intelligence.
138. As already indicated in the text, Mrs Woodcock knew about the 'Hush Hush Men' staying in the house. That her husband and Keenlyside did not know is untenable. Mrs Woodcock, *An Officer's Wife in Ireland*, p. 20.
139. The Dublin Metropolitan Police Report on his death lists McLean as a captain in the Intelligence Dept. TNA: PRO CO 904/168/1.
140. Doyle WS.
141. Collins Papers, NEG 545 POS 917.
142. *Ibid.*
143. *Belfast Telegraph*, 23 November 1920.
144. James Doyle WS 771.
145. Beaslai Critique, part 2, p. 52.
146. Traynor WS.
147. Thornton WS.
148. Beaslai, *Michael Collins and the Making of a New Ireland*, vol. 2, p. 88. Broy describes seeing Collins soon afterwards 'in a morose mood, with his hands on each side of his head, moving slowly left and right, and the automatic pistol in his pocket hitting against the table. Then he suddenly jumped up and said: "We'll just have to carry on."'
149. Beaslai Critique, part 2, p. 51.
150. *Ibid.*
151. *Ibid.*
152. Jeune Memoir.

Chapter Six
1. Adapted from Donal O'Kelly, 'The Dublin Scene: War amid the Outward Trappings of Peace', in *The Kerryman, With the I.R.A. in the Fight for Freedom: 1919 to the Truce* (Tralee, 1949), p. 27.
2. Traynor WS. David Neligan was scathing about the performance of McKee's Brigade. 'The leadership of the Dublin Brigade failed miserably so far as making war on the Auxiliaries was concerned. The latter came and went without let or hindrance' (Neligan WS 380).
3. *Ibid.*
4. *Ibid.*
5. *Ibid.*
6. *Ibid.*
7. Aherne WS.
8. Daly WS.
9. Dalton WS.
10. Vinnie Byrne WS.
11. Edward Kelleher WS 477.
12. Leonard WS.

13. For the killing of Doran, see Dolan WS, Vinnie Byrne WS and Thornton WS.
14. Ben Byrne WS.
15. *Ibid.*
16. Neligan, *The Spy in the Castle*, p. 121.
17. Thornton WS.
18. Jeune Memoir.
19. Macready, *Annals of an Active Life*, vol. 2, p. 514.
20. Sturgis, *Diaries*, p. 90.
21. Macready, 16 December 1920. Macready–Wilson correspondence.
22. Macready to Sir Henry Wilson, 18 December 1920. Macready–Wilson correspondence. Winter assumed control of Special Branch on 27 December 1920. War Diary of the General Staff and Dublin District. TNA: PRO WO 35/90.
23. Macready–Wilson correspondence.
24. Sturgis, 3 January 1921, *Diaries*, p. 104.
25. Record of the Rebellion/Intelligence, which recorded that Special Branch 'continued to work for the Army but was responsible to a new master, the Chief of Police. Consequently the driving power behind the agents gradually diminished.'
26. Military Intelligence said that 'for personal reasons it was wholly unpopular among the personnel of the Special Branch, and unfortunately personal considerations can rarely be left out of account in questions connected with secret service' (Record of the Rebellion/Intelligence). Macready wrote that 'Boyd is naturally not too pleased' (Macready–Wilson correspondence, 18 December 1920).
27. Record of the Rebellion/Intelligence.
28. Greenwood to Lloyd George. Lloyd George Papers, F/19/2/321.
29. Fisher's Supplementary Report, 11 February 1921. Lloyd George Papers, F/17/1/9.
30. *Ibid.*
31. *Ibid.*
32. *Ibid.*

33. Sturgis, 19 August 1920, *Diaries*, p. 25.
34. Winter, *Winter's Tale*, pp. 337–8.
35. At a Dublin inquest on an RIC sergeant. *Northern Whig*, 24 June 1920.
36. Igoe's Police Service file. TNA: PRO T164/25/20.
37. Stapleton WS.
38. Anderson in a letter of 13 December 1921 in the Grant–Sturgis Papers. I am grateful to Dr Michael Hopkinson for allowing me access to his copies of this material.
39. Igoe's Police Service file. TNA: PRO T164/25/20.
40. Traynor WS.
41. Stapleton WS.
42. *Ibid.*
43. Vinnie Byrne WS.
44. Dalton WS.
45. *Ibid.*
46. Igoe's Police Service file. TNA: PRO T164/25/20.
47. Beaslai Critique, part 2, p. 51.
48. *Ibid.*
49. Beaslai Critique, part 2, p. 67.
50. Traynor WS.
51. Broy WS 1280.
52. Nancy Wyse-Power WS 587.
53. Broy WS 1280.
54. *Ibid.* The British file on Broy's arrest and his subsequent detention and investigation is at TAN: PRO CO 904/44.
55. Swindlehurst Diary, and Neligan, *The Spy in the Castle*, p. 108.
56. Broy WS 1280.
57. Neligan, *The Spy in the Castle*, p. 109.
58. Broy WS 1280.
59. *Ibid.*
60. Sturgis, 13 February 1921, *Diaries*, p. 125.
61. *The Times*, 11 February 1921.
62. Broy WS 1280.
63. *Ibid.*
64. Neligan, *The Spy in the Castle*, pp. 130–2.
65. *Ibid.*, p. 130.
66. *Ibid.*, p. 135.

67. *Ibid.*, p. 137.
68. Slattery WS.
69. Daly WS.
70. Slattery WS.
71. Thornton WS.
72. Vinnie Byrne WS.
73. Leonard WS.
74. White WS.
75. Ben Byrne WS.
76. Vinnie Byrne WS.
77. Record of the Rebellion/Intelligence.
78. For these centres, see Report on the Intelligence Branch, pp. 65–9.
79. Record of the Rebellion/Intelligence.
80. *Ibid.*
81. *Ibid.*
82. Report on the Intelligence Branch, p. 24.
83. Macready to Anderson, 5 and 9 March 1921. TNA: PRO CO 904/188.
84. Anderson to Macready, 8 March and 9 April 1921. TNA: PRO CO 904/188.
85. Christy Harte WS 2.
86. Report on the Intelligence Branch p. 25.
87. Record of the Rebellion/Intelligence.
88. *Ibid.*
89. *Ibid.*
90. *Ibid.*
91. *Ibid.*
92. Winter, *Winter's Tale*, p. 303.
93. This was the British army raid of a flat in Longwood Avenue, off the South Circular Road, which captured Mulcahy's attaché cases that also contained plans for spreading typhoid and IRA operations in England.
94. Beaslai Critique, part 2, pp. 88–9.
95. Noyk WS.
96. Traynor WS.
97. For this raid, see Report on the Intelligence Branch, pp. 54–6, and Noyk WS.
98. Noyk WS.
99. Thornton WS.
100. Beaslai Critique, part 2, p. 88.
101. Beaumont WS.
102. Thornton WS.

103. Record of the Rebellion/Intelligence.
104. Winter, *Winter's Tale*, p. 305.
105. TNA: PRO CAB 24/123 CP 2934.
106. Winter, *Winter's Tale*, p. 329.
107. *Ibid.*, pp. 329–30.
108. *Ibid.*, p. 329. Winter's sentiments echoed those of Yeats in his poem 'Easter, 1916' when he wrote:

That woman's days were spent
In ignorant good-will,
Her nights in argument
Until her voice grew shrill.
What voice more sweet than hers
When, young and beautiful,
She rode to harriers?

109. Margery Greenwood to Law, 28 September 1920. Bonar Law Papers, 103/3/29.
110. Winter's description of Childers, *Winter's Tale*, p. 345.
111. *Ibid.*, p. 328.
112. *Ibid.*
113. D.A. MacManus, *Life in Ireland during her Final Fight for Freedom: A Personal Episode*. Mulcahy Papers, P7/D/52.
114. Report on the Intelligence Branch, p. 42.
115. For Winter's account of the Fovargue episode, see *Winter's Tale*, pp. 305–6.
116. *The Times*, 4 April 1921.
117. O'Malley, *On Another Man's Wound*. O'Malley shared a cell in the Castle with Fovargue.
118. Swindlehurst Diary.
119. *Ibid.*
120. *Ibid.*
121. *Ibid.*
122. *Ibid.*
123. Donnelly WS.
124. *Ibid.*
125. *Ibid.*
126. Report on the Intelligence Branch, p. 46.
127. Christopher Fitzsimons WS 581.
128. Paddy O'Connor WS 813.
129. An account of the attack is in the National Library of Ireland, Collins Papers NEG 545 POS 915.

130. Montmorency, *Sword and Stirrup*, p. 343.
131. *Ibid.*
132. *Ibid.*, pp. 348–9.
133. *Ibid.*, p. 350.
134. *Ibid.*, p. 348.
135. The photograph and letter are in the Beaslai photograph collection in the National Library of Ireland.
136. Montmorency, *Sword and Stirrup*, p. 357.
137. Ben Byrne WS.
138. Montmorency, *Sword and Stirrup*, p. 358.
139. Macready to Anderson 21 February 1921. TNA: PRO CO 904/188.
140. Volunteer GHQ Intelligence's nickname for Lees. Vinnie Byrne WS.
141. Ben Byrne WS.
142. *Ibid.*
143. MacDonnell WS.
144. Beaslai Critique, part 2, pp. 44–5.
145. Padraic O'Farrell, *The Sean MacEoin Story* (Place, 1981), p. 49.
146. *Ibid.* For Collins's instructions to the Longford IRA about hostage taking, see Beaslai Critique, part 2, p. 85.
147. Dalton WS and Ben Byrne WS.
148. Dalton WS.
149. Traynor WS and Daly WS.
150. Dalton WS. Stapleton WS. Daly WS.
151. Michael Lynch, National Library of Ireland, MS 22117 (1).
152. William J. Stapleton, 'Michael Collins's Squad', *Capuchin Annual* (1970), p. 373.
153. Dalton WS.
154. *Ibid.*
155. McCrae WS.
156. Stapleton, 'Michael Collins's Squad', p. 356.
157. Leonard WS.
158. *Ibid.*
159. Michael Lynch Statement, National Library of Ireland, MS 22117 (1).
160. Leonard WS.
161. Michael Lynch Statement, National Library of Ireland, MS 22117 (1).
162. Noyk WS.
163. Macready, *Annals of an Active Life*, vol. 2, p. 537.
164. *Ibid.*, p. 538.
165. *Ibid.*
166. *Ibid.*
167. Sturgis, who sympathised with Winter's difficulties, recorded on 17 December 1920 that 'he is not enough of an idol to his people who all seem to be on the make and work not as a loyal team but individually' (*Diaries*, p. 93).
168. Macready to Anderson, 8 April 1921. TNA: PRO CO 904/188.
169. Sturgis, *Diaries*, pp. 157–8.
170. *Ibid.*, p. 180.
171. Comment on Tudor, 14 March 1921. Comment on Cope, 24 September 1920. Macready–Wilson correspondence.
172. TNA: PRO CO 904/188.
173. Report on the Intelligence Branch, p. 28.
174. Macready to Anderson, 11 April 1921. TNA: PRO CO 904/188.
175. Traynor WS.
176. *Ibid.*
177. Dan McDonnell WS. According to Slattery WS Collins's reservations about the Custom House operation made him reluctant to commit the Squad to it.
178. Daly WS and Transcript of Mulcahy in conversation with Daly. Mulcahy Papers, P/b/178.
179. Colley WS.
180. Traynor WS and Daly WS.
181. Colley WS.
182. Slattery WS.
183. Vinnie Byrne WS.
184. *Ibid.* Many of the Volunteers arrested at the Custom House were caught after their hands were found to be smelling of petrol.
185. Daly WS.
186. Colley WS.
187. Daly WS.

Chapter Seven

1. Paddy Rigney, '"The ASU" in The National Association of the Old IRA', *Dublin Brigade Review* (1939).

2. O'Connor WS.
3. Lawless WS and Plunkett WS.
4. Dan McDonnell WS.
5. *Ibid.*
6. *Freeman's Journal,* 27 June 1921.
7. She had given the information to Paddy Drury, a Crow Street Intelligence officer. Michael Stack, Written Statement 525. Bureau of Military History. Hereafter Stack WS. O'Connor WS and White WS also record the maid as the source of information.
8. Stack WS.
9. Thornton WS.
10. Long Papers, 947/308.
11. Thomson Weekly Intelligence Report. TNA: PRO CAB 24/120 CP 2859.
12. Addison Memorandum to the Cabinet, 13 April 1921. TNA: PRO CAB 24/122 CP 2829.
13. Montague Memorandum to the Cabinet, 14 April 1921. TNA: PRO CAB 24/122 OP 2840.
14. Macready to Greenwood, 27 April 1921. Lloyd George Papers, F/19/4/10.
15. Greenwood to Lloyd George, 10 May 1921. Lloyd George Papers, F/19/4/10.
16. *Ibid.*
17. Anderson to Greenwood, 11 May 1921. Lloyd George Papers, F/19/4/10.
18. Sturgis, 4 October 1920, *Diaries,* p. 51.
19. Wylie. TNA: PRO CO 904/177/2.
20. Colonel Dan Bryan WS 947.
21. Sturgis, 19 May 1921, *Diaries,* p. 180.
22. Montmorency, *Sword and Stirrup,* p. 356.
23. Bryan WS.
24. Jeune Memoir.
25. Collins to de Valera, 26 June 1921. Foulkes Papers, 7/24.
26. Sturgis, *Diaries,* p. 184.
27. *Ibid.*
28. Winter, *Winter's Tale,* p. 333. Joseph McGuiness in his WS 607 asserts that the attack, in which he participated, occurred after 'we received information one morning that a touring car would be coming from Dublin Castle via Thomas Street to the Viceregal lodge and that some important personage would be travelling in it. We got instructions that we were to attack this car.'
29. *Ibid.,* p. 338.
30. TNA: PRO CAB 24/123 CP 2983.
31. There are full records of this meeting in both CAB 27/107 and the Lloyd George Papers, F31/1/42.
32. Tom Jones, 15 June 1921, Report to Prime Minister on the Irish Situation Committee meeting earlier in the day. Lloyd George Papers, F/25/1/42.
33. TNA: PRO CAB 24/123 C.P. 2983.
34. *Ibid.*
35. *Ibid.*
36. *Ibid.*
37. Cabinet Secretary Hankey to Lloyd George. Lloyd George Papers, F/25/1/42.
38. Report of Irish Situation Committee, 15 June 1921. CAB 27/107.
39. Tom Jones to Lloyd George, 15 June 1921. Lloyd George Papers, F/25/1/42.
40. Macready to Frances Stevenson, 20 June 1921. Lloyd George Papers, F/3 6/2/19.
41. Memorandum by Colonel Sir Hugh Elles, Commandant of the Tank Corps Centre, submitted to the Cabinet by the Secretary of State for War, 24 June, 1921. TNA: PRO CAB/24/185 C.P. 3075.
42. *Ibid.*
43. *Ibid.*
44. Anderson to Greenwood, 15 June 1921. TNA: PRO CO 904/232.
45. *Ibid.*
46. *Ibid.*
47. In a letter dated 16 June 1921 captured by British Intelligence in the raid on de Valera's house on 22 June 1921. TNA: PRO CO 904/23 (7).

48. *Ibid.*
49. Anderson to Sturgis. TNA: PRO CO 904/232.
50. *Ibid.*
51. *Ibid.*
52. Winter, *Winter's Tale*, p. 339.
53. Sturgis, *Diaries*, p. 192.
54. Winston Churchill, *The World Crisis: The Aftermath* (London, 1929), p. 290.
55. For this episode, see Colley WS, Daly WS, Henderson WS and Leonard WS.
56. Winter, 1 July 1921. TNA: PRO HO 317/60.
57. Thomson, 23 June 1921. TNA: PRO CAB 24/125 CO 3074.
58. Thomson, 23 June 1921. TNA: PRO CAB 24/125 CO 3074.
59. Thomson, Irish Intelligence Summary, Special Supplementary Report No. 259, 1 July 1921. Lloyd George Papers, F/46/9/25.
60. *Ibid.*
61. *Ibid.*
62. Greenwood to Frances Stevenson, 29 June 1921. Lloyd George Papers, F19/5/7.
63. For Childers, see both the official life by Andrew Boyle, *The Riddle of Erskine Childers* (London, 1977), and Jim Ring, *Erskine Childers* (London, 1996).
64. Boyle, *The Riddle of Erskine Childers*, p. 255.
65. Thomson, Irish Intelligence Summary, Special Supplementary Report No. 259, 1 July 1921. Lloyd George Papers, F/46/9/25.
66. *Ibid.*
67. Greenwood to Lloyd George, 4 May 1921. Lloyd George Papers, F/4/5/21.
68. Greenwood to Lloyd George, 5 July 1921. Lloyd George Papers, F/19/4/5–6.
69. Colonel Brind, 5 July 1921. TNA: PRO CAB 24/126/3109.
70. *Ibid.*
71. *Ibid.*
72. Barton handwritten account in the Childers Papers, 7833/51.
73. For this operation, see Colley WS, Daly WS, Henderson WS and Leonard WS.
74. Henderson WS.
75. Leonard WS. O'Connor WS says the planned operation was on an even bigger scale than that of 24 June, encompassing the entire Brigade and the entire city with extra heavy Volunteer parties attacking places where Auxiliaries were known to congregate. These included Kidd's Café and the Royal Winter Gardens, a fashionable restaurant attached to the Theatre Royal near O'Connell Bridge.
76. Darling, *So it Looks to Me*, p. 211.
77. *Ibid.*, p. 212.
78. *Ibid.*
79. *Irish Times*, 12 July 1921.
80. Noyk WS.

Conclusions

1. Francis Costello (ed.), *Michael Collins: In his Own Words* (Dublin, 1997), p. 20.
2. Taylor to French, 19 April 1920. French Papers, JDF8.
3. *Ibid.*
4. Report on the Intelligence Branch, p. 51.
5. Report on the Intelligence Branch, pp. 51–2.
6. Record of the Rebellion/Intelligence.
7. Keith Jeffery, 'British Military Intelligence following World War One', in *British and American Approaches to Intelligence* (Basingstoke, 1987), p. 74.
8. Macready to Sir Henry Wilson, 24 August 1920, in a 'Report on the Situation in Ireland'. Lloyd George Papers, F/180/5/10.
9. Darling to Hemming, Irish Office London, 9 August 1921. TNA: PRO CO 904/232.
10. Winter, *Winter's Tale*, p. 323.
11. *Ibid.*
12. Wyse-Power WS.
13. Report on the Intelligence Branch, p. 73.

14. Record of the Rebellion/Intelligence.
15. History of the Fifth Division, Imperial War Museum.
16. Macready wrote that 'Many a time I urged that some members of the Cabinet should take a trip to Dublin, if only to gather some idea of the atmosphere of the place of which they, together with every person who had not crossed the Channel, were in complete ignorance' (*Annals of an Active Life*, vol. 2, p. 470).
17. History of the Fifth Division. Imperial War Museum.
18. Duff, *Sword for Hire*, p. 77.

BIBLIOGRAPHY

Primary Sources

Bureau of Military History, Cathal Brugha Barracks, Dublin
Witness Statements

Maurice Aherne 483
Liam Archer 819
Dulcibella Barton 936
Robert Barton 979
Annie Barrett 1133
J.N. (Sean) Beaumont 709
John Bolger 1745
Eamon Broy 1280, 1285
Sean Brunswick
Annie Bryan 805
Dan Bryan 947
Bernard Byrne 631
Christopher Byrne 642
Joseph Byrne 461
Thomas Byrnes 564
Vinnie Byrne 493
James Carragher 613
Harry Colley 1687
Patrick Collins 506
Paddy Daly 814
Charles Dalton 434
Joseph Dolan 663
Simon Donnelly 481
Martin Finn 921
George Fitzgerald 684
Christopher Fitzsimons 581
Peter Forlan 316

Captain E. Gerrard 348
Bernard Golden 281
Jerry Golden 522
Christopher Harte 2
Frank Henderson 821
Robert Holland 280 and 371
Joseph Hyland 644
Edward Kelleher 477
John Kenny 1693
Michael Knightley 835
Sister Eithne Lawless 414
Joe Lawless 1043
Patrick Lawson 667
Joe Leonard 547
Michael Lynch 511
Pat McCrae 413
Patrick Mannix 308
T.J. McElligott 472
Mick McDonnell 225
Patrick McHugh 664
Joseph McGuiness 607
Charles McQuaile 276
Patrick Mullan 621
Dan McDonnell 486
Lily Mernin 441
Paddy Mulcahy 1468
David Neligan 380

Michael Noyk 707
Laurence Nugent 907
Brigid O'Mullane 450
Paddy O'Connor 813
Geraldine O'Donnell 861
Michael O'Flanagan 908
Brigid O'Reilly 454
John Plunkett 865
Robert Purcell 53
Thomas Reidy 1422
Peter Reynolds 350
Daniel Ryan 1673
Sean Saunders 817
Frank Saurin 715
James Slattery 445
Eugene Smyth 334
Michael Stack 525
William Stapleton 822
Michael Staines 944
Frank Thornton 615
Oscar Traynor 340
Liam Tobin 1753
Richard Walsh 400
George White 956
Nancy Wyse-Power 587

Bodleian Library, Oxford
Strathcarron (i.e.
    Macpherson) Papers

House of Lords Record Office
Bonar Law Papers
Lloyd George Papers

Imperial War Museum
French Papers
Robert Jeune Memoir
Loch Papers
J J.P. Swindlehurst Diary
Henry Wilson Papers
Macready Correspondence
Douglas Wimberley Papers

Liddell Hart Archive, London
    University
Foulkes Papers

*The National Archives,
London*
Anderson Papers
Cabinet Papers
Colonial Office Papers
Home Office Papers
War Office Papers
Winter Correspondence
Wylie Papers

National Library of Ireland
Beaslai Papers
Collins Papers
Michael Lynch Memoir
Noyk Papers
O'Donoghue Papers

University College, Dublin
Mulcahy Papers
O'Malley Notebooks
Trinity College, Dublin
Childers Papers

*Wiltshire Records Office
Trowbridge*
Long Papers

Secondary Sources

Books
Abbot, Richard, *Police Casualties in Ireland 1919–1922* (Cork, Mercier, 2000)
Adams, R.J.Q., *Bonar Law* (London, John Murray, 1999)
Andrew, Christopher, *Secret Service: The Making of the British Intelligence Community* (London, Hodder & Stoughton, 1985)
Andrews, C.S., *Dublin Made Me: An Autobiography* (Dublin, Mercier, 1979)
Augusteijn, Joost, *From Public Defiance to Guerrilla Warfare: The Experience of Ordinary Volunteers in the Irish War of Independence 1919 to 1921* (Dublin, Irish Academic Press, 1996)
Beaslai, Piaras, *Michael Collins and the Making of a New Ireland*, 2 vols (London, Harrap, 1926)
Bennett, Richard, *The Black and Tans* (London, Four Square Books, 1961)
Blake, Robert, *The Unknown Prime Minister: The Life and Times of Andrew Bonar Law 1858–1923* (London, Eyre & Spottiswoode, 1955)
Bowden, Tom, *The Breakdown of Public Security: The Case of Ireland 1916–1921 and Palestine 1936–1939* (London, Sage, 1977)
Boyle, Andrew, *The Riddle of Erskine Childers* (London, Hutchinson, 1977)
Breen, Dan, *My Fight for Irish Freedom* (Dublin, Poolbeg, 1989)
Brennan, Robert, *Allegiance* (Dublin, Brown & Nolan, 1950)
Clarke, Kathleen, *Revolutionary Woman: An Autobiography* (Dublin, O'Brien Press, 1991)
Coogan, Tim Pat, *Michael Collins: A Biography* (London, Roberts Rinehart, 1990)
Costello, Francis, *Enduring the Most: The Life and Death of Terence MacSwiney* (Dingle, Brandon Books, 1995)
—— (ed.), *Michael Collins: In his Own Words* (Dublin, Gill & Macmillan, 1997)
—— *The Irish Revolution and its Aftermath 1916 to 1923* (Dublin, Irish Academic Press, 2003)
Dalton, Charles, *With the Dublin Brigade 1917–1921* (London, Peter Davies, 1929)
Dangerfield, George, *The Damnable Question: A Study in Anglo-Irish Relations* (London, Constable, 1977)
Darling, Sir William, *So it Looks to Me* (London, 1952)
Deacon, Richard, *The British Secret Service* (London, Grafton, 1991)
Deasy, Liam, *Towards Ireland Free* (Cork, Royal Carbery Books, 1973)
—— *Brother against Brother* (Dublin, Mercier, 1982)
Doherty, Gabriel (ed.), *Michael Collins and the Making of the Irish Free State* (Cork, Mercier, 1998)
Duff, Douglas V., *Sword for Hire* (London, John Murray, 1934)
Dwyer, T. Ryle, *Michael Collins: The Man who Won the War* (Cork, Mercier, 1990)
Forester, Margery, *Michael Collins: The Lost Leader* (Dublin, Gill & Macmillan, 1971)
Foster, E.C., *Let the Boy Win his Spurs: An Autobiography* (London, 1976)
Gleeson, James, *Bloody Sunday* (London, Four Square, 1962)

Griffith, Kenneth, and O'Grady, Timothy, *Curious Journey: An Oral History of Ireland's Unfinished Revolution* (London, Hutchinson, 1982)

Hardy, Captain J.L., *I Escape!* (London, Cherry Tree Books, 1938)

Hart, Peter, *The IRA and its Enemies: Violence and Community in Cork 1916–1923* (Oxford, Oxford University Press, 1998)

Holmes, Richard, *The Little Field-Marshal: Sir John French* (London, Jonathan Cape, 1981)

Hopkinson, Michael, *The Irish War of Independence* (Dublin, Gill & Macmillan, 2002)

—— (ed.), *The Last Days of Dublin Castle: The Diaries of Mark Sturgis* (Dublin, Irish Academic Press, 1999)

Jones, Tom, *Whitehall Diary*, vol. 3, *Ireland*, ed. Keith Middlemas (Oxford, Oxford University Press, 1971)

Keegan, John, *Intelligence in War: Knowledge of the Enemy from Napoleon to Al-Qaeda* (London, Knopf, 2003)

Kendle, John, *Walter Long, Ireland and the Union 1905–1920* (Montreal, Glendale Publishing, 1992)

McColgan, John, *British Policy and the Irish Administration 1920–1922* (London, HarperCollins, 1983)

Macready, Sir Cecil Frederick Nevil, *Annals of an Active Life*, 2 vols (London, Hutchinson, 1924)

Mansergh, Nicholas, *The Unresolved Question: The Anglo-Irish Settlement and its Undoing* (New Haven, CT and London, Yale University Press, 1991)

Menzies, Mrs C. Stuart, *As Others See Us* (London, Herbert Jenkins, 1924).

Mitchell, Arthur, *Revolutionary Government in Ireland: Dail Eireann 1919–1922* (Dublin, Gill & Macmillan, 1995)

Montmorency, Hervey De, *Sword and Stirrup: Memories of an Adventurous Life* (London, 1936)

Morgan, Kenneth, *Consensus and Disunity: The Lloyd George Coalition Government 1918–1922* (Oxford, Oxford University Press, 1979)

Mulcahy, Risteard, *Richard Mulcahy (1886–1971): A Family Memoir* (Dublin, Aurelian Press, 1999)

Neilson, Keith (ed.), *Go Spy the Land: Military Intelligence in History* (Westport, CT, Praeger, 1992)

Neligan, David, *The Spy in the Castle* (London, MacGibbon & Kee, 1968)

O'Connor, Frank, *The Big Fellow: A Life of Michael Collins* (London, Nelson, 1937)

O'Donoghue, Florence, *No Other Law: The Story of Liam Lynch and the Irish Republican Army 1916–1922* (Dublin, Anvil, 1954)

O'Halpin, Eunan, *The Decline of the Union: British Government in Ireland, 1892–1920* (Dublin and Syracuse, Gill & Macmillan/Syracuse University Press, 1987)

—— *Head of the Civil Service: A Study of Sir Warren Fisher* (London, Routledge, 1989)

O'Mahony, Sean, *Frongoch: University of Revolution* (Dublin, FDR Teoranta, 1987)

O'Malley, Ernie, *On Another Man's Wound* (Dublin, Anvil, 1990)

Philips, W.A., *The Revolution in Ireland 1906–1923* (London, Longmans, 1923)

Porter, Bernard, *Plots and Paranoia: A History of Political Espionage in Britain 1790–1988* (London, Unwin Hyman, 1989)

—— *The Vigilant State: The London Metropolitan Police Special Branch before the First World War* (London, Weidenfeld & Nicolson, 1987)

Ring, Jim, *Erskine Childers* (London, John Murray, 1996)

Seth, Ronald, *Anatomy of Spying* (New York, Dutton, 1963)

Shulsky, Abram, *Silent Warfare: Understanding the World of Intelligence* (Washington, Brasseys, 1993)

Taylor, Rex, *Michael Collins* (London, Four Square, 1958)

The Kerryman, *Cork's Fighting Story* (Tralee, The Kerryman, 1949)

—— *Dublin's Fighting Story* (Tralee, The Kerryman, 1949)

Thomson, Basil, *Queer People* (London, Hodder & Stoughton, 1922)

—— *The Scene Changes* (London, Collins, 1939)

Townshend, Charles, *The British Campaign in Ireland 1919–1921* (Oxford, Oxford University Press, 1975)

Valiulis, Maryann, *Portrait of a Revolutionary: General Richard Mulcahy and the Founding of the Irish Free State* (Dublin, Irish Academic Press, 1992)

Wheeler-Bennett, Sir John, *John Anderson, Viscount Waverley* (London, Macmillan, 1962)

Winter, Sir Ormonde, *Winter's Tale: An Autobiography* (London, Richards Press, 1955)

Woodcock, Mrs Caroline, *An Officer's Wife in Ireland* (Dublin, Galago, 1994)

Articles

Bowden, Tom, 'Bloody Sunday – a Reappraisal', *European Studies Review*, 2 (1972)

Breen, Dan, 'Irish Leaders of our Time, 4: Sean Tracey', *An Cosantoir*, 5/5 (May 1945)

Harvey A.D. 'Who were the Auxiliaries?', *Historical Journal*, 35 (1992)

Henderson, Frank, 'Irish Leaders of our Time, 5: Richard McKee', *An Cosantoir*, 5/6 (June 1945)

Hiley, Nicholas, 'Counter-Espionage and Security in Great Britain during the First World War', *English Historical Review*, 101 (1986)

Jeffery, Keith, 'Intelligence and Counter-Intelligence Operations: Some Reflections on the British Experience', *Intelligence and National Security*, 2/1 (January 1987)

Kavanagh, Sean, 'The Irish Volunteers' Intelligence Organisation', *Capuchin Annual* (1969)

Leeson, David, 'The "Scum of London's Underworld"? British Recruits for the Royal Irish Constabulary, 1920–21', *Contemporary British History*, 17/1 (Spring 2003)

Lowe, W.J., 'Who were the Black and Tans?', *History Ireland* (Autumn 2004)

McKenna, Kathleen, 'The Irish Bulletin', *Capuchin Annual* (1970)

Mulcahy, Richard, 'Conscription and the General Headquarters Staff', *Capuchin Annual* (1968)

—— 'Chief of Staff', *Capuchin Annual* (1969)

O'Doherty, Liam, 'Dublin Brigade Area 1920', *Capuchin Annual* (1970)

O'Donoghue, Florence, 'Reorganisation of the Irish Volunteers 1916–1917', *Capuchin Annual* (1967)

O'Halpin, Eunan, 'British Intelligence in Ireland, 1914–1921', in Christopher Andrew and David Dilks (eds), *The Missing Dimension: Government and Intelligence Communities in the Twentieth Century* (London, Macmillan, 1984)

O Luing, Sean, 'The "German Plot" 1918', *Capuchin Annual* (1968)

—— 'Thomas Ashe', *Capuchin Annual* (1967/8)

Popplewell, Richard, 'Lacking Intelligence: Some Reflections on Recent Approaches to British Counter-Insurgency 1900–1960', *Intelligence and National Security*, 10/2 (April 1995)

Putkowski, Julian, 'A2 and the Reds in Khaki', *Lobster*, 27 (1994)

—— 'The Best Secret Service Man We Had', *Lobster*, 28 (1995)

Silvestri, Michael, 'Sir Charles Tegart and Revolutionary Terrorism in Bengal', *History Ireland* (Winter 2000)

—— '"The Sinn Fein of India": Irish Nationalism and the Policing of Revolutionary Terrorism in Bengal', *Journal of British Studies*, 39/4 (October 2000)

Snoddy, Oliver, 'Three By-Elections of 1917', *Capuchin Annual* (1967)

——, 'National Aid 1916–1917–1918', *Capuchin Annual* (1968)

Stapleton, William J., 'Michael Collins's Squad', *Capuchin Annual* (1970)

Townshend, Charles, 'Bloody Sunday – Michael Collins Speaks', *European Studies Review*, 9 (1979)

—— 'The Irish Republican Army and the Development of Guerrilla Warfare, 1916–1921', *English Historical Review*, 94 (1979)

Newspapers

Belfast Telegraph, *Freeman's Journal*, *Irish Independent*, *Irish Times*, *Northern Whig*

INDEX

A2 Branch GHQ GB, 72–3
Addison, Christopher, 221
Aherne, Maurice, 179–80
Ames, Lieutenant Peter, 146, 151–2, 153, 171, 174
  Bloody Sunday, 156–7
An t-Oglac, 20, 141
Anderson, Sir John, 90, 97, 101–2, 116, 135, 207, 244
  Bloody Sunday, 163
  and coercion policy, 227
  Igoe Gang, 185
  spy payments, 195
  strategy, 88, 92–3
  team of, 140
  and Truce negotiations, 221, 222, 228–9, 235
  and Winter, 183, 213, 225, 242–3
Andrews, Todd, 149, 157, 173
Angliss, Lieutenant H., 174
Anglo-Irish Treaty, 1921, 7, 49, 176, 187, 228
Anglo-Irish War, 17, 18, 20, 22, 26–8, 29, 53, 92, 241
  Bloody Sunday, 141–77
  British policy, 23, 26–8, 84, 87–9, 91–3, 100, 104, 141, 143, 176–7, 183, 184, 218, 243–5
  course of; Jan.–July 1920, 64–96; July–Nov. 1920, 97–140; Nov. 1920–Mar. 1921, 178–218; May–July 1921, 219–38
Arbour Hill Military Prison, 189–90
Archer, Liam, 51–2, 79
Arnold, Sidney, 73, 74
Ashe, Thomas, 7, 8–9, 24, 124
Atwood, P., 103
Auxiliaries, 45–9, 93, 112–14, 129, 141, 178, 194
  attacks on, 53, 56, 179, 180, 204, 220, 229, 237

Bloody Sunday, 152–3, 155, 162–8, 173–4, 243
  and Broy, 188–91
  and Collins, 118
  confidence of, 143
  and Cope, 223–4
  Custom House attack, 216–18
  effects on population, 241–2
  intelligence officers, 105
  IRA hostages, 182
  Montmorency, 204–7
  raids, 196–8
  spies, 146
  Truce, 238

Baggallay, Captain G.T., 131, 158, 170, 171, 174
Balbriggan, County Dublin, 107, 148
Balfour, Gerald, 225, 226–7, 244
Barrett, Ben, 29, 76, 192–3
Barry, Kevin, 125–6, 173, 175
Barry, Tom, 118, 123
Barry's Hotel, 38
Barton, Agnes, 232
Barton, Charles, 232
Barton, Detective Sergeant John, 22, 24, 58, 61, 65, 192–3
Barton, Robert, 93, 231–2, 234, 235, 236
Beal na Blath, 123
Beaslai, Piaras, 39, 152, 176
Beaumont, William, 197
Beggar's Bush barracks, 113, 115, 166–7, 188, 214
Begley, Denis, 153, 154, 155
Bell, Alan, 81–2, 96, 99, 195
Bennett, Lieutenant, 151–2, 153, 156–7, 171, 174
Bennett, Major George, 146
Bewley, Charles, 170
Birkenhead, Lord, 93

Black and Tans, 49, 92, 98, 107, 112, 120, 184, 206
  effects on population, 241–2
  reprisals, 147–8, 149
Bloody Sunday, 58, 121, 132, 141–77, 179, 205, 240, 242–3
  assessment of, 172–7
  British funerals, 168–9
  courts martial, 170–2
  Croke Park shootings, 164–6, 168, 176
  intelligence gathering, 145–7
  internments, 182–3
  IRA deaths, 167–8
  map of assassination area, 142
  planning, 148–51
Boddington, Capt H.F., 103
Bolster, Frank, 181, 211
Bonar Law, Andrew, 23, 26–8, 84, 88, 141, 143, 225, 244
  resignation, 221
Boyce, James, 170, 171
Boyd, General, 103, 147–8, 182, 231
  Bloody Sunday, 159, 163
  Commander, 183–4, 241
  curfew, 108
  and 'dirty tricks', 127
  Truce, 236
Breen, Dan, 17, 20, 32, 43, 99, 112, 137, 143, 195, 202
  search for, 130, 131–7
Brennan, Robert, 47, 78, 79, 110, 112
Bridewell, 167
Brien, Supt Owen, 46, 64, 65
Brind, Colonel, 163, 182, 228, 235–6
British Army, 26, 180–1, 227, 228–9, 240
  Bloody Sunday, 164, 168–9
  and coercion, 242
  Directorate of Intelligence, 47, 48, 50, 64, 68–9, 71–3, 175–6, 206, 241–3; dual system, 104–5, 241; Neligan joins, 191–2
  prisoner interrogations, 198–204; Squad targets, 53, 56; under Winter, 194–204, 212, 213
  freedom of movement, 107, 207
  harassment of, 144
  internment, 182–3
  under Macready, 83
  reinforcements, 26

spies in, 51
  and Truce, 238
Brooke, Frank, 93–4, 97
brothels, 47, 129
Broy, Colonel, 238
Broy, Eamon, 12, 32, 37
  capture, 188–91
  and Collins, 18–19, 21, 25, 47, 49, 117, 119, 123, 138
  on Crimes Branch Special, 66–7
  on G Division, 22, 40–1, 64
  German Plot, 14–15
  as spy, 9–11, 46, 65, 240
Brugha, Cathal, 8, 9, 16, 21, 25, 32, 176
  Bloody Sunday, 148, 151, 152, 163
  Cabinet assassination scheme, 15, 207–8
  and Collins, 187–8
  search for, 195
Bruton, Detective Sergeant, 95, 125
Bulfin, Sir Edward, 89
Burton, Major Stratford, 48
Byrne, Ben, 55, 63, 139, 158, 181–2, 193, 206, 208
  Lees assassination, 207
Byrne, Charlie, 43–4, 45
Byrne, Captain Christy, 159, 172
Byrne, Eddie, 181
Byrne, Inspector-General Sir Joseph, 16, 23, 30–1
Byrne, Vinnie, 26, 32, 33, 54, 55, 56, 57, 58, 60, 80, 180, 181
  Barton ambush, 192–3
  Bell assassination, 81, 82
  Bloody Sunday, 152, 156–7
  Brooke assassination, 93–4
  Coffey ambush, 95
  confession, 59
  Custom House attack, 216–17
  on Daly, 193–4
  and Hardy, 110
  and Igoe, 186
Byrnes, Daisy, 72, 77
Byrnes, Jack ('John Jameson'), 72–7, 80, 107, 231

Café Cairo, 146
Caffrey, John, 210
Caldow, John, 162
Caldwell, Paddy, 43
Cameron, Major Cecil, 103, 109, 194

Capel Street Municipal Library, 12
Carew, Major, 103, 157, 171
Carolan, Professor, 132, 133, 134, 135
Carpenter, P., 103
Carson, Sir Edward, 13, 23
Casement, Sir Roger, 12, 70, 77–8, 139
Central Hotel, 48
Chamberlain, Austen, 225, 226–7, 229
Chesterton, G.K., 238
Childers, Erskine, 199, 224, 232–5
Childers, Molly, 232–5
Children's Hospital, 152, 163
Christian, officer, 136
Churchill, Winston, 89, 93, 229
Civil War, 235
Clancy, Peadar, 20, 83–4, 132, 136, 141, 144, 178
  Bloody Sunday, 152
  captured, 165–6
  death of, 167–8, 176, 181, 187, 203, 242–3
Clarke, Kathleen, 6, 7
Clarke, Tom, 1–2, 3, 6, 18
Clune, Archbishop Patrick, 175, 221
Clune, Conor, 152, 153, 165–6
  death of, 167–8, 203, 242–3
Coffey, Detective Sergeant, 95, 125
Collevin Dairies, 39
Colley, Harry, 215, 217–18
Collins, Hannie, 5
Collins, Michael, 7, 202
  acting President, 187–8
  Ashe funeral, 8–9
  and Childers, 234
  death of, 123
  early life, 5–6
  evades capture, 35, 116–23
  Finance minister, 21, 39, 40, 81, 197
  German Plot, 14, 15
  Home Affairs minister, 16
  intelligence war, 11–12, 18–19;
    assessment of, 239–45; Director, 3,
    35–63, 97–140; and G Division, 21–2,
    23–6, 28; Jan.–July 1920, 64–96;
    July–Nov. 1920, 97–140; Nov.
    1920–Mar. 1921, 178–218; May–July
    1921, 219–38
  in IRB, 5–7
  lifestyle, 37–8

  map of territory of, 34
  and McKee, 19–20
  personality of, 36–8, 123
  private life, 116
  Rising aftermath, 2, 3–4
  secrecy and control of, 39–41
  and Soloheadbeg, 17
  and Truce negotiations, 228, 230–1, 237–8
  see also Squad
Collins, Michael, Sr, 5
communism, 71, 72–3
Connolly, James, 1
Connolly, Joe, 25
Conroy, Jimmy, 63, 180, 181, 206
Coogan, Tim Pat, 72, 75
Cope, 'Andy', 86, 88, 91, 97, 140, 213
  Bloody Sunday, 163
  Truce negotiations, 222–4, 227–30, 231, 235–6
Cork IRA, 29, 91–2, 118, 121–3, 126–7, 130–1, 145, 147
  Deasy, 121–3
  Fermoy ambush, 26, 27
  Hales, 138–9
  Lindsay kidnap, 100
  spy shot, 77, 80
Cotton, Arthur, 94
Coughlan, Captain F.X., 157, 158
Crawford, Major, 162–3
Crippen, Dr, 139
Croke Park shootings, 164–6
Crozier, Brig-Gen F.P., 155
Cullen, Tom, 38, 41, 57, 77, 123, 136, 189, 197–8
  analysis of reports, 52–3
  and Byrnes, 75, 76
  dinner search, 117–18
  and Hardy, 110, 112
  role of, 42, 43, 44
  spy dossiers, 145, 147
Cullenswood House, 39
Cumann na mBan, 189, 241, 243
Curzon, Lord, 93, 244
Custom House, attack on, 188, 193, 214–18, 219, 240

Dail Eireann, 16, 23, 81, 240
  Bloody Sunday, 148
  Loan, 131, 234

offices captured, 198
penalty for membership, 225, 226
suppressed, 27–8, 30, 35, 46, 93, 207
Dalton, Charlie, 43, 44, 45, 56, 58, 145–7, 180
 Bloody Sunday, 159–61
 and Igoe, 186–7
 MacEoin capture, 208, 209–10
Dalton, Emmet, 196–7, 209, 210–12
Dalton, Jim, 130
Daly, Paddy, 62–3, 95, 96, 113, 125, 136, 237
 Bell assassination, 81–2
 Bloody Sunday, 151, 172, 180
 Brooke assassination, 94
 Byrnes assassination, 76
 Custom House attack, 215, 216, 217, 218
 French ambush, 32–3
 leadership of, 192–4, 219
 MacEoin capture, 209
 Roberts ambush, 95
 Squad training, 25, 26, 29–30, 56
Darling, William, 89, 98, 237–8, 242
de Valera, Eamon, 9, 14, 16, 27, 75, 176, 222, 228
 arrest and release, 229, 231
 and Childers, 234
 escape, 21
 return from USA, 187–8, 212–13
 treatment of, 225
 and Truce negotiations, 223, 230–1, 235
 to USA, 25
Deasy, Liam, 121–3
Dempsey, Jim, 153, 155
Devlin, Liam, 38
Devlin's pub, 38, 121–2
Dolan, Joe, 43, 45, 57, 76, 82, 137, 138
 arms shortage, 219–20
 Bloody Sunday, 157–8
Dominic, Father, 124
Dominion Home Rule, 88, 92, 97
Donnelly, Simon, 151, 202–3
Doran, William, 181
Dowling, 'Chummy', 146, 153, 160, 161–2, 174
Dowling, Joe, 12
Doyle, James, 159
Doyle, Sean, 29, 59, 156, 204, 216, 217

Dublin Brigade, IRA, 18, 74, 104, 105, 140, 141, 223
 arms, 20, 127, 219–20
 ASU, 179, 180, 193, 197–8, 204
 Bloody Sunday, 148–64, 176
 Custom House attack, 214–18, 219
 double agent, 200–1
 Grafton Street attack, 229
 HQ, 124
 intelligence gathering, 42–4, 145
 under Mulcahy, 9, 11
 O'Connell St attack plan, 237
 response to Auxiliaries, 113–14
 and Squad, 53, 56
 under Traynor, 178–9
Dublin Castle administration, 16, 26–8, 30, 35, 42, 143, 188, 191–2, 215
 Bloody Sunday, 159, 163–4, 165–6, 169, 174
 Collins exposed to, 75
 courts martial, 170–2
 effects of Squad, 239
 German Plot, 13–15
 intelligence, 97; dual system, 183–4; and G Division, 64–5; and Special Branch, 69–77; and Thomson, 71
 interrogations, 198–204
 Montmorency in, 205–6
 Redmond appointment, 61–3
 reform, 23, 83, 84–9
 and RIC, 30–1
 spies in, 12, 48–50, 51
 and Truce negotiations, 222–4, 225, 227–30, 235–6
 Tudor and Winter in, 140
 wedding in, 52
Dublin District Special Branch, 194
Dublin Metropolitan Police (DMP), 10, 19, 21, 31, 49, 61, 86, 88, 104, 194, 205
 decline, 99
 intelligence (see G Division, DMP)
 reform, 83, 89–90
Dublin Typographical Society, 124
Dublin Whiskey Distillery, 39
Duff, Douglas, 119–20, 244–5
Duggan, Eamon, 11–12, 14, 21, 121, 197, 235, 236
Duke, Henry, 12, 14
Dundalk IRA, 225

Dunne, Miss, 48
Dwyer, James, 223, 228

Easter Rising, 1916, 1–3, 11, 14, 16, 42,
    64, 68, 149, 188, 204–5
  and Barton, 233
  Castle file on, 48
  Collins, 6
  feuds, 130
  Thomson report on, 70
Eastwood Hotel, 159
Edgeworth-Johnstone, commissioner, 61,
    86, 89, 91, 191
Elles, Colonel Sir Hugh, 227, 242, 244
Ellis, John, 139
Ennis, Tom, 16, 25, 157, 204, 217
Etchingham, Sean, 238
  see also Anglo-Irish War

Farrell, Catherine, 156, 157
Fenians, 69
First World War, 13, 24–5, 92, 128, 158,
    204
  Childers, 199, 233
  conscription, 11, 12
  Hardy, 114
  MI5, 69–70
  Tudor, 84, 90
  Winter, 89, 90, 103
Fisher, Sir Warren, 85–9, 97, 184, 244
Fitzgerald, Captain, 162, 174
Fitzgerald, Desmond, 112
Fitzgerald, Martin, 222, 223
Fitzmaurice, Constable, 137
Fitzpatrick, auctioneer, 152–3, 165–6, 168
Flanagan, Captain Paddy, 151, 159–61,
    179, 219
Fleming family, 132, 135, 137
Fleming's hotel, 38
Fogarty, Michael, Bishop of Killaloe, 130
Foley, Michael, 12
Forlan, Head Constable Peter, 49–50, 113
Fovargue, Vincent, 200–1
Freeman's Journal, 111, 120, 121, 172,
    220, 222
French, Lord, 13, 19, 22–3, 47, 52, 61, 70,
    82, 93, 94
  Ashtown ambush, 31–3, 43, 63, 81
  and British policy, 26–8, 89
  and Fisher, 85, 89

and hunger strike, 83–4
and intelligence system, 15–16, 86
and Macready, 83
restrictions on, 98
and RIC, 30–1
Frongoch camp, 6, 8, 11, 138
Fuller's Restaurant, 48

G Division, DMP, 1–2, 9, 19, 30, 39, 46,
    69, 72, 81, 125, 143, 240
  and Collins, 21–2, 23–6, 43
  effects of Squad, 239
  German Plot, 14–15
  Jan.–July 1920, 64–96
  July–Nov. 1920, 97–140
  Redmond assassination, 61–3
  spies in, 10–11, 40, 49–50, 65, 188–91
Gaelic Athletic Association (GAA), 149,
    151, 164–5
Gaelic League, 38
Galway IRA, 186–7
Garnin, Cadet, 155
Gavan Duffy, Mrs, 243
Gay, Tommy, 12
George V, King, 27, 231, 233, 236
germ warfare, 127–8
German Plot, 12, 13–15, 21
Golden, Bernard, 48–9
Gough, Peter, 210
Government of Ireland Act, 1920, 104,
    184, 221
Greene, James, 160, 161, 170, 171
Greenwood, Margery, 199
Greenwood, Sir Hamar, 83, 85, 88–9, 90,
    98, 116, 140, 244
  ambush planned, 136
  Bloody Sunday, 163
  and coercion policy, 213, 225, 227
  and de Valera release, 229
  and King, 190
  optimism, 141, 143, 182, 183
  Sinn Fein spy, 231
  and Squad, 130
  and Truce negotiations, 222, 235
Gregory, Augusta, Lady, 10
Gresham Hotel, 149, 158–69, 163, 171–2,
    174, 175
Griffin, Jimmy, 158
Griffin, Joseph, 145
Griffin, Paddy, 63

Griffith, Arthur, 7, 9, 14, 79, 108, 130,
    143, 197, 228, 231
  and Hardy, 110–12
  imprisonment, 176, 187, 235
  treatment of, 225
  and Truce negotiations, 221
Grocers and Vintners Association, 38
Guilfoyle, Joe, 43, 45, 179–80

Hales, Sean, 138, 200
Hales, Tom, 138–9
Hally, Detective Sergeant, 22
Hardinge, Lord, 31
Hardy, Frank Digby, 109–12
Hardy, Captain Jocelyn ('Hoppy'), 114–15,
    138, 152, 166, 168, 180, 190
interrogations, 200, 203
Harper-Shore, Captain F., 103, 131
Harte, Christy, 195
Harte, Tom, 138
Hayes, Kathleen, 162
Hegarty, Sean, 126–7
Henderson, Arthur, 175
Henderson, Frank, 20, 22, 144, 237
Hill Dillon, Major S.S., 49, 68–9, 80, 99,
    184
  assassination attempt, 98
  defective ammunition, 127
  'hotline', 116
Hoey, Daniel, Detective Sergeant, 22, 24,
    26, 28
Hogan, Sean, 32–3
Holmes, Mr, 134
Hue and Cry, 117
Hughes, James, 43
Humphreys, Travers, 170
hunger strikes, 166
  Ashe, 8
  MacSwiney, 124–5
  Mountjoy, 3–4, 8, 124, 125
Hyde, Sean, 146
Hyem, P., 103
Hyland, Joe, 117, 212, 217

Igoe, Eugene (Gang), 185–7, 225
Irish Banks Court, 81
Irish Brigade, 12, 77–8, 79
Irish Bulletin, 105, 126, 129
Irish Engineering Union, 179
Irish Independent, 111, 120

Irish National Aid and Volunteers'
    Dependants Fund, 6–7
Irish National Foresters, 38
Irish Republican Army (IRA), 61, 204,
    214, 230
  GHQ reorganised, 144
  and Igoe Gang, 185–7
  Intelligence Division, 11–12, 39, 53,
    64–96, 97–140, 179–80, 180, 241;
    areas of responsibility, 48; intelligence
    gathering, 44–7; officers, 43–8; spies
    of, 48–9; spies within, 77–80, 128–30
  interrogations of, 198–204
  penalty for membership, 225
  popular support, 242
  postal raid, 51
  prisoners' hunger strike, 83–4
  tax-collectors raided, 82–3
  and Truce negotiations, 235, 240
Irish Republican Brotherhood (IRB), 11, 18,
    22, 24, 29, 39, 78, 122, 208
  Collins in, 5–6, 7
  intelligence officers, 43
  penalty for membership, 225
  and Squad, 60
Irish Situation Committee, 89, 225–8, 240,
    242
Irish Times, 238
Irish Volunteers, 8–9, 11, 12, 18, 20,
    22–3, 26, 29
  arms smuggling, 232
  attack on G Division, 24–6
  Collins as Intelligence Director, 3, 14,
    21–2, 35–63
  Easter Rising, 1–3
  intelligence, see Irish Republican Army:
    Intelligence Division
  and Soloheadbeg, 16–17
  suppressed, 46, 93
  see also IRA
Isham, Lt-Col Ralph, 73, 75, 76
Ivanhoe Hotel, 204

'Jameson, John', see Byrnes, Jack
Jeffrey, Keith, 241
Jennings, Lt-Col, 159, 172
Jervis Street Hospital, 219
Jeune, Captain Robert, 108, 132, 135, 146,
    160, 176, 182, 224
  Bloody Sunday, 153, 161–2, 174

Jones, Tom, 225
Jury's Hotel, 121, 201–2

Kavanagh, Joseph, 12, 40–1, 49, 65, 152, 188
Keenlyside, Captain, 146, 159–61, 174
Keenlyside, Mrs, 160–1
Kell, Captain Vernon, 16, 69–70
Kelleher, Ned, 43
Kells, Detective Henry, 83, 125
Kelly, Colonel, 98, 126–7, 138, 139
Kelly, warder, 210
Kennedy, Mick, 25, 181
Kennedy, Paddy, 44
Keogh, Tom, 25, 32, 57, 58, 62–3, 95, 155, 181–2, 192
    Bell assassination, 81–2
    Bloody Sunday, 153–4, 158
    Brooke assassination, 93–4
    Lees assassination, 207
    MacEoin capture, 208, 211
    as Squad leader, 193–4
Kidd's Buffet, 48, 146
Kilcoyne, Tom, 76
Kilmainham Gaol, 105, 169–70, 203
King, Captain W.L., 113, 114–15, 152, 166, 168, 190
Kirwan's pub, 38, 119, 132
Knightly, Michael, 111–12

Lawless, Eithne, 152–3
Lawless, Joe, 18, 25–6, 107, 135
Lawrence of Arabia, 9
Lees, Captain Cecil, 207
Lemass, Sean, 158
Leonard, Joe, 32, 56, 96, 180, 237
    Barton ambush, 192–3
    Bloody Sunday, 155–6
    Byrnes assassination, 76
    MacEoin capture, 209, 210–12
    Ryan assassination, 181
    Squad training, 25, 29–30
Lewes Gaol, 6, 7
Limerick IRA, 43, 130, 131
Linacre, Brigadier, 109
Lincoln Gaol, 21
Lindsay, Mrs, 100, 126
Lloyd George, David, 6, 12, 13, 19, 23, 83, 86, 184, 229, 231, 233
    assassination plan, 182

and Bloody Sunday, 177
Irish policy, 87–8, 89, 91, 93, 104, 143, 244
suppresses Dail, 27–8
and Treaty, 228
and Truce negotiations, 220–2, 224, 230, 235, 236
and Winter, 101, 103
Loch, General, 68
Lockhart, L.K., 101, 224
Logue, Cardinal, 16
London and North Western Hotel, 204
Long, Nurse, 134, 135
Long, Walter, 12–14, 15, 23, 62, 70, 77, 84, 93, 220, 244
Longford IRA, 42–3, 208
Lynch, Denis, 39
Lynch, James, 131
Lynch, John, 131, 146, 174
Lynch, Liam, 130–1, 143
Lynch, Michael, 39, 209, 211, 212
Lyons, Denis, 5

McCarthy, Detective Sergeant, 190–1
McCarthy, Miss, 38, 78
McCarthy, Sergeant, 62
McCormack, Captain Patrick, 158–9, 168, 174–5
McCormack, Mrs, 174–5
McCrae, Pat, 95, 158, 173
    MacEoin capture, 210–12
MacCurtain, Thomas, 28
MacDermott, Sean, 1, 2, 3, 18
MacDonald, Matty, 158
McDonnell, Daniel, 43, 50, 129–30, 172, 219–20
    Bloody Sunday, 157–8
McDonnell, Mick, 6, 20, 25, 28, 29, 55, 56, 57, 58, 81, 82
    Barton ambush, 192, 193
    French ambush, 31–2, 33
    to London, 207–8
MacEoin, Sean, 207–12
McGee, Peter, 43
McGrane, Eileen, 189, 198
McGuinness, Joe, 7
McGurk, Quartermaster, 178
Mackay, Anthony, 58
McKee, Dick, 9, 16–17, 22, 25, 29, 39, 83, 113, 136, 145, 179, 209

Bloody Sunday, 147, 148, 149–50, 152
 and Breen, 132, 135
 captured, 165–7
 and Collins, 19–20, 24
 death of, 167–8, 176, 181, 187, 203,
  242–3
 French ambush, 31–2
 heads Dublin Brigade, 11, 43, 124
 leadership of, 141
 and Tobin, 42
 Traynor deputy, 144
McKee, Moira, 152
McKenna, Kathleen, 105–6
McKenna, Rose, 73, 74
Mackey, Mr and Mrs, 54
McLean, Billy, 153, 155, 163
McLean, Captain Donald, 135, 162, 174
MacLysaght, Edward, 152, 168
McMahon, intelligence officer, 146, 153–4,
  171
MacMahon, James, 16, 31, 86, 88, 174
 and Truce negotiations, 223, 228, 236
McNamara, Detective Sergeant James, 12,
  46, 49, 65–6, 121, 145, 238, 240
 and Hardy, 138
 and Redmond, 62
 on the run, 191
MacNeill, Eoin, 235
Macpherson, Ian, 19, 23, 26–8, 30, 31,
  83
 kidnap plan, 243
McQuaile, Charles, 51
Macready, General Nevil, 84, 97–8, 102,
  127, 143, 199
 Bloody Sunday, 163, 164
 and coercion policy, 225–7, 228–9, 242
 and Collins, 119
 complaints of, 212–14
 dual intelligence system, 104, 183, 194
 Dublin Castle reform, 84–9
 heads army in Ireland, 83
 Lindsay kidnap, 100
 police reform, 89–90
 policy of, 90, 91, 93, 147–8, 176, 244
 protection of officers, 107, 207
 spy payments, 195
 and Truce negotiations, 222, 235
 and Winter, 224
MacSwiney, Terence, 28–9, 124–5, 126,
  143

Maguire, Sam, 139
Malaya, 241
Mannix, Constable Patrick, 49, 145
Mansion House, 16, 22, 163
Markievicz, Countess, 14, 198–9
martial law, 92–3, 183, 213, 225–8
Mater Hospital, 135–6, 217, 219
'Maudie', 145–6, 151–2, 160
Maye, governor of Kilmainham, 105,
  170
Mayfair Hotel, 220
Mellows, Liam, 238
Mernin, Lily, 48, 75, 145, 240
MI5, 69–70, 71, 102
Mills, Major, 164–5
Moira Hotel, 48
Monaghan, Andy, 153, 154, 155
Montague, Edwin, 143–4, 221–2, 244
Montgomery, Colonel, 160, 170, 174
Montmorency, Hervey de, 204–7, 223
Mooney, Brigadier Sean, 237
Moran, Paddy, 171–2
Moreland, Geo., 55, 180
Morris, Cadet, 155
Mountjoy Gaol, 8, 166
 hangmen, 139
 hunger strike, 83–4, 124, 125
 interrogations, 135, 201
 MacEoin imprisonment, 208–12
Moynihan, Paddy, 50–1
Mulcahy, Paddy, 214
Mulcahy, Richard, 8, 9, 11, 15, 17, 19, 20,
  21, 39, 197, 202
 on assassinations, 107
 Bloody Sunday, 147, 149, 151, 152,
  163, 175, 176
 brother in GPO, 214
 and Byrnes, 74
 and Collins, 23–4, 36, 37, 38, 187–8
 counter-measures, 144
 Dail suppression, 28–9
 and Deasy, 122
 and London plan, 208
 and McKee, 141
 papers seized, 116, 127, 182, 196
 search for, 105, 123–4, 127–8, 195
 and Soloheadbeg, 16–17
 and Squad, 56, 58–9
Mulloy, Bryan, 80–1, 107
Munro, governor of Mountjoy, 211

Murphy, Greg, 12
Murray, Lieutenant, 146, 160–1, 162, 174

Neligan, David, 52, 61, 63, 97, 118, 129, 137
    Bloody Sunday, 167
    Broy capture, 189–90
    and Hardy, 114
    joins secret service, 191–2
    Lloyd George assassination plan, 182
    as spy, 49, 65, 131, 145, 240
New Ireland Assurance Society, 42
Newbury, Captain, 155–6, 174
Newbury, Mrs, 155–6, 163, 174
Newell, Tom 'Sweeney', 186–7
Noble, Lieutenant W., 103, 157, 172, 173
Noyk, Michael, 35, 37, 105, 196, 212, 238
    Bloody Sunday trials, 169–72
Nugent, Laurence, 129, 172–3
Nunan, Sean, 21

Ó Muirthile, Sean, 78, 79
O'Brien, Art, 73
O'Brien, Denis, 22
O'Callaghan, Donal, 126–7
O'Connell, Sean, 152
O'Connor, Batt, 118
O'Connor, Lord Justice, 222
O'Connor, Rory, 74, 238
O'Donoghue, Florence, 56, 130, 139
O'Donovan Rossa, Jeremiah, 8
O'Driscoll, Dinny, 153, 155
O'Hanrahan, Harry, 11, 12, 14
O'Hanrahan, Michael, 11
O'Hegarty, Diarmuid, 238
Oliver, Sir Roland, 170
O'Malley, Ernie, 114–15
O'Malley, Kit, 196–7
O'Neill, Bob, 44
O'Neill, Con, 43
O'Neill, Larry, 163
O'Reilly, Joe, 6, 41, 74
O'Reilly, Mick, 181, 206
Osgood, Molly, see Childers, Molly
O'Shaughnessy, Thomas, 52
O'Sullivan, Diarmuid, 50–1
O'Sullivan, Gearoid, 39, 152, 238
O'Sullivan, Detective Inspector Philip, 180–1

O'Sullivan, Tahdg, 121–2, 123
O'Toole Gaelic Football Club, 197

Palestine, 113, 241
Paris Peace Conference, 19, 23, 71, 233
Pearse, Patrick, 1, 8
Peel, intelligence officer, 146, 153, 155, 174
Percival, General, 138, 139
Pierrepont, Thomas, 139
Pike, Robert, 137
Plunkett, Sir Horace, 233
Plunkett, Jack, 128
Plunkett, Joseph, 1, 2, 3, 6
Portland Gaol, 234
Post Office, 50–2, 214
Price, intelligence agent, 136
Price, Ivon, 68
Price, Leonard, 146, 160, 162, 174
Purcell, Superintendent, 22, 189
Putkowski, Julian, 73, 75, 77

Quinlisk, Henry, 77–80, 107, 231

Reddy, Captain, 74
Redmond, Assistant Commissioner William, 61–3, 66, 77, 86, 94, 99
Republican Outfitters, 136, 166
Republican Police, 194, 198, 202–3
Restoration of Order in Ireland Act, 97, 100
Revell, Detective Sergeant Richard, 95, 125
Reynolds, Sergeant, 146
Richmond Barracks, 129
Roberts, Albert, Assistant Inspector General, 95
Robinson, Seamus, 17–18, 19, 32
Roche, Sergeant, 137
Rotunda Hospital, 1–2
Rotunda Rink, 51
Royal Exchange Hotel, 174
Royal Irish Constabulary (RIC), 16, 23, 26, 64, 88, 104, 184
    ageing, 68
    attacks on, 29, 53, 54, 91, 137, 206–7
    Bloody Sunday, 164–6
    and Collins, 18–19, 117
    Crimes Branch Special, 66–8, 69, 194
    Igoe Gang, 185–7

intelligence on, 44–5, 46
low morale, 99
MacEoin arrest, 207–12
protection of G Division, 61
reform, 89–90
reprisals, 92, 107, 147–8
Smith in charge, 30–1
Soloheadbeg, 16–17, 243
spies in, 49–50, 130, 191
see also Auxiliaries
Royal Marine Hotel, 97
Russell, Sean, 178
Bloody Sunday, 148–50, 161, 163, 164, 166, 172
Ryan, John, 144, 181–2
Ryan, Martin, 50, 51

St Andrew's Hotel, 207
St Patrick's Training College, 132, 134
Saurin, Frank, 43, 48, 80, 156–7, 161
Savage, Martin, 32–3, 57
Seton, Malcolm, 101–2
Shaw, Celia, 106
Shaw, Sir Frederick, 13, 30, 83, 84
Shelbourne Hotel, 48
Shortt, Edward, 13, 16, 31, 225
Sinn Fein, 17, 19, 27, 30, 52, 65, 79, 99, 100, 101, 191, 194
anti-RIC campaign, 67–8
Byrnes on, 74
and Childers, 233
and coercion threat, 228
conscription protest, 12
convention, 1917, 9
on defensive, 104, 108, 143
elections, 7, 184; 1918, 3, 15, 16, 242; 1921, 222
Fisher's attitude to, 87–8
German Plot, 14
and Igoe Gang, 185–7
and IRA, 90
land courts, 87
prisoner interrogations, 198–204
raids on, 24, 28
RIC boycott, 26
seen as communist, 71
spies of, 86
suppressed, 46, 87, 93
Thomson's spy in, 231–5

and Truce negotiations, 177, 221, 222–4, 230–1, 235–6
and Volunteers, 22–3
and Winter, 213
Slattery, Jim, 25, 28, 32, 57, 58, 59, 82, 96, 181
Bloody Sunday, 153–5
Brooke assassination, 93–4
Custom House attack, 216, 217
and Daly, 192–4
RIC ambush, 206–7
second in command, 193–4
Smith, Sean, 153
Smith, Thomas, 162
Smith, Commissioner T.J., 23, 31, 86, 88, 89, 91
Smuts, Jan, 236
Smyth, Divisional Commissioner Gerard, 91–2, 131, 132
Smyth, Major G., 132, 133, 134
Smyth, Patrick, detective sergeant, 22, 24, 25–6
Soloheadbeg ambush, 16–17, 18, 19, 25, 26, 243
Special Branch, 13, 15–16, 69–77
Bloody Sunday, 157, 182–4
under Winter, 104, 108, 143, 147, 183–4, 241
Special Branch Dublin District, 103, 104, 108, 143, 146–7
Squad, The, 6, 39, 40, 125, 138, 139, 141, 204, 219
activities of, 53–60
allowances, 54
assessment of, 239
authorisation of, 41–2, 53
Bell assassination, 81–2
Brooke assassination, 93–4
and Broy capture, 190
Byrnes assassination, 76
Cabinet assassination scheme, 207–8
characteristics of members, 57–60
Custom House attack, 215–18
daily life, 55, 94–6
established, 29–30
French ambush, 31–3
HQ, 55–6
and Igoe Gang, 185–7
intelligence gathering, 43, 145–7
Lees assassination, 207

MacEoin escape plan, 207–12
post-Bloody Sunday, 180–2
recruitment, 56
Redmond assassination, 62–3
reprisals, 137
size of, 63
tensions within, 192–4
training of, 56, 57–9
Wilson assassination, 3–4
see also Bloody Sunday
Stack, Michael, 220
Stack, Mrs, 155, 156
Standard Hotel, 56, 62–3
Stapleton, Bill, 59–60, 63, 94, 181, 209,
    210
    Bloody Sunday, 155–6
    on Igoe Gang, 185–6
Stevenson, Frances, 231
Straw, Jack, 107
Strickland, General, 98, 126–7, 138, 147
strikes, 93
Sturgis, Mark, 88, 97, 127, 148, 150, 183,
    190
    Bloody Sunday, 163, 164
    and Collins, 119
    pessimism, 184
    and Truce negotiations, 222, 223, 229,
        237
    and Winter, 140, 213
Summerhill Dispensary, 180
Supple, Detective Chief Inspector, 190
Sweeney, Joe, 4
Swindlehurst, Private J.P., 201

Tams, Captain, 204
Taylor, Sir John, 31, 86, 239
Teeling, Frank, 153, 155, 163, 171, 172
Tegart, Charles, 101–3, 244
Thomson, Basil, 13–14, 15, 27, 30, 81, 86,
    99
    attitude to war, 121, 143
    Dublin agents, 194, 231–2
    and Hardy, 110, 111, 112
    heads Special Branch, 69–77
    'hotline', 116
    on Sinn Fein, 230–1
    and Winter, 102–3
Thornton, Frank, 38, 40, 44–5, 46, 119,
    136, 144, 197–8
    assassinations, 137

Bloody Sunday, 148, 175
    and Byrnes, 75, 76
    on Collins, 123
    and Daly, 192
    dinner search, 117–18
    Dublin Guard, 219
    Percival ambush, 139
    recruiting agents, 47
    Redmond assassination, 62
    role of, 42–3, 44, 52–3, 182
    spy dossiers, 145–7
    and Truce, 220, 238
Thorpe, A., 103
Tipperary IRA, 17, 19, 20, 26, 131
    Soloheadbeg ambush, 16–18
Tobin, Liam, 2, 3, 38, 39, 40, 80, 110,
    136, 137, 138, 147, 181
    Bell assassination, 82
    Bloody Sunday, 167
    breakdown, 145
    Brooke assassination, 93–4
    and Byrnes, 74, 75–6
    dinner search, 117–18
    and hangmen, 139
    and Hardy, 112
    and Igoe, 186
    role of, 41–2, 43, 44, 45, 52–3, 207–8
    and spies, 129–30
    and Truce, 238
Traynor, Oscar, 144, 152, 166, 176,
    178–9, 185, 188, 193, 237
    Bloody Sunday, 175
    Custom House attack, 214–18
    Dublin Guard, 219
    evades capture, 196–7
    illness, 220
    MacEoin capture, 209
Treacy, Sean, 17–18, 20, 32, 43, 99, 112,
    143, 195
    search for, 130, 131–7
Truce, 1921, 28, 176, 191, 194, 212,
    218, 239, 241
    agreed, 236, 238
    movement towards, 219–38
Tuam, County Galway, 92
Tudor, General Hugh, 49, 119, 136, 183,
    237, 244
    Auxiliaries, 93, 190
    Black and Tans, 91–2, 147
    Bloody Sunday, 163

HQ, 98–9, 140
Igoe Gang, 185
  Macready on, 213
  and MacSwiney, 124
  Police Adviser, 89
  policy, 90–1, 242
  and Truce negotiations, 222, 236
  and Winter, 101
typhoid bacillus, 127–8

Umbreville, Ralph, 224
United States of America (USA), 130, 191,
  232, 233

Vaughan's Hotel, 38, 42, 118–19, 121,
  138, 168, 195, 238
  Bloody Sunday, 152–3

Walsh, David, 128
Walsh, Jack, 44
Walsh, William, Archbishop of Dublin,
  213
Walter House, 39
War of Independence, see Anglo-Irish War
Wharton, Detective Thomas, 29
Whelan, Thomas, 170, 171, 172
White, George, 193
Whitman, Walt, 238
Wicklow Hotel, 48, 181
Wilde, Lieutenant L.E., 158–9, 168, 175
Williamson, James, 170, 171
Wilson, Captain Lea, 1–2, 3–4
Wilson, Lieutenant-Colonel Walter, 103,
  104, 108, 143, 147, 157, 196
  Bloody Sunday, 163, 174, 182–4
Wimberley, Major-General Douglas, 98
Wimborne, Viceroy, 12, 14

Winter, Colonel Ormonde, 89–90, 91, 92,
  98–100, 139, 143, 190, 244
  activities of, 125
  agents of, 105
  ambushed, 224–5
  and Auxiliaries, 112–14
  Bloody Sunday, 163, 166, 170, 171,
  172, 173, 185
  bugging, 204
  and Collins, 116–17
  and de Valera release, 229
  and Hardy, 109, 110, 112
  head of intelligence, 101–3, 108–9,
  183–4, 194–204, 212, 213, 240–1,
  243
  HQ, 140
  and Igoe, 187
  interrogations, 198–9
  IRA deaths, 242–3
  and MacSwiney, 124
  personality, 140
  search for Breen and Treacy, 135, 136,
  137
  and Squad, 130–1
  and Truce negotiations, 222, 224–5,
  230
  use of bloodhounds, 116
Woodcock, Caroline, 146
Woodcock, Colonel, 146, 159–60, 174
Woodcock, Mrs, 159–60, 161, 169, 170,
  171
Worthington-Evans, Sir Laming, 225, 227
Wylie, William, 126, 222–3
Wyse-Power, Charles, 170
Wyse-Power, Mrs, 243

Young, Patrick, 165–6, 167, 168